ROSES IN COLOUR AND CULTIVATION

ROSES

IN COLOUR AND CULTIVATION

By

T. C. MANSFIELD

———

WITH

80 PLATES IN COLOUR

AND

37 ILLUSTRATIONS

COLLINS 14 ST. JAMES'S PLACE LONDON

PRODUCED BY
ADPRINT LIMITED LONDON

First published 1943
Revised edition 1946
Reprinted 1947

PRINTED IN GREAT BRITAIN BY
W. S. COWELL LTD IPSWICH AND LONDON

CONTENTS

Note on the Use of the Visor

To render identification easy, a transparent visor is included in each book, divided up into lettered squares.

To use the visor, place it over the plate with the top white line in line with the top of the plate. At the foot of the plate will be found the letters indicating the squares in which the variety against which the letters stand is to be found.

PREFACE

The second book of the series "The Garden in Colour" has presented from the point of view of its colour reproductions problems quite different from those met with in the first book of the series.

As in the first book, the plates are made from actual colour photographs, and all exposures were made under studio conditions in order that constant factors in lighting could be obtained. The heat engendered by the batteries of lights seemed to have the power to imbue the subjects with the temperaments of fractious film stars, and even the charm of the photographer failed to render them tractable, their petals moving with a speed which to the jaded mind of the author seemed to be comparable with that of light, but which on measurement proved to be only 1/40th of an inch per second, but quite enough to present a problem to which an answer had to be found.

In particular the species roses proved to be of exceptional difficulty; buds would open; petals would fall; stamens would wither, and generally the photographer's lot assumed hazards which were only surmounted by infinite patience and the expenditure of a very large measure of time. Nor, indeed, were all the roses endowed with the same peculiarities of temperament. It can be said that one very famous rose would *not* photograph. No less than seven attempts were made, and on each occasion it seemed to exhibit a different phase of fractiousness. It is probable that the particular process has never before been so extensively used in such work, the exposures in many cases being in the nature of from 40 to 60 seconds.

No attempt has been made to "gild the lily," and the only "dressing" done is that shown in Plate 68, which was used to show how bad dressing can spoil an otherwise good rose. It should be remembered in judging colours that most roses exhibit a certain variation in colour between individual flowers, and that the individual flowers photographed were individually matched for colour, and no attempt has been made to add brightness to the original colour to obtain brilliance and make a striking picture, and that as far as the inks used in reproduction will allow, accuracy rather than brilliance has been the first criterion. Thus what deficiencies still exist in portraying the rose in the

7

fullness of its beauty are those inherent in trying to reproduce upon paper the glow which exists only in the living velvet of the petals of the rose.

I feel sure that I voice the opinion of my friend, the photographer John Hinde, when I say that if we have given you the rose less overpainted than before, if we give you the rose in all its aspects, in the bud, half-opened, full-blown, the rose in fact as you would see it in your garden, then we have done all we set out to do.

It is particularly important that the colours should not be judged by artificial light, the best light in which to view them being a good *clear north* light, *not* sunlight.

A certain measure of criticism may be levelled at the composition of some of the pictures. It has been necessary to adopt certain grouping to include the largest number of varieties possible. Simulated natural backgrounds have been used to replace the usual black velvet or "cut out" backgrounds, as experience has shown that such backgrounds give a better atmosphere in which colour may be adequately judged.

At first sight many of the so-called "red" roses may appear disappointing in colour. We feel sure, however, that the policy of not exaggerating and intensifying colours is the right one to be adopted, and claim a larger measure of faithfulness in reproductive representation of the colours than has hitherto been achieved.

The author gratefully acknowledges the help given ungrudgingly by the following, to whom his sincere thanks are due:

Mr. and Mrs. Courtney Page of the National Rose Society.
Col. F. R. Durham, The Secretary, The Royal Horticultural Society.
The late Rev. Father Kynaston, Downside Abbey, for species roses.
Mr. R. L. Harrow, Director, Royal Horticultural Society's Gardens, for species and other roses.
Mr. J. H. Wilson and Miss Durrant of the British Colour Council, for facilities enabling accurate colour matching.
C. H. Weller, Esq., Willsbridge, Bitton, Somerset, for species and other roses and proof correction.
G. F. Harkness, The Rose Gardens, Hitchin, for species and other roses.
Wilfrid Hinde, Esq., for roses.

Baltonsborough,
Somerset.
December, 1942.

PREFACE TO THE SECOND EDITION

. I feel that, upon the occasion of the publication of the second edition of this book, I must convey my thanks to my many correspondents, both known and unknown to me, who have tendered their advice, criticism, and, not least, correction.

All these points have been taken into account, and in the new edition minor inconsistencies have been eliminated.

Many of my correspondents have had considerable experience of growing roses "upon their own roots," and I cordially invite them to write to me upon this subject at greater length, as this is one phase of rose-growing upon which sound, attested evidence on a widespread scale is missing.

I shall be pleased to answer such letters as I may receive, as time permits.

Glastonbury,
 Somerset.
  July, 1946.

CHAPTER I

THE ROSE: HISTORICAL

THE rose is the most beloved of all flowers, beloved indeed for its fragrance, freshness and form; beloved by artists, poets, singers, lovers, and not least by gardeners. Were it not for the vicissitudes chronicled in the Preface, we might add photographers to this impressive list, but one cannot be certain that the passive patience and monumental immobility of these admirable people can be shaken by even the beauty of the rose.

The name "Rose," or to give the genus its botanical name, "Rosa," is possibly derived from the Celtic word "rhod," having as its meaning red, a colour which is predominantly the colour of the rose; or from the Greek "rhodon," a rose tree. The rose in one or other of its forms is endemic to almost every country in the world, with the possible exception of parts of South America and the tropics. Thus with almost the whole world as its habitat and with a popularity still wider spread, its history should be a study of increasing popularity and widening scope and beauty.

One of the earliest references to the rose appears in the Book of Wisdom, "Let us crown ourselves with rosebuds before they be withered," which probably refers to the Roman practice of crowning the heads with wreaths of roses at ceremonial banquets.

FitzGerald's translation of the *Rubáiyát* of Omar Khayyám gives us the reference:

> "I sometimes think that never blows so red
> The Rose as where some buried Caesar bled,"

—a clear link between the still predominant colour and flower, and a reference by implication to the desire of the rose for firm fertile soil.

Herodotus tells us of a double rose which grew in the gardens of Midas—generally agreed to have been the Cabbage Rose, R. centifolia—which he says had sixty leaves and "surpassed all others in fragrance."

Theophrastus in his *Enquiry into Plants* writes, "Among roses there are many differences, in the numbers of petals, in roughness, in beauty of colour, and in sweetness of scent. Most have five petals, but some have twelve or twenty, and some a great many more than these; for there are some, they say, which are even called 'hundred-petalled.' . . . Roses can be grown from seed which is to be found below the flower in the 'apple.' . . . As, however, the plant comes slowly from seed, they make cuttings of the stem, as has been said, and plant them. If a bush is burnt or cut over, it bears better flowers; for if left to itself it grows luxuriantly and makes too much wood."

This is probably the first reference to methods of pruning and propagation and certainly indicates the early cultivation of the rose.

It is significant that the Island of Rhodes, to which the rose gave its name, had the representation of a rose upon its coins.

The Romans, too, praised the rose in no less measured terms. Pliny in his *Natural History* writes, "The essential points of difference in the rose are the numbers of the petals, the comparative number of thorns on the stem, the colour and the smell. The number of the petals, which is never less than five, goes on increasing in amount, till we find one variety with as many as a hundred, and thence known as *centifolia*."

Suetonius tells us that Nero spent the fantastically large sum of four million sesterces upon roses for a single feast. Indeed it is certain that the rose was cultivated on quite a considerable scale that its blooms might be used at festivities. Crowned with wreaths of roses, filled with strong wine, the imprudent might resort to confidences whispered *sub rosa*. Both the rose and the phrase have persisted.

The rose has been prominently featured in English heraldry. The badges of Edward I, Henry IV, Edward IV, Henry VII, Henry VIII, Edward VI, and Queen Elizabeth, all featured the rose in one form or another. Nevertheless it is far from probable that the rose became the emblem of England by the deliberate choice of the most appropriate national flower. It is said that Edmund, Earl of Lancaster, was sent by the King of France in the thirteenth century to the city of Provins, to punish the citizens for the murder of its mayor. Remaining there for some time, he took as his badge on his return to England the red rose of Provins. It was probably the Damask Rose. The Rose of York was probably chosen for its distinctive difference, possibly without the dramatism given to it in Shakespeare's *Henry VI*.

It can be said without fear of contradiction that, in spite of the introduction of numberless plants from all parts of the world, the popularity of the rose has increased rather than decreased. The earliest printed catalogue is of Gerard's garden at Holborn, dated 1596, which gives a list of sixteen roses with Latin names. These were described with their English names in *The Herball or General Historie of Plantes* in 1597.

Double roses appear in records as far back as it is possible to go. They are abnormal flowers in that many or all of their stamens are metamorphosed into petals. In the case of the so-called green rose, Rosa chinensis viridiflora, the petals, stamens, and even seeds are metamorphosed into leaves.

The attention centred upon classical writers at the Renaissance influenced gardeners to pay attention to the remarks of Theophrastus that though roses could be grown from seed they were more easily propagated from cuttings, so that new varieties were only obtained by "sporting," and there was little advance in rose production. It was in Holland that the practice grew up of growing roses from seed, when new plants sprang up from accidental cross pollination, until finally the stage was reached when cross pollination became the practice. There is, of course, no fixation in the resulting generation, and with repeated cross pollinations more uncertainty resulted. Thus the only fixation of a given form could be secured by vegetative reproduction. This could be done by means of cuttings, or layers, or by detaching the suckers if any were produced. The general practice became grafting or budding, the latter in particular. This was done, and is still practised, on Manetti or briar stocks.

If one wished to point a moral, and so far I have resisted the temptation to mention the "Wars of the Roses," I should add that in spite of centuries of disturbances, upheavals, turmoils, the rose has persisted and improved, to become an ever-living symbol that, come what may, beauty shall not perish from the earth, and that of all the works of man none is greater than that in the trials and tribulations through which he has passed, he has still found time, nay, made time, not, I think, for gain, to produce the modern rose as a permanent memorial to all that is good and beautiful in life; for while the rose lives, so will man's thoughts turn from horrors and fears, and devices and stratagems, to return to the beauty which abides in the mind, and urges him on to produce that which is better and still more beautiful.

CHAPTER II

ROSES OF THE PAST WHICH HAVE INFLUENCED THE MODERN ROSE

THE species of Rosa probably number approximately two hundred, and are of wide distribution, but of these only about twenty have contributed to the important hybrids which have become so essential to the present-day rose garden. On the whole, it would seem to be best to divide them empirically into two classes: (*a*) those blooming in the early summer, and (*b*) those flowering continuously from May onwards to November.

Into the first class fall:—

ROSA ALBA (the White Rose) was introduced in 1597 and is endemic to Central Europe, and to-day still found in old cottage gardens. The single flowers, which are generally not of the purest white, being flushed pink towards the centre, are produced in abundance, and are somewhat flat in appearance. R. alba is very hardy, and though it appreciates good feeding will grow reasonably well in even a poor soil. R. alba is presumed to be a hybrid between R. canina var. dumetorum and R. gallica, and generally bears five grey-green leaflets to each leaf; its flowers, borne in corymbs, are said to have been a source of attar of roses. A semi-double form also exists. Its varieties, carnea, Celestial and Maiden's Blush, have all distinct pink, semi-double, sweetly-scented flowers.

R. ARVENSIS (the Ayrshire Rose) is a native of Europe, including Britain; is extremely hardy and produces clusters of single white flowers, each about two inches in diameter, borne upon trailing branches, with almost evergreen leaves normally composed of seven leaflets. It generally flowers in June and can be grown in poor soil. It may be used because of its free growth for covering arches. Double-flowered forms (probably hybrids) are Bennett's Seedling—which has small semi-double flowers—and Dundee Rambler, with double white flowers with rose edges.

R. BANKSIAE (the Banksian Rose) is an evergreen climbing white rose, a native of China, and was introduced into Britain in 1807 and named after Lady Banks. It bears many-flowered clusters of small white or yellow flowers, upon stems almost devoid of spines. R. Banksiae flowers upon the old wood, and not then, as a rule, until it is well established. It is unfortunately not suited to exposed positions, and is most suitable for sheltered walls, and should be grown in deep rich soil. It should not be pruned; thinning only is necessary.

The varieties of R. Banksiae are:—R. Banksiae var. albo plena, with small double white sweetly but modestly scented flowers; R. Banksiae var. lutea, with small double yellow flowers. The variety lutescens has small single yellow flowers and the variety normalis similar white flowers.

R. CENTIFOLIA (the Cabbage Rose) forms bushes up to six feet in height, is probably a native of the Eastern Caucasus, and is certainly the oldest garden rose known. Its leaves are generally made up of five leaflets, each up to two inches in length. It produces large, nodding, many-petalled flowers, never reflexed, and the original species is thought to have had large double rose-pink flowers. It requires hard pruning and good cultivation, and is delightfully scented; is said to have been grown extensively at Mitcham for the preparation of rose-water. It seems to have been introduced into Britain in 1596, but certain hybrids are known to have been in cultivation before that date.

R. CENTIFOLIA VAR. MUSCOSA (the Moss Rose) is said to have been unknown in Britain before the beginning of the eighteenth century, the first apparent mention being in a catalogue of R. Furber of Kensington in 1724. The many varieties of R. centifolia var. muscosa will be found in the Glossary. All are exceptionally attractive in the bud form, the typical mossy calyx and flower stalk being the especial outstanding feature.

R. CENTIFOLIA VAR. PROVINCIALIS (the Provence Rose) is one of the earliest known roses, and is popularly supposed to have been brought from Syria by Thibaut le Chansonnier to be cultivated in the gardens at Provins.

R. DAMASCENA (the Damask Rose) is one of the oldest of known roses; its origin cannot be traced, though it is thought to have been introduced into Europe from the gardens of Damascus by the Crusaders. Johnson attributes the date of its introduction into Britain to be 1524, when he says it was introduced by Linacre. The Damask Rose grows to six feet in height with long arching green stems, with large leathery green leaflets, generally in fives, and bears fragrant pale-pink to red many-petalled flowers in clusters. It is exceptionally hardy, and should not be pruned but thinned as necessary. It is said to have been grown extensively in various countries as a source of attar of roses.

R. GALLICA (the French or Garden Rose) has long been known
in Europe and can be clearly distinguished by its dwarf compact habit, its thick dark green leaves, and the comparative
smallness of its few thorns. It is very hardy, requires little
pruning, and good culture. The flowers, which are semi-double,
vary from pink to red. The varieties are dealt with fully in the
Glossary. Good culture and thinning result in the production
of good flowers. Rosa gallica is one of the parents of the Hybrid
China Rose, the other parent being R. indica var. chinensis;
it also provided parentage to the Hybrid Bourbon type, the
other parent being R. bourbonia.

The Hybrid China Roses are all strong growers, making fine
pillar roses, and flower in June and July.

The Hybrid Bourbon type are very robust, have fine broad
green foliage and large handsome flowers, and make good pot
roses, standards and pillars.

R. HEMISPHAERICA is also known as R. sulphurea, and is the double
yellow Persian Rose, said to be a cultivated form of R. Rapinii.
It produces wreathed sulphur-yellow double flowers, but
requires a warm and sheltered position, light pruning, and a
rich soil, generally against a wall. R. hemisphaerica may not
in itself be a rose which by parentage has influenced the modern
rose; it certainly did by its colour concentrate attention upon
the production of good self-coloured yellow roses.

R. LUTEA (the Austrian Briar) is also known as R. foetida and
forms a bush of about four to six feet in height, with small green
sharply toothed, round leaflets, from five to nine to each leaf,
and bears deep-yellow flowers about $2\frac{1}{2}$ inches in diameter.
It occurs in widely spread localities from the Crimea to Tibet.
R. lutea flowers in June, and the flowers have a slightly
unpleasant scent. Pruning consists of thinning only. R. lutea
is very subject to black spot and should not be planted with
other roses. R. foetida has provided the yellow colouring in
many hybrids, particularly in the Pernetiana roses.

R. MULTIFLORA (the Polyantha or Japanese Rose) forms a wide
spreading bush with leaves consisting of from five to eleven
leaflets, and bears loose heads of white honey-scented flowers.
R. multiflora has influenced garden roses very considerably,
being a parent of many of the polyantha and "multiflora" types.
Exceptionally hardy, it produces its flowers upon the new wood.

R. PENDULINA (also known as R. alpina) forms a thornless bush of
some four to six feet in height, with leaves composed of from
five to nine large coarse leaflets, and bears large single, rich

Hybrid Tea Rose, Shot Silk

Three Species Roses

Rosa lutea **ABJNLMPQ**   Rosa spinosissima var. lutea **CDGH**
              Rosa lutea var. bicolor **EFKLOP**

pink, very fragrant flowers. It produces bright red pear-shaped fruits in autumn. With R. indica, R. pendulina has produced the Boursault roses. These have long, almost thornless flexible stems, and produce clusters of double flowers. They are exceptionally hardy, and will do comparatively well upon poor soil, though they also repay good cultivation.

R. RUBIGINOSA (the Sweet Briar) is widely spread throughout Europe. It forms a bush up to eight feet in height, much branched, with leaves of from five to seven leaflets, smelling sweetly. The single flowers, which in the type are bright pink, are approximately two inches in diameter, and are followed by bright red fruits. They form good hedges and gave rise to the Penzance Briar hybrids raised by the late Lord Penzance.

R. SEMPERVIRENS (the Evergreen Rose) is a rose generally climbing or decumbent, with large green shining leaves, and bearing clusters of large white, scented flowers. It is reputed to have been introduced into Britain in 1629. The varieties make fine pillar, climbing or weeping roses and require little or no pruning.

R. SETIGERA (the Prairie Rose) is a native of Central North America, and in Britain reaches a height of approximately eight feet. Its greyish foliage and large bright-pink flowers, which fade white, borne in loose corymbs, make it extremely attractive, and its hardiness is exceptional. R. setigera is a parent, with R. Wichuraiana, of the well-known American Pillar.

R. SPINOSISSIMA (the Scots or Burnet Rose) is also known as R. pimpinellifolia and makes a densely spiny bush with sweetly-scented milk-white flowers profusely produced. The leaves, consisting of from five to eleven small leaflets, are very attractive. It forms a most attractive dwarf hedge and grows well in almost any poor soil when its height becomes negligible. The fruits are black and round. It can be freely propagated from either seed or suckers, and is the parent of the Burnet Roses of various colours.

R. WICHURAIANA (the Memorial Rose) is a native of China and Japan discovered by Doctor Wichura in 1860. It is of trailing habit and bears shining leaflets, which are almost evergreen, in leaves of from seven to nine. The flowers, borne in corymbs, are white with bright yellow anthers and sweetly scented. R. Wichuraiana has given rise to one of the most popular groups of hybrids in the world. Crossed with other types it has produced such roses as Dorothy Perkins, Minnehaha and Excelsa. Generally flowering in late summer, they prove invaluable and, apart from the removal of dead and weak wood, require little pruning until they become too thickly crowded.

17

The second division (the continuous-flowering varieties) includes:—

R. BOURBONIA (the Bourbon Rose) is a hybrid between R. indica and R. gallica. It is said to have been found growing in a hedge on the Isle of Bourbon (now Réunion). Seedlings raised from it were grown by a M. Jacques, gardener to M. le duc de Neuilly, and introduced into Britain in 1828 as l'Ile de Bourbon Rose. It produces semi-double brilliant rose-pink flowers of great fragrance, and is the parent of a very large number of roses of good form and clean colours, which are generally exceptionally good in autumn. R. bourbonia mated with R. gallica, R. centifolia, and R. damascena produced the Hybrid Bourbon Roses; these crossed with R. chinensis produced the Hybrid Perpetuals.

R. BRACTEATA (the Macartney Rose) was introduced into Britain by Lord Macartney in 1765 and is still little known to amateurs. With evergreen glossy leaves, it will climb to fifteen feet in height upon a sheltered wall, and produce large single white flowers generally borne singly and centred by golden stamens. Not of great hardiness and seldom producing much seed in its woolly orange-red fruits, its chief claim to inclusion is that it was one of the parents of that marvellous rose Mermaid which has inherited also its thorns, which resemble an eagle's beak. The hybrid bracteata roses may be very severely pruned without fear of preventing them from flowering. The best method is to thin out the old wood in spring, removing any frost-damaged tips.

R. CHINENSIS (the China or Monthly Rose) was introduced from China late in the seventeenth century. It is a low-growing rose with leaves shining green above, and bears its double flowers in loose panicles. The colour varies from white to red, but its outstanding contribution is that it flowers almost continuously from June to the winter. R. chinensis needs little pruning and is best grown upon its own roots, and while it usually gets little attention, it does repay in generous measure the good culture which occasionally falls to its lot. The influence of the long flowering period of R. chinensis is felt in the Hybrid Perpetual roses, and from them transmitted to the Hybrid Teas. The Hybrid Perpetuals are particularly hardy and can be grown well out of doors in the northern states of America, but the Hybrid Teas need protection if grown in the middle states north of the Ohio. In Britain they may be grown in all parts of the country without fear of winter loss.

R. chinensis is also the name given to that section which was known as the Tea Rose (Rosa odorata). R. chinensis (odorata) is, where the climate allows it, evergreen, and bears white, yellow or pink tea-scented flowers. The first variety to be introduced into Britain was the pink one in the early nineteenth century. All the plants need protection from frost and cutting winds, and careful spring pruning. These, too, have had their influence on the modern rose by cross pollination with the Hybrid Perpetual types.

R. CHINENSIS VAR. MINIMA (the Fairy Rose), known also as R. Lawranceana, is a China Rose in miniature, and grows to about one foot in height, bearing rose-red flowers of double form in perfect miniature. R. chinensis var. minima forms a good edging for rose beds and has the same continuous habit of flowering as R. chinensis, producing its small but perfectly shaped flowers in unending succession. Little pruning is required, except an occasional thinning of the old wood.

R. MOSCHATA (the Musk Rose) is the wild briar of the Himalayas, extending westward to Southern Europe, and makes a bush with arching or climbing branches and produces musky-scented single white flowers in groups of seven. It grows to a great height, sometimes reaching thirty feet. Some of the hybrids of this type make very good climbers. Pruning consists of eliminating the dead wood and removing the tips of the strong basal shoots.

R. NOISETTIANA (the Noisette or Champney's Rose) is a hybrid of American origin, between R. chinensis and R. moschata, introduced into Britain in 1820. Its chief characteristics are its free growth and its many-flowered corymbs of sweetly-scented flowers of white, pink, red or yellow. Well-known Noisettiana hybrids are the Maréchal Niel, Mme Alfred Carrière, William Allen Richardson. R. Noisettiana flowers upon ripened lateral wood, so that all old wood should be preserved, removal of damaged and unsound wood being sufficient.

R. RUGOSA (the Japanese Rose) is a native of China and Japan and makes a bush of some six feet in height, with bright green large leaves with from five to nine leaflets, each heavily ribbed and of very attractive appearance. The flowers, which are produced in few-flowered corymbs, are large and vary from white to purplish rose. R. rugosa is very hardy, will grow anywhere, and requires little pruning. The seed pods are particularly attractive. The rugosa hybrids make exceptionally fine hedges.

These are the chief ancestors of the modern rose; each has played its part in adding strength, hardiness, beauty of shape or of colour, or of improved habit. As a rule the usual garden roses in named horticultural varieties have little to recommend them by way of foliage or habit; they are grown for their chief beauty, their flowers. They are attacked by insects and by fungi, and it is essential, therefore, that they should be grown in prepared beds where they can be pruned and well cared for. The roses for mixed borders should be the species roses, though here again some are subject to certain diseases which render them subjects for individual culture. The Glossary of Roses gives full details of the individual requirements of each rose, and should be carefully studied where any doubt exists.

Finally, even should the rose be subject to twice as many forms of diseases, and half a dozen times as many insect enemies, it would still be worthy of every care bestowed upon it. The rose demonstrates for all time the gardener's love of beauty, his skill, his painstaking care, his generosity, his tenderness towards the weak, and his mastery of climatic conditions, for he who plants a seed places his faith in a providence which he knows will in the fullness of time provide an answer. The modern rose is the answer to myriads of such questions, and who cannot say that man's work upon the rose has not only improved the rose, but has also improved him ?

CHAPTER III

SUGGESTIONS FOR GROWING ROSES

FOR reasons obscure to the author, it seems to have been the practice to begin all books designed to encourage gardeners to grow roses with a long series of don'ts. The author suggests that the primary aim of this chapter may be summarised in the one word "Do." Indeed, he would suggest that:

> "'Tis better to have loved and lost
> Than never to have loved at all"

applies just as much to the rose as to any other charmer, and presents the suggestions made herein with the object of eliminating the fatal word "lost." Tradition has hedged the rose with a quickset of difficulty, which exists in the imagination only. The rules are simple; where there is soil upon which a dock will grow in the sun, there also will grow a rose. It is perfectly true that some roses are not easy to grow, that some are subject to disease, that some are tender and some fickle; it is equally true, however, that there are many from which all may choose some which will fit with certainty any given set of circumstances and delight their proud owner with their generosity of colour, scent, and form, in a way which no other flower can do.

Let us begin, then, from the beginning, with the advice "Do." Having decided that we are going to grow roses, we must, of course, have some slight knowledge of the type of rose which will best suit our purpose. If the patient reader has survived the tedium of the last chapter, which served to introduce him to his rose's pedigree, he will be delighted to find that he need consider for the moment three main classes of roses only. These we will call Bedding roses, Climbing roses and Shrub roses.

Bedding roses we may roughly describe as those which vary from nine inches to three feet in height, and which should be grown as far as possible together. They include as the main constituent groups the Hybrid Tea roses, the Tea roses, the Hybrid polyantha roses, and the Hybrid Perpetual roses.

Climbing roses, which are inadequately named since they do not climb, may be said to be those of such strong growth and development that their long shoots may be trained to cover a support, and include, in addition to the so-called climbing forms of the groups mentioned under Bedding roses, Hybrid multiflora roses, Hybrid wichuraiana roses, Noisette roses, Banksian roses, and Hybrid bracteata roses.

The Shrub class may roughly be described as those roses which are labelled species, and which may be called the "wild roses" of this and of other lands.

Mrs. Beeton's recipe for jugged hare begins, if my memory does not play me false, "First catch your hare," and this would indeed seem to be good advice to the cook, comparable with the advice given to the would-be rose-grower, "First choose your roses," but I cannot echo the advice. The prime consideration should be that of site, and by that I mean soil and aspect; if you are free to choose a site, choose one which is open and unshaded and situated away from trees; if you are limited as to space, make the best of what you have and select the nearest approach to an open and unshaded site as your small space will allow. In most cases the basic soil will have to remain, for no one to-day can face the prohibitive cost of the importation of the perfect soil. If you already possess a retentive heavy loam, give thanks for it and till it well, for thus will you get good roses. Roses, fortunately, have no really exclusive requirements as to soil. If your soil should be clay, if it is well drained and suitably manured, again you will produce good roses. If your soil should be a light one it should be well manured and mulched with a moisture-retaining mixture during the flowering season, and again you should produce good roses.

If you have a chalky soil you will have, of course, to feed it well, but chalky soils have the advantage of warmth and you should still produce good roses. Thus it can be seen that whatever the set of circumstances with which you have to contend, you will have some advantage which is lacking in certain other combinations of circumstances.

Roses are gross-feeding plants, and it is essential, if the finest blooms are to be produced, that they are well fed. The soil in which they grow must be well drained but retentive of moisture. Roses grow well on clay but not in clay. Roses appreciate a well-limed soil. Here we briefly state some of the most important cultural items. Let us now prepare the site to allow for these points and ensure our own success.

Assuming we have as our basic soil a heavy retentive loam, we must dig it deeply and thoroughly. Here we should use the double digging system, retaining the existing top soil at the top but thoroughly breaking up the second spit. Figure 1 shows how this is done. Into each run of six square yards of the bottom spit dig in one bushel of well-littered manure, and break up thoroughly.

Into the top spit, which should be left rough to be affected as much by frost as possible, dig in one bushel of well-rotted manure to each run of eight square yards, and finish off by dressing the surface after digging with four ounces of slaked lime to each square yard of surface. This should ensure complete success.

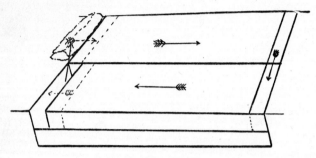

I—DOUBLE DIGGING

If your soil consists of heavy clay, treat similarly, digging into each spit such lightening material as may be readily available, such as sand, wood ashes, or burnt soil; leave the top spit rough and allow it to be well frozen so that it may readily crumble.

Should the soil be sandy, the problem presented is quite different, since it is of little use to dig in manure deeply, and after digging the second spit a thick layer of turf should be placed over it, grass side downwards, and then chopped into pieces about the size of one's fist before the final spit is replaced above it. Into the top spit dig in well-littered stable manure, at the rate of one bushel for each eight square yards. On this kind of soil the maximum benefit is obtained by yearly top dressings, and it is recommended that well-rotted cow manure be used for this purpose if available, again at the rate of one bushel to eight square yards, and dug into the top soil. Under these circumstances very good roses can be grown in sandy soils, but it is also recommended that in all light soils wood ashes should also be incorporated at frequent intervals. The four-ounce dressing of slaked lime for each square yard of soil is again necessary.

If your soil is chalky you should aim at getting good tilth in the top twenty inches of soil. Between the first and second spits turf should be incorporated as in the case of sandy soil, and into the top spit well-rotted cow manure at the rate of one bushel for each eight square yards. After digging, apply a dressing of four ounces of lime to each square yard of soil. Similarly, this type of soil benefits by annual top dressings, particularly of well-rotted cow manure at the same rate, together with a similar dressing of loam. All preparatory work should be done as far as possible in the early autumn, and should be finished approximately a month before the earliest time for planting.

Gardeners are pre-eminently sociable people, rose-growers are probably even more so. The rose-grower will willingly discuss with you the way in which he obtains his remarkable results. Do not disdain the advice given by your neighbours—in all probability they have similar soil assets or liabilities, and the general advice given here cannot hope to legislate for every problem. If you find a friend producing roses of an exceptional standard, with a basic soil similar to your own, it would be most unwise to discount his advice, which is most certainly to be easily obtained.

Generally speaking, the best month in which to plant roses in Britain is in November, for planting at such a time secures the best display possible the following summer. It is quite true that roses may be planted during suitable weather at any time from late October to early April, but it is safe to say that where the general climate is suitable for November planting it does give the best and quickest results. I know of one rose garden in which every tree was moved during early August, transported a distance of six miles and replanted without the loss of a single tree, and with really remarkable results the following year, but I would venture to suggest that this is quite insufficient evidence for making this a common practice, for the gardener in question was of the type who would have probably succeeded in growing a coconut palm at the North Pole!

While I strongly urge that adequate cultivation can only be given to dwarf roses within the standard confines of the specially prepared rose bed, and deprecate the practice of growing dwarf rose trees in the mixed border, I feel that the species roses are better grown, where it is desired to feature them in the garden, in the mixed shrubbery borders, or as specimens in isolated positions. Many of the species and hybrid species make excellent hedges of varying heights according to the type cultivated. But the cultivation of roses is not confined to rose beds, shrubberies, and specimen plants, nor to walls, pillars and pergolas.

One of the most fascinating hobbies for the amateur is the pot culture of roses. Every owner of a greenhouse could in normal times indulge this hobby with the certainty that in interest at least he would profit much by it. Such a method does enable the grower to obtain very good quality roses, unspoilt by inclement weather conditions, long before outdoor blooms are obtainable. The greenhouse to be used may be slightly heated or may be a "cold" house, though in the latter case very early blooms should not be anticipated.

Hybrid Tea Rose, Violinista Costa

Hybrid Bracteata Rose, Mermaid

Roses intended for forcing should be potted at the end of September. If they are bought especially for the purpose, unpack on arrival, soak the roots in water, after having removed any broken or damaged roots, and having trimmed back any long thick roots to a maximum length of six inches, prepare the John Innes' Standard Potting Compost in the following way: Take seven parts sterilised loam, three parts sterilised peat, two parts sand, and add one quarter pound of the John Innes' Base, which may be bought from a nurseryman's sundriesman, and three-quarter ounce of powdered chalk per bushel of the mixture (a bushel is that quantity of soil which can be held by a box twenty inches wide, twenty-two inches long and five inches deep when filled level). This mixture will be found very suitable for all purposes. If sterilised soil is not used, good unsterilised loam may be used, but it should be understood that the John Innes' Base is balanced for use with sterilised loam, and though better results will be obtained with unsterilised soil and the John Innes' Base than by haphazard methods of culture, I urge the use of sterilised loam where possible.

If the grower desires a mixture of ordinary character which can be used as a parallel for control culture, I suggest: one bushel of turf loam, one-third bushel of peat or leaf mould, half bushel of well-rotted stable manure, one-sixth bushel of wood ash, and one-third bushel of sharp sand. Do not make the mixture too fine in character by passing through a sieve; use a coarse sieve if using one at all.

Select some good clean eight-inch pots, and try the roots of the roses to see whether they will be overcrowded. If overcrowding is obvious, trim back the roots so that they are neither bent nor overcrowded in the pot. In the bottom of each pot place a layer of drainage material—which should also be sterile—amounting to two inches in depth, and then a layer of soil of approximately four inches in depth well firmed down. Spread the roots over this and pack the soil firmly to one inch below the rim of the pot. Plunge the potted roses in ashes out of doors in a sheltered position, generally along a sheltered north wall. If possible, place a piece of slate or asbestos beneath the drainage hole of each pot to prevent the access of worms to the pot. Protect the plants from frost as far as possible since they will stand out of doors until late November.

During the last week in November take the pots into the greenhouse and after one week cut them back to within two or three buds or eyes from the base, in the case of Teas, Hybrid Teas or Hybrid Perpetuals, removing in the process all weak or straggly growths, and making sure that the topmost eye on each branch is one which points directly outwards to the rim of the pot. In the case of the Polyantha roses cut out any weak or straggly growths, any which crowd the centre of the bush, and remove the unripened ends of the shoots.

Where the house is heated, the temperature should be maintained at approximately 50° F. during the day and 40° F. by night until the roses have started into growth, when the day temperature should be 75° F. and the night temperature 50° F. During certain sunny days in spring, temperatures will rapidly rise and a careful watch must be kept to see that, on such days, ventilation is given to keep the temperature as constant as possible. Humidity must also be carefully regulated. Kept too dry, a house will quickly house Aphis, Thrips and Red Spider; too moist, it will encourage the onset of mildew, which is generally encouraged by quick changes of temperature. Each night place in the house the water with which it is necessary to water and spray the roses *next* day in order that it shall be at the right temperature. Water if necessary, but spray with a syringe in the morning and afternoon of each day. Watering should always be done when the pots give a ringing tone when tapped with the knuckles.

Pot-grown roses require feeding, and I recommend for the purpose the John Innes' Dry Feed at the rate of eight teaspoonfuls per pot every fourteen to twenty-one days. This should not be applied until the roses are making strong growth and are in bud, though essentially the problem is to supply such plant foods at the time the rose requires it. A certain amount of disbudding will need to be carried out when the buds begin to develop. Look at each shoot and you will generally find that there is a group of small buds clustered together. If the terminal bud is sound, well formed and shapely, let it remain, and remove the smaller ones; if it appears deformed, remove it and select another well-formed one to develop. Treat each shoot similarly. This will ensure large well-formed flowers. If the roses are to be grown for decorative purposes, in pots, drastic disbudding is unnecessary.

As soon as the roses have finished flowering, take them out of the house and put into a cold frame to harden off, and replace in their sheltered north aspect when suitably hardened; continue to feed while growth is taking place. Re-pot in the last week in September in new compost and treat exactly as before.

Hybrid Tea Rose, Ophelia

A curious sport from Dame Edith Helen
It is from "sporting" of this kind that some new varieties are obtained

CHAPTER IV

ROSES FOR SPECIFIC PURPOSES

IN Chapter II a short account has been given of the parents of the modern rose. It now becomes necessary to write at some greater length of the descendants of these roses.

Perhaps the first of these which should be mentioned is the Hybrid Perpetual rose. Before the advent of the Hybrid Tea rose, the Hybrid Perpetual rose was outstanding. The first Hybrid Perpetual roses were produced by M. Laffay in 1837, and, as their name indicates, they were of cross-bred origin and were reputed to be the result of crossing the Hybrid Bourbon roses or the Hybrid Chinese with the Damask Perpetuals. The fact that they produced blooms for a longer period than the normal summer-flowering roses led to their being given the name Hybrid Perpetual.

Hybrid Perpetual roses are distinguished by their vigorous growth and rather large many-petalled flowers which are usually of one colour only. Generally speaking, they yield few blooms in the late summer and autumn, and have been outstripped in garden value by the newer Hybrid Tea and Pernetiana roses which display a far greater range of colour and which flower for a much longer period. Notwithstanding this, they still elicit admiration, for they grow into strong vigorous bushes two feet or more in height, with large handsome and generally fragrant blooms. The Hybrid Perpetual roses are good roses for town gardens, and grow so vigorously that they should be planted at least two feet apart.

Perhaps the best known of the Hybrid Perpetual roses are Frau Karl Druschki (white), Hugh Dickson (crimson), Mrs. John Laing (pink), and Ulrich Brunner (rose-red).

The second type of modern rose and the most popular is the Hybrid Tea rose. The Hybrid Tea rose is of much more recent origin than the Hybrid Perpetual and was first produced by crossing the Hybrid Perpetual type with the Tea-scented China rose. This was done by M. H. Guillot, who in 1867 crossed the Hybrid Perpetual rose Mme Victor Verdier with the Tea rose Mme Bravy and called the resultant cross "La France." The following crosses inherit much of the vigour of the Hybrid Perpetual, together with the long flowering period of the Tea roses.

Cross breeding has now been carried on to a considerable extent with the Pernetiana roses and Polyanthas so that the Hybrid Tea section is now a group comprising an immense number of varieties often differing greatly in habit of growth and form. Generally speaking, however, it may be said that the Hybrid Tea rose is a vigorous rose which flowers profusely in June and July, and then occasionally until September, when it again produces a very fine display of flowers. For a time growers concentrated upon producing roses of good form and brilliant colouring, and for a while fragrance was deemed of secondary consideration, but more recently much has been done to remedy the early lack of fragrance in the Hybrid Tea rose. One of the earlier faults was that the petallage of the Hybrid Tea rose was slight, but it may be stated generally that the fuller-petalled Hybrid Tea roses are less free in flowering than the "thinner" varieties.

Of the better-known Hybrid Tea roses one may name as examples:—

Betty Uprichard	La France
Caroline Testout	Madame Butterfly
Dame Edith Helen	Mrs. Henry Bowles

The third group is that known as the Pernetiana Roses. The first variety was raised by M. Pernet-Ducher, a famous French rose-grower, who hybridised a Hybrid Perpetual rose with the Austrian Briar, Rosa lutea. The actual cross was the Hybrid Perpetual rose Antoine Ducher with the double form of R. lutea called the Persian Yellow. The resultant rose was Soleil d'Or. This was followed by crossing with the Tea rose, and thus into both classes came the tints or orange and copper which had hitherto been unattainable.

The outstanding characteristics of the Pernetiana rose are its moderately vigorous growth, its prickly stems, its deep-green leaves, which are generally proof against mildew, and its flowers of very bright colouring. Nearly all the finest yellow roses belong to this group, together with those of orange and apricot shades. As indicated earlier, the Austrian Briar, Rosa lutea, is particularly liable to black spot, and it seems to be the general experience of rose-growers that the Pernetiana roses have inherited a greater tendency to black spot than other types.

Many of the Pernetianas are "thin," but are still worth growing for their intense colouring. Some of them are very sweet-scented, but the scent is characteristically like that of ripe apricots. One of the earliest of the Pernetiana group was Juliet, now rarely grown, but which impressed itself upon my mind many years ago with its brilliant combination of rose and old gold.

As examples of the best known Pernetianas we quote:—

Christine (gold)
Condesa de Sastago (orange-flame and gold)
Federico Casas (orange and copper)

Golden Emblem (yellow)
Julien Potin (yellow)
Mrs. G. A. van Rossem (orange and apricot)

HYBRID MUSK ROSES

This is a delightful group of roses raised by the late Rev. J. H. Pemberton, which are vigorous in growth and very free-flowering with a long flowering period. They are of mixed parentage, R. moschata being one of the parents. Some of the more vigorous types grow to a height of four feet and produce flowers which may be excused their somewhat small size in view of their great abundance. Perfectly hardy, they need little attention and are a continual delight to the eye.

Of the best known are:—

Clytemnestra (dark reddish-rose, opening salmon-rose)
Cornelia (old rose)
Danaë (buds yellow, flowers pale yellow)

Eva (dark red)
Felicia (pink shaded yellow)
Moonlight (lemon-white)
Penelope (pink shaded salmon)

POLYANTHA POMPON ROSES

This group sprang from a dwarf form of Rosa multiflora which, with its clustered heads and long-flowering tendency, provided an extremely useful class of brightly coloured roses for mass effect. Cameo (salmon-pink), Coral Cluster (pale pink), Ellen Poulsen (cherry-rose), Little Dorrit (coral to salmon), Orleans Rose (crimson), Paul Crampel (orange-scarlet), are examples.

The original climbing Polyantha is that to which is attached the story that the type was found growing in a Japanese garden by an English engineer who sent it home to a friend. The unique possibilities of this rose were appreciated by Charles Turner, who distributed it as Crimson Rambler. Prior to this there had been introduced into Britain in 1880 Rosa Wichuraiana, a very vigorous creeping rose with white, fragrant flowers and flowering in the late summer. Based upon these two there sprang into life a series of hybrids, the wichuraiana ramblers, which in themselves provided a new and entrancing class of hardy roses of great vigour and intense floriferousness typified by Albéric Barbier (creamy-white), Dorothy Perkins (rose-pink), Dr. W. van Fleet (blush), Emily Gray (golden-yellow), Lady Godiva (blush), Minnehaha (deep pink), and Paul's Scarlet Climber (scarlet).

More recently the Dwarf polyantha type has been crossed with the Hybrid Teas and produced the Hybrid polyantha type which has large semi-double flowers and vigorous growth and a long flowering period. Typical of the group are: Else Poulsen (rose-pink), Karen Poulsen (brilliant scarlet), Donald Prior (crimson), Salmon Spray (salmon-pink), Van Nes (carmine).

Sufficient has been said of the parentage of the modern rose to provide a background for the division into types for specific purposes. There remains only to mention the climbing roses, which are of two types: firstly those which by nature are vigorous and of strong growth, and secondly the climbing "sports" which are variations of dwarf or bush roses and liable in the event of incorrect treatment to revert to dwarf characteristics.

Of the first class may be quoted as examples:

Allen Chandler (scarlet) Lemon Pillar (pale yellow)
Gloire de Dijon (yellow) Zéphirine Drouhin (carmine-
Lady Waterlow (salmon-blush) pink)

Of the climbing sports may be quoted:

Caroline Testout (pink) Mme Butterfly (pink to apricot)
Lady Hillingdon (apricot- Mme Edouard Herriot (terra-
yellow) cotta)
Mme Abel Chatenay (pale Ophelia (salmon-flesh)
salmon-pink)

Thus it can be seen that because of their habit and other characteristics inherited from their ancestors, certain roses are more fitted than others for use for specific purposes, and one can roughly divide all the types of roses into the following groups:—

(I) DWARF-GROWING ROSES
   (*a*) For bedding purposes (*c*) Polyantha roses for bedding
   (*b*) For growing in pots (*d*) Hybrid polyantha roses

(II) ROSES MAKING SUITABLE STANDARDS

(III) CLIMBING ROSES
   (*a*) For walls (*b*) For pillars, arches, pergolas

The task of selecting individual roses is an invidious one since every rose has an intrinsic beauty and is therefore worth growing, and any list selected as giving the best twelve, fifty or one hundred roses must exclude many which another group of selectors would include. The lists which follow must, therefore, be regarded only as representative of the types which are suggested for their various purposes. Fuller details of all the varieties will be found in the Glossary at the end of the book, but the preliminary lists will aid the would-be grower to select a group of suitable varieties which reference to the Glossary will enable him to confirm or reject.

By far the largest group to consider is the group which we have called Bedding roses. Here the best plan would appear to be to

Hybrid Bourbon Rose, Zéphirine Drouhin; the so called "Thornless Rose"

Hybrid Tea Rose, Ville de Saverne

divide them into colour groups, since the prime need of the selector is to select by colour; the lists which follow are, therefore, arranged in colours. Unless marked to the contrary all are Hybrid Tea roses.

WHITE, CREAM OR SLIGHTLY TINTED ROSES

Abol (very fragrant)
Clarice Goodacre (fragrant)
Elizabeth Arden
  (slightly fragrant)
Frau Karl Druschki (H.P.)
McGredy's Ivory
Mme Jules Bouché
  (slightly fragrant)
Mrs. Herbert Stevens
  (slightly fragrant)
Olive Cook
  (slightly fragrant)

BLUSH, FLESH, PALE YELLOW, SULPHUR OR CHROME SHADES

Barbara Richards (maize-yellow) (very fragrant)
May Wettern (light-pink) (slightly fragrant)
Mrs. Oswald Lewis (canary-yellow) (very fragrant)
Ophelia (salmon-flesh) (very fragrant)
Rex Anderson (cream) (very fragrant)

PINK AND SALMON-PINK SHADES

Caroline Testout
  (slightly fragrant)
Dame Edith Helen
  (very fragrant)
E. J. Ludding (fragrant)
Hector Deane (very fragrant)
Lady Sylvia (fragrant)
Lal (fragrant)
McGredy's Pink (fragrant)
Mme Abel Chatenay
  (very fragrant)
Mme Butterfly (very fragrant)
Mme Henri Guillot (fragrant)
Mrs. Edward Laxton (fragrant)
Mrs. Henry Bowles (fragrant)
Mrs. Henry Morse
Mrs. L. B. Coddington
Picture
Pink Dawn (fragrant)
The Doctor (fragrant)
Velsheda (fragrant)

YELLOW, AND YELLOW SHADES

Aureate (fragrant)
Christine (Pernetiana)
Directeur Guérin (fragrant)
Geheimrat Duisberg (Pern.)
  (fragrant)
Golden Dawn (Tea)
Goldenes Mainz (fragrant)
Julien Potin (Pernetiana)
  (fragrant)
Lady Hillingdon (Tea)
Lucie Marie (fragrant)
Margaret Dickson Hamill
McGredy's Yellow (fragrant)
Mme Nicolas Aussel (fragrant)
Mrs. Beatty (fragrant)
Mrs. Wemyss Quin (Pernetiana)
  (fragrant)
Oswald Sieper (fragrant)
Phyllis Gold (fragrant)
Président Charles Hain
  (fragrant)
President Herbert Hoover
  (fragrant)
Sir Henry Seagrave (fragrant)

ROSE, ORANGE AND COPPER SHADES

Apricot Queen (fragrant)
Betty Uprichard (fragrant)
Catalonia (fragrant)
Comtesse Vandal (fragrant)
Emma Wright (fragrant)
Fred Walker (fragrant)
Ladylove (fragrant)
Lesley Dudley (fragrant)
Mrs. A. R. Barraclough
    (fragrant)
Mrs. Sam McGredy (fragrant)
Rose Berkeley (fragrant)
Rose d'Amour (fragrant)
Sunrise (fragrant)

LIGHT CRIMSON

Anna Neagle (fragrant)
Charles P. Kilham (fragrant)
General MacArthur
    (very fragrant)
Gerald Hardy (fragrant)
J. C. Thornton
J. H. Bruce (fragrant)
Lieut. Chauré (very fragrant)
Major Shelley (fragrant)
Margaret McGredy (fragrant)
McGredy's Triumph (fragrant)
Richmond (very fragrant)
Southport (slightly fragrant)
W. E. Chaplin

DARK RED

Captain Sassoon (fragrant)
Christopher Stone (fragrant)
Covent Garden
Crimson Glory (fragrant)
Etoile de Hollande (fragrant)
Hadley (very fragrant)
Malar Ros (fragrant)
President Boone (very fragrant)
President Jac Smits

DWARF ROSES WITH A COMBINATION OF RED, YELLOW AND COPPER

Angèle Pernet (Pern.) (frag.)
Angels Mateu (fragrant)
Atlantida (fragrant)
Autumn (fragrant)
Brasier (fragrant)
Condesa de Sastago (Pern.)
    (fragrant)
Duchess of Atholl (fragrant)
Edith Nellie Perkins (fragrant)
Federico Casas (fragrant)
Lady Forteviot (fragrant)
Luis Brinas (fragrant)
McGredy's Pride (fragrant)
Mme Edouard Herriot (Pern.)
Mme Joseph Perraud (fragrant)
Mrs. G. A. van Rossem (fragrant)
Ninon Vallin (fragrant)
Pilar Landecho (fragrant)
Simone Guérin (Pern.) (fragrant)
Violinista Costa

Within the scope of the dwarf bedding varieties may be selected the following, which thrive in partly shaded sites:

Caroline Testout (pink)
Emma Wright (orange)
George Dickson (crimson)
Margaret Dickson Hamill
    (yellow)
Mme Ravary (yellow)

Hybrid Tea Rose, Walter Bentley

A new Hybrid Tea Rose, Norman's 137B

The following dwarf varieties are good for town or suburban gardens:

Bertha Gorst (crimson-cerise)
Betty Uprichard (salmon-pink)
Caroline Testout (pink)
Dame Edith Helen (pink)
Etoile de Hollande (dark red)
Frau Karl Druschki (H.P.) (white)
General MacArthur (red)
Gloire de Dijon (Tea) (yellowish-flesh)
Golden Dawn (yellow)
Hugh Dickson (H.P.) (crimson)
Lady Sylvia (apricot to pink)
Margaret Dickson (H.P.) (white to flesh-pink)
Mme Butterfly (pale pink, apricot and gold)
Mme Edouard Herriot (Pern.) (coral-red and yellow)
Mrs. John Laing (H.P.) (soft pink)
Ophelia (pale salmon, shaded rose)
Ulrich Brunner (H.P.) (geranium-red)

Hybrid polyantha roses:

Else Poulsen (rose-pink)
Karen Poulsen (crimson-scarlet)
Kirsten Poulsen (cherry-red)

DWARF ROSES FOR EXHIBITION PURPOSES

The starred varieties are especially recommended.

*Barbara Richards (maize)
Comtesse Vandal (pale pink deepening to reddish copper)
Dame Edith Helen (pink)
*Directeur Guérin (creamy-yellow)
Earl Haig (crimson-red)
*Frau Karl Druschki (H.P.) (white)
*George Dickson (crimson)
*Golden Dawn (Tea) (lemon-yellow)
*Hugh Dickson (H.P.) (crimson)
*Julien Potin (Pern.) (primrose-yellow)
Lady Inchiquin (pink and orange)
Malar Ros (dark crimson)

Maréchal Niel (Noisettiana) (golden-yellow)
*McGredy's Ivory (ivory)
McGredy's Yellow (pale yellow)
*Mrs. A. R. Barraclough (carmine-pink)
Mrs. Beatty (pale yellow)
*Mrs. Charles Lamplough (white-lemon)
Mrs. Foley Hobbs (Tea) (white tipped pink)
*Mrs. Henry Bowles (rose)
Mrs. Henry Morse (rose-pink)
Mrs. John Laing (H.P.) (rose-pink)
*Mrs. Sam McGredy (orange-scarlet)
Olive Cook (lemon-white)

Oliver Mee (salmon-pink)
*Oswald Sieper (lemon-white)
Percy Izzard (cream to yellow)
*Phyllis Gold (golden-yellow)
*Portadown Fragrance (orange to scarlet)
President Boone (deepening scarlet)
*Président Charles Hain (yellow and cream)
*Rev. F. Page-Roberts (saffron-yellow)

Rex Anderson (cream)
*Sam McGredy (cream and buff)
*Sir Henry Seagrave (primrose-yellow)
*The Doctor (silvery rose)
The General (blood-red and orange)
Walter Bentley (deep pink)
*W. E. Chaplin (crimson)
*William Moore (deep pink)
William Orr (crimson)

DWARF ROSES FOR GROWING IN POTS UNDER GLASS

Charles P. Kilham (orange-red)
Frau Karl Druschki (H.P.) (white)
Hinrich Gaede (red and orange)
Julien Potin (golden-yellow)
Katherine Pechtold (orange, rose and gold)
Lady Hillingdon (Tea) (apricot, yellow and fawn)
Ladylove (rose-pink shaded apricot)
Lady Sylvia (flesh-pink)
Lal (salmon-pink)

Mme Butterfly (pink and apricot)
Mme Edouard Herriot (terra-cotta and rose)
Mme Joseph Perraud (orange shaded pink)
Mrs. A. R. Barraclough (carmine-pink)
Mrs. Herbert Stevens (white)
Mrs. John Laing (H.P.) (rose-pink)
Mrs. Sam McGredy (orange-scarlet)
Ophelia (salmon-flesh)
Richmond (bright crimson)

DWARF POLYANTHA ROSES (POLYANTHA POMPON) FOR BEDDING PURPOSES

Baby Betty (rose, yellow centre)
Cameo (salmon-pink)
Conchita (salmon)
Coral Cluster (coral-pink)
Eblouissant (dark red)
Edith Cavell (crimson)
Ellen Poulsen (rose-pink)
Gloire du Midi (orange)
Golden Salmon Improved (salmon)

Katharine Zeimet (white)
Kersbergen (very dark red)
Little Dorrit (coral-salmon)
Mrs. W. H. Cutbush (rose-pink)
Orleans Rose (geranium-red)
Paul Crampel (orange-scarlet)
Pride of Hurst (coral-pink)
Sparkler (bright red)

Varieties marked "S" are single-flowered varieties which should be kept apart from other types.

S Alice Amos (cerise)
Anne Poulsen (bright pink)
S Betty Prior (carmine)
S Bonnie Jean (carmine)
Cécile Brunner (blush)
S Cheerio (brick-red)
S Dainty Maid (carmine)
Donald Prior (crimson scarlet)
Else Poulsen (rose-pink)
Eugénie Lamesch (yellow edged carmine)
S Fairy Cluster (pale pink)
Folkestone (scarlet)
Fortschritt (salmon and yellow)
Fuchsine Guy (bright pink)

S Karen Poulsen (scarlet)
S Kirsten Poulsen (cherry-red)
Locarno (orange-scarlet)
Orange Triumph (orange-red)
Perle d'Or (nankeen-yellow)
S Pink Delight (shell-pink)
Poulsen's Pink (pink and gold)
Poulsen's Yellow (buttercup-yellow)
S Salmon Spray (salmon-pink and carmine)
Springtime (pale pink)
S Van Nes (carmine)
Yvonne Rabier (white)

The following dwarf-growing roses make very fine standards. Standards are generally budded on two types of stocks, Rugosa and Briar. The rugosa standards are the more suitable for light loamy soils, the briars for the heavier types of loamy soils. Standard roses require approximately the same type of attention as their dwarf prototypes.

Angels Mateu (flame and gold)
Barbara Richards (maize)
Bertha Gorst (crimson-cerise and gold)
Betty Uprichard (coppery-pink and salmon)
Captain Sassoon (dark crimson)
Caroline Testout (pink)
Charles P. Kilham (orange-red)
Christopher Stone (dark crimson)
Comtesse Vandal (pale pink deepening to reddish-copper)
Directeur Guérin (creamy yellow)
Duchess of Atholl (orange shaded rose)
Edith Nellie Perkins (red shaded cerise)

Etoile de Hollande (dark red)
Frau Karl Druschki (H.P.) (white)
General MacArthur (crimson-scarlet)
George Dickson (crimson)
Golden Dawn (Tea) (lemon-yellow)
Golden Emblem (Pernetiana) (golden-yellow)
Hadley (crimson)
Hugh Dickson (H.P.) (crimson)
Lady Forteviot (yellow and apricot)
Lady Sylvia (flesh-pink)
Lal (salmon-pink)
Major Shelley (cerise-scarlet)

Margaret Dickson Hamill (straw)
Margaret McGredy (geranium-lake)
May Wettern (salmon and pink)
McGredy's Ivory (ivory)
McGredy's Pink (rose-pink and gold)
McGredy's Triumph (orange and scarlet)
McGredy's Yellow (pale yellow)
Mme Abel Chatenay (salmon-pink)
Mme Butterfly (pink and apricot)
Mme Edouard Herriot (terra-cotta and rose)
Mme Joseph Perraud (orange shaded pink)
Mrs. A. R. Barraclough (carmine-pink)
Mrs. Edward Laxton (old rose and salmon)
Mrs. Foley Hobbs (Tea) (ivory and pink)

Mrs. G. A. van Rossem (orange and yellow)
Mrs. Henry Morse (rose-pink)
Mrs. Herbert Stevens (Tea) (white)
Mrs. John Laing (H.P.) (rose-pink)
Mrs. Sam McGredy (orange and scarlet)
Ophelia (flesh-pink)
Oswald Sieper (lemon-white)
Phyllis Gold (golden-yellow)
President Boone (deepening scarlet)
President Hoover (orange-yellow, shaded pink)
Rex Anderson (cream)
Shot Silk (cerise, shaded salmon)
Southport (scarlet)
The Doctor (silvery-rose)
Violinista Costa (scarlet, shaded gold)
William Orr (crimson)

The following Hybrid polyantha roses make very good standards:

Donald Prior (crimson-scarlet)
Else Poulsen (rose-pink)
Karen Poulsen (scarlet)
Kirsten Poulsen (cherry-red)

Locarno (orange-scarlet)
Orange Triumph (orange-red)
Perle d'Or (pinkish-yellow)
Van Nes (carmine)

In addition, the following wichuraiana ramblers make exceptionally fine weeping standard rose trees:

Albéric Barbier (cream and yellow)
Dorothy Perkins (rose-pink)
Evangeline (pale pink)
Excelsa (crimson-rose)
François Juranville (fawn-pink)
Hiawatha (crimson, white eye)

Lady Gay (rose-pink)
Lady Godiva (blush, white eye)
Léontine Gervais (salmon-pink and yellow)
Marjorie Foster (scarlet)
Minnehaha (deep pink)
Sanders' White (white)

The nature of the different types of climbers has already been noted, and it is, therefore, proposed to divide them into those which may be used for specific purposes. It should again be pointed out that there are no climbing roses. Roses which are thus called are suitable for training against walls, over arches or pergolas, and it is simply the vigour of their growth which makes them suitable for the purpose.

Roses suitable for training against walls which face north:

Aimée Vibert (white)
Albéric Barbier (cream)
Allen Chandler (scarlet)
Conrad F. Meyer (silvery-rose)
Dr. W. van Fleet (soft pink)
Félicité-et-Perpétue (creamy-white)
Gloire de Dijon (buff)
Hugh Dickson (crimson)
Mary Wallace (rosy pink)
Mermaid (sulphur-yellow)
Mme Alfred Carrière (white and blush)
Tausendschon (rose-pink)

Roses suitable for training against walls which face east:

Ards Rover (dark crimson)
Caroline Testout (pink)
Dr. W. van Fleet (soft pink)
Gloire de Dijon (buff)
Gruss an Teplitz (crimson)
Mermaid (sulphur-yellow)
Mme Alfred Carrière (white)
Paul's Scarlet Climber (scarlet)
Thelma (coral-pink)
William Allen Richardson (orange-yellow and white)

Roses suitable for training on walls facing south and east:

Banksiae lutea (yellow)
Chaplin's Pink Climber (pink)
Fortune's Yellow Rose (orange-yellow)
Lady Hillingdon (Climbing) (apricot-yellow and fawn)
Lady Waterlow (salmon-blush and carmine)
Maréchal Niel (golden lemon-yellow)
Mermaid (pale sulphur-yellow)
Miss Helyett (rosy pink)
Mme Abel Chatenay (salmon-pink)
Mme Butterfly (pink and apricot)
Mme Grégoire Staechelin (pale coral-pink)
Ophelia (flesh-pink)
Pax (white)
Phyllis Bide (pink shaded yellow)
René André (yellow shaded orange)
Souvenir de Claudius Denoyel (crimson)
William Allen Richardson (orange-yellow)
Zéphirine Drouhin (carmine-pink)

Roses suitable for training as pillars, on arches or trellis:

Albéric Barbier (cream)
Albertine (salmon)
Allen Chandler (scarlet)
American Pillar (rose)
Caroline Testout (pink)
Chaplin's Pink Climber (pink)
Crimson Conquest (crimson)
Dorothy Perkins (rose-pink)
Dr. W. van Fleet (blush-pink)
Easlea's Golden Rambler (gold flushed with red)
Emily Gray (golden-yellow)

Evangeline (pale pink)
Excelsa (crimson)
François Guillot (yellowish-white and pink)
François Juranville (fawn-pink)
Gardenia (creamy yellow)
Gerbe Rose (deep pink)
Hiawatha (crimson, white eye)
Hugh Dickson (crimson)
Jersey Beauty (pale yellow)
Lady Godiva (blush)
Lady Waterlow (salmon-blush and carmine)
Lemon Pillar (lemon)
Léontine Gervais (yellow, rose-tinted)
Marjorie Foster (scarlet)
Mary Hicks (crimson)
Mary Wallace (rose-pink)

Mermaid (sulphur-yellow)
Minnehaha (deep pink)
Miss Helyett (rosy pink)
Mme Abel Chatenay (salmon-pink)
Mme Alfred Carrière (white)
Mme Butterfly (Climbing) (pink and apricot)
Mme Grégoire Staechelin (pale coral-pink)
Ophelia (flesh-pink)
Paul's Scarlet Climber (scarlet)
Purity (white)
Sanders' White (white)
Tea Rambler (coppery pink)
Thelma (pale coral-pink)
The New Dawn (soft pink)
Zéphirine Drouhin (carmine-pink)

Climbers for growing in pots or under glass:

Caroline Testout (pink)
Fortune's Yellow (orange-yellow)
Lady Hillingdon (Climbing) (apricot, yellow and fawn)
Maréchal Niel (golden lemon-yellow)
Mermaid (sulphur-yellow)

Mme Abel Chatenay (Climbing) (salmon-pink)
Mme Butterfly (Climbing) (pink and apricot)
Ophelia (Climbing) (flesh-pink)
William Allen Richardson (orange-yellow)

Roses suitable for forming hedges:

(a) LOW HEDGES

Betty Prior (carmine)
Dainty Bess (pink)
Donald Prior (crimson-scarlet)
Else Poulsen (rose-pink)

Kirsten Poulsen (cherry-red)
Van Nes (carmine)
The Scotch Roses (see Rosa spinosissima)

(b) FOR TALLER HEDGES

Cornelia (old rose)
Eva (dark red)
Felicia (china-pink)
Hugh Dickson (crimson)
Joyous Cavalier (scarlet)
Moonlight (lemon-white)

Penelope (shell-pink)
Penzance Briars (see Rosa rubiginosa)
Rugosa roses and hybrids (see Rosa rugosa)

CHAPTER V

CHOOSING THE VARIETIES

TO write a chapter devoted to choosing appropriate roses for a rose garden would at first sight appear to be a case of arrant "padding" and a mere repetition of what has gone before. Such, however, is not the case. In a family so large as the rose family, there are many diversities of character, many weaklings, many strong and willing youngsters, a few worthy greybeards, a number of temperamental beauties, a few finicks, and a host of patient maids-of-all-work. Each has its place in an ordered community, and each its definite usefulness. Perfection can be, among human beings, a very terrifying possession and can make its possessor a most uncomfortable neighbour. Fortunately there is no perfect rose, search though we may.

Before we settle down to a discussion on the choice of the roses it is most desirable to grow, if there is to be any limit at all, it would be as well to consider how, that is to say in what circumstances, we are to prepare to grow them.

We have earlier indicated that we consider the only way in which one may grow dwarf bush roses with success is in specially prepared beds, and we repeat this with greater fervour, adding that in these beds we should grow roses and roses alone. One should add to this that the roses themselves should be planted to produce an effect as a harmonious whole and be subject to conditions of culture, and the normal pruning which will render them floriferous and active.

Certain divisions of the normal bedding roses into classes with vigorous, medium and weak growth now appear to add to the troubles of the would-be selector, and because of the existence of these variations it is of paramount importance to state a set of arbitrary rules which should govern the planting of any rose bed or garden.

The first rule is that, within limits, the roses should be planted as closely together as possible. Amplified this means that though the closest distance for planting certain varieties may be stated to be eighteen inches apart, this is the correct and maximum distance, as there is no advantage to be gained by planting such varieties, say, twenty-four inches apart. Certain vigorous varieties require thirty inches of space between them and their next nearest neighbours if the best results are to be obtained. Standard and half-standard roses should be three feet apart.

If rose beds are being designed especially, it is wise to keep these measurements in mind, so that the beds may accommodate the roses to be planted in them with correct spacing. It should not be necessary to add that a similar distance to the distance between the plants should be left at the edges of the beds.

But in addition to the factors already mentioned there remains the question of colour. As a rule the most satisfactory method is to grow within the confines of one bed—which should be a simple geometrical shape—only one kind of rose, and to obtain contrast between the beds themselves. In the confines of the small garden this is not always possible and the roses within the beds may have to be of two colours or even more, or perhaps completely mixed.

Some of the plates in this book, in particular those numbered 15, 33, 45 and 69, indicate the colours of roses which should not be so mixed. Thus Plate 69, showing the roses Ulrich Brunner, Rex Anderson, and Silver Jubilee, shows quite clearly how it is completely inadvisable to use crimson and yellow roses in close association. Moreover, Plate 38 shows that even different kinds of crimson roses must be associated with the nicest care, though Plate 39 shows that this may be done with a measure of success. As a rule the best associate for the crimson rose is a white one, and pink shades and cream ones blend well. Plate 33 shows how an association of yellow shades can be very disappointing, but Plate 32 shows how it can also be successful. In certain roses a number of shades of colour blend together to form an enchanting picture, but as a rule there is a dominant colour. It is this dominant colour which is the operative factor and should be considered when choosing another rose with which to associate it. Here the use of a colour chart is of considerable help. The roses pictured in the plates are, as far as printer's ink and reproduction methods will allow, of the same tone of colour as the rose itself. If the colour is matched to the colour chart—and the numbers quoted in the Glossary are the matching colours of the Horticultural Colour Chart—the actual association of colour can be judged before the planting is planned, and the rejection or acceptance of an idea will result almost automatically.

In addition, in the composite plates, that is, in those which contain the pictures of more than two kinds of roses, a piece of paper placed over one or other of the three associated kinds will often be found to provide in the two remaining varieties the colour association it is desired to obtain, though the association of the three kinds is disappointing. This can be readily seen by placing a piece of paper over the rose Enid in Plate 13.

40

Species Rose

Rosa mirifica, known as the Sacramento Rose

Hybrid Tea Rose, Madame Butterfly

Where the garden consists of a number of beds the deeper colours, particularly the crimsons and reds, should be kept as far as possible in the centre beds and not planted in the outer beds with an interleavening of lighter colours. Colour associations are, however, factors which express individual predilections, and, fortunately, in such matters there still remains freedom of opinion and room for originality. The test which the rose-grower should apply is not whether this or that book recommends a particular association, but whether the contiguity of any two colours is pleasing to him, and gratifies his own particular colour sense.

Certain individuals obtain a large measure of real pleasure from the relation of certain colours which affrights others, and it would be an extremely intolerant person who would deny them that satisfaction.

To summarise, try out your proposed colour associations, if you are able, before you translate them into terms of living roses; thus you will save yourself much disappointment. A word of warning also: do not judge the colour of a rose by the colour it appears to have in the subdued light of a show tent—you will find that in the garden it is apt to look quite differently; neither must you judge its colour under artificial light—quite often under such circumstances the blue-content of the crimsons is eliminated, and a crimson rose will appear to be an intense scarlet. The last warning is one which is seldom given, but nevertheless a most appropriate one. Roses associated together bear flowers in all stages of development; buds, perfectly formed flowers and full-blown roses existing upon the bush at the same time. The dominant factor is the colour of the full-blown rose, and it is, therefore, that colour which should always be considered in association with another. In the reds this will always be a little bluer than the rose in its bud stage, and certainly a little less intense. As far as reproduction will allow, the nurseryman who specialises in roses tries to give in illustrations as clear an idea of the colour of a rose as the process will allow. Unfortunately, in order to obtain, shall we say, a look of freshness, colours are brightened, and the result becomes a fresher-looking picture but a poor medium by which to judge the actual colour.

But all these methods are but a poor substitute for what in normal times is the simplest way of all. Find the time, before you plan your rose beds, to visit the gardens of a nurseryman who specialises in growing roses. Here you can see for yourself in nature's actual colours and under garden conditions all the colour associations you have in your mind, and you will come away with the knowledge that neither artist nor photographer, nor printer, nor poet, can bring before your eyes a picture which can in any real measure catch one-tenth of the glory which the rose alone can show you.

To return, however, to the question of choosing the roses! We have discussed vigour and colour, and we must now consider stocks. Bush and standard roses are usually budded upon the stock, that is, the stem and root, of another type of rose. This may be either briar, laxa, rugosa, or Manetti. Briar, or canina as it is sometimes called, is outstandingly good, but Manetti for certain purposes is not so good, as, though for a while it gives very good results, with age deterioration takes place very quickly. Laxa is said to encourage rose rust. Manetti stocks are, however, very suitable for roses used in greenhouses and for climates with warm and equable temperatures. Rugosa stocks are suitable for soils which are lighter than those normally used for rose-growing, but are not considered to be such good stocks for bush roses.

In Eastern North America a favourite stock is a variety of R. multiflora. Thus it can be seen that a diversity of stock also exists, and that the appropriate stock varies with the purpose for which the rose is to be grown and the country in which it is to be produced. Thus it is wise when choosing a source of supply not to buy imported roses, but to buy roses which have been produced in one's own country, not for reasons of patriotism but from the commonsense point of view that the man on the spot knows his local conditions a great deal better than the remote, if polite, stranger.

Now for a word about roots. The root system of the rose is its means of supply, and should be a network of fibres. Thick massive roots are to be deprecated. The good rose should have three or four strong roots, a mass of fibrous roots and four to five canes of equal strength. If the rose has been frequently transplanted there is little doubt that it will possess both the root system and the strong canes, but it would be unreasonable to expect that such roses should be obtained at a price which could hardly show the grower the cost of their frequent transplanting! Do not assume, either, that roses grown, say, in the north or east of the country will have preponderating advantages over those grown, shall we say, in the south or west. It is possibly true that those grown in the north and east may be rather more hardy, but if so it is equally certain that those grown in the south and west will have rather better ripened wood. Thus you may see that there are no definite advantages to be gained except those dictated by the suitability of the stock and the quality of the canes and roots.

So far we have dealt only with bush roses. Bush roses are also grown as standards, and here the roses are budded on to longer canes of briar or rugosa and form upright-growing heads on stout stems of about forty inches in height. Standards on rugosa usually form exceptionally large heads and require immediate staking after planting. Upright standards are, therefore, to be regarded as bush roses on long stems and present the same picture as the bush rose of the same variety, with its flowers produced considerably above ground level. They can be used with advantage to obtain variation in height in beds of Hybrid Tea roses, to form avenues close to paths where their beauty and fragrance can be appreciated without attendant backache. Standards should have the same fibrous roots recommended for the dwarf roses, and good stout stems with three to five active stems at the head.

Climbing Roses are really, as has been previously stated, strong-growing variations of the dwarf roses, and are not available in all varieties. The colour is in each case the same as that of the appropriate dwarf-growing variety. They can scarcely be called suitable for rapidly clothing arches or pergolas.

For this purpose the best class is the rambler. The rambler produces its flowers in clusters and is a fast and vigorous grower, and very suitable for any purpose where quick cover is required. The ramblers really comprise two classes, the wichuraiana and polyantha types, which for this purpose may be regarded as one class. Climbing roses should have the same type of roots as the dwarfs, and should have from three to five strong canes for their heads which should be of from four to eight feet in length. Climbers with thin and weakly growth should be rejected.

Weeping standards are climbing or rambling roses budded on long briar or rugosa stems, or occasionally trained to grow upon a single parent stem. They can be trained to grow upon umbrella-like frames and present a pleasant picture grown centrally in beds or in isolated positions in the lawns. The root systems should be plentiful and fibrous, the stems stout and strong, and the heads vigorous. If these items are satisfactory, correct and efficient planting, good culture and careful attention will ensure complete satisfaction to the gardener.

To conclude: choosing roses consists, in the main, of first of all choosing those varieties which satisfy the senses—primarily that of sight, secondarily that of smell—and relating these varieties to a specific purpose. It also consists of choosing the best-grown plants for the project, and though it is no part of this book's purpose to suggest either the rose-grower or the place from which the roses should be obtained, it must be pointed out that roses which satisfy the conditions stated can be obtained from all reputable rose-growers. But that is not the end; the complement to a good start is good culture, for it is idle to deny a good plant efficient care and attention, and then blame the original grower!

CHAPTER VI

PLANTING ROSES

THE best time for planting roses has already been discussed and it has been conceded that, generally speaking, November is the best month. Do not panic, however, if the month passes and the ground is frozen hard, and your roses have not arrived. Rose-growers also have hearts, and I know many who steadfastly refuse to send out trees in unsuitable weather. This applies equally to other months, for no advantage can be gained by receiving roses in such spells. Of course, it may happen that the weather should change after the roses have been despatched and they will arrive in unsuitable weather. Fortunately, the nurseryman takes precautions against this and packs his trees with moss and litter about the roots, with the stems strawed to prevent damage by bruising and from frost. If your plants should arrive during a spell of frost, do not open the parcel, soak it with water and place it in a frost-proof shed or cellar, covered with a sack or two. In such a way roses will keep for two or three weeks.

But it may happen that your beds are not ready and the weather is suitable for planting; in that case the plants should be "laid in." In this case unpack carefully, taking care not to damage the plants as they are separated. Remove the labels and fix them nearer to the tops of the canes so that they may not be buried and become indecipherable, soak the roots in water for thirty minutes, and open a trench and bury the roses leaning towards one side of the trench, so that all the roots and one-third of the stems are completely covered with soil. They should then be safe until the time is ripe for planting.

But all these things may not happen. The roses may arrive during perfect weather, at a time when the beds are just ready for planting. In this case open the packages in a shed away from wind and sun and stand the roots in a bucket of water for a period of from thirty to sixty minutes. Shorten any exceptionally long roots, remove any damaged roots or suckers, remove all leaves and seed pods, and cover the roots of each group with a piece of sacking so that they cannot be parched by the wind or sun. When planting the roses keep the bulk under the sacking, removing only those which are immediately required. Dig a hole large enough to take the roots when fully outspread, remembering that the point at which the plant was originally budded should be sufficiently low in the hole to be one inch below the surface of the soil when it is filled in. Distribute the roots evenly around the hole and fill in a little fine soil to which has been added half a pound of bone meal per bushel, fill in a further two inches of the ordinary soil over the roots, and tread firmly down around the stock. Now fill in the depression with the ordinary soil of the bed and tread in firmly. Roses *must* be firmly planted, and the soil around them should after they are planted be an integral part of the surrounding bed.

Generally speaking, the depth of the holes in which the roses are to be planted will vary between three and four inches; but examination of the plants will show quite clearly the depth to which they were originally planted, and this depth should be adhered to, provided that it does take the point at which the stock was budded just below the surface of the soil.

When stakes are required, these should be driven into the hole in which the rose is to be planted before the rose is put in. This removes the possibility of damage to the roots of the rose. When the tree is first tied it should be done loosely until it has finally settled in place, when it may be firmly tied.

For a while after planting, sinking may take place around the stock; this should be filled in from time to time so that water does not stand in the depression. Freshly planted roses become loosened in the soil as the result of frost and they should be systematically firmed after such frosts, provided that the soil is not too wet. A good plan is to protect freshly planted trees with a layer of leaves. A good thick layer drawn up around the trees is necessary, and to avoid them being lifted away by the wind they should be well covered with a layer of soil.

Standard roses may be planted slightly deeper than bush roses; indeed, it is advantageous so to do. Climbing roses (which excludes the rambler types) which are to be planted against walls should be situated at least six inches from the base of the wall in a carefully prepared site. This should be a hole approximately two feet square, and if the soil is light it should be freely "fed" with turf and decayed manure, to thoroughly enrich it as explained in Chapter III. Into the top spit should be incorporated two ounces of bone meal, or half a pound of basic slag added to the surface soil and forked in.

The wichuraiana ramblers are probably the most easily grown of all the roses. They are, however, particularly gross-feeding plants needing deep rich soil, and the site for each rose should be prepared as for climbers. The tree should be planted so that its topmost roots are approximately three inches below the top of the

45

soil. It should be trodden firmly in as in the case of a bush rose, and the surface soil well covered with a layer of well-rotted manure. The shoots should be shortened by about one-third of their complete length immediately after planting, but complete pruning should not take place until the spring.

The polyantha (pompon) roses are splendid bedding roses, producing clusters of small but brightly-coloured single, semi-double or double flowers during summer and autumn. They are splendid for filling formal beds on the lawns or for edging beds planted with other and more vigorous varieties. The polyantha (pompon) roses should be planted exactly in the same way as described for bush roses and require similar treatment. The same applies to the Hybrid polyantha roses, which, lightly pruned, make splendid floriferous bushes of about three feet in height.

We have made it clear that the best month in which to plant roses is undoubtedly the month of November. Sometimes this is impractical, or, for one reason or another, impossible, and one is often asked how late in the spring roses may be planted with any degree of success. An instance I can quote with certainty of successful planting late in the spring is of a large planting which took place in the first week in May, and provided very good-quality blooms in late July; but in this case all necessary precautions were taken to ensure success.

Roses planted very late in the spring should consist only of the Hybrid Tea roses or Tea roses, and should be specially "retarded." Nurserymen will in normal times have many varieties available which can be supplied retarded in this way. These are generally lifted from the positions in which they have been growing, and then frequently moved to prevent them breaking into growth. They will generally be found to have been pruned before they have been despatched, but if this has not been done they should be pruned before planting (see Chapter VII).

Before the roses are received, prepare the rose beds as described earlier, taking great care that the manure used is the most well-rotted which can be obtained, and incorporating in the top spit four ounces of bone meal per square yard. After having completed the work, leave the top spit rough for two or three days so that drying may take place. In suitable fine weather tread or roll firm and rake fine and even. Prepare sufficient fine, dry, leafy soil and add two ounces of superphosphate of lime to each gallon of soil (that is, four ounces per bucketful). When the roses arrive, place them in buckets of water and allow the roots to soak for from four to six hours. Take out the necessary holes, loosen the soil at the foot of the holes and spread about an inch of the finely-prepared soil over the base. When the roses have been sufficiently soaked, place one in turn in the middle of each hole, spread out the roots and cover with another inch layer of the finely-prepared soil, treading in firmly. Using fine, dry soil, fill the hole and tread as firmly as possible. Immediately after planting, water well in but tread no more. After a few days, dress the surface around each plant with a two-inch layer of well-decayed manure.

For the guidance of all desiring to plant late in the spring, the following approximate dates are given:

All early varieties, Hybrid Perpetuals, should be planted not later than mid-March in most seasons.

All Teas and Hybrid Teas should be planted not later than mid-April in even the most severe season, and the grower should take every reasonable precaution to see that they are given every possible attention and opportunity to become quickly established.

All real gardeners have in them an overwhelming desire to see that their charges grow and flourish. It is this desire which ensures that the good gardener is capable of performing miracles, but these miracles require two other attributes in the gardener in addition to the desire to see success. They are painstaking care and a real love of plants. Every good gardener I know, and each day I feel more inclined to thank God that there are so many of them, has all the attributes of a patient and sympathetic nurse, the ruthless precision of a great surgeon, and the meticulous attention to detail of a great artist.

CHAPTER VII

PRUNING

YOU will remember that Theophrastus had noted that burnt-over roses were improved in the future by the burning, and that this was a clear indication of the treatment needed by certain types of roses. It has been noted in connection with other plants that as they get past maturity they become less and less virile, and less floriferous. In the case of the rose you can quite easily observe that the strong shoot flowers profusely during its second year, but gradually deteriorates in successive years, getting weaker progressively up the stem. Soon a stronger shoot springs into life lower down the stem, and the process of atrophy in the older stem is accelerated, until in the course of time it would cease to exist. This would be nature's way of effecting pruning, and is, of course, slow in its application. Scientifically, there is a good reason for the strength of the stems which spring from the lower levels, since it is quite obvious that the plant has to perform a greater amount of work in lifting sap to a greater height than a lesser one, and that the nearer the base of the rose the stronger the new stem will be. It must also be obvious that there is limit to the number of such stems which can be formed without subjecting the plant to gross overwork. This is one of the reasons for pruning. Pruning, therefore, consists of two separate operations:

(a) Thinning, or the removal of all dead, weakly, unripe or unwanted shoots.

(b) The shortening of the remaining shoots to encourage virile growth which will produce flowers of the best quality and quantity.

It must also be obvious that, since roses are grown for a variety of purposes, and have sometimes in the first few years of their lives to build up a contour which will determine their shape for years to come, pruning to encourage growth and flowering must vary not only with the type of the rose itself, but also with regard to the purpose for which it is grown. It is quite wrong to assume, as many do, that the pruning of roses is only done to assure tidy and neat plants. Efficient pruning will determine not only the number of shoots which the plants will carry during the ensuing summer, but the size, number and quality of the flowers which the plant

Three Hybrid Polyantha Roses

Pink Karen **ABCDFG**
Else Poulsen **GHJKLMNORS**
Enid **PQTU**

Climbing Polyantha Rose, Phyllis Bide

will bear, and it may be stated as a corollary that the harder the pruning the stronger the new growths which will be made. Put in another way, "Spare the knife and spoil the rose."

The factors to be borne in mind when pruning, then, are these:

(a) The character or type of the rose.

(b) The purpose for which it is grown, e.g. as a decorative bush, as a pillar, for its bedding effect, or for exhibition purposes.

It will also be apparent that the times of pruning must vary with the latitude and altitude, and that plants growing in southern parts will need to be pruned before those growing in the north. A good general rule is stated to be that in the southern counties pruning of Hybrid Perpetual and Hybrid Tea roses of all types should be done approximately during the second week in March. As one proceeds farther north, this may be deferred at such a rate that in North Scotland it should be done in the second week in April.

Tea roses, polyanthas and Bourbons are a little more tender and should be pruned a week later than these dates, as should climbing roses growing on south and west walls, with a further deferment of a week for those growing on north and east walls.

The correct tool to use is the pruning knife, well whetted and with the keenest cutting edge, but unless you are skilled in its use it is better to employ a good pair of sécateurs. Rolcut sécateurs are ideally suited for the purpose. In addition, a pair of flexible but fully protective gloves which fit easily are necessary, since these can save a number of very nasty scratches and wounds.

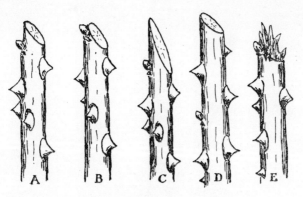

2—PRUNING CUTS—A—The correct pruning cut
B—Cut too close to eye
C—Cut too long
D—Too much wood above eye
E—Ragged cut

Every cut made in pruning must be made above an "eye" or bud or joint, and must slant away from the eye at an angle. Fig. 2 shows the correct and incorrect ways.

Generally speaking, the cut should be made immediately above an outward-pointing eye except in the case of roses with very lax growth which should be pruned just above an inward-pointing eye.

By examination you will speedily be able to classify all your roses into three classes:

- (a) Those with strong growth;
- (b) Those with medium growth;
- (c) Those with weak growth.

Successful pruning undoubtedly depends upon this classification of vigour since, in the case of Hybrid Tea roses in particular, the main object must be to encourage growth of medium strength which will give blooms of good size and colour. Thus it can be seen that the strong-growing roses will retain more dormant eyes than the medium-growing ones, and the weakest growers will be pruned most severely of all. The Glossary gives in all cases an indication to which class the rose belongs.

It is, of course, essential that all dead wood, all weak wood, and all unripe wood should be completely removed, and in this

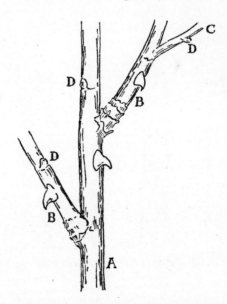

3—(A) Main stem, (B) Lateral stems, (C) Sub-lateral stems, (D) "Eyes"

connection it should be pointed out that "ripe" wood is that which is produced early in the growing season and which has time to become hardened. Unripe wood is that produced by autumn growth and is best removed.

For garden purposes pruning should not be so severe as for exhibition purposes, and in the summary which follows at the end of this chapter roses for exhibition purposes are dealt with under pruning instruction *E*.

Fig. 3 shows the meaning of the terms used in the pruning instructions, and these should be made a part of the gardener's normal vocabulary.

First pruning of all roses with the exception of wichuraiana ramblers, Climbing Tea roses, Climbing Hybrid Tea roses and polyantha roses, which have been planted in the autumn, should be severe, and they should be pruned to leave only two to three eyes per stem, generally leaving stems of about two inches in length. Dwarf roses planted in the spring should be pruned extra severely, only one or two eyes per stem being left, and, if pruned after they are planted, the ground around them should be trodden firm.

Climbing Tea and Hybrid Tea roses should have the shoot tips removed, but should not be otherwise pruned during the spring after planting.

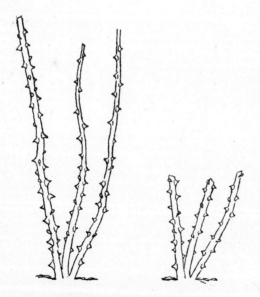

4 AND 5—PRUNING MAIDEN PLANT AFTER PLANTING

Wichuraiana ramblers, whether planted in the autumn or spring, should be pruned to half their total length and tied with wide distribution. In the following autumn, when well provided with basal shoots, the older growths may be then cut out.

Polyantha and Hybrid polyantha roses should be cut back so as to leave a maximum of six inches of stem length from the base.

HYBRID PERPETUAL ROSES, HYBRID TEA ROSES, TEA ROSES, NOISETTES AND PERNETIANAS

PRUNING FOR GARDEN PURPOSES

G.P.A. Time of spring pruning should be determined from p. 49. For garden purposes the general requisite is that the rose should be allowed to form as shapely a plant as possible, and that it should bear the largest possible number of flowers consistent with good quality. For this purpose the general instruction covering all this type of rose should be that all dead, weak and immature shoots should be removed in their entirety from the base and that any congestion in the centre of the plant should be relieved. If shoots have a tendency to cross one another, one at least should be eliminated. The strong remaining shoots should be shortened to leave four to six eyes, and such shoots as remain should be chosen to impart symmetry to the plant.

Autumn pruning should only consist of removing old and dead wood to facilitate the ripening of the new wood. An example of a rose needing such treatment is Julien Potin.

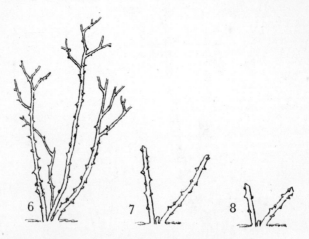

6—ESTABLISHED PLANT OF MODERATE GROWTH BEFORE PRUNING
7—PRUNED FOR GARDEN PURPOSES AS G.P.A.
8—PRUNED FOR EXHIBITION PURPOSES AS E.A.

G.P.B. The less vigorous varieties require harder pruning than the more vigorous ones, and with the stronger-growing varieties six to eight dormant buds may be left on each stem, but otherwise pruning is done exactly as in the case of the less vigorous type dealt with under *G.P.A.* An example of a rose needing such pruning is Federico Casas.

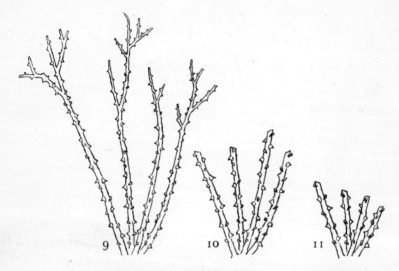

9—ESTABLISHED PLANT OF VIGOROUS GROWTH BEFORE PRUNING
10—PRUNED FOR GARDEN PURPOSES AS G.P.B.
11—PRUNED FOR EXHIBITION PURPOSES AS E.B.

G.P.C. Very vigorous varieties require even lighter pruning still, the general instruction applying to the removal of old and weak wood being identical, but extra special care should be taken to see that the centre of the plant is not overcrowded. Long, strong shoots from the base should be reduced to eight or nine inches in length, ending in an eye which points outwards, and four to five can be left on the laterals on the remaining and older shoots. Attention should be paid to the need for keeping a symmetrical plant. An example of a rose needing such pruning is Frau Karl Druschki.

G.P.D. Roses which have a lax habit may be pruned as in *G.P.B.*, but rather more stems may be left in the centre of the plant.

G.P.E. Climbers. Little or no pruning need be done to these roses. Dead wood should be removed and such wood as threatens to overcrowd the plant removed after the flowering

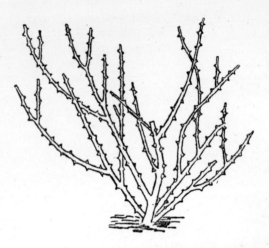

12—ESTABLISHED PLANT OF VERY VIGOROUS GROWTH
BEFORE PRUNING

period in the summer. Lateral growths should be pruned back to four buds in March.

G.P.F. Polyantha and wichuraiana pompons should be pruned for bedding purposes very close to the ground each year after the first pruning, which should not be severe. For other decorative purposes where height is not required to be controlled, the removal of the old flower stems and thinning of the old wood at the base is all that is necessary.

The climbing varieties require only the dead wood and some of the older stems removed to prevent overcrowding. An example of a rose needing this pruning is Gloria Mundi.

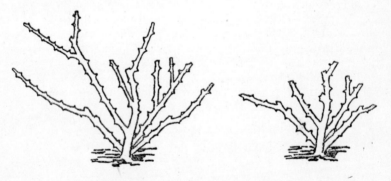

13—PRUNED FOR GARDEN PURPOSES AS G.P.C.
14—PRUNED FOR EXHIBITION PURPOSES AS E.C.

54

G.P.G. Hybrid polyantha roses and certain species roses, indicated by these letters, require very little pruning, dead wood only being removed, and the removal of the tips of the old shoots which have bloomed being sufficient. An example of a rose needing this pruning is Salmon Spray.

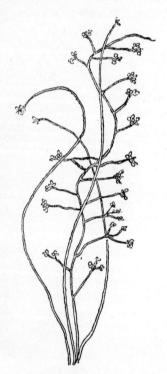

15—WICHURAIANA RAMBLER CLASS
G.P.H. BEFORE PRUNING

16—WICHURAIANA RAMBLER CLASS
G.P.H. AFTER PRUNING

G.P.H. Wichuraiana ramblers of the type which bloom on the new wood of the previous year should have all the growth which has flowered during the year removed at the base. The new growths should be securely tied in place. The tips of the new growths may be removed if necessary in spring. An example of a rose needing this pruning is Dorothy Perkins.

G.P.I. Certain types of wichuraiana ramblers bloom also on the lateral shoots as well as from the new shoots of the previous year, and beyond the removal of the very old wood and shortening of the lateral shoots to four eyes need little or no pruning; in fact, they are better without it. An example of a rose needing this pruning is Albéric Barbier.

G.P.J. Wichuraiana climbers again need little or no pruning except the removal of the very old or useless wood and a shortening of the laterals to approximately six inches. An example of a rose needing such treatment is Paul's Scarlet Climber.

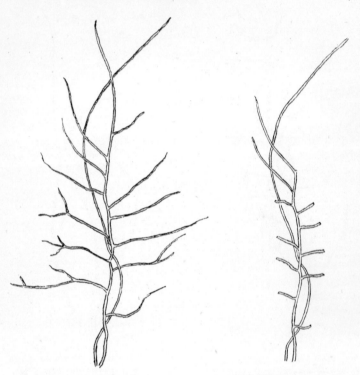

17—WICHURAIANA RAMBLER CLASS   18—WICHURAIANA RAMBLER CLASS
     G.P.I. BEFORE PRUNING   G.P.I. AFTER PRUNING

G.P.K. Standard roses of upright growth may be pruned as for the appropriate dwarf roses. In particular, attention should be paid to all roses which fall in the *G.P.A.* class; see that they are cut back almost to the stock. Shapely heads should be encouraged by judicious pruning. Very seldom is much more growth left beyond the point of the previous year's pruning.

G.P.L. Weeping standard roses should be pruned hard back the first season; in successive years the new growth only should be left, except where the older growths may be required to render

Billy Boy (Hybrid Tea) **ABFCDGH**
Dainty Maid (Hybrid Polyantha) **FJKLMPQ**

Hybrid Tea Rose, Home Sweet Home

the head symmetrical. All unwanted older growths should be cut back tight to the head. Long shoots which trail on to the ground should be shortened.

All other roses will be found with their detailed pruning instructions under their class in the Glossary.

PRUNING ROSES FOR EXHIBITION PURPOSES

General instructions for all roses: Remove all dead, weakly and damaged wood.

E.A. Plant should be thinned to allow room for the new growths which are to develop, and the stronger and well-ripened shoots of the previous year's growth should be cut back to two or three eyes. Toward the latter end of May the blind shoots, that is those without flower buds, should be removed and only the most promising should be allowed to remain. See p. 52.

E.B. These are stronger-growing varieties and should be similarly treated except that three to four eyes should be left upon each shoot. Removal of the blind shoots should be similarly undertaken as for the weaker-growing type. See p. 53.

E.C. The still stronger-growing types should have the strong basal shoot shortened to a maximum of six inches, and two to three eyes should be left upon the laterals of the older wood. Particular attention should be paid to the centre of the plant to see that it is not overcrowded. If it is found that too many shoots are produced to give flowers of high quality, some should be removed in addition to the blind shoots, which should, in any case, be removed. See p. 54.

In the case of species roses and their varieties, pruning instructions will be found fully detailed in the Glossary and these instructions should be consulted if there is any doubt.

In addition to the general pruning of the plants, roses do require a large measure of care to ensure that they will keep healthy and strong, and that they should flower well. Roses which have been established for some time benefit from mulching in spring, though this process may be harmful to freshly planted trees. A rose which is in vigorous growth may be given a mulch with benefit, but the soil should be loosened in its top inch before the two- to three-inch layer of well-rotted manure is applied round the stem, but not touching it, over a radius of about one foot.

The hoe should be used as frequently as possible during dry periods, but in no case should deep hoeing be practised.

During the spring attention should be given to any obvious errors in pruning—certain dormant buds may not develop and a further cut may become necessary. Young growths which develop inwards in consequence should be rubbed off. Weak straggly growths should be weeded out.

Nearly all roses produce during the summer a number of long shoots which cannot be expected to produce flowers during the current year, and will have the effect of preventing the flowering wood from producing its second crop of flowers. These shoots, if less than two feet long, should be tipped, or reduced to that length if longer.

When roses are cut for decorative purposes they should be cut with stems as long as possible, as this acts as an additional pruning and encourages free flowering.

During the autumn still further attention may be given to the bush roses which have produced further long or whiplike growths. These should be shortened so that they do not provide a means whereby the wind may cause them to chafe other growths, or to loosen the tree in the soil. Dead or useless wood which appears may be removed then rather than await the arrival of spring.

The sketches are self-explanatory and deal with all the phases of the pruning of roses.

One cannot leave the consideration of pruning without giving some account of the development of a type of pruning recently used both in this country and America, which seems to give a measure of greater simplicity and the benefit of considerably more growth to the ordinary gardener. Briefly the theory is as follows: The moisture raised by the root of the rose contains only a part of the constituents which will eventually make up the growth of the rose. The sap, as we may call it, is lifted in the structure of the plant until it eventually reaches the leaves, which by the process of photosynthesis proceed to construct from the air the material needed to build up the plant, mainly consisting of sugars. As the reconstructed sap is diffused into the plant it is transported to all parts of the plant where the sugar is converted into starch and helps to build the structure. Thus the whole plant, roots, stem and leaves, work together in harmony, and any interruption of this harmony must be regarded as harmful to the plant. Hence any removal of stems or leaves is to be regarded as definitely bad. A further function of the leaves and the shoot tips is their ability to manufacture hormones which exercise a very considerable influence upon the ready growth of the plant. If we take this theory for granted it is logical that pruning can only discourage the growth of the rose and prevent it from really showing its natural characteristics. It has been stated earlier in this chapter that examination of a rose which is unpruned will show that the best roses are borne on the stoutest and strongest of stems. By examination it can be seen that the old stems produce thin laterals which in their turn produce small flowers, but had we continued to watch from year to year we should have found that the bigger the bush grew in size the larger and stronger the new shoots produced would be, and the larger the flowers produced by these shoots. Thus the reason for pruning can be stated to be to encourage the plant to produce longer and stronger new growth. If we concentrate all the stored-up material in the body of the plant into the growth of one or two new shoots we shall make certain that these growths are strong. Nevertheless, we shall have robbed the plant of nearly all its capacity for obtaining new material for reconstruction for a considerable period, and logically there is no reason to suppose that there is gain by so doing. In fact, it can only be held that such treatment so enervates the plant that it will become exhausted in a comparatively short period.

In long pruning only two kinds of cuts are made. The first is to remove old or dead wood from the plant or to remove unwanted shoots from the side of the stem. Such a cut is made as close to the good wood or the stem as is possible without cutting into it. The second kind of cut is that made to remove a small piece of dead wood above a good eye. This cut is made sloping away from the eye and not towards it, generally one-eighth of an inch above it. The general rules for long pruning may be stated as follows:—

L.P.A. Newly planted roses of all types and weakly plants. Such plants should not be pruned until after the eyes have started to shoot. This may be as late as April. All wood which is dead should be cut away, and any wood in which the eyes have not started to grow should be removed. Nothing else should be done. When the rose buds begin to appear those produced on thin stems should be removed, but the leaves and stems themselves should remain.

L.P.B. To prune large-flowered bush roses and all but the weakest growth. The date of pruning is unimportant, but it should be finished by the middle of April as far as it is possible, or there will be a tendency of the sap to bleed. Pruning here amounts to the removal of all dead and diseased wood and any exhausted wood which has produced no good shoots the previous year. All laterals which branch are reduced to single shoots, leaving the strongest in existence.

L.P.C. Pruning dwarf polyanthas, Hybrid polyanthas, single roses and briars and all species roses. This kind of pruning should be complete before the middle of April. Pruning consists of removing old diseased and exhausted wood, and the removal of old flower stems. If the bush appears to be crowded, thin branches may be removed to allow a freer circulation of air. Where polyantha pompons and Hybrid polyantha roses are required for bedding purposes uniformity can be encouraged by more severe pruning.

L.P.D. Standards. These are pruned exactly as for *L.P.B.* but additional attention must be given to the shapeliness of the head. Here it is obvious that all strong outward shoots must be pruned to an outward eye, irrespective of whether the eye has started into growth or not. Extra strong shoots may have to be shortened, always to allow the growing eyes to reserve the general shape of the tree.

L.P.E. Pruning of climbers and ramblers except the climbing sports. These should be pruned in November. The long new shoots are always retained, all short shoots which have flowered are cut back to the main stem unless the stronger shoots are insufficient to maintain the growth of the plant, in which case the short shoots are cut back to two or three eyes. All dead wood is completely removed and any old wood which has not thrown long new canes is cut away from the base.

L.P.F. Pruning of climbing sports. These are pruned during the winter, and all that is necessary is to remove dead and exhausted wood and any thin side shoots.

CHAPTER VIII

PROPAGATION OF ROSES

ROSES may be propagated in the same way as most other plants:—

  (a) From seed
  (b) From cuttings
  (c) By budding
  (d) By grafting

In Chapter II it has been explained that the propagation of roses from seed was one of the reasons for the speedy introduction of new varieties, because, first of all, of the accidental cross pollination of different varieties, and finally because of controlled hybridisation designed to produce new varieties. Thus it is impractical for the rose-grower to reproduce individual hybrid roses of a given type from seed. He can, of course, grow on seedlings from the seed his roses will produce quite freely, but he does not know what these may produce. He combines one rose with another with a certain design in view, but often a very large batch of seedlings will produce few, if any, roses of any real merit. Thus the amateur may, if he follows out this practice, find that he may have to grow many hundreds of seedlings to produce a single good rose. The cross pollination is performed by taking the pollen from the anthers of one rose grown under glass by means of a fine camel-hair brush and dusting it upon the stigma of another kind of rose from which the stamens have been removed. This is the seed parent.

In actual practice the roses which it is desired to hybridise should be grown in a greenhouse, as indicated in Chapter III. After potting, the roses should be pruned within three weeks and should be brought into flower at the same time, as near the end of March as possible. When the flowers have just passed the bud stage, the rose which it is desired to make the seed parent should have the stamens removed and should be covered with a muslin or paper bag to prevent the entry of insects with undesired pollen. In three to four days the pollen from the rose which it is desired to make the other parent may be introduced by means of a fine camel-hair brush, the bag being removed for the purpose but being replaced immediately afterwards, and being left for approximately a week afterwards. The seed pods should be left on the plants until they are almost ready to fall, when they should be removed and stored with their stalk ends firmly embedded in sand until sowing time arrives in November.

The compost should be three parts loam, three parts sand, one part leaf mould, one part charcoal. Prepare a shallow box with an inch layer of drainage material and fill with the compost to half an inch from the top. Plant the seeds about one inch apart and cover with a layer of finely sifted compost. Firm the soil over the seeds, water them well, cover with a sheet of glass and keep in a house with a fixed temperature of from 55° to 60° F. When the seedlings have three to four leaves, pot on, one to each pot, using 2-inch to 2½-inch pots with a similar compost, and placing them near the glass, grow on until the roots are well developed, when they may again be potted on to 3-inch pots in a similar soil with the addition of a little bone meal. Harden off gradually in June and plant them out in a sheltered but sunny spot in July. By October, buds should be available for budding on stocks if desired, but some time will necessarily elapse before the value of the cross may be determined. This waiting period can be shortened by the process of inarching. To do this the seedlings should be planted near the side of the pots at their first potting, and when well rooted, generally in three weeks to a month, should be knocked out of the pot and placed with the soil ball intact and a little fresh soil in a piece of sacking about six inches square, which should be wrapped round the roots and firmly secured with raffia. This should then be tied to a strong briar or Manetti stock so that the stem of the seedling touches the stem of the briar and is kept growing. At the point of contact make a T slit in the stem of the stock, insert the stem of the seedling and tie firmly with raffia. Quite quickly union will be effected and the head of the stock can be cut off just above the graft and the seedling can be separated by cutting away at its point of contact with the stock; its container can then be removed. From eight to ten weeks after this has been done, the stock should possess a good head which should flower in good time and prove or disprove the value of the cross pollination.

Though seed as a means of producing garden roses is not practical, species roses may be grown in this way, and though minor variations may occur, the process is in the main the most suitable way of increasing or replacing stock. The hybrids of the species may show greater variation in their progeny, however.

Vegetative reproduction of garden roses is the general method used, and the simplest method is by cuttings of the stem, though this has definite disadvantages in certain cases. This method may be adopted at various times of the year, and the various methods are described. During the months of July and August four- to six-inch lengths of stems which have just flowered should be cut from the parent tree with a very keen knife, and all the leaves with the exception of the top two removed. The leaflets upon these should be reduced if they are large; the buds should all remain. The stems should be then inserted, to a depth of half their length, into a very sandy soil near the edges of a 5-inch pot. The soils should be pressed down very firmly and the soil well watered. The pots should be placed in a closed frame or in a greenhouse under a handlight and kept reasonably moist, but not wet. Three to four weeks will usually be sufficient for them to produce roots. The preparations Seradix A and Hortomone A applied as described will aid in the production of good root systems, but are not essential to good rooting. When rooted, the cuttings should be potted into 5-inch pots with soil a little more generous—that is, containing less sand and more leafy loam—and gradually hardened off in an outdoor frame.

Autumn cuttings are made somewhat longer, any length from six to ten inches being suitable. A narrow trench with straight back about four inches deep is prepared in a sheltered border, which can be left fallow, and the base covered with a layer of sharp sand into which the ends of the cuttings are inserted, and the trench is then firmly filled in and the cuttings left undisturbed. Rooting will be much slower, and it should not be taken for granted that when growth takes place in the spring rooting has commenced, though it is likely to follow fairly soon after. The cuttings should not be removed until the following autumn when they may be taken to permanent quarters. This method is particularly applicable to the rambler roses, and gives very good results in most cases. The advantage of roses upon their own roots is that every shoot is of the true rose, there being no "suckers." Such roses are not infrequently of short life, but often produce bushes of outstanding merit.

The chief commercial method of producing roses is by "budding." This consists of incorporating the bud from one tree into the stem of another. Bush and standard roses are produced in this way. The best stock to use is undoubtedly briar, and so the first step consists of producing the briars. These may be bought, grown from seed collected from briar hedgerows, grown from cuttings of briar produced as previously described, or from strong young briars obtained from the hedges in October or November. Thus the preliminaries must be made a considerable time before the budding is done so that the stocks are available.

Seedling briars are undoubtedly best. They are generally, if the roses are to be dwarfs, cut back to form strong root stocks. The head is left upon the root stock and the bud is inserted in the main root stem below the head and slightly below the normal soil level. In the case of standards and half-standards, the buds are inserted in the young side stems, right in the angle they make with the main stem, so that the object must be to select briars with straight stems and to trim off all the side growths except two or three which emerge at a height of from three feet to four feet from the ground. These are left unpruned. If rugosa stock is used, the buds are inserted in the main stems and three buds are usually used.

In the photographs (Plates 17, 18 and 19) which illustrate the process it has been necessary, in order to show the T cut, the insertion of the shield and the method of tying, to make these cuts on the front of the side growths, but it should be pointed out that the correct position for the T cut and the insertion of the shield is as near the joint of the side stem with the main stem as possible. This discourages the growth of briar buds from the joint.

Having selected the appropriate briars, the next problem is to choose the correct time and the best type of buds to insert. Generally the best months for budding are July and August, but much depends upon the ripeness or otherwise of the available buds. The best buds to use are those taken from a flowering stem of the rose at the time when it is bearing a full-blown rose. The best buds this stem bears are generally about half-way down. The leaves and petiole may be left on to serve as a handle by which the bud may be held. Turn the shoot upside down, and with a very keen knife cut from approximately one inch above the bud (that is below the bud in its growing position), cut out bud, finishing about three-eighths of an inch below it. The leaves may now be removed, but the petiole may be left. This is technically called the "guard," and is used to protect the bud and as a means of inserting the bud in the T cut. The sliver of wood which lies inside the bark is next removed and the bark and bud left un-bruised and uninjured. This is technically known as the "shield." The shield may be made slightly smaller by trimming, so that approximately three-quarters of an inch of bark remain below the bud (as it grows), and three-eighths of an inch above it. It is important that the buds should be kept plump and fresh, and the stems should be kept plunged in water while the work proceeds. The buds should not be allowed to become dry and should be inserted in the T cuts as soon as prepared.

The cuts in the stems of the stocks in which the buds are placed

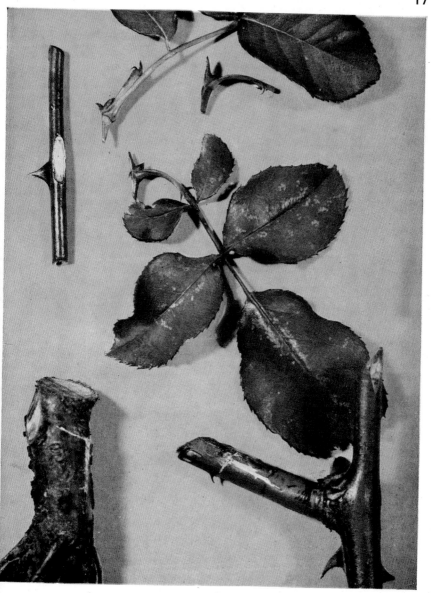

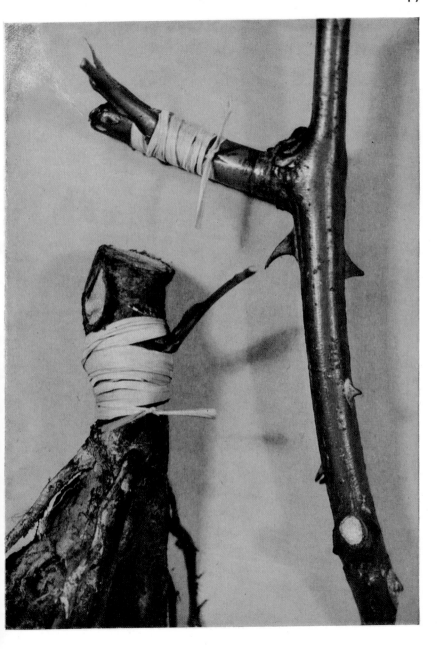

Pernetiana Rose, Afterglow

are all T-shaped with the cross-cut at the top made first. The bark is carefully lifted on each side of the down-stroke to allow the prepared bud to be inserted. This is done by taking the bud by the guard and slipping it into the T cut from the top so that it fits cleanly into the stock and makes a trim fit. In the case of bush roses only one bud is inserted; with standards two or three, one on each of the side growths, are inserted. The final process is to tie the bud in place with raffia in such a way that the lips of the T cut lie flat upon the back of the shield of the bud. Plates 18 and 19 illustrate this.

Plates 18 and 19 show the growths trimmed off—for photographic purposes these had to be eliminated so that detail should be clear. It is important to note that the briar must be allowed to continue to grow and that no growths upon which buds have been inserted may be cut back. Thus the dwarf briar stock keeps its top growth and the standard stock keeps its full side stems until all growths have ceased for the year, when the entire stock or branch in which the bud has been inserted should be cut off an inch from the bud. The tie is then cut to prevent strangling of the stock. Normally the bud will not start into growth until the following spring, but in the case of standards the growth made should be supported by tying with a loose loop of raffia to a stick tied to the stock and protruding above it. If this is not done a sharp gust of wind may whip the "take" out of its socket. In the case of bush roses no support is necessary. Where buds on standards have failed to "take," the branches should be cut back to the main stem and not allowed to remain.

Grafting is sometimes used to provide roses for cultivation under glass, and is an operation of considerable interest, being almost identical with the operation used for grafting fruit trees. Here briar stocks are firmly potted in 3½-inch pots in early autumn, using a good standard rose compost. The pots are then plunged in a bed of ashes in a sheltered position out of doors and well watered in. They must not be allowed to become dried out. The pots are brought into a heated greenhouse in November and are then ready for grafting. The scions are pieces of the particular rose it is desired to propagate, of ripened wood, that is growth which has been made during the early summer, and they should be about 1½ inch in length and contain one eye, but no more. Several methods of grafting are possible, and the method to be used to accomplish a perfect union between the scion and the stock may vary.

The most usual method is whip-grafting, and here the essential factor is that the scion and the stock should be of similar diameter.

First cut the briar stock off 2 inches above soil level with a horizontal cut with a pair of Rolcut sécateurs. Now, with a really keen knife, cut the stump with an upward cut so that a thin wedge is made at the top, thus:—

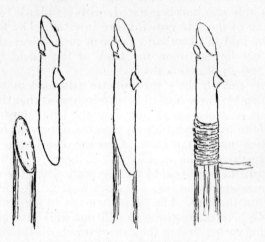

19, 20 AND 21—WHIP-GRAFTING

Do this with one stroke of the knife. It is well worth while to practise this cut on similar material first if one has not performed the operation before. Then take a scion of suitable size and make a similar cut at the bottom end in such a way that the bud is not removed or damaged. The art in making these cuts is to see that the two sections are of identical shape. Now the union may be made. To do this, place the cut part of the scion on the cut part of the stock so that the two surfaces fit flush and the bark at the edges of the scion exactly meets the bark edges of the stock. If this is done correctly, the stock and the scion will make what appears to be a continuous stem. They may now be tied together. Wet some raffia and let one end lie along the stem from the ground, and starting from the top of the junction wind the other end round and round the united pair, finishing well below the junction and finally tying to the loose end. Some practice may be necessary before a successful graft is established.

Where the stock and scion are different in diameter rind-grafting can be used. Here the stock is cut off two inches above the soil level and a slitting cut made in the side of the bark. The scion is prepared exactly as before but is pushed into the slit with the cut side to the wood side of the briar and bound firmly in place with raffia.

Three Species Roses

Rosa pineliensis **ABEFK**
  Rosa agrestis **BCGJKNO**
    Rosa blanda var. hispida **DHKLPQ**

Polyantha Pompon Rose, Baby Betty

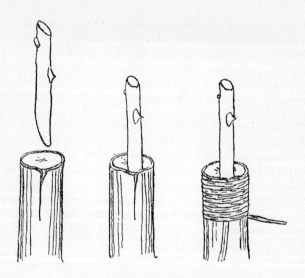

Where the stock is too big to allow the employment of either of the foregoing methods, wedge-grafting is the simplest method to adopt. Here the scion is chosen with two or three eyes, but should not exceed two inches in length. Cut back the stock as before

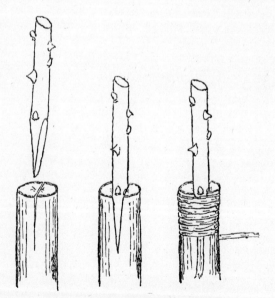

25, 26 AND 27—WEDGE-GRAFTING

and split it down the middle with a sharp knife to a depth of one inch. The scion should be cut to a sharp wedge with a cut on both sides and inserted in the slit so that the bark on each side of the wedge touches the bark on each side of the end of the split in the stock. The union should be firmly bound in position with raffia and the exposed cut parts should be covered with grafting wax.

The grafted plants should be kept in the house with a moderate temperature of approximately 60° F., evenly maintained with a moist atmosphere. No ventilation should be given except when the temperature and humidity can be maintained, until March, when the house may be given increased ventilation as the weeks progress. When the shoots show good growth and root development is obvious, the trees may be repotted and grown on.

Grafted trees may be planted out, if it is desired after repotting, about the third week in May.

CHAPTER IX

ROSE DISEASES AND PESTS

THE rose is subject to a large number of more or less serious diseases, and is prey to a considerable number of pests. Just, however, as the finest way to acquire a prepossession that one suffers from a number of incurable maladies oneself is to dig and delve deeply into a medical journal, so one can, if so minded, become as affected by the chapter of the ills and evils which may befall the rose, that one can imagine one's roses affected by them all. As a rule only four of the diseases need be considered seriously, and each has its appropriate treatment.

It is axiomatic that the healthy rose is less subject to disease and pests than the ill-cared-for one, and the first essential of the combat against rose diseases should undoubtedly be to see that all the needs of the rose are fully met. These have been previously outlined and should be followed with care.

FUNGI. Certain of the rose diseases are due to the action of tiny plants which are called fungi. These may be called "un-green" plants and resemble in character the mushroom or toadstool. You are probably aware that it is only through the agency of the chlorophyll, or the green colouring matter in the leaf, that the normal plant can build up the organic matter required for its development. It follows, therefore, that these fungi must either be parasitic and derive the substances upon which they exist from a plant already containing chlorophyll and able to construct its carbohydrates from carbon dioxide and water by the process which is known as photosynthesis, or they must be saprophytic and obtain their organic food from dead or decaying organic material.

There are, of course, other diseases which may be the result of certain dietary deficiencies, and taken as a whole the diseases of roses may be regarded as similar to those affecting human beings, and yielding to treatment, except inoculation, in a similar fashion. For example, the disease "ringworm" is caused by a microscopic fungus, and is easily cured with appropriate treatment. "Rickets" is undoubtedly due to dietary deficiency, in similar fashion to "chlorosis" in certain plants. Here the cure is to remedy the deficiency.

Fungi do not produce seeds in the generally accepted sense of the word; they produce myriads of microscopic spores by various means. These spores may be wind-borne, carried to the leaf by rain, or insects, and though at first the leaves will show no signs of attack, the process of growth will continue until the spore-bearing part of the fungus comes to the surface and the spores are scattered in myriads around, when all the elements necessary for the epidemic stage are present. It is clear, therefore, that the aim of the gardener should be to prevent the early infection.

For this reason it is necessary to examine the first sources of infection. It is obvious that even in the cleanest of gardens infection cannot be avoided since spores can be wind-borne, and persist in the diseased leaves of the previous year, or even in the tissues of the plant itself as mycelium.

The obvious method is to collect and burn all leaves from affected bushes, and to cut out all diseased wood during the winter months, but, while so doing, the usual precautionary sterilisation measures should be taken or the surgery may only spread the disease. It should be quite clear, however, that once any disease caused by a fungus, other than common mildew, exists in a plant it can only be eliminated by surgery and that all spraying with fungicides only aims at spreading evenly over the plant tissues a poisonous substance which will prevent the germination of any new spores deposited upon the surface. It will be apparent, therefore, that spraying can only be effective as long as the material sprayed remains upon the surface and that as soon as the spraying compound has been washed off by a shower of rain it is no longer effective.

MILDEW. The most important of the rose diseases is undoubtedly mildew, both in roses grown in the open and those grown under glass. The earliest symptom of the disease is the appearance of whitish spots upon the leaves which spread and cover the whole of the leaf, and then spread rapidly over the young growth with consequent interference with the production of flowers. There is considerable difference in the susceptibility of various kinds of roses to the attacks of mildew, some of the newer glossy-leaved wichuraiana hybrids being almost immune while the softer-leaved quicker-growing types are attacked.

To reduce the incidence of the disease roses should be pruned so that air may circulate freely and the plant may be open to sunlight. As mildew is an external disease, when caught at the onset, it may be rubbed off with the fingers, preferably dipped in a powder of flour of sulphur, though this cannot be done if the disease is widespread. Various sprays may be recommended:—

Three Hybrid Tea Roses

Gloaming **BCFG**

Lady Barnby **JKNO**   Charles P. Kilham **LMPQ**

Fruits of Species Roses

Rosa virginiana BCDFGH

Rosa caudata JKNO

Rosa blanda LMPQ

1. Potassium Sulphide (Liver of Sulphur) -   - 1 ounce
   Water   -   -   -   -   -   -   - 2 gallons

which should be mixed just prior to spraying and used while the colour is still liver-brown. If it is to be used as a fungicide, that is for plants already attacked by the disease, one ounce of soft soap should be added to the mixture. The mixture should not be used where it can come into contact with white lead paint, which it will blacken. This mixture should be used as soon as the leaf buds are developed and at intervals of seven days afterwards.

2. A spray which is increasing in popularity is Bicarbonate of Soda in the proportion of one ounce to ten gallons of water, similarly used.

Ammoniacal Copper Carbonate is also used, and Lime Sulphur and Bordeaux mixtures; details of the methods of preparation are given on p. 74. It should be pointed out, however, that some of the liquid colloidal copper preparations are clean to handle and, used in conjunction with a wetting compound, exceptionally effective. Bouisol is particularly good for controlling rose mildew.

BLACK SPOT. The second disease in importance is doubtless black spot, which generally appears at mid-summer and can be diagnosed by the somewhat circular purpled brown patches which appear on the surface of the more mature leaves. Some leaves are completely covered and drop off; such a defoliation is usually followed by the growth of buds which would normally remain dormant throughout the winter with a consequent weakening of the rose.

The spores of the disease winter in the soil. It is therefore important that the fallen leaves should be collected and burnt; the soil should be dressed with freshly slaked lime at the rate of ¾ lb. per square yard in November, and during January the leafless plants and the soil should be drenched with a solution of Copper Sulphate at the rate of three ounces to four gallons of water. The roses should again be sprayed with a similar mixture during the third week in February.

The total development period of the disease is about fourteen days, and to be effective, any spraying which is done must be done at shorter intervals than this, when the Potassium Sulphide mixture or Bouisol may be used.

A mixture which is very popular and useful for the control of black spot and rose rust may be made from two ounces fluid Bouisol, three ounces fluid Sulsol, and two ounces soft soap to five gallons of water. It has the additional merit of controlling mildew and green fly.

A mulching with an inch layer of peat moss litter, or with fresh lawn cuttings in early May, and repeated at intervals, is also said to discourage the advent of black spot.

ROSE RUST is one of the commonest of rose diseases, and is so called because of the rusty appearance of the patches on the leaves. The treatment accorded to diseased plants should be exactly that recommended for black spot above, but care should be taken when spraying that the underside of the leaves is completely wetted by the spray.

When swellings appear on the stems of the roses at or near ground level the disease known as CROWN GALL is present. By some this is not regarded as affecting the efficient growth of the rose, but is comparable to the formation of a callous after wounding. Nevertheless the formation of a large mass of material under the stimulus of the bacteria would seem to point to a misapplication by the plant of material not primarily destined for the purpose, and discouragement at least would seem indicated. The treatment—and none better is known—is to cut away the gall with a sharp knife and to paint the wound with Stockholm tar to prevent re-infection.

BLACK OR DOWNY MILDEW is a more serious disease than ordinary mildew and is seen on roses grown under glass. The rose begins to wilt and the leaves to fall freely without apparent reason. Closer examination will disclose the presence of irregular brown or purplish-brown spots on the upper surface of the leaves, with corresponding whitish-grey downy patches below. It spreads with rapidity. All dead and infected material should be burned and the plant sprayed with the Potassium Sulphide mixture and the plants given free ventilation. Vaporised Sulphur is also used as a treatment.

LEAF SCORCH attacks only the leaves of the plants, on which small yellow-green patches appear at first. These increase in size, become more yellow, change to brown surrounded by a red or purple line. It rarely appears in epidemic form, but the defoliation of the plant sometimes causes a second growth which is definitely harmful, and the onset of the disease must be checked. All diseased leaves should be gathered or stripped from the plant and burned. The ground around the plant should be drenched with Copper Sulphate solution, and the trees sprayed in the spring as the leaves appear with the Potassium Sulphide solution.

DIE-BACK is a disease which affects the shoots of roses, particularly Ramblers, to such an extent that cases have been reported in which five to six feet of the shoots have become dead and

Three old but good Roses

Caroline Testout (Hybrid Tea) **ABEF**   Climbing H.T. Rose, Lady Waterlow **CDGH**
Common China Blush **KLMOPQ**

Three Species Roses

Rosa californica **CEF**
Rosa chinensis viridiflora **KNO**   Rosa multibracteata **GHMLPQ**

blackened. It is again the work of a fungus. The control indicated is that the diseased branches should be cut out and burned, and the tree sprayed with Bordeaux mixture in the autumn, with following sprays of Ammoniacal Copper Carbonate in spring.

STEM CANKER appears to be a disease much more widespread in America and forms yellowish-brown patches on the stems, sometimes with a purple edge, but generally without. These patches develop to show the characteristic lesions. All cankered wood should be cut away and burned.

The treatment indicated is to drench with strong Bordeaux mixture in autumn and again in early spring; subsequent spraying should be done with Ammoniacal Copper Carbonate.

BROWN CANKER usually appears at a point just above the union between scion and stock as a slight discoloration which gradually deepens to black with a waterlogged appearance, and swelling and cracking of the bark takes place. The disease is not fatal as a rule, but leads to a very severe falling-off of both quantity and quality of the blooms, the leaves of affected plants often being light green. No cure exists for the disease, but its incidence is lessened if the graft union is above the level of the soil, humidity apparently being a controlling factor. Soil in which affected plants have been grown should be sterilised if it is to be used again for the same purpose. Infected stock should be burned.

CHLOROSIS is one of the few diseases which are not due to bacteria or fungi. It has been previously pointed out that the plant depends upon its chlorophyll for the adequate manufacture of the carbohydrates necessary for its effectual growth. When chlorosis affects roses, leaves lose their green colouring and become wholly or partly yellow, consequently losing their power of carbon assimilation, and the plant literally starves to death. Roses seldom show signs of chlorosis except in calcareous soils, but it is undoubtedly not the presence of chalk, but the absence of iron content in such soils which is the contributory factor in the causation of chlorosis, since it is demonstrable that trace elements of iron salts are essential if the plant is to possess adequate chlorophyll. The cure is to add to the soil one ounce of iron sulphate per plant in granules about the size of a pea, and to spray the plant with a solution of Iron Sulphate at the rate of one ounce to six gallons of water until the symptoms abate.

BRONZING is a symptom of overfeeding, usually met with in young roses forced under glass, and is marked by the bronzy discoloration of foliage with subsequent dropping-off. Attention should be given to feeding.

THE MIXTURES mentioned as preventives are:

(a) Copper Sulphate Wash. Three ounces of powdered Copper Sulphate to four gallons of water. It should not be applied to plants with leaves. Add copper sulphate to one quart of hot water in an earthenware vessel. Add cold water to four gallons.

(b) Ammoniacal Copper Carbonate can be prepared by adding two ounces of Copper Carbonate to one pint of ·880 ammonia and a quarter-pint of water, which should then be bottled. When required for use it should be added to sixteen gallons of water, and should be used at once.

(c) Bordeaux mixture is made by adding one pound of copper sulphate, one pound of stone lime to each ten gallons of water, and should again be used immediately after mixing.

The copper sulphate should be crushed and dissolved in a quart of hot water in an earthenware vessel, and sufficient water then added to make up to five gallons. The lime should be slaked with a little water, more water added to bring it to a creamy consistency and then sufficient water added to bring the quantity to five gallons, and added to the copper sulphate solution. As any free copper sulphate present in the solution scorches foliage, a test should be made of the clear liquid when it has settled to detect the presence of free copper sulphate. Any bright iron surface dipped in the liquid will show a copper deposit if this is so, and a little more lime should then be added. A more definite test is to add a little potassium ferrocyanide solution to a little of the clear solution left after precipitation, when no discoloration should take place; if, however, a reddish-brown colouring is observed, more lime should be added until the test shows no discoloration. To avoid clogging, spray liquid should be passed through a very fine brass sieve.

Other recommended fungicides are:

Bouisol, one fluid ounce to two and a half gallons of water for mildew or black spot.

Sulsol, one and half ounces to two and a half gallons of water for rose rust.

Both these should be used in conjunction with the wetting compound.

Lime sulphur spray is better used from a concentrated prepared form, and many proprietary brands are available from which to choose.

The character of spraying varies according to the purpose for which one is spraying. Obviously, with all preventives such as Ammoniacal Copper Sulphate, Bouisol, Sulsol or Bordeaux mixture, the object must be to distribute as fine a spray as is possible so that the whole leaf may be protected by a thin film of the protecting solution.

The Potassium Sulphide solution must be similarly applied, and for this purpose it is necessary that the spray should be directed both above and below the leaves.

Where poison sprays are used, a similar fine spray should be employed, so that the surfaces of the leaves are coated with a thin but even layer of the poison, in order that the insect may eat the maximum quantity.

Where the spray is to be employed against aphides and their kindred, spraying should be coarser so that every part of the bush is adequately reached.

Thus the spray should be applied by means of a syringe fitted with an appropriate nozzle for producing a fine or coarse spray, and one feels that the best method of selecting an appropriate syringe or Knapsack Sprayer is to see one demonstrated before purchase.

INSECT PESTS AFFECTING ROSES

The most important of the insect pests which affect roses are without doubt the eight or nine kinds of APHIDES, or GREEN FLY to give them the name generally applied. A superficial account of the methods of reproduction of the aphides is necessary to explain the reason for certain intervals in spraying.

In the spring a wingless female appears and produces, without the aid of a male partner, a number of living young which mature to become other wingless females, until the plant becomes smothered. The wingless forms then give rise to winged forms which migrate to other plants and produce similar wingless creatures.

At the end of the season sexual females and males are produced. The females, which are wingless, upon fertilisation produce eggs which are deposited upon the plant and remain dormant in the bud axils; when fresh they are elongated egg-shaped and green or yellow in colour, but become eventually black and shiny, and give rise to the next year's generations.

The rate of reproduction of green fly is prodigious, and it is fortunate that they have in addition to the gardener many other enemies. Unfortunately, too, they have at least one group of friends—the ants.

Sprays which are used to kill green fly usually act by clogging the breathing pores and thus slowly suffocate them. Thus death does not take place quickly and during the passage of the parent to oblivion more young are frequently born which are unaffected by the spray. Thus it can be seen that only by persistent spraying can real freedom from plant lice be conferred upon the rose.

Among the natural enemies of the rose aphides are the Ladybird beetles, larvae (niggers), Hover flies, Lacewing flies, and certain Chalcid flies. The Ladybird beetles and larvae both feed upon the aphides continuously. The Hover-fly maggots feed ravenously upon them and resemble green, grey, or greyish-red leeches. The larvae of the Lacewing fly also create great havoc among them, and the Chalcid flies lay their eggs in the bodies of the aphides and the resultant maggots consume them internally.

All these creatures should be encouraged. On the principle that he who is not for is against, ants should be exterminated wherever met, since they undoubtedly "nurse" the aphides and encourage their distribution for the benefit of the honeydew they produce. Paradichlorbenzine inserted in the nests provides a certain lethal end, and should be sparingly inserted in the nests three times in the space of one month. Failing this, Naphthalene should be similarly used.

Sprays which are used for the discouragement of green fly must be mild since more damage can often be caused by the spray than by the green fly. The best spray to be used is made by boiling one pound of quassia chips completely covered by soft water and pouring off and straining the liquid at intervals. Dissolve half a pound of soft soap in soft boiling water and add the quassia solution, making the total liquid up to ten gallons by adding soft water. The spray should be used twice at two-day intervals, and finally the trees sprayed with clean soft water to clear the fly.

Nearly all insects breathe through a series of pores called spiracles, and sprays for their discomfiture are designed to clog these pores. In certain cases sprays contain stomach poisons for the eating insects.

BEETLES. The following beetles attack roses and can do considerable harm:—

THE ROSE BEETLE, which can be found in rose-blossoms in dull and damp weather, is a shining coppery-green colour with occasional cream markings on the wing cases, and about half an inch in length. It causes damage to the rose both in its adult and larval stages, the adults eating the anthers and the petals of the roses, and the larvae the roots.

THE COCKCHAFER is about twice as big, with a black head and thorax, the abdomen marked at the sides with black and white lines, and the wing cases are reddish-brown with four longitudinal ridges. The grubs or larvae are six-legged, white and thick with a large head and swollen bladder-like tail end.

THE SUMMER CHAFER is about half the size of the Cockchafer and of reddish-brown colour. The larvae are similar to, but smaller than, those of the Cockchafer.

THE GARDEN CHAFER is about half an inch in length with a green body and brown wing cases.

The only remedy for the adult beetles is hand-picking. The Cockchafer and the Summer Chafer can be collected from the bushes in the daytime; the Rose Chafer in the rose on dull days, and the Garden Chafer at the end of the day. The grubs can be tempted out of the soil by placing reversed turves covered with soil over their haunts, when they can be removed and killed. The larvae can be killed by forking in Naphthalene at the rate of approximately two ounces per square yard.

Several WEEVILS also attack roses, and the remedy for the adults is to shake the trees after having placed tarred boards beneath them, and for the grubs in the soil by a similar application of Napthalene as recommended above.

LEAF-CUTTER BEE. This insect, which usually constructs a tunnel in a decaying section of wood, old mortar or even in the ground, cuts almost circular pieces from the leaves of roses with which to line the tunnel. As a child I found it quite instructive to watch the insects at work and follow them to their respective homes. The process of destruction at night was left to persons more mature, but the remedy to-day remains the same.

SAWFLIES. There are four varieties which are known to attack roses:—

THE LEAF-ROLLING SAWFLY, which lays its eggs on the leaves. The larva, while immature, rolls the leaf about it to form a cylindrical protection. The leaf withers and dies, and the larva migrates to another leaf. So severe has been the attack in some cases that the bushes have been killed.

The remedy is to hand-pick the leaves when curling is obvious and to burn them. The grub when mature falls to the ground and forms a cocoon in the soil. There is little doubt that the cocoons are frequently introduced in the soil which sometimes surrounds the briar stock. This should be washed away before planting.

Spraying with a nicotine wash will kill a proportion of the larvae, but by far the most certain method is to hand-pick the curled leaves when they are first observed and to burn them.

THE ROSE SLUGWORM is the name given to the larva of another sawfly which attacks roses. It can be recognised by its pale yellow-green colouring, with a central dark longitudinal line, and its orange head. It attacks the tissues of the rose leaves, generally leaving the upper or lower skin intact. The first symptom is the blotching of the leaves and an ensuing whiteness, followed by browning and shrivelling. There are generally two broods per year, the first in the month of June, the second in August. Fortunately, the pest is easily controlled by spraying with a nicotine wash. The larvae fall to the ground when mature and pupate in the soil in oval cocoons. The soil should be treated with Naphthalene to destroy them, as previously described.

THE ROSE EMPHYTUS. The larvae of this sawfly cause much damage to rose trees by eating away all the tissues of the leaves, except the midrib. They may be distinguished by their wrinkled dark green bodies with pale green sides, spotted white, somewhat enlarged at the front towards the brown-yellow and black head. The legs are white with dark marks, and the grub holds to the leaf by the front feet and curls the remainder of its body into the air when in movement, but remains curled beneath the leaf when at rest. When mature the grubs enter the branches, so killing that part of the growth above them. The remedy is to spray with a nicotine wash, to remove all dead wood in the winter and to fumigate the soil with Naphthalene, and to hand-pick the grubs when they are observed.

THE ROSE-SHOOT SAWFLY has a larva which produces quite a different kind of damage to the rose tree, making its home in the pith of the shoots, and emerging when mature by a direct hole to the bark. Fortunately, it is of rare occurrence. The only treatment is to remove the shoots attacked and to burn them. The soil beneath the affected tree should be treated with Naphthalene as previously described.

MOTHS. The caterpillars of a large number of familiar moths are often found upon the leaves and buds of rose trees. They may affect the roses in any one of three ways, by:

(a) consuming the foliage;
(b) eating into the unopened blooms;
(c) tunnelling into the leaves.

Of the first class, the Brindle Beauty
Dagger Moth
Gold-Tail Moth
Lackey Moth
Pale Tussock Moth
Shoulder-Stripe Moth
Swallow-Tail Moth
Vapourer Moth
Winter Moth

all produce caterpillars which are definitely injurious. In almost all cases the most effective treatment is hand-picking, regard being taken that the undersides of the leaves are carefully examined. Spraying with an arsenate of lead wash in cases where plants are infested is the best deterrent, and many proprietary brands of paste are available with appropriate directions for the application of the wash.

A spray may be made by dissolving one ounce of arsenate of soda in three quarts of water, and two ounces of acetate of lead in a similar quantity of water, when the two quantities should be mixed. The solution, which is poisonous, should be carefully stored. Dusting with Derris dust is also sometimes recommended.

The second class comprises generally the caterpillars or "maggots" of a group of small moths known as the TORTRIX MOTHS. Some of these are the brown, green and yellow Rose Grubs.

Unfortunately, the presence of the grubs is generally only detected when their depredations become apparent and the leaves are spun together and the buds spoiled. By far the best procedure is to spray twice at weekly intervals in the second and third weeks in April with a nicotine spray made by adding one ounce 90 per cent nicotine and two ounces of soft soap to ten gallons of water. A heavy spraying should be given.

ROSE LEAF-MINER. Another pest which may be encountered is the Rose Leaf-Miner, the maggot of which forms a twisting track of pale green with a darker middle line in the leaves of roses. Spraying does not effect a cure, and when bushes are badly affected the damaged leaves should be hand-picked and burned.

THE FROG-HOPPER OR CUCKOO-SPIT INSECT is often the cause of considerable damage to the rose. It is easily recognised by the curious frothy spittle-like mass with which it surrounds and protects itself. The insect, a quite active yellowish-green ovoid creature, is endowed with a sucking mouth and by continually drawing sap from the stem causes it to become weakened and deformed. The best method of control is to syringe freely with a nicotine wash.

SCALE INSECTS can be very destructive either to roses grown under glass in the case of one species, or in the open in the case of another species, but generally appear only upon roses which have been neglected. The correct treatment is to spray with a paraffin jelly, which is best bought prepared, when the leaves are not present, or to hand-pick and burn affected leaves when the trees are in growth.

MEALY BUGS sometimes affect roses under glass, lodging in the crevices and leaf axils, covering themselves with white wool. When observed the white patches should be painted with methylated spirit.

RED SPIDER. Another insect which affects both outdoor roses and roses under glass is the Red Spider. A minute sucking insect, it causes first a mottling of the leaves, as it dwells in colonies, and finally the leaf yellows and falls off. In or out of doors the treatment is to spray with Volck, which is perfectly harmless to plant life and easy to use.

THE ROSE LEAF-HOPPER usually makes its presence obvious by the marbling of certain of the leaves of the tree, and during hot weather the leaves not infrequently fall, and prejudice the proper development of the wood. The insect moults several times, and examination of the underside of the leaf usually discloses certain grey dried-up cast skins of the insects. The appropriate treatment is to spray with a nicotine and soft soap wash.

THRIPS, OR BLACK FLY, can also do damage to roses. They are small insects with black bodies and four slender wings. They thrive best in a dry atmosphere, and spraying with cold water can be effective. In the case of severe attacks a nicotine wash should be used as a spray.

A summary of the appropriate treatments for various pests is given below:—

Aphides. Spray as indicated on p. 76.

Beetles. Hand-picking. Dig in Naphthalene at the rate of two ounces per square yard.

Weevils. Shake on to tarred boards. Treat soil with Naphthalene as above.

Leaf-Cutter Bee. Destroy nests.

Sawflies. Hand-pick; spray with nicotine wash made by adding one ounce of 90 per cent nicotine and two ounces of soft soap to ten gallons of soft water. Dress soil with Naphthalene.

Three red Hybrid Tea Roses

Gerald Hardy **ABEF**   Hadley **CDGH**
         Colonel Sharman-Crawford **KLOP**

Hybrid Tea Rose, Crimson Glory

Shoot Borer. Remove damaged shoots and burn them.

Caterpillars. Spray with arsenate of lead paste, made into a wash as indicated on p. 79.

Leaf-Miner. Hand-pick leaves affected and burn them.

Frog-Hopper. Use a nicotine wash spray.

Scale Insects. Spray with paraffin jelly when out of leaf. Hand-pick when in leaf.

Mealy Bug. Paint with methylated spirit.

Red Spider. Spray with Volck.

Leaf-Hopper. Spray with nicotine wash.

Thrips. Spray with nicotine wash.

CHAPTER X

THE GENERAL MAINTENANCE OF ROSES

THE best method to deal with this question would appear to be to follow the yearly life cycle of the rose from dormancy to dormancy, and this is the procedure we propose to adopt.

The month of *January* is generally a very quiet one from the point of view of the rose-grower, and no work can be done if there is frost in the ground. Where beds have been forked over they may be top-dressed as necessary; the manure to be used should be as old and as rotten as is possible.

Trees should be inspected to see if the wind and rain have loosened the stocks in the ground, and they should be suitably firmed in appropriate weather. Arches and pergolas should be looked over and any repairs effected as the weather allows.

In the greenhouse, grafting—where practised—should begin in the third week. Pot roses may be pruned and be brought into the house. Roses already brought in will be starting into growth and careful watering and ventilation will become necessary. Any sign of insect pests will make it necessary to fumigate the house with a recommended fumigant.

February will also bring its toll of trees loosened in the ground by the frost; these should be firmed in during suitable dry weather. Climbers should be tied securely where they have become loosened.

All pot roses should by now be pruned and brought into the house. Roses may still be grafted under glass. Ventilation of the houses should be continued, care being taken to avoid any sudden and excessive changes of temperature. Mildew may make its appearance in the house, and a first spraying should be made with a fungicide.

The month of *March* is probably the busiest of the year. Late planting is taking place, and pruning should be done during the month. Remember that a good general rule to learn is "Spare the wood and spoil the rose." Where roses are to be planted this month, prune hard before planting, and plant very firmly. All dried leaves, twigs and refuse of any kind should be removed. Trees protected from frost should have such covering removed before the end of the month. Where the soil is light it is advisable

Three Hybrid Tea Roses

Dame Edith Helen **ABEF**　　　　　　　　Profusion **CDGH**
Lal **KLMOP**

Three bright Hybrid Tea Roses

Mrs. Edward Laxton **EFJK**

Elite **CDG**
Duchess of Atholl **LMPQ**

to give it a dressing of well-decayed manure. Ventilation of houses should be carefully attended to. Seedlings should be transplanted.

The month of *April*, generally a variable month, provides enough changes to be entertaining to everyone, and the rose-grower is no exception. Trees are now bursting into growth and require constant protection against the visitation of insects and other pests. The new growth is delicate and easily damaged, and insecticides should be mild and harmless to the new growth.

Unwanted eyes should be rubbed off and suckers from the parent stock removed. To do this loosen the soil, if in doubt, and trace the growth back to its point of emission from the stock. As a rule it may be easily distinguished by its thinner and greener appearance than the true rose and the fact that its leaves are composed of from seven to nine leaflets. The rose itself generally has only five leaflets.

Roses pruned in March should be examined to see if terminal buds are really "live," and where necessary to ensure a live terminal bud, cut back still further. This may be particularly necessary in the case of the ramblers. Where inward-growing buds have started into growth in such a manner as to suggest that the middles of the plants will be crowded, the buds pointing inwards should be rubbed out. All prunings should be burned.

The beds may be dressed lightly with soot, which should be forked in on the surface, and whether this is done or not the surface should be lightly hoed. All bushes should be firmed where they are found to be loose. Freshly planted roses should not be given manure in any form, but established trees may be given, after a shower of rain, diluted liquid cow manure.

Roses in the houses will need attention. Watering will become more frequent, and careful feeding must take place. Ventilation should be adequate and in keeping with the changeable weather. Spraying to prevent mildew and other diseases should be practised regularly.

The month of *May* will bring buds in plenty and troubles in legions. Trees should be hand-picked for pests, and where they are inaccessible to the hands, spraying with a recommended insecticide should be resorted to. Disbudding—the rubbing-out of buds—should be commenced as soon as it is obvious which buds are likely to mature best. The feeding of all trees with liquid manures may now take place. The growth of standard roses should be carefully watched to see that each shoot has plenty of room for development.

In the case of newly-planted roses, the staking of standards should be made secure. With newly-planted bush roses watering should be resorted to during dry periods to encourage efficient growth. Syringe freely to encourage the plants to break. Water given to roses in houses should be reduced to prevent excessive growth, and plants which have flowered in pots should be hardened off and then removed to the open. Roses attacked by mildew must be sprayed with regularity.

June is the month in which roses start to flower in quantity in the garden. The maiden trees, which are to provide roses for exhibition, should be systematically disbudded; control must be exercised by spraying to discourage disease and pests. The ground should be hoed in dry weather and the feeding of the plants continued. Roses from pots may be planted out even at this late stage. Blooms which are cut for decorative purposes should be cut with at least three-quarters of the whole flowering stem to ensure a succession of good-quality flowers.

July provides the month in which the rose is in fullest flower, and much work can be found to do in the rose garden. Old flowers should be removed exactly in the same way as blooms are cut. Spraying must be continued. If the month is dry, watering may have to take place to encourage good growth, and spraying is always beneficial to the rose if not done in fullest sunshine.

Rambler roses which have flowered may be pruned, all the growths which have flowered being removed to give the younger and more virile growths a chance to harden. Grass cuttings may be spread over the rose beds as a mulch and hoed in at the end of a week as a means of retaining moisture in the soil.

August roses have, as a rule, but a short life, and hoeing and mulching may continue to give the plants assistance. Budding of stocks should be done during the month, preferably on the cooler days. Cuttings of roses may also be taken this month. The pruning of rambler roses should be completed.

The foliage of roses should be kept as clean as possible, and spraying should be practised whenever possible with clean rainwater where no disease is detected, and with fungicide wherever disease is present. All pot roses located in the open should be carefully watered, and if intended for growth indoors in winter should have their flower buds removed.

During *September* the roses will again produce a crop of flowers and will continue to do so until quite late in the year if they are given appropriate treatment. Hoeing and mulching with grass clippings should be continued; weak useless shoots should be cut out; dead blooms should be removed and spraying to keep the foliage as clean as possible should be regularly practised. Dead wood should be removed from climbing roses.

Usually "black spot" can be found in evidence during this month, and affected leaves should be removed and burned, and trees sprayed with the fungicide recommended.

The preparation of new beds for the next year can be undertaken, and the work pushed on. Where roses are required as late as possible during the year, disbudding should be continued, only the most likely buds being allowed to remain on the plant. Roses requiring repotting should be treated during the month and should be removed from budded stocks.

October can be used for the preparation of beds for the succeeding season. Lists of roses required for the next season should be prepared. Cuttings of briars for the next year's stocks may be taken as well as cuttings of the rose. Cuttings already rooted may be planted out. All fallen leaves, twigs and branches should be collected and burned. Liquid manuring should be discontinued and the ground dressed with two ounces of bone meal and one ounce of flowers of sulphur per square yard, forked in lightly. Climbers should be inspected and nailed up where necessary. Extra long shoots of dwarf roses should be shortened to prevent whip in the wind. Roses which need protection should be treated with bracken, or such protective covering as is available. Cuttings already rooted should be planted out in permanent quarters.

November is the principal month for planting, and this should be commenced as far as possible. After planting the beds should be dressed with manure, leaves or bracken to afford such protection as is possible.

Late-budded stocks should be protected by drawing up the earth around them. Rose borders should be dressed with manure and forked over. Transplanting, where desired, should be done this month. Where disease has been experienced and the leaves have fallen, the bushes and soil should be drenched with a solution of copper sulphate. Beds which require it should be limed with slaked lime at the rate of four ounces per square yard. Roses in pots which are to be forced should be pruned and brought into the greenhouse.

December is generally a month in which to take stock of achievements, and push on with delayed work as the weather will allow. Planting may still take place; beds may still be dressed with manure. Care must be taken to see that all climbers share in the good things given to the dwarfs, and special care should be given to climbers against walls.

An indication only has been given of the work to be accomplished month by month. The actual details of the way in which it should be carried out have been dealt with elsewhere.

28—HIGH-CENTRED WIDE-PETALLED REFLEXED

29—GLOBULAR REFLEXED

Three Dwarf Polyantha Roses

Lady Reading **ABCEFGHJ**
Ellen Poulsen **JKLMNRS**
Orange Triumph **PQTU**

McGredy's Yellow (Hybrid Tea) **BCDGH**

Mrs. Herbert Stevens (Tea) **EFJK**

Francesca (Hybrid Musk) **LMPQ**

30—HIGH-CENTRED WIDE-PETALLED OPEN

31—HIGH-CENTRED IMBRICATED REFLEXED

32—HIGH-CENTRED WIDE-PETALLED
SEMIGLOBULAR

33—HIGH-CENTRED
REFLEXED

34—HIGH-CENTRED WIDE-PETALLED
SEMIGLOBULAR REFLEXED

35—OPEN WIDE-PETALLED
(CAMELLIA-SHAPED)

Julien Potin (Pernetiana) ABEFGH
Goldenes Mainz (Hybrid Tea) CDJNOPQ

Three Hybrid Polyantha Roses

Salmon Spray **ABE**   Kirsten Poulsen **BCDFGH**
                 Else Poulsen **JKLMNOPQ**

36—MANY-PETALLED (FULLY DOUBLE)
GLOBULAR

37—HIGH-CENTRED SPIRALLED REFLEXED

NOTES ON THE USE OF THE GLOSSARY

The inclusion of a rose in this Glossary should not be taken as an indication that it may be obtained from any commercial grower. It may be taken for granted, however, that it remains in cultivation, either in amateur or professional gardens or in the gardens of horticultural establishments.

For ease of reference, hybrid garden roses have been listed alphabetically. Hybrid species roses have been given cross references in the alphabetical list, but are fully described under the species name.

In all cases the following information is given, where it is available.

(1) The name of the introducer, and date. Thus: *Evans* 1926. (Roses that appear post-dated will not come into commerce before the year indicated.)

(2) Whether evergreen or deciduous under normal conditions. Thus: *D.* or *E.*

(3) The height:

SG.	short growth
MG.	medium growth
VG.	vigorous growth
TG.	tall growth
EG.	exceptionally tall growth
C.	climber

Examples of such growths are:—

SG.	Captain Kilbee-Stuart
MG.	Dame Edith Helen
VG.	Edith Nellie Perkins
TG.	Caroline Testout
EG.	Hugh Dickson

(4) Whether fragrant:

SF.	slightly fragrant
MF.	moderately fragrant
F.	fragrant
VF.	very fragrant
TF.	tea-scented
NF.	without scent

(5) Pruning instruction for general garden purposes, thus: *GPA.*, etc. (see pp. 52–57); and in some cases instruction for long pruning: *LPA.*, etc. (see pp. 59, 60).

(6) Pruning instruction for exhibition purposes: *EA.*, etc. (see p. 57).

(7) Colour, as matched by the Royal Horticultural Society's Colour Chart.

(8) Purpose. Whether best suited for:

A.	arch
B.	bedding
Banks.	covering banks
C.	climber
Cut.	cut flower
E.	exhibition
G.	growth as garden specimen
H.	hedge
House.	greenhouse cultivation
P.	pergola
Pot.	pot culture
Pr.	pillar
S.	specimen
S.Sh.	specimen shrub
St.	standard
T.	trailer
W.	wall rose
Wst.	weeping standard

(9) Months of flowering.

In addition, the following abbreviations are used in the introductory chapters and in the Glossary:

comm.	commemorative name
H.P.	Hybrid Perpetual
H.S.	hybrid of species
H.T.	Hybrid Tea rose
N.	Noisettiana
Pern.	Pernetiana
S.	species
T.	Tea rose

A GLOSSARY OF ROSES

ABOL (Hybrid Tea). A fine white rose, sometimes slightly tinted with pink before fully opening, with a fine fragrance. The flowers, which are freely produced upon bold stems, are well shaped and the foliage is resistant to mildew.
Evans 1926. *D. MG. VF. GPB. EB. White. B. June-October.*

ABRICOT (Hybrid Tea) forms a vigorous upright-growing bush with glossy green foliage and bears medium semi-double flowers of apricot and bright salmon-pink, with the reverse of the petals coral-red.
Barbier 1929. *D. VG. F. GPB. EB. — B. June-October. Hardy.*

ACICULARIS (needle-pricked) (Species), N. America, derives its name from its needly spines and forms a dense and compact shrub of up to four feet in height with glaucous foliage and bearing large solitary flowers of deep rose of about two inches in diameter, followed by red pear-shaped fruits.
Lindley 1805. *D. VG. F. Prune only to shape. — S. May-June. Hardy.*

ACICULARIS VAR. BOURGEAUIANA (comm.), W. Canada, is also var. Sayi, and has similar habit, slightly larger flowers of paler rose-pink, and bears upon very prickly stems its rounded red fruits.
— —. D. EG. F. Prune only to shape. — S. May-June. Hardy.

ACICULARIS VAR. NIPPONENSIS (from Nippon), Japan, is also known as the Fujiyama Rose, and shows signs of being a rugosa hybrid, bearing similar flowers of bright rose-red.
— —. D. EG. F. Prune only to shape. — S. May-June. Hardy.

ADENOSEPALA (with glandular sepals) (Species), Europe, is strong-growing with large handsome grey-green leaves and bears freely large deep pink flowers which are followed by bright-scarlet beautiful fruits.
Wooton and Standley —. D. EG. F. Prune lightly. — S. June-July.
[Hardy.

ADMIRATION (Hybrid Tea) has light green glossy disease-resisting foliage and produces very large full cream flowers, tinted and shaded and streaked with fiery red.
McGredy 1922. *D. MG. VF. GPB. EB. Cream. B.E. June-October.*

ADOLF GRILLE (Hybrid polyantha) produces its clustered heads of large double semi-globular bright-carmine flowers on compact but strong bushes, with dark green plentiful foliage.
Kordes 1939. *D. VG. SF. GPG. — — B.G. June-September. Hardy.*

ADORA (polyantha pompon) is dwarf but free-growing and produces flame-pink buds which open to rose-pink double pompon flowers, and is freely scented.
Beckwith 1936. *D. MG. VF. GPG. — — B. June-October. Hardy.*

ADORATION (H.T.) is the American name for Ile de France, which see.

ADRIAN REVERCHON (Lambertiana) is a climbing or pillar rose with single rose-pink flowers borne in profusion.
Lambert 1909. *D. VG. MF. GPI. — — Pr. July. Hardy.*

ADVANCE (H.T.) has large, double, high-centred flowers of nasturtium-red, shaded with deep rose-pink, and with the reverse of the petals of that colour. Growth is vigorous, erect and branching, and foliage dark green.
Le Grice 1941. *D. VG. SF. GPB. EB. — B.E. June-September.*

AENNCHEN MULLER (polyantha pompon) is a very continuous-flowering dwarf rose-pink polyantha rose of great attractiveness.
Schmidt 1907. *D. MG. NF. GPC. GPG. — — B. June-Oct. Hardy.*

AFTERGLOW (Pernetiana) produces long-budded and long-stemmed flowers of pale amber flushed without with deep pink, and has handsome shiny mildew-proof foliage. A sport from Mrs. Sam McGredy, it has all its parent's good points.
Le Grice 1938. *D. MG. F. GPB. EC. 606/2 and 420/2. June-October.*
[Hardy. Pl. 20.

AGNES (Hybrid rugosa) is a hybrid between Rosa rugosa and the Persian Yellow, and produces large double amber-yellow fragrant flowers within a frame of much-notched green foliage.
Saunders 1900. *D. EG. VF. Prune lightly. — S. June-July. Hardy.*

AGNES EMILY CARMAN (see R. rugosa).

AGRESTIS (field) (Species), Europe, is also known as R. sepium, and makes a bush of from four to six feet in height with grey-green foliage, small bright-red thorns, and clusters of pale pink single flowers which are followed by bright red fruits.
Savi —. D. EG. MF. Prune only to shape. 622. S. June. Hardy. Pl. 21.

AGRESTIS VAR. BELGRADENSIS (of Belgrade) is similar in habit of growth, but has shiny green foliage and coral-red thorns. The flowers, which are single, vary between white and very pale pink.
— —. D. TG. MF. Prune only to shape. 622/3. S. June. Hardy.

AGRESTIS VAR. GIZELLAE (comm.) has a similar habit of growth, but the foliage is dark green, much veined, and the flowers are white.
— —. D. TG. MF. Prune only to shape. White. S. June. Hardy.

AIMÉE VIBERT (Noisettiana) has small double pure white flowers, often deepening to cream in the centre, and is a climbing rose of exceptionally vigorous form.
Vibert 1828. *D. VG. NF. GPC. — — P.Pr. June-July. Hardy.*

ALBA (white) (Species), S. Europe, is probably a natural hybrid between R. canina var. dumetorum and R. gallica and makes a fine bush of from six to eight feet in height, bearing large, sweetly-scented salver-shaped flowers of clear white, sometimes tinged with pink. The leaflets number five, and are large and of glaucous colour; the fruits which follow the flowers are elongated and bright-red in colour. R. alba is also known as the Jacobite Rose.

Linnaeus —. D. TG. F. Prune only to shape, as specimen bush or pillar.
[White. S. June. Hardy.

ALBA PLENA, S. Europe, is a semi-double-flowered form which has been found growing as a wildling in Britain, and is otherwise similar.

— —. D. TG. F. Prune only to shape. White. S. June. Hardy.

ALBA CARNEA (flesh-pink) is similar, but has semi-double flowers of pale rose-pink, and shapes into an exceptionally attractive bush.

— —. D. TG. F. Prune only to shape. Pink. S. June. Hardy.

ALBA CELESTIAL is another very good variety, with flowers of slightly deeper pink, and is somewhat more double in appearance.

— —. D. TG. F. Prune only to shape. Pink. S. June. Hardy.

ALBA MAIDEN'S BLUSH is one of the loveliest of all the old roses. Known as far back as 1597, its semi-double flowers deepen from pink-flushed white to pale salmon-pink.

— —. D. TG. F. Prune only to shape. Pink. S. June. Hardy.

ALBA VAR. SUAVEOLENS (sweet-smelling), S.E. Europe, is the source of attar of roses, and otherwise resembles the type.

— —. D. TG. F. Prune only to shape. Pink. S. June. Hardy.

ALBÉRIC BARBIER (wichuraiana rambler) has the most pleasing glossy, dark-green foliage, and smothers itself in well-shaped lemon-yellow buds, opening to creamy-white flowers. It is most admirable for covering arches and pergolas and makes an excellent weeping standard; in fact of all weeping standards it is my own personal favourite. It blooms on the lateral shoots as well as the new shoots, and beyond shortening the laterals to four or five buds should be left as much as possible unpruned.

Barbier 1900. D. C. NF. Detailed. 403/3 to 2/3. C.P.Wst. June-July.
[Hardy.

ALBERTII (comm.) (Species), Turkestan, makes a bush of some three to four feet in height, with graceful branches clad in small foliage made up of from five to nine leaflets, and long sharp red thorns. The flowers, which are approximately $1\frac{1}{4}$ inches in diameter, are white or pale cream.

Regel —. D. VG. MF. Prune only to shape. White. S.Pr. June. Hardy.

ALBERTINE (wichuraiana rambler) produces cluster-heads of bright salmon rose-shaded flowers above foliage of bright, glossy green. It is seldom troubled with mildew.

Barbier 1921. D. C. F. Cut out all wood which has flowered, during autumn.
[C.Pr.Wst. July. Hardy.

ALBERT MAUMENÉ (see R. Hugonis).

ALEZANE (Hybrid Tea) produces large double flowers of apricot, shaded with coppery-red, with a red-brown reverse veined with yellow, and is a good vigorous rose.
Pahissa 1934. *D. VG. MF. GPA. EA. — — E.B. June-Sept. Hardy.*

ALICE AMOS (polyantha pompon) has single flowers of bright pink, with distinct white eyes, and resembles a dwarf and refined American Pillar.
Prior 1923. *D. VG. MF. Prune sparingly. — B. June-Sept. Hardy.*

ALICE HARDING (Hybrid Tea) is a pleasant yellow rose of good habit and fine colour, and is likely to be very popular.
Mallerin 1936. *D. VG. NF. GPA. EA. — — E.B. June-Sept. Hardy.*

ALIDA (H.T.) has very double bright-red flowers of long pointed shape, which last well, and are borne upon vigorous plants of branching habit, with mid-green foliage.
Lens 1938. *D. VG. SF. GPB. EB. — B.E.G. June-September. Hardy.*

ALIDA LOVETT (wichuraiana rambler) is a large-flowered climber, with bright pink flowers, which makes a fine pillar or hedging rose.
Van Fleet 1905. *D. EG. NF. Remove all growth which has flowered during*
[*the summer. — — C.Pr. June. Hardy.*

ALLEN CHANDLER (H.T.) is a very vigorous rose suitable for growth as a pillar or as a hedge rose. It produces clusters of from three to four bright scarlet flowers. It requires little pruning beyond the removal of the dead wood and such old growth as may cause it to become crowded.
Prince 1924. *D. EG. F. Detailed. 724. Pr.H. June. Hardy.*

ALLEN'S FRAGRANT PILLAR (Climbing H.T.) has large double flowers of bright cerise, toning to yellow at the base, borne singly or in small groups on vigorous climbing plants, with attractive ample shiny dark bronze-green foliage.
Allen 1931. *D. C. MF. GPE. — — Pr.W. June-September. Hardy.*

ALLEN'S GOLDEN CLIMBER (H.T.) is a climbing rose with very glossy green leaves and large full flowers of deep orange-red. It is a fine free-flowering variety suitable for training upon a wall or pergola, or growing as a pillar.
Allen 1932. *D. EG. F. As for Allen Chandler. — — P.Pr.W. June-Sept.*
[*Hardy.*

ALOIS JIRASEK (H.T.) is of medium growth, producing full flowers of dark orange. Foliage is glossy green.
Bohm 1931. *D. MG. F. GPB. EB. — BE. June-September. Hardy.*

ALPINA (see R. pendulina).

AMADIS (Boursault) produces upon thornless stems clusters of semi-double purplish-red flowers early in the season.
Laffay 1829. *D. VG. NF. Thin after flowering. — — A.H.Pr. June.*
[*Hardy.*

AMALIA JUNG (H.T.) produces flowers of intense crimson-red of good shape, colour and fragrance, but is no better and little worse than many newcomers.
Leenders 1934. *D. VG. VF. GPA. EA. B.E. July-September. Hardy.*

AMELIA EARHART (see Président Charles Hain).

AMÉLIE GRAVEREAUX (see R. rugosa).

AMERICAN PILLAR (wichuraiana rambler) is a most vigorous variety producing canes often exceeding ten feet in length. The foliage is glossy green and the clustered flowers are bright rose-pink with a white eye, and it can provide as impenetrable a thicket as ever Christian had to surmount. It is exceptionally hardy, but is liable to die back after reaching four years of age. It is exceptionally easy to propagate from cuttings and should be kept in all stages for replacements. Given plenty of space, it will give generously of colour.
Van Fleet 1905. *D. C. NF. Remove dead wood and very old growth only. —*
[A.P.Pr. July. Hardy.

AMPÈRE (H.T.) has large fully double orange-red flowers with an orange-yellow exterior flushed with carmine, and is of very striking appearance.
Meilland 1937. *D. MG. MF. GPD. EB. —— B. June-Sept. Hardy.*

AMULETT (H.T.) is a shapely, fiery red, long-budded rose, with shiny green foliage and vigorous growth.
Tantau 1930. *D. VG. MF. GPA. EA. —— B. June-Sept. Hardy.*

AMY ROBSART (see R. rubiginosa).

ANDERSONII (comm.) (Hybrid of Species) (see R. arvensis). *Pl.* 60.

ANEMONAEFLORA (anemone-flowered) (Species), China, is a double-flowered pale pink or white climbing rose with its flowers produced in large clusters. It was originally discovered growing in a garden in China and is reputed to be a hybrid of R. laevigata and R. multi-flora. The distinctive feature of the flowers is that the inner petals are shorter than the outer ones. R. anemonaeflora can under favour-able circumstances be evergreen, but requires a sheltered position against a wall.
Fortune 1846. *D. EG. MF. Remove only the dead wood.* 625/2. *W. June.*

ANEMONE (see R. laevigata sinica).

ANEMONOIDES (resembling the anemone) is a hybrid between R. laevigata and R. indica and is a climbing rose with pale-pink single flowers.
Schmidt 1896. *D. EG. F. Remove only the dead wood. — W. June.*

ANGÈLE PERNET (Pernetiana) has large loose flowers of pale orange-red shaded with chrome-yellow, is of good habit and is free-flowering. The foliage is a shiny, attractive bronze-green and is damp-resistant; the flower a fine autumn rose.
Pernet-Ducher 1924. *D. MG. MF. GPB. EB. — B. June-Sept. Hardy.*

Hybrid Polyantha Rose, Else's Rival

Hybrid Tea Rose, Eternal Youth

ANGELITA RUAIX (H.T.) has large high-centred, double, deep orange-yellow flowers of attractive shape, borne upon vigorous branching plants with varnished deep green foliage.
Dot 1940. *D. VG. SF. GPB. —— B.G. June-September.*

ANGELS MATEU (Pernetiana) produces large full blooms of an exquisite combination of orange and old rose, to which no pen can do justice.
Dot 1934. *D. VG. VF. GPA. EA. — B. June-September. Hardy.*

ANNA NEAGLE (H.T.) is a good attractive rose of bright currant-red, yellowing at the base of the petals. It is of free-growing habit and produces its flowers upon long stiff stems. In addition, to render it even more attractive, it is very resistant to disease.
McGredy 1937. *D. VG. GPA. —— B. June-September. Hardy.*

ANNE OF GEIERSTEIN (see R. rubiginosa).

ANNE POULSEN (Hybrid polyantha) is a magnificent bedding rose with vigour, a long flowering period and great beauty in its clusters of bright pink, semi-double, crimson-shaded flowers. Its growth is strong and upright and its bright green foliage is resistant to mildew.
Poulsen 1935. *D. VG. VF. GPA. — 724. B. June-September. Hardy.*

ANNETTE GRAVEREAUX (Pernetiana) produces large pale lemon-yellow flowers shaded with deep orange-yellow, is very vigorous in growth and has fine glossy green foliage.
Leenders 1929. *D. VG. MF. GPA. EA. — E. June-September. Hardy.*

ANNIE DREVET (H.T.) has attractive but thin cupped flowers of nasturtium-red, with the reverse of the petals of cadmium-yellow, produced upon vigorous erect and branching plants with glossy deep green foliage.
Caron 1938. *D. VG. SF. GPB. —— B. June-September. Hardy.*

ANNIE DUPEYRAT (Pernetiana) has bright green glossy foliage, is a vigorous grower, and produces flowers of large size, full and fair, of a fine shade of orange shaded well with deep pink.
Mallerin 1934. *D. VG. MF. GPA. EA. — B. June-September. Hardy.*

ANNIE JEBENS (H.T.) produces much glossy green foliage and has flowers of great fullness on erect stems, of bright carmine red, with a golden reverse to the petals.
Kordes 1932. *D. MG. MF. GPB. EB. — B. June-September. Hardy.*

ANTINEA (H.T.) has large full flowers, on strong upright stems, of orange-pink shading to yellow at the base. The foliage is green and glossy and clothes a shapely and vigorous bush which flowers for a considerable period.
Gaujard 1934. *D. VG. GPA. EA. — E.B.Pot. June-September. Hardy.*

ANTONIN DVORAK (H.T.) has persistent flowers of great size of light pink flushed with orange, and forms a bushy plant with glossy green foliage.
Bohm 1933. *D. VG. GPA. EA. — B. June-September. Hardy.*

Apeles Mestres (Climbing Pernetiana) is a climbing rose with great globular sunflower-yellow flowers on strong-growing canes, with glossy deep green foliage. It must, however, be grown in a position where it gets a maximum of sunlight. Here it will give back a proportion of the sunlight it takes.

Dot 1926. *D. C. Prune as lightly as possible. — — W. June-September.*

Aphrodite (H.T.) has long-pointed vermilion buds which open into large, semi-double, coral-red flowers, shaded with gold. The flowers are borne several together on a long stem above dark green, glossy foliage.

Easlea 1928. *D. VG. VF. GPA. — — B. June-September. Hardy.*

Apothecary's Rose (see R. gallica var. officinalis).

Apricot Glow (wichuraiana climber) is a vigorous climber with long strong stems and polished green foliage, which bears large apricot double flowers, with a basal toning of orange, fading to pink.

Brownell 1936. *D. C. SF. GPJ. — — Pr.W. June-July. Hardy.*

Apricot Queen (H.T.), produces its salmon and old-gold flowers upon long stiff stems on a good vigorous bush. The foliage is not liable to disease.

Howard & Smith 1939. *D. VG. SF. GPA. — — B. June-Sept. Hardy.*

Arch Reventos (H.T.) has pure yellow well-shaped buds, on plants of free branching habit. Foliage is polished deep green and growth vigorous.

Leenders 1935. *D. VG. MF. GPB. EB. — B.E. June-September.*

Ards Rambler (Climbing H.T.) is a climber of good growth with large flowers of carmine-rose.

Dickson 1908. *DC. VG. F. Prune as lightly as possible. P.W. June-Sept.*
[Hardy.

Ards Rover (Climbing H.P.) is a fine climber of vigorous growth with large crimson flowers of good substance. Foliage is large and of good appearance.

Dickson 1894. *D. C. VG. NF. Prune as lightly as possible. — P.W.*
[June-September. Hardy.

Arethusa (see R. chinensis).

Aribau (H.T.) is a fine rose with long buds singly borne upon strong, erect stems above reddish-green foliage. Little or no disbudding is required for exhibition purposes, as the fiery-red brilliant flowers are produced before the laterals.

Dot 1937. *D. MG. F. GPB. EB. — B.E. June-September. Hardy.*

Ariel (H.T.) produces large, globular, double flowers of bright golden-yellow with flame shading and streaked with crimson in the centre and on the outside of the buds. The foliage is dark glossy green and resistant to disease.

Bees 1921. *D. VG. MF. GPA. — 5/2. B. June-September. Hardy.*

Hybrid Tea Roses, Faience **ABEFKLOP**
Cherry **CDGH**

Madge Whipp **EFJK**

George Dickson **CDGH**
W. E. Chaplin **KLMPQ**

ARKANSANA (from Arkansas) (S.), Western United States, is a dwarf-growing rose of some two to three feet with pink flowers, fading to white, borne in corymbs. The leaflets number from seven to eleven and are grey-green in colour and are borne on very thorny stems. The flowers are followed by small bright-red fruits.

Porter —. D. VG. SF. GPG. — — G. May-June. Hardy.

ARMOSA (see R. chinensis Hermosa).

ARNDT (polyantha) bears its pale flesh-pink flowers in large corymbs upon a tree which is half climber. The foliage is a good dark green, the growth vigorous, and the flowering season long.

P. Lambert 1913. D. C. NF. Remove old, unripened or unnecessary shoots in [early spring. — Pr. June-Sept. Hardy.

ARNOLD (see R. rugosa).

ARNOLDIANA (H.S.) (see R. rugosa) is a hybrid of parentage R. rugosa × R. bourbonia and makes a strong-growing upright bush with corymbs of semi-double reddish-purple flowers each of about two inches in diameter.

Rehder —. D. VG. MF. Prune as lightly as possible in March. — — [S. June-July. Hardy.

ARRILAGA (H.P.) is one of the more recent hybrid perpetual roses with a charming fragrance. The foliage is of good, strong green, the growth vigorous and upright, the buds are large, the flowers very large double and well shaped and of bright glowing pink.

Schoener 1929. D. VG. VF. GPA. EA. — — B.E. June-Sept. Hardy.

ARVENSIS (of the field) (S.), Europe, is also known as R. repens, or more commonly the Ayrshire Rose, and comprises in general a group of very hardy and vigorous semi-climbing or trailing roses which will thrive amazingly in poor soil. The somewhat large bronzy-blue foliage is almost evergreen, and the clusters of white flowers are most freely produced in June. R. arvensis can be suitably used for covering an arch, and requires little pruning beyond the removal of the dead wood and occasional thinning in February.

Hudson 1762. D. C. NF. Detailed. White. S. June. Very hardy.

ARVENSIS VAR. ANDERSONII (S.) is a hybrid of R. arvensis which makes a large and shapely bush of some five or six feet in height and produces large clusters of very large bright-pink flowers with golden stamens. Requires only light pruning.

(Garden origin) —. D. EG. F. Detailed. S. June. Very hardy. Pl. 60.

ARVENSIS BENNETT'S SEEDLING (S.) is also known as R. Thoresbyana, and is similar in growth and habit, but produces clusters of small, double white flowers and is delightfully scented.

Bennett 1840. D. C. F. Detailed. White. S. June. Very hardy.

ARVENSIS CAPREOLATA (S.) is also known as the Roebuck Rambler, and will sprawl wide and sometimes rise to a height of twenty feet. The white flowers are freely produced in corymbs.

Bean —. D. C. NF. Detailed. White. S. June. Very hardy.

Aspirant Marcel Rouyer (H.T.) bears its large, pointed, fully double flowers singly on strong stems with much glossy, bronzy foliage. The flowers are apricot, deepening to reddish-orange at the centre, with the exterior flesh colour, shaded and veined with yellow.
Pernet-Ducher 1919. *D. VG. MF. GPA. — B. June-September. Hardy.*

Asun Galindez de Chapa (H.T.) has a long bud, is fully double, and is salmon-pink with a deeper reverse shading to yellow at the base. The flowers are borne in threes or fours on stout stems clad with shiny, deep green foliage.
Ketten 1923. *D. VG. MF. GPA. — June-September. B. Hardy.*

Atlanta (multiflora rambler) is a climber with coppery-orange buds which open to large flesh-pink full flowers. The foliage, which is small and of glossy deep green, is particularly attractive.
Williams 1927. *D. C. NF. Prune as lightly as possible. P.Pr. June-Sept.*
[Hardy.

Atlantida (H.T.) is a fine shade of coppery-salmon shaded with peach; the buds are long and well shaped, and the blooms retain their colour well. Growth is vigorous and the foliage free from disease.
Pahissa 1939. *D. VG. F. GPA. EA. — BG. June-September.*

Attar of Roses (H.T.) proclaims that the scent is the thing; the flowers, of moderate size, are cream tinted with pink; the foliage is deep dark green, but the scent is divine.
B. R. Cant 1936. *D. VG. VF. GPA. — Cream. B.S. June-Sept. Hardy.*

Attraction (H.T.) has bright yellow full flowers shaded with orange, the buds of which are frequently touched with carmine-crimson. It is a dwarf-growing variety and exceptionally good for bedding.
Dickson 1931. *D. SG. MF. GPA. — — B. June-September. Hardy.*

Auguste Gervaise (wichuraiana rambler) bears clusters of very large semi-double flowers, shading from cream to salmon-pink and orange-yellow. In growth it is strong, and is most profuse in flowering; it should be pruned to leave the best of the old shoots.
Barbier 1918. *D. C. NF. Detailed. — — C.P.Pr. June-July. Hardy.*

Auguste Kordes (Climbing polyantha) produces clusters of fiery scarlet semi-double flowers on almost thornless stems clad with shiny green disease-resistant foliage. Pruning should consist of the removal of the dead wood and elimination of crowded shoots.
Kordes 1928. *D. C. MF. Detailed. — — C.P.Pr. June-July. Hardy.*

Augustine Guinoisseau (H.T.), often described as a white La France, is very vigorous, floriferous, and produces large white flowers tinted with flesh-pink.
Guinoisseau 1889. *D. VG. F. Prune lightly. G.S.B. June-July. Hardy.*

Augustus D. Hartmann (H.T.) has very double, cupped blooms of metallic red, borne singly, and large green disease-resistant foliage.
B. R. Cant 1914. *D. VG. F. GPA. — — B. June-September. Hardy.*

AUNT HARRIET (wichuraiana rambler) is an old-fashioned name for a vigorous almost thornless climber with clusters of rather small semi-double crimson-scarlet flowers with white eyes.
Van Fleet 1918. *D. C. F. Prune lightly. — S.C. July. Hardy.*

AUREATE (H.T.) has large, perfectly shaped flowers of deep yellow, shaded with orange, with dark green disease-resistant foliage.
Dickson 1932. *D. VG. F. GPA. EA. — B. July-September. Hardy.*

AURELIA CAPDEVILLA (H.T.) has satin-pink flowers shaded with salmon.
Dot 1933. *D. VG. F. GPA. — — B. July-September. Hardy.*

AURORA (Hybrid Musk) has sprays of semi-double canary-yellow flowers, borne upon a bush of some four feet in height with disease-resistant foliage. Prune as little as possible.
Dot 1933. *D. EG. VF. Detailed. — — July-September. Hardy.*

AURORA BOREAL (H.T.) is a lightly-petalled variety of upright, vigorous growth, with bright crimson and orange colouring, shaded with gold at the base. The foliage is resistant to disease and thrives well in rainy districts.
Munné 1935. *D. VG. F. GPA. — — B. July-September. Hardy.*

AUSONIUS (Hybrid multiflora) is a semi-climbing rose suitable as a pillar with clusters of semi-double yellowish pink flowers with large white centres. Requires only very light pruning.
Lambert 1932. *D. EG. F. Detailed. — — Pr. July. Hardy.*

AUSTRIAN COPPER BRIAR (see R. lutea).

AUSTRIAN YELLOW BRIAR (see R. lutea).

AUTUMN (H.T.) has buds of burnt orange shaded with deep pink or carmine and others slightly paler. The flowers are borne on an upright bush with glossy green resistant foliage.
Coddington 1930. *D. MG. F. GPB. EB. 672/1. B.G. June-Sept. Hardy.*

AUTUMN DELIGHT (Hybrid Musk) makes a stout bush of some four feet in height with large clusters of creamy-white flowers. Autumn Delight should be pruned as little as possible and makes a good hedge.
Bentall 1933. *D. VG. VF. Prune lightly. — H.B. June-Sept. Hardy.*

AVIATEUR BLÉRIOT (wichuraiana rambler) has bright glossy foliage and bears its light-orange flowers in clusters. The long new shoots should be preserved, as it is upon the laterals of these that it flowers.
Fauqué 1910. *D. C. NF. Detailed. — P.Pr.C. June. Hardy.*

AVOCA (H.T.) has long pointed buds developing to fully double sweet-scented crimson flowers.
Dickson 1907. *D. EG. MF. GPA. — B. June-September. Hardy.*

AYRSHIRE Rose (see R. arvensis).

Baby Albéric (polyantha pompon). The first of the "babies" is now sufficiently old to be becoming nearly grown-up, and produces clusters of small yellow buds which open to creamy-white double flowers.
Chaplin 1932. *D. VG. NF. GPF. — — B. June-September. Hardy.*

Baby Betty (polyantha pompon) is a charming little rose of clean pale-yellow, tinted at the edges of the petals with rose and red. It is of vigorous growth and very suitable for bedding.
Burbage Nurseries 1929. *D. VG. F. GPF. — — B. June-Sept. Hardy.*
[*Pl.* 22.]

Baby Château (Hybrid polyantha) bears its clustered heads of large double dark-crimson flowers upon strong upright and branching plants, with varnished bronze-green ample foliage.
Kordes 1936. *D. VG. SF. GPG. — — B.G. June-September. Hardy.*

Baby Elegance (polyantha pompon) produces clustered heads of pale orange-yellow flowers on thorny bushes bearing glossy green foliage. The height is medium, seldom exceeding eighteen inches.
Hobbies 1912. *D. VG. MF. GPF. — — B. June-September. Hardy.*

Baby Faurax (polyantha pompon) is of similar dwarf growth but has clustered double flowers of amethyst- and steel-blue, reverting at times to red.
Lille 1924. *D. VG. MF. GPF. — — B. June-September. Hardy.*

Baby Lyon Rose (polyantha pompon) produces its clustered heads of double coral-red and deep yellow in some profusion on dwarf bushes.
Turbat 1916. *D. VG. F. GPF. — — B. June-September. Hardy.*

Baby Mine (polyantha pompon) is a dwarf sport of Cécile Brunner, and produces clusters of small, double, sulphur-yellow flowers shading to butter-yellow, on compact bushes bearing light green shiny foliage.
Moore 1929. *D. VG. F. GPF. — — B. June-September. Hardy.*

Ballerina (Hybrid Musk) is a delightful hybrid musk rose producing large clusters of small pink single flowers with clear white eyes on bushes of some three feet in height.
Bentall 1937. *D. VG. — GPH. — — S. June-September. Hardy.*

Baltimore Belle (Hybrid setigera) is a rose of American origin with large single or semi-double flowers of buff-yellow, fading to white, making a fine climber, or towering bush.
Feast 1843. *D. EG. F. GPH. — — S.C. July-August. Hardy.*

Banksiae (named after Lady Banks) is an evergreen climbing rose bearing clusters of small white or yellow flowers. It is most suitable for a sheltered wall, and pruning should consist only of thinning where necessary.
Aiton 1807. *E. C. F. Detailed. — — W. May-June.*

Banksiae var. albo-plena is similar in all respects but has small double white flowers, and var. lutea has equally beautiful yellow flowers.
— 1807. E. C. F. As above. — — W. May-June.

Three modern red Hybrid Tea Roses

J. H. Bruce **ABEF**   Glory of Rome **CDGH**

Mrs. George Geary **KLOP**

Tea Rose, Golden Dawn

BARBARA (H.T.) is an attractive medium-size rose with double, bright red flowers, the exterior of the petals being of pale yellow.
Paul 1923. *D. MG. F. GPB. — — B. June-September. Hardy.*

BARBARA RICHARDS (H.T.) is a very full rose of maize-yellow flushed with rose, with long pointed blooms, the outsides of which are buff. It is very floriferous and sweetly-scented, but is at times liable to hang its head.
Dickson 1930. *D. VG. VF. GPB. EB. — G.B.E.S. June-Sept. Hardy.*

BARBARA ROBINSON (H.T.) produces its long pointed creamy buds, several on a stem, opening to creamy-white, large, double flowers.
Dickson 1925. *D. VG. F. GPA. — White. B. June-September. Hardy.*

BARCELONA (H.T.) has deep red, cup-shaped blooms with deeper shading, and is lighter on the outside of the petals. The flowers are large, lasting, and sweetly-scented, and borne on strong stems.
Kordes 1932. *D. VG. VF. GPA. EA. — G.E.B. June-September. Hardy.*

BARON DE WASSENAER (see R. muscosa).

BARONESSE H. VON GEER (H.T.) produces groups of flowers of the type of Mme Abel Chatenay, of pale flesh colour with an exterior of vermilion, on a bush of upright growth.
Leenders 1922. *D. VG. MF. GPA. EA. — S. June-September. Hardy.*

BARONESS ROTHSCHILD (H.P.) has its flowers frilled with foliage, and its soft-rose cup-shaped flowers, shaded with white, are borne on strong, stout stems.
Pernet 1867. *D. EG. NF. GPC. — — S. June. Hardy.*

BARONNE DE VIVARIO (polyantha pompon) is delightful in its combination of dark green foliage and clusters of clear white flowers.
Soupert and Notting 1925. *D. MG. NF. GPF. — — B. June-September.*
[Hardy.

BEAUTÉ D'AUTOMNE (polyantha pompon) is a dwarf with large clusters of bright rose-pink flowers on short stems bearing shining green disease-resistant foliage on a bush of some twelve to eighteen inches.
Turbat 1918. *D. MG. NF. GPF. — — B. June-October. Very hardy.*

BEAUTY OF NEW SOUTH WALES (polyantha pompon) is another dwarf with clustered heads of bright crimson flowers, each with a distinguishing white eye.
Knight 1931. *D. SG. MF. GPF. — — B. June-September. Very hardy.*

BECKY (H.T.) has long pointed buds of deep rose opening to single flowers of gleaming rose-pink, and is of exceptionally good habit.
Beckwith 1925. *D. VG. MF. GPA. — — B. June-September. Hardy.*

BEDFORD CRIMSON (H.T.) is held to be of superior shape to Etoile de Hollande, and is of good deep velvety crimson and retains its colour well.
Laxton 1926. *D. VG. VF. GPA. — 821/2. B. June-September. Hardy.*

BEDFORDIA (H.T.) produces its nicely-shaped salmon-pink flowers with great freedom, on shapely bushes of upright growth.
Laxton 1931. *D. VG. F. GPA. — — B. June-September. Hardy.*

BEGGERIANA (comm.) (S.), N.W. Asia, makes a very prickly bush of some six feet in height and bears clustered, single, white flowers of about the size of a penny. The combination of its pale green foliage and its deep crimson fruits renders it most attractive.
Schrenk 1888. *D. EG. MF. Prune lightly. — — S. July. Hardy.*

BELINDA (Hybrid Musk) is another delightful long-flowering rose, making a strong bush of some six to seven feet in height with bright green leaves and clustered heads of soft-pink flowers. Requires very little pruning other than the removal of dead wood, and makes a fine hedge.
Bentall 1936. *D. EG. F. Detailed. — — S.H. June-October. Hardy.*

BELLA (beautiful) (S.), N.W. China, is a large six- to eight-foot shrub, resembling R. Moyesii in growth, bearing in sprays large, solitary, single flowers of bright pink. Pruning should be a minimum.
Rehder & Wilson —. *D. EG. NF. Detailed. — — S. July. Hardy.*

BELLE CUIVRÉE (H.T.) has long pointed medium-sized buds opening in full to medium flowers of coral-red shaded bronzy-yellow, and is of free branching habit.
Pernet-Ducher 1924. *D. VG. F. GPA. — — B. June-September. Hardy.*

BELLE DES JARDINS (see R. centifolia).

BELLE POITEVINE (see R. rugosa).

BELVEDERE (Hybrid polyantha) is a very large-flowered double red rose, with darker shading, with its flowers borne in large clusters on dwarf plants.
Kiese 1928. *D. VG. NF. GPF. — — B. June-October. Hardy.*

BEN ARTHUR DAVIS (H.T.) is an attractive garden rose, with semi-globular double flowers shading from cream at the edges of the petals to deep yellow, with pink at the base. Growth is vigorous, erect and branching, and foliage shining deep green.
Bostick 1935. *D. VG. MF. GPB. — — June-September. Hardy.*

BEN CANT (H.P.) has a very vigorous upright growth and produces sweetly-scented, deep crimson flowers of good form.
B. R. Cant 1938. *D. EG. NF. GPA. EA. — B.E. June-Sept. Hardy.*

BÉNÉDICTE SÉGUIN (H.T.) is of strong upright growth with reddish-bronze foliage, and produces very large globular flowers of yellow-ochre shaded with deep orange.
Pernet-Ducher 1918. *D. VG. NF. GPA. EA. — B.E. June-Sept. Hardy.*

BENNETT'S SEEDLING (see R. arvensis).

BENTALL'S SCARLET (H.T.) is one of the brighter of the so-called "scarlet" roses and has buds of pleasing shape and upright and vigorous growth.
Bentall 1935. *D. VG. MF. GPA. EA. — B.E. June-September. Hardy.*

BERGER'S ERFOLG (see R. rugosa).

Hybrid Tea Rose, Hortulanus Budde

Three Dwarf Polyantha Pompon Roses

Gloire du Midi **ABCEFG**

Little Dorrit **HJKLMNO**

Hurst Gem **OPQRSTU**

BERNICE (H.T.) has pointed buds which develop to semi-double fragrant flowers. The outer petals are cream shaded with pink, and the inner ones yellow shaded with carmine, and the plant is upright-growing and tall.
Pemberton 1927. *D. EG. F. GPA. EA. — B.E. June-September. Hardy.*

BERNICE (polyantha pompon) is a bedding rose with large clusters of small, double, rounded, deep cerise-pink flowers, borne upon dwarf but vigorous bushes, with shining pale green foliage.
Nicolas 1937. *D. MG. VF. GPF. — — B. June-October. Hardy.*

BERTHA GORST (H.T.) is bright cerise-red, shaded with gold towards the base and with good satiny texture, is a good grower and free from disease.
Beckwith 1933. *D. EG. NF. GPA. EA. — B.E. June-Sept. Hardy.*

BERTHA TURNER (H.T.) has glossy green disease-resistant foliage and bears its peach-coloured, cup-shaped double flowers with great freedom on upright trees.
Pemberton 1925. *D. EG. F. GPA. — B. June-September. Hardy.*

BERTHE DE FORGE (H.T.) has well-shaped buds of coral, opening to double flowers of deep orange with salmon reverse.
Chambard 1934. *D. VG. MF. GPA. EA. — B. June-September. Hardy.*

BERTRAM PARK (H.T.) has single flowers of bright crimson-pink shaded yellow at the base, in small clusters on bushes of upright and vigorous growth.
Burbage Nurseries 1927. *D. VG. MF. GPA. — — B. June-Oct. Hardy.*

BESSIE CHAPLIN (H.T.) has large, very double, well-rounded flowers of bright pink deepening at the centre, and is of upright growth, with green foliage and almost thornless.
Chaplin 1921. *D. MG. F. GPB. EB. — B.E. June-September. Hardy.*

BESS LOVETT (wichuraiana climber) has large double open globular flowers of crimson-pink, borne upon vigorous climbing plants with shining deep-green foliage.
Van Fleet 1915. *D. C. MF. GPJ. — — A.P.Pr.W. July-Aug. Hardy.*

BETTER TIMES (H.T.) has large, very full, well-shaped flowers of cerise-red and is probably the best of the Columbia descendants, as its scent, vigour and healthy growth make it outstanding.
Hill 1934. *D. VG. F. GPA. EA. — B.E. June-September. Hardy.*

BETTY HULTON (H.T.) is of upright, vigorous growth, with large deep-green leaves, and bears long pointed buds and saffron-yellow double flowers held high in the centre. In addition, it is very sweetly scented.
Dickson 1923. *D. VG. VF. GPA. EA. — B.E. June-September. Hardy.*

BETTY PEARSON (H.T.) has perfectly shaped blooms of cream deepening to apricot in the centre.
Burbage Nurseries 1929. *D. VG. F. GPA. EA. — B.E. June-September.*

Betty Prior (Hybrid polyantha) is a very vigorous single, carmine rose, opening to pink, with its flowers borne in large trusses. It is a comparatively tall-growing variety and is in good company with Kirsten Poulsen.
Prior 1934. *D. TG. NF. GPF. — — B.H. June-October. Hardy.*

Betty Sutor (H.T.) makes a strong, upright bush, with much light-green glossy foliage; produces long pointed buds opening to large double cone-centred, pale rose-pink scented flowers, variously borne.
McGredy 1929. *D. VG. MF. GPA. EA. — B.E. June-October. Hardy.*

Betty Uprichard (H.T.) is still one of the most popular of roses, with large light green glossy foliage, strong growth, pointed buds, and large semi-double to double flowers of pale salmon-pink with carmine reverse.
Dickson 1922. *D. VG. VF. GPA. EA.* 626/2-626. *B.E. June-September.*
                                                        [*Hardy. Pl.* 46.

Beverley Nichols (H.T.) is a most ladylike rose of peaches and cream with a fine discerning scent, and is upright and of moderate growth.
Burbage 1939. *D. MG. MF. GPA. EA. — B.E. June-Sept. Hardy.*

Bianca (H.T.) has a long-pointed flower of white, tinted with cream and pink, and is delightfully scented.
Pemberton 1927. *D. VG. VF. GPA. — White. B.E. June-Sept. Hardy.*

Billy Boiler (H.T.) has not so far been met in cultivation in this country, but has a very high reputation in Australia. The flowers, which are abundantly borne, are reported to be bright red and the growth to be vigorous.
Clark 1927. *D. VG. — — — — —*

Billy Boy (H.T.) produces many semi-double flowers of brilliant buttercup-yellow above bright green glossy foliage and is one of the best of all yellow roses for massing.
Beckwith 1926. *D. VG. F. GPA. — B. July-September. Hardy. Pl.* 15.

Bishop Darlington (Hybrid wichuraiana) has large semi-double flowers shading from cream to pale pink within, and light pink and pale gold without. The foliage is typical of the group, of medium size and glossy, and the growth vigorous, making it suitable for growing as a pillar rose.
Thomas 1926. *D. C. MF. GPF. — — Pr. June-October. Hardy.*

Black Bess (multiflora rambler) is a pillar rose of vigorous growth, with very dark crimson, scented, semi-double flowers, borne in clusters. Foliage is deep bronze-green.
Kordes 1939. *D. C. MF. GPJ. —* 929-824. *Pr. July-August. Hardy.*

Black Boy (Climbing H.T.) is another rose of Australian origin, with large semi-double cupped flowers of very dark smooth crimson, shading to maroon. It is of very vigorous growth, and is an admirable climber in a warm, sunny position.
Clark 1919. *D. C. VF. GPF. — — C. June-September. Hardy.*

BLACK KNIGHT (H.T.) is another very dark-red rose, with high-centred semi-globular flowers, produced upon very vigorous and erect plants with deep-green foliage.
Hillock 1934. *D. TG. VF. GPC. — — B. June-September. Hardy.*

BLANCHE DOUBLE DE COUBERT (see R. rugosa).

BLANCHE MOREAU (see R. muscosa).

BLANDA (smooth) (S.), N. America, is an almost thornless rose with mauve-pink flowers of about two inches in diameter, borne singly or in small clusters on a bush of some six feet in height, with leaves five- or seven-parted. The flowers are followed by bright red fruits.
Aiton 1773. *D. EG. MF. GPF.* 527/2. *S. July. Hardy. Pl.* 21 *&* 24.

BLANDA VAR. GLABRA (smooth) is similar but has light green foliage, red thornless branches and large, single, pink flowers.
— —. D. EG. F. GPF. — — S. July. Hardy.

BLANDA VAR. MICHIGANENSIS (from Michigan) is similar but the flowers are of somewhat deeper pink with the petals rather wider and more overlapping.
— —. D. EG. F. GPF. — 628/1. *S. July. Hardy. Pl.* 53 *&* 70.

BLAZE (Hybrid wichuraiana) is a most vigorous climber with semi-double flowers of cupped shape, resembling Paul's Scarlet Climber, of bright scarlet. It should be pruned of the old main wood only when new canes are available.
Jackson & Perkins 1933. *D. C. F. Detailed. — — C.P. June-July.*
[*Hardy.*

BLOOMFIELD ABUNDANCE (H.T.) bears a decided resemblance to Cécile Brunner in both colour and shape, but is larger in its flowers. The attractive flowers are double salmon-pink, with an orange base, and are freely produced both singly and in clusters upon exceptionally vigorous plants with varnished dark-green foliage.
Thomas 1920. *D. EG. MF. GPC. — — B.S. June-September. Hardy.*

BLOOMFIELD COURAGE (Hybrid wichuraiana) produces large clusters of small dark-red flowers with white eyes along the whole branch. Prune lightly, retaining the old shoots and four to five eyes on the laterals.
Thomas 1935. *D. C. NF. Detailed. — — C. June. Hardy.*

BLOOMFIELD DAWN (Climbing H.T.) is a pillar rose with single, pink, scented flowers with a yellow centre and rose-pink reverse.
Thomas 1931. *D. EG. MF. GPC. or GPG. — — G.S.Pr. June-Sept.*
[*Hardy.*

BLOOMFIELD FLAME (H.T.) has large nasturtium-red flowers, paling at the centre to orange. Growth is exceptionally vigorous and leaves are shining coppery-bronze.
Thomas 1930. *D. EG. MF. GPC. or GPG. — — G.S. June-Sept. Hardy.*

BLOOMFIELD LUSTRE (Climbing H.T.) is a climbing rose with double salmon-pink flowers shading to deep yellow at the base. Growth is vigorous and foliage ample and green.

Thomas 1931. *D. C. MF. GPE. — — C.P.Pr.W. June-September. Hardy.*

BLOSSOM (H.T.) is a very dwarf rose with full, well-shaped flowers of medium size, of peach-blossom pink, tinted yellow at the base within, and yellow and pale pink without.

Beckwith 1925. *D. SG. F. GPD. — — B. June-September. Hardy.*

BLUSHING BRIDE (H.T.) is of vigorous, bushy, compact habit, with light-green resistant foliage, with long pointed buds and conical-centred flowers of clear white, faintly flushed with pink at the centre.

Dickson 1918. *D. VG. NF. GPA. — — B. July-August. Hardy.*

BLUSHING LUCY (wichuraiana rambler) is a late-flowering rambler producing large trusses of pale pink double flowers which last well.

Williams 1938. *D. C. F. GPH. — P.Pr.C. July-August. Hardy.*

BLUSH QUEEN (H.T.) makes an almost thornless dwarf bush with deep green foliage and very large, very double, very high-centred blush-pink solitary flowers on short stems.

F. Cant. 1924. *D. SG. F. GPD. — — B. July-September. Hardy.*

BLUSH RAMBLER (multiflora rambler) bears semi-double pale pink cupped flowers in large clusters on short stems and is a very vigorous climber.

B. R. Cant 1903. *D. C. NF. GPE. — — P.Pr.H. July. Hardy.*

BOHEMIA (H.T.) has large semi-double solitary flowers of a pure rose-pink colour on good stems, on a vigorous and very thorny bush with small bronze-green foliage.

Bohm 1928. *D. VG. MF. GPA. — — B. July-September.*

BOHM'S TRIUMPH (H.T.) is another very large, dark red, full rose of good shape on stiff stems, borne on a vigorous well-shaped bush.

Bohm 1934. *D. VG. VF. GPA. EA. — B.E. July-September. Hardy.*

BOLERO (H.T.) has large, double, cupped flowers of nasturtium-red with a gold reverse, is of vigorous, erect and branching growth, and has dark green foliage and long flowering period.

Gaujard 1937. *D. VG. SF. GPB. — — B. June-September. Hardy.*

BONFIRE (wichuraiana rambler) is a most vigorous rambler which excels in producing long clusters of upwards of twenty flowers of bright scarlet-red. All old wood should be removed after flowering.

Turbat 1928. *D. C. NF. Detailed. — — C.P.Pr.H. Early July. Hardy.*

BONNIE JEAN (Hybrid polyantha) produces large clusters of single cerise-carmine flowers with white eyes and is of vigorous growth, normally reaching three feet in height.

Archer 1937. *D. VG. NF. GPA. — — B.H. July-September. Hardy.*

BORDERER (Hybrid polyantha) is another rose of Australian origin bearing its flowers in small clusters. The individual flowers are small and cup-shaped, semi-double and of salmon-fawn and pink.

Clark 1918. *D. MG. MF. GPB. — — B. July-September. Hardy.*

Boule de Neige (N.) has full medium-size flowers of pure white shaded with pale green and is of vigorous growth.
Lacharme 1867. D. VG. NF. GPA. — White. G.S. July. Hardy.

Bouquet d'Or (H.T.) produces perfectly shaped light golden flowers from buds which are deep gold.
Lippiatt 1922. D. VG. MF. GPA. — — B. July-September. Hardy.

Bourbonia. The following roses are all hybrids of the Bourbon Rose introduced in 1828. Generally speaking, all are particularly good in autumn.

Bourbonia Madame Isaac Pereire has very large, full, sweetly-scented flowers of deep rose-pink, shaded with rose-carmine, and is very hardy. Should be pruned by thinning, but as the type flowers on the lateral wood, old wood should be only tipped.
Margottin 1880. D. TG. VF. Detailed. — — P.Pr.S. July-Sept. Hardy.

Bourbonia Souvenir de la Malmaison has very large double flowers of silvery-pink, deepening to rose in the centre, and should be pruned similarly.
Beluze 1843. D. TG. VF. Detailed above. — G.P.S. July-Sept. Hardy.

Bourbonia Souvenir de la Malmaison Rose Pink is very similar but with flowers of rose-pink.
— —. D. TG. VF. Detailed above. — G.Pr.S. July-September. Hardy.

Bourbonia Zéphirine Drouhin is a very vigorous thornless rose with flowers of carmine pink.
Bizot 1873. D. C. VF. Detailed above. — H.B.P.Pr.S.W. July-Sept.
[Hardy. Pl. 7.

Boursault Roses are roses of climbing or pillar types resulting from the hybridisation of Rosa alpina. They are good for walls with northern aspects. The flowers are produced in large trusses. An example is Amadis, which will be found dealt with under that name. Flowering takes place during July and little or no pruning is required.

Boutonnière (H.T.) has small shapely double flowers of deep salmon-pink, freely borne upon erect bushes with dark green polished foliage.
Lammerts 1940. D. VG. SF. GPC. — — B.G. June-October. Hardy.

bracteata (bracted) (S.), N.W. China, is known as the Macartney Rose and is a vigorous climber of some tenderness suitable for a warm wall. The flowers, which are continuously borne in summer, are large, single, and of clear white. May be pruned severely when necessary.
Macartney 1875. E. C. NF. Detailed. White. W. July-August.

bracteata Mermaid is a hybrid of clear pale yellow with golden stamens but is larger, is very hardy and is notable as the finest of all the large single climbers.
Paul 1918. E. C. F. Detailed above. — W.H.Pr.S. July-September. Pl. 4.

BRASIER (H.T.) has fragrant, very double, good-shaped flowers of bright
carmine, shaded with scarlet and gold. The foliage is resistant and
the plant vigorous and undamaged by wet conditions. Fades in sun.
Mallerin 1937. *D. TG. F. GPC. EC. — B.E.St. July-Sept. Hardy.*

BREAK O' DAY (Hybrid polyantha) bears clusters of semi-double
globular flowers of bronzy-pink, passing with age to pale pink.
Growth is vigorous, erect and branching, and the ample foliage is
green.
Archer 1937. *D. VG. SF. GPG. — — B.G. June-October. Hardy.*

BREEZE HILL (wichuraiana climber). In my youth Gloire de Dijon
was a great favourite, and Dr. van Fleet's Breeze Hill is a still
greater rose. Its large double flowers are produced in clusters and
are of the same deep cream with a hint of salmon and pink. A fine
rose for a wall or arch which should be pruned but very lightly.
Van Fleet 1927. *D. VG. F. Detailed. — — C.W. July-Sept. Hardy.*

BRENDA (see R. rubiginosa).

BRIARCLIFF (H.T.) has well-shaped flowers of deep rose-pink paling
towards the outside, with citron shading at the base. The flower is
exceptionally large and borne singly on a strong stem.
Briarcliff 1926. *D. VG. F. GPA. — — B. July-September. Hardy.*

BRIDESMAID (T.). This tea-scented rose has a large flower of globular
shape with imbricated petals of clear pink, and is exceptionally good
when grown under glass or as a pot rose.
Moore 1893. *D. MG. F. GPA. EA. — E.Pot. July. Hardy.*

BRIGHTNESS (see R. spinosissima).

BRILLIANCY (H.T.) is a compact but vigorous-growing rose with good
shape, full double flowers of brilliant crimson and fine scent.
Le Grice 1936. *D. MG. VF. GPA. EA. — B.E. July-September. Hardy.*

BRILLIANT RED (H.T.) has high-centred and reflexed double flowers
of bright crimson-scarlet, borne from vigorous, erect and branching
plants with clear green foliage.
Lens 1938. *D. VG. SF. GPB. — — B.G. July-September. Hardy.*

BRUNONII (Brown's) (S.), Himalayas, is a most vigorous climbing rose
producing clusters of single white, scented flowers on strong green
canes with pale green leaves. R. Brunonii is also known as the
Musk Rose of Nepal and is best grown on a sunny wall.
Lindley 1822. *D. C. VF. GPF. — White. W. June. Tender.*

BURGUNDIACA (see R. centifolia var. parvifolia).

BURGUNDY (polyantha pompon) produces large clusters of very deep
red, very double flowers on short dwarf compact bushes.
Howard & Smith 1939. *D. SG. NF. GPF. — — B.E. July-Sept. Hardy.*

BURNET Rose (see R. spinosissima).

BUSH FIRE (wichuraiana rambler) is another Australian rose resembling Excelsa, with enormous clusters of bright red, double flowers with central yellow zones, but it flowers much earlier.
Clark 1917. *D. C. NF. GPF. — — P.H. July. Hardy.*

BUSYBODY (H.T.) lives up to its name by producing with profusion a large number of small but perfectly formed chrome-yellow flowers in unending succession on compact free-growing bushes of vigorous growth, of Australian origin.
Clark 1927. *D. MG. F. GPA. — — B. July-September. Hardy.*

CABBAGE ROSE (see R. centifolia).

CALEDONIA (H.T.) is an exceptionally well-shaped, high-centred, fully-double, white rose, borne in solitude on a long and strong stem. The foliage is large, dark green, and resistant to disease, and the growth vigorous.
Dobbie 1928. *D. VG. F. GPA. EA. White. B.G.E. July-Sept. Very hardy.*

CALIFORNIA (H.T.) has extra large wide petalled, semi-double open flowers of golden-orange, borne upon tall branching, vigorous plants with shiny dark green foliage.
Howard & Smith 1937. *D. TG. MF. GPC. — — B.G. July-Sept. Hardy.*

CALIFORNICA (from California) (S.), N.W. America, makes a bush of from four to eight feet in height, and bears large clusters of deep pink flowers with small foliage. The flowers are followed by bright red round fruits.
Chamisso and Schlechtendahl —. *D. TG. F. GPE. — 31/3. S.Sh. June-*
[*July. Hardy. Pl. 26*

CALIFORNICA FLORE PLENO is a variation which has flowers which are similar in colour but are double and semi-double.
Rehder —. *D. TG. F. GPE. — — S.Sh. June-July. Hardy.*

CALLISTO (Hybrid Musk) is a delightful shrub of branching habit of some three to four feet in height with dark green foliage which produces clusters of double golden-yellow flowers along the stem.
Pemberton 1920. *D. TG. F. GPC. — S.Sh. July-October. Hardy.*

CALOCARPA (see R. rugosa var. calocarpa).

CAMEO (polyantha pompon) is a very dwarf rose suitable for bedding which produces clustered heads of small double pink flowers.
De Ruyter 1932. *D. SG. NF. GPF. — B. July-September. Hardy.*

CAMILLA SCHNEIDER (H.T.) makes a vigorous upright bush with plenty of large green foliage and produces its large full double conical-centred blooms of clear bright blood-red each on a long stout stem.
Kordes 1922. *D. TG. MF. GPA. EA. — B.G.E. July-Sept. Hardy.*

CANADIAN JUBILEE (H.T.) is a variety raised in Canada, with large double flowers of Indian red with a yellow base, fading to pink as the flower ages. The plant is, however, subject to black spot.
Dunlop 1927. *D. VG. MF. GPA. — — B.G. July-September. Hardy.*

CANARY (H.T.) has high-centred flowers of light golden-yellow shading to canary-yellow, developing from light gold buds tinged with cerise. It is of strong upright and branching growth.
Dickson 1929. *D. VG. MF. GPA. —— B.G. July-September. Hardy.*

CANDEUR LYONNAISE (H.P.) has large long-pointed buds of clear white, sometimes with a trace of very pale yellow, developing to very large double flowers each borne in solitude.
Croibier 1914. *D. EG. NF. GPC. EC. White. B.E. July.*

CANIGO (H.T.) is an attractive very double white rose of extremely dwarf growth with a long flowering period and moderately scented.
Dot 1927. *D. SG. MF. GPD. EB. White. B.E. July-September.*

CANINA (dog-rose) (S.) is the Dog Rose of England and is spread widely throughout Europe and Western Asia. It produces vigorous canes generally well equipped with thorns and provides the understock for most of our bush and standard roses. The flowers vary from very light to very dark pink, borne in sprays of two or more, and are followed by large bright red fruits.
Linnaeus —. *D. EG. MF. ———— June. Hardy.*

CANTABRIGIENSIS (see R. Hugonis).

CAPRICE (H.T.) is a fine vigorous bush of upright growth with well-shaped large flowers singly borne, of two tones of orient red.
Leenders 1934. *D. EG. MF. GPC. EC. — G.B.E. June-Sept. Hardy.*

CAPTAIN BLOOD (H.T.) has high-centred semi-globular double flowers of deep blood-crimson, borne upon vigorous branching bushes, with ample dark green tough foliage.
Melville Bros. 1938. *D. VG. VF. GPB. EB. — B.E.G. July-Sept. Hardy.*

CAPTAIN CHRISTY (H.T.) is one of the oldest of the H.T.'s and still retains its charm for many who prefer the older and more sober subjects. The flowers are large, very full and globular in shape, of pale flesh-pink, deepening in the centre. Growth is very vigorous and the flowering period long.
Lacharme 1873. *D. TG. MF. GPA. —— G.B. June-September. Hardy.*

CAPTAIN F. S. HARVEY-CANT (H.T.) produces very large high-centred flowers of peach-pink with deep pink reverse, on bushes of strong and vigorous growth and flowering well throughout the season.
F. Cant 1923. *D. VG. F. GPA. EA. — G.E. June-September. Hardy.*

CAPTAIN GLISSON (H.T.) has large high-centred semi-double flowers of pale yellow, deepening at the centre, produced from vigorous plants with ample dark green foliage.
Hill 1935. *D. MG. SF. GPB. —— B.G. July-September. Hardy.*

CAPTAIN HAYWARD (H.P.) has large, loosely-petalled flowers of light scarlet-crimson, of good form, on strong vigorous bushes of medium height.
Bennett 1893. *D. VG. F. GPA. EA. — G.B.E. June and later. Hardy.*

Three fine Roses of pale tone

Mabel Morse (Hybrid Tea) **BCFG**

Clarice Goodacre (Hybrid Tea) **JKNO**   Percy Izzard (Hybrid Tea) **LMPQ**

Hybrid Tea Rose, Los Angeles

CAPTAIN KILBEE-STUART (H.T.) is a moderate grower with very large, very full, high-conical-centred crimson-scarlet flowers borne in solitude on medium stems almost devoid of thorns. Foliage is glossy deep green.
Dickson 1922. *D. SG. F. GPB. EB. — B.E. June-September. Hardy.*

CAPTAIN RONALD CLERK (H.T.) has semi-double, high-centred flowers of bright vermilion-red and is exceptionally good in its free flowering propensities.
McGredy 1923. *D. VG. MF. GPA. — — G.B. June-September. Hardy.*

CAPTAIN SASSOON (H.T.) has high-centred fragrant, double flowers of deep crimson-scarlet, and is of vigorous growth.
Gaujard 1938. *D. VG. VF. GPB. — — B.G. June-September. Hardy.*

CAPTAIN THOMAS (Climbing H.T.) is a pillar rose with single cream flowers, borne in clusters upon vigorous canes, with polished bright-green foliage.
Thomas 1938. *D. C. MF. GPE. — — Pr. July-August.*

CARESS (H.T.) produces its loose, well-shaped, buttercup-yellow flowers, tinted with rose, and shaded with light salmon rose at the borders, on strong upright stems.
Dickson 1935. *D. VG. MF. GPA. EA. — G.B.E. June-September. Hardy.*

CARILLON (H.T.) has semi-double flowers of bright flame, developing to coral-pink, and is a very fine variety for bedding.
Jackson & Perkins 1935. *D. MG. MF. GPB. — — B. July-Sept. Hardy.*

CARITO MACMAHON (H.T.) has high-centred very double bright-yellow flowers borne in profusion on strong bushes of upright growth.
Dot 1934. *D. MG. F. GPA. EA. — B.E. July-September. Hardy.*

CARL KEMPKES (Hybrid polyantha) has clustered heads of bright crimson, semi-double flowers, paling slightly with age, borne upon compact plants of vigorous habit, with polished deep green foliage.
Kordes 1937. *D. VG. SF. GPG. — — B.G. June-September. Hardy.*

CARMELITA (H.T.) has very fine large, double, vivid red flowers borne on strong stems and is of exceptionally strong bushy growth and is a fine rose for both garden and greenhouse.
Spanbauer 1933. *D. VG. VF. GPA. — — Pot.House.G. July-Sept. Hardy.*

CARMEN (see R. rugosa).

CARMINE PILLAR (multi-rambler) produces its carmine-red flowers several on each stem. The flowers are large, single, fragrant, and the growth very vigorous.
Paul 1895. *D. C. MF. GPH. — — P.Pr.A. June-July. Hardy.*

CARNIVAL (H.T.) has high-centred reflexed double flowers of orange, passing to pink at the edges of the petals. Growth is vigorous and erect, and foliage is shining bright green.
Archer 1939. *D. VG. SF. GPB. — — B.G. June-September. Hardy.*

CAROLINA (S.) Eastern N. America, is a vigorous shrub with stout prickly canes, small, rather thin, pointed leaves and bright carmine flowers about two inches in diameter. R. carolina increases by producing suckers and its flowers are followed by bright red rounded fruits.
Linnaeus (known in 1726). *D. VG. NF. GPG. — — S. June-July. Hardy.*

CAROLINE TESTOUT (H.T.) is still one of the most popular of everyday roses, its vigorous growth, erect habit, free flowering and hardiness proving of sufficient commendation when added to its large silvery satin-pink globular flowers, with their sweet scent, and deeper centres.
Pernet-Ducher 1890. *D. TG. SF. GPC. EA.* 627/3-2. *G.E. June-September.*
[*Hardy. Pl.* 25.

CARRIE JACOBS BOND (H.T.) produces delightfully scented well-shaped buds of crimson-scarlet and lasts well when cut. It is of vigorous and free growth, and of exceptional charm.
Howard & Smith 1935. *D. VG. VF. GPA. EA. — Pot.E.G. July-Sept.*
[*Hardy.*

CATALONIA (H.T.) has large globular flowers of bright cardinal-red shaded with gold, which last well, and are borne on vigorous bushy plants bearing much large deep green foliage.
Dot 1933. *D. VG. VF. GPB. EA. — G.B.E. June-September. Hardy.*

CATHCART BEDDER (H.T.) has shapely semi-double flowers of deep salmon-pink, borne upon strong bushy plants with bronze foliage.
Austin & McAslan 1939. *D. VG. SF. GPB. — — B. June-Sept. Hardy.*

CATHERINE SEYTON (see R. rubiginosa).

CATHRINE KORDES (H.T.) makes a vigorous upright tree, with dark green plentiful foliage which is resistant to disease, producing with some regularity if not prodigality large double flowers of glowing scarlet tinged with gloom, which break from blood-red buds.
Kordes 1930. *D. VG. MF. GPB. EA. — G.B.E. June-September. Hardy.*

CAUDATA (with tail) (S.), China, makes a very tall bush of from six to ten feet in height with scented foliage and bears small clusters of pale rosy-red flowers of about two inches in diameter, which are equally fragrant and are followed by long inverted-pear-shaped fruits.
Baker —. *D. EG. F. GPG. — — S. June. Hardy. Pl.* 24.

CAVALIER (H.T.) has large, double, globular flowers shading from deep cream at the edges of the petals to deep orange-yellow at the centre. Growth is vigorous with ample glossy green foliage.
Samtmann 1939. *D. VG. VF. GPB. — — B.G. June-September. Hardy.*

CECIL (Pernetiana) produces large, single, golden-yellow flowers in large clusters on a bush of compact vigour with shiny disease-proof foliage.
B. R. Cant 1926. *D. VG. NF. GPB. — — G.B. June-Sept. Hardy. Pl.* 61.

Cécile Brunner (polyantha pompon) has stood the test of time and still remains dear to the heart and attractive to the eye. The flowers, which are pale pink at the edges, are shaded pale rose on a yellow ground at the centre, and are borne in clusters on long stems. If left unpruned eventually forms a large bush, but can be kept very dwarf. *Ducher* 1880. *D. VG. MF. GPF. — 420/3. June-August. Hardy.*

Celestial (see R. alba).

Centifolia (hundred-leaved) is the old Cabbage Rose or Provence Rose, and it is the oldest garden rose known. R. centifolia probably originated in the Caucasus and was first grown in cultivation in Persia. It is from experiences of R. centifolia that Pliny makes his observations on the conditions under which roses should be grown. The beauty of the varieties of R. centifolia is freely acknowledged, its fragrance is exceptional, and the fact that botanists place the date of its introduction in England as 1596 points to its hardiness and persistence. The flowers of the variety generally accepted as being the original species are large, very double, inclined to nod, rounded and incurved and of bright rosy-pink, paler at the edges. The tree grows to a height of about six feet and seems to thrive on good cultivation and vigorous pruning.
——. *D. EG. VF. GPC. —— S. June-July. Very hardy.*

Centifolia major is a variety with larger fuller flowers with petals which overlap like the leaves of a cabbage.
— 1596. *D. EG. VF. GPC. —— S. June-July. Very hardy.*

Centifolia var. muscosa (see R. muscosa).

Centifolia var. parvifolia (with little foliage) is the Burgundy Rose, sometimes known as R. burgundiaca, making a compact bush of some eighteen inches in height, with very fully-petalled pompon-like flowers of clear pink.
Ehrhardt —. D. SG. F. GPF. —— S. July. Hardy.

Centifolia parvifolia "Pompon de Saint François" is the same in all respects but in the colour of the flowers, which are light red.
——. *D. SG. F. GPF. —— S. July. Hardy.*

Centifolia var. provincialis (the Provence Rose) numbers among its varieties the following:—

Centifolia provincialis Belle des Jardins has the typical flowers of purple-red, variegated with carmine and striped with white.
Guillot 1872. *D. EG. VF. GPC. —— S. June-July. Very hardy.*

Centifolia provincialis Konigin von Danemark has similar flowers of pale flesh-pink deepening towards the centre.
Booth 1898. *D. EG. VF. GPC. —— S. June-July. Very hardy.*

Centifolia provincialis nana De Meaux Pink is in effect a miniature version of the Cabbage Rose with similar colouring and seldom exceeding two feet in height. It is also known as the Pompon Rose.
Sweet 1814. *D. SG. F. GPG. —— S. June-July. Hardy.*

CENTIFOLIA PROVINCIALIS NANA PETITE DE HOLLANDE is rather larger in growth but has similar small flowers of rose-pink cupped flowers and makes quite a good low hedge of three to five feet.
——. *D. TG. F. GPC.* —— *H. June-July. Hardy.*

CENTIFOLIA PROVINCIALIS ROSEA is the Pink Provence Rose with large double rose-pink sweetly-scented flowers.
——. *D. EG. VF. GPC.* —— *S. June-July. Hardy.*

CENTIFOLIA PROVINCIALIS RUBRA is similar in growth with somewhat smaller flowers of rich red.
——. *D. EG. VF. GPC.* —— *S. June-July. Hardy.*

CENTIFOLIA PROVINCIALIS "UNIQUE BLANCHE" is similar in all respects but in the colour of the flowers, which are white.
Grimwood 1777. *D. EG. VF. GPC.* —— *S. June-July. Hardy.*

CERASOCARPA (with horned carpels) (S.), Central China, has long canes bearing shining green foliage, and bears large clusters of densely packed, smallish, creamy-white flowers.
Rolfe —. *D. C. NF. GPG.* —— *C. July.*

CERES (Hybrid Musk) produces large clusters of pale blush-pink flowers deeply shaded with yellow, and has an exceptionally long flowering period.
Pemberton 1914. *D. TG. F. GPG.* —— *H.S. July-October. Hardy.*

CHALLENGER (H.T.) produces its very large, wide-petalled, deep crimson, high-centred flowers on good stems from vigorous upright and branching plants with deep green foliage.
B. R. Cant 1938. *D. VG. VF. GPB. EB.* — *B.E.G. June-Sept. Hardy.*

CHAMELEON (H.T.) is an unusual rose with scented foliage, free branching habit and clustered buds, which open to toothed-petalled flame-coloured flowers edged with bright pink.
Dickson 1918. *D. TG. NF. GPC.* —— *S.B. June-August. Hardy.*

CHAMI (Hybrid Musk) has large sprays of bright rose-pink flowers on attractive bushes of some two to three feet in height, and carries an exceptionally strong scent of musk.
Pemberton 1929. *D. VG. NF. GPG.* —— *B.S. July-October. Hardy.*

CHAMISSO (Lambertiana) makes an exceptionally fine bushy pillar of about eight feet in height, bearing many small, round, orange buds which open to medium-size, semi-double flowers of flesh-pink, with a pale yellow centre. Foliage is bronze to bronze-green.
Lambert 1922. *D. EG. F. GPG.* —— *S. June-October. Hardy.*

CHAMPNEY'S Rose (see R. Noisettiana).

CHAPEAU DE NAPOLÉON (see R. muscosa cristata).

CHAPLIN'S CRIMSON GLOW (wichuraiana climber) has clustered heads of semi-double deep crimson flowers with a white base, and makes a fine rose for pillar or pergola.
Chaplin 1930. *D. C. NF. GPJ.* —— *Pr.P.A. July. Hardy.*

CHAPLIN's PINK CLIMBER (wichuraiana climber) produces clustered heads of semi-double pink flowers which do not fade, and is a most attractive and desirable plant for pillar or arch or pergola.
Chaplin 1929. *D. C. NF. GPJ. — — Pr.P.A. July. Hardy.*

CHARLES CRETTÉ (H.T.) has very large flowers of mid-rose of velvety texture, upon vigorous bushes.
Chambard 1917. *D. VG. F. GPB. — — B.E. June-September. Hardy.*

CHARLES H. RIGG (H.T.) has large vermilion-scarlet well-formed flowers shading to pink, and is of vigorous upright growth.
Chaplin 1931. *D. VG. VF. GPB. EB. — B.G.E. June-September. Hardy.*

CHARLES K. DOUGLAS (H.T.). On a vigorous, upright bush bearing dark green foliage, resistant to disease, are borne the large scarlet crimson-flushed, fully double flowers. A good rose, with a long and persistent flowering period.
Dickson 1919. *D. VG. VF. GPB. EB. — B.G.E. June-September. Hardy.*

CHARLES P. KILHAM (H.T.) is a fine rose of grand shape and distinctive colouring, with good growth and foliage resistant to mildew. The colour is dull orange-red, shaded with dull scarlet, and the flower hovers in an atmosphere of the old tea-scented rose.
Beckwith 1926. *D. VG. MF. GPB. EB.* 623/1-623. *B.G.E.St. June-Sept.*
[*Hardy. Pl. 23.*

CHARLOTTE E. DEDEM (H.T.) has large wide-petalled, high-pointed, semi-double, open flowers of deep golden-yellow. Growth is vigorous and erect and foliage of polished green.
Buisman 1937. *D. VG. SF. GPB. — — B.G. June-September. Hardy.*

CHARLOTTE KLEMM (see R. chinensis).

CHARMAINE (polyantha pompon) has deep pink buds in clusters, opening to full medium-size double pink flowers shaded with salmon. Foliage is bright shiny green and the average height does not greatly exceed two feet.
Burbage Nurseries 1929. *D. VG. MF. GPF. — — B. June-Sept. Hardy.*

CHARMER (H.T.). Gaiety being the keynote of this charmer, it is proper that it should be clad in pink, cerise and yellow; that it should have the fragrance of sweet peas, and that it should, in addition to charm, have distinction.
Dickson 1934. *D. VG. F. GPA. — — B. June-September. Hardy.*

CHASTITY (Climbing H.T.) is a fine climbing hybrid tea rose with strong vigorous habit, and neat flowers of good shape, pure white in colour, shading to lemon-yellow at the base.
F. Cant 1924. *D. C. F. GPE. — White. C.W. June. Very hardy.*

CHÂTILLON RAMBLER (wichuraiana rambler) produces many clusters of small, semi-double, cupped flowers of delicate salmon-pink, on strong canes well provided with thorns and good green foliage, which has the drawback of mildewing in certain localities.
Nonin 1913. *D. VG. MF. GPH. — — A.Pr. June-July. Hardy.*

Châtillon Rose (Hybrid polyantha) has enormous bunches of semi-double clear pink flowers with white eyes, on dwarf and compact bushes which seldom exceed two feet in height.
Nonin 1923. *D. VG. MF. GPG. — — B.G.H. June-Sept. Hardy.*

Cheerful (H.T.) is a grand name for a rose which resembles Caroline Testout in its habit, shape and size of bloom. The flowers are of terra-cotta pink, which does not fade, and overspreads a base of pure orange.
McGredy 1915. *D. MG. F. GPC. — — B.G. June-Sept. Very hardy.*

Cheerio (Hybrid polyantha) is a good vigorous grower with clusters of single flowers of brick-red shaded with gold, with good green foliage which is not subject to disease. Its good distinctive colour, its fragrance, its complete imperturbability in face of heavy rain, and its resistance to disease, give it every characteristic necessary in a good outstanding rose. Height does not exceed three feet.
Archer 1938. *D. VG. F. GPG. — — B.G.H. June-September. Hardy.*

Chérie (Hybrid polyantha) is a very beautiful crimson-scarlet sport of "Else Poulsen," which it resembles in all other respects.
Morse 1931. *D. VG. NF. GPG. — — B. June-September. Hardy.*

Cherokee Rose (see R. laevigata).

Cherry (H.T.) has large flowers with a characteristic high centre, the upper face of the petals being carmine-pink, the lower side of yellow which deepens to sunflower-yellow at the base. The flowers are borne on medium stems and the foliage is plentiful and of good green.
McGredy 1928. *D. VG. MF. GPB. EB.* 0621-3/3. *G.B.E. June-September.*
[*Very hardy. Pl.* 37.

Chestnut Rose (see R. Roxburghii).

Chieftain (H.T.) has outstanding grace of form, long upright stems, fine colour and fragrance, and cuts well. The petals are long and bright red, touched in the open bloom with orange-scarlet. Gives no impression to the eye at least of blueing, and was one of the most satisfactory before the camera.
Montgomery 1936. *D. VG. VF. GPB. EB. — G.B.E. June-Sept. Hardy.*

chinensis (Chinese) (S.), is also known as R. indica var. sinensis—a somewhat paradoxical name—but more commonly as the Monthly Rose, and its continuous flowering propensities have given it deserved popularity. The following varieties and hybrids number among them the best still in cultivation. They flower from June to October, and often later, and can be equalled by no other rose in this respect. They should be thinned rather than cut back, and this is best done in early April.

chinensis Arethusa has medium-yellow flowers in groups, shaded with apricot, and is of vigorous growth.
Paul 1903. *D. VG. F. Detailed. — G. June-October. Hardy.*

CHINENSIS CHARLOTTE KLEMM has semi-double medium flowers in groups, of fiery-red shaded dull orange and crimson, and produces its flowers with exceptional freedom.
Turke 1905. *D. VG. F. Detailed. — G. June-October. Hardy.*

CHINENSIS COMMON CHINA BLUSH bears its full, large, double flowers in loose many-flowered sprays, and is probably one of the best of the group.
Parsons 1796. *D. VG. F. Detailed. — 527/2-3. B.C. June-October. Hardy*
[*Pl.* 25

CHINENSIS COMTESSE DU CAYLA has its semi-double flowers freely borne in groups, and its vivid colouring renders it one of the most beautiful of all roses. The flowers are copper and nasturtium-red and the opened flowers red-gold and pink within, and yellow without.
Guillot 1902. *D. VG. MF. Detailed. — — G. June-October. Hardy.*

CHINENSIS CRAMOISIE SUPÉRIEURE bears its large, double, crimson flowers in large clusters and is in every way a good rose.
Plantier 1834. *D. VG. MF. Detailed. — — G. June-October. Hardy.*

CHINENSIS DUCHER has fully double, flat, white, smallish flowers produced in clusters.
Ducher 1870. *D. VG. MF. Detailed. — White. G. June-October. Hardy.*

CHINENSIS FABVIER has semi-double crimson flowers with a white eye and is fragrant.
Laffay 1832. *D. VG. F. Detailed. — — G.B. June-October. Hardy.*

CHINENSIS FELLEMBERG has rosy-crimson semi-double flowers, and is otherwise similar.
Fellemberg 1851. *D. VG. F. Detailed. — — G.B. June-October. Hardy.*

CHINENSIS FRAU DR. SCHRICKER has large double flowers of carmine shaded with coppery red.
Felberg-Leclerc 1927. *D. VG. VF. Detailed. — — G.B. June-October.*

CHINENSIS HERMOSA, sometimes known as Armosa, produces clusters of small to medium high-centred double flowers of delicate blush-pink, and will always remain a personal favourite among a distinctive and very precious group.
Marcheseau 1840. *D. VG. F. Detailed. — 628/3 to 628/1. B. June-October.*
[*Hardy.*

CHINENSIS INDICA SANGUINEA, also known as Miss Lowe's variety, is one of the oldest roses in commerce and is probably a wild species. Its bright-red single flowers are gloriously scented and produced with great freedom.
— —. D. VG. VF. Detailed. — — B.C. June-October. Hardy.

CHINENSIS IRENE WATTS has white flowers shaded with salmon-pink, and is a quite dwarf variety.
Guillot 1896. *D. SG. F. Detailed. — — B.C. June-October. Hardy.*

CHINENSIS LAURETTE MESSIMY produces large, double, bright rose-pink flowers tinted with yellow at the base.
Guillot 1894. *D. VG. MF. Detailed. — — B. June-October. Hardy.*

CHINENSIS MADAME DE LA VALETTE has large golden-yellow flowers shaded with coppery-red and is delightfully scented.
Schwartz 1910. *D. VG. F. Detailed. — — B.G. June-October. Hardy.*

CHINENSIS MADAME EUGÈNE RESAL has large double flowers of variable colour from nasturtium-red to bright pink, on an orange-yellow ground. Sport from Laurette Messimy.
Guillot 1896. *D. VG. MF. Detailed. — — B. June-October. Hardy.*

CHINENSIS MRS. BOSANQUET has white flowers tinted with flesh colour.
Laffay 1832. *D. VG. F. Detailed. — White. B. June-October. Hardy.*

CHINENSIS OLD CRIMSON CHINA has flowers of dark velvety crimson and produces large sprays of flowers. It cannot, at least in this country, be said to be either one of the best or easiest of growers.
Curtis 1789. *D. MG. F. Detailed. — — E.G. June-October. Hardy.*

CHINENSIS ORIENTAL QUEEN is one of the most recent additions to the rank of the China hybrids and has double flowers of good form of orange-scarlet with a yellow base fading to carmine.
Beckwith 1926. *D. VG. NF. Detailed. — — B.G. June-September. Hardy.*

CHINENSIS QUEEN MAB has apricot flowers shaded with orange.
Paul 1896. *D. MG. NF. Detailed. — — B. July-September.*

CHINENSIS VAR. MINIMA (Lawranceana) is a miniature China Rose and the smallest of all cultivated roses. The original species is said to be extinct but may well be that variety at present known as R. Roulettii Doncaster's variety, which is paler than R. Roulettii and slightly taller in growth.
Sweet 1810.

CHINENSIS VAR. MINIMA OAKINGTON RUBY has ruby-crimson flowers perfectly double in form but less than three-quarters of an inch in length when in bud, and one inch across when fully open. Grown in rich soil it is apt to grow at least one foot in height, but poor soil and pruning keep it in character.
Bloom 1933. *D. SG. F. Detailed. — 724/2. G. June-October. Hardy.*

CHINENSIS VAR. MINIMA PEON is known in America as Tom Thumb and is similar except that its crimson-scarlet flowers are borne in clusters and have a white eye.
De Vink 1935. *D. SG. NF. Detailed. 724/3. G. June-October. Hardy.*

CHINENSIS VAR. MINIMA POMPON DE PARIS is similar to Oakington Ruby, but its leaves are finer and its perfectly-shaped flowers are rose-pink.
— —. D. SG. F. Detailed. — 627. G. June-October. Hardy.

CHINENSIS MINIMA VAR. ROULETTII is the smallest of all roses. Found by M. Correvon in Switzerland in 1829, it is a perfect miniature seldom exceeding three inches in height, when able to produce many flowers of rose-pink in quick succession.
Correvon 1829. *D. SG. F. Detailed. — 628/2. S. June-October. Hardy.*

Three Hybrid Tea Roses

Golden Melody **ABCDGH**
McGredy's Yellow **EFGJK**
McGredy's Ivory **NOLMPQ**

Three Hybrid Tea Roses

Mrs. Henry Bowles **BCFG**
W. F. Dreer **JKNO**   Betty Uprichard **LM**

CHINENSIS VIRIDIFLORA is also known as R. monstrosa and is in effect
a green rose. The flowers are double green, and seem to be made up
of serrated-edged green leaves, tinted with bronze. A curiosity no
doubt, but one which always fascinates, and provides its flowers
with such frequency as to fascinate often.
Bembridge & Harrison 1856. *D. MG. NF. Detailed.* 62/2 *to* 00961. *S.*
[*July-Sept. Pl.* 26.

CHINENSIS WHITE PAT is of very dwarf growth and produces semi-double
flowers of creamy white in profusion.
Henderson 1879. *D. SG. MF. Detailed. White. S. June-September.*

C. H. MIDDLETON (H.T.) is an attractive deep-crimson double rose of
high pointed form, of vigorous bushy growth, with dark glossy
foliage, and of fine old-rose scent.
B. R. Cant 1939. *D. VG. VF. GPB. — — B.G. June-Sept. Hardy.*

CHRISTINE (Pern.) is a grand rose to bring us back. True, the flowers
are small, but they are of purest gold; they are but moderately
fragrant, but they are borne on long stems for a very long period;
but you may have guessed that Christine is one of the author's
particular favourites. To make the story complete it should be added
that the foliage is as lovely as the rose and is always free of disease.
McGredy 1918. *D. MG. MF. GPB. —* 606/1. *B.St. June-Sept. Hardy.*

CHRISTINE PRIOR (H.T.) has large semi-double or double flowers, with
high conical centre of deep rose-red, tinted with yellow and peach,
with yellow at the base.
McGredy 1924. *D. VG. F. GPB. — — B. June-September. Hardy.*

CHRISTINE WRIGHT (Climbing H.T.) has large double pink flowers
borne several on a stem, resembling Caroline Testout but with the
colour of the wild rose predominant. Is of very vigorous growth and
moderately fragrant.
Hoopes & Thomas 1909. *DC. MF. GPE. —* 625/2. *W.A. June-July.*
[*Hardy.*

CHRISTOBEL (H.T.) also has very large shapely flowers, of deep apricot-
yellow with deeper shading. Growth is extra strong and bushy,
and the flowering period prolonged.
Croibier 1937. *D. TG. NF. GPC. — — B.G. June-October. Hardy.*

CHRISTOPHER STONE (H.T.) has long-pointed buds, semi-double flowers
of dark crimson scarlet; the petals are of fine form and the colour
well retained.
Robinson 1934. *D. VG. F. GPB. EB.* 827-826/2. *B.E. June-Sept. Hardy.*

CHRISTOPH WEIGAND (H.T.) has very double high-pointed flowers of
pale silvery-pink and flowers with continuity.
Weigand 1928. *D. VG. MF. GPA. EA. — G.B.E. June-Sept. Hardy.*

CILLY MICHEL (H.T.) is a brilliant combination of nasturtium-red,
coral-red, and orange, with its large flowers borne on strong and
long stems.
Felberg-Leclerc 1928. *D. VG. MF. GPB. EB. — G.B.E. July-Sept. Hardy.*

CINNAMONEA (cinnamon-brown) (S.), Europe, Asia, makes a most ornamental bush of some six feet in height, with brown spineless stems and green leaves, divided into five or seven leaflets, bearing single pink or deep-pink to red flowers either solitarily or in few-flowered clusters. The flowers are fragrant and followed by small, round, bright red fruits.

Lindley —. D. EG. F. GPG. or LPC. —— S. June-July. Hardy.

CINNAMONEA VAR. PLENA is similar with double flowers.

CITRON (H.T.) has globular but not full flowers of biscuit-yellow, flushed with coppery orange, produced upon vigorous plants with red bronze foliage.

Gaujard 1933. D. VG. MF. GPB. —— B.G. June-September. Hardy.

CLARA CURTIS (H.T.) has very large, very double flowers of golden-yellow borne on long strong stems.

Dickson 1922. D. MG. MF. GPB. EB. — G.B.E. June-Sept. Hardy.

CLARA D'ARCIS (H.T.) has large, fully double flowers with wide petals of bright rose-pink, deepening at the centre, and with a trace of yellow at the base. Flowers very freely and has a spicy fragrance.

Pernet-Ducher 1932. D. VG. VF. GPB. EB. — G.B.E. June-Sept. Hardy.

CLARIBEL (H.S.) is a derivative from R. rugosa suitably pictured in Plate 70.

Beckwith 1901. D. VG. SF. GPC. —— H.S. June. Hardy. Pl. 70.

CLARICE GOODACRE (H.T.) is a rose which has stood the test of time and remains one of the best white roses. Flowers of medium size and completely double, of ivory white shading to chrome yellow, are borne on long strong stems.

Dickson 1916. D. VG. F. GPB. EB. White. G.B.E. June-Sept. Hardy.
[Pl. 43.

CLEMATIS (wichuraiana rambler) is a rambler which produces very large clusters of small dark red flowers with outstanding white eyes. Growth is exceptionally vigorous.

Turbat 1924. D. C. NF. GPI. —— A.P. June-July. Hardy.

CLIMBING SPORTS.

The following climbing sports are available from varieties which will be found described under the appropriate name in the alphabetical list. The climbing sports seldom flower as freely as the parents, but quite often the flowers are even finer and larger. A good general instruction with regard to pruning is that they should not be pruned during the year of establishment and then only as indicated under pruning instructions *LPF.* or *GPE.* For record purposes the name of the introducer and date is given.

Climbing Briarcliff (H.T.)	...	...	*Parmentier* 1929
,,	Captain Christy (H.T.)	...	*Ducher* 1881
,,	Captain Hayward (H.P.)	...	*Paul* 1906
,,	Captain Ronald Clerk (H.T.)...		*Austin & McAslan* 1934
,,	Caroline Testout (H.T.)	...	*Chauvry* 1901

Climbing	Cécile Brunner (polyantha pompon)	*Hosp* 1894
,,	Charles P. Kilham (H.T.) ...	*Morse* 1934
,,	Christine (Pern.)	*Willink* 1936
,,	Columbia (H.T.)	*Vestal* 1923
,,	Crimson Glory (H.T.) ...	*Millar* 1942
,,	Daily Mail Scented (H.T.) ...	*Archer* 1930
,,	Dame Edith Helen (H.T.) ...	*English* 1932
,,	Duchess of Atholl (H.T.) ...	*Howard Rose Co.* 1933
,,	Else Poulsen (Hybrid polyantha)	*Ley* 1932
,,	Emma Wright (H.T.)	*Stanway Rose Garden* 1932
,,	Etoile de France (H.T.) ...	*Howard* 1915
,,	Etoile de Hollande (H.T.) ...	*Leenders* 1931
,,	Frau Karl Druschki (H.P.) ...	*Laurenson* 1906
,,	General MacArthur (H.T.) ...	*Dickson* 1923
,,	Gloria Mundi (polyantha pompon)	*Lens* 1934
,,	Golden Emblem (Pern.) ...	*Armstrong* 1927
,,	Golden Ophelia (H.T.) ...	*Hage* 1924
,,	Gruss an Teplitz (H.T.) ...	*Storrs & Harrison* 1911
,,	Hadley (H.T.)	*Teschendorff* 1927
,,	Hoosier Beauty (H.T.)	*Gray* 1925
,,	H. V. Machin (H.T.)	*Dickson* 1919
,,	Independence Day (Pern.) ...	*Murrell* 1932
,,	Irish Fireflame (H.T.)	*Dickson* 1916
,,	Joseph Guy (is a climbing sport of Auguste Kordes)	*Nonin* 1929
,,	Lady Ashtown (H.T.)	*Bradley* 1909
,,	Lady Hillingdon (T.)	*Hicks* 1917
,,	Lady Sylvia (H.T.)	*Stevens* 1933
,,	La France (H.T.)	*Henderson* 1894
,,	Little Dorrit (polyantha pompon)	*Hillier* 1933
,,	Los Angeles (Pern.)	*Warner* 1925
,,	Mabel Morse (H.T.)	*Ley* 1932
,,	Madame Abel Chatenay (H.T.)	*Easlea* 1917
,,	Madame Butterfly (H.T.) ...	*E. P. Smith* 1925
,,	Madame Edouard Herriot (Pern.)	*Ketten* 1921
,,	Mrs. Aaron Ward (H.T.) ...	*Dickson* 1922
,,	Mrs. G. A. van Rossem (H.T.)	*Verschuren* 1935
,,	Mrs. Henry Bowles (H.T.) ...	*Dobbie* 1929
,,	Mrs. Henry Morse (H.T.) ...	*Chaplin* 1929
,,	Mrs. Henry Winnett (H.T.) ...	*Bernaix* 1930
,,	Mrs. Herbert Stevens (T.) ...	*Pernet-Ducher* 1922
,,	Ophelia (H.T.)	*Dickson* 1920
,,	Paul Crampel (polyantha pompon)	*Tantau* 1937

Climbing	President Herbert Hoover (Pern.)	*Cant* 1937
,,	Queen Alexandra (H.T.) ...	*Harkness* 1931
,,	Radiance (H.T.)	*Griffling* 1926
,,	Richmond (H.T.)	*Dickson* 1912
,,	Rodhatte (polyantha pompon)	*Grootendorst* 1925
,,	Rose Marie (H.T.)	*Pacific Rose Co.* 1927
,,	Shot Silk (H.T.)	*Knight* 1931
,,	Souvenir de Claudius Pernet (Pern.)	*Western Rose Co.* 1925
,,	Souvenir de Georges Pernet (Pern.)	*Pernet-Ducher* 1927
,,	Souvenir de H. A. Verschuren (H.T.)...	*Howard & Smith* 1927
,,	Sunburst (H.T.)	*Stuartson* 1915
,,	Sunstar (H.T.)	*Dickson* 1925
,,	Talisman (H.T.)	*Dixie Rose Co.* 1933
,,	Wilhelm Kordes (H.T.) ...	*Wood & Ingram* 1927

CLINOPHYLLA (with limp leaves) (S.), India, makes a rounded compact bush with greenish stems unvexed by many thorns and above neat green foliage, and bears its clear-white flowers, centred with golden stamens, followed by elongated orange-red fruits.
——. *D. TG. NF. GPE. —— White. S. June.*

CLOVELLY (H.T.) has blooms of good shape, fully double and of light rose-pink, borne on long strong stems. It is very sweetly scented and may be said to be vigorous and not subject to mildew.
Hicks 1924. *D. VG. VF. GPB. EB. — G.B.E. June-September. Hardy.*

CLYTEMNESTRA (Hybrid Musk) is another hybrid musk rose of good habit approximating three and a half feet in height and covered with good dark green foliage. The flowers, borne in considerable clusters, develop from coppery buds to chamois-yellow and are exceptionally fragrant.
Pemberton 1915. *D. TG. VF. GPE. —— S.G. June-October. Hardy.*

COLETTE CLÉMENT (H.T.) has single or semi-double flowers of bright orange-nasturtium and is an exceptionally fine variety for bedding purposes, being at its best in autumn.
Mallerin 1931. *D. VG. F. GPB. —— B. June-September. Hardy.*

COLONEL CAMPBELL WATSON (H.T.) has well-shaped conical-centred flowers of clear pink, shaded with salmon-rose and bright carmine, and is of vigorous growth and fragrant.
Bees 1937. *D. VG. F. GPB. EB. — G.B.E. June-September. Hardy.*

COLONEL DAZIER (H.T.) has large flowers of good form, very double, of pale flesh with the underside of the petals of bright rose, shading to golden-yellow at the base.
Ketten 1927. *D. VG. F. GPB. EB. — B.G.E. June-September. Hardy.*

COLONEL LINDBERGH (polyantha pompon) is a sport from Juliana and has clustered heads of salmon-orange semi-double flowers of medium size.
Den Ouden 1928. *D. VG. NF. GPF. — — B. June-September. Hardy.*

COLONEL NICHOLAS MEYER (H.T.) has well-shaped full double flowers of geranium-red deepening to intense red, and is of vigorous growth and exceptionally fragrant.
Sauvageot 1934. *D. VG. VF. GPB. — — B. June-September. Hardy.*

COLONEL OSWALD FITZGERALD (H.T.) in a martial array still holds pride of place in spite of advancing years for its well-formed dark crimson flowers and resistant foliage.
Dickson 1917. *D. VG. NF. GPB. — — B. July-September. Hardy.*

COLONEL SHARMAN-CRAWFORD (H.T.) is not just "another red rose." The flowers are of good form, of glowing crimson shaded with deep red, and its colour is well retained. Growth is erect, moderately vigorous, foliage plentiful and green, and the flowers freely produced all the season.
Dickson 1933. *D. MG. VF. GPB. — 724. B.Pot. June-Sept. Hardy. Pl.* 27.

COLUMBIA (H.T.) would appear to have everything the others have. Its large, full, well-shaped flowers of glowing rose-pink, its fine habit, its persistent flowering combine to make it, in spite of its age, an outstanding variety.
Hill 1916. *D. VG. VF. GPB. — — B.House. June-September. Hardy.*

COMMANDANT FÉLIX FAURÉ (H.P.) has dark crimson double flowers with vermilion shading which is well retained, and remains one of the best of the red hybrid perpetuals still in cultivation, if only for its outstanding fragrance.
Boutigny 1902. *D. VG. VF. GPC. — — B.G. July-September. Hardy.*

COMMON CHINA BLUSH (see R. chinensis). *Pl.* 25.

COMTESSE DE CASTILLEJA (Pern.) has large cupped flowers of orange, passing to golden red, is intensely fragrant and has dark green disease-resistant foliage, strong upright growth and free flowering proclivities beyond the ordinary.
Chambard 1926. *D. VG. VF. GPB. — — G.B. July-September. Hardy.*

COMTESSE DU CAYLA (see R. chinensis).

COMTESSE VANDAL (H.T.) has large, gloriously shaped flowers of reddish-orange edged with pale pink and golden without. It is of good growth, does not object visibly to rain, but is subject unfortunately to mildew, which can, of course, be controlled.
Leenders 1932. *D. VG. MF. GPB. — — G.B. July-September. Hardy.*

CONCHITA (polyantha pompon) has clustered heads of very persistent clear-salmon double flowers, borne with prodigality on vigorous bushy plants with glossy green foliage.
Jordan 1935. *D. VG. F. GPF. — — B. July-October. Hardy.*

CONCORDIA (H.T.) has large semi-double well-rounded flowers of glowing pink, paling to silver-pink at the edges, borne solitarily on long stems. Its growth is upright, thorny and vigorous, and its flowering prodigal.

Brix 1924. *D. VG. F. GPB. — — B. July-September. Hardy.*

CONDESA DE SASTAGO (Pern.) has the interior of its petals of orange-flame to turkey-red, with the underside of gold. Is vigorous in growth, fragrant, resistant to disease, does not mind rain and is exceptionally free-flowering.

Dot 1934. *D. VG. F. GPB. — — G.B. July-September. Hardy.*

CONQUEROR (H.T.) has semi-double flowers of saffron-yellow which passes to pale yellow as the flower ages. Is sweetly scented and of vigorous growth.

Chaplin 1929. *D. VG. F. GPB. — — — B. July-September. Hardy.*

CONRAD F. MEYER (see R. rugosa).

CONSTANCE (Pern.) bears, upon a vigorous bush with glossy green foliage, full, double flowers with high centres of brilliant canary-yellow turning to golden-yellow.

Pernet-Ducher 1915. *D. VG. MF. GPB. — — B. June-Sept. Hardy.*

CONTRAST (H.T.) has double high-pointed flowers of pink shaded with coppery-orange, with the reverse of the petals of white similarly shaded. Growth is vigorous, erect and branching, and foliage large and of glossy green.

Howard & Smith 1937. *D. VG. SF. GPB. — — B.G. June-Sept. Hardy.*

COPPER GLOW (wichuraiana climber) has large double flowers of long-pointed shape, of golden copper. Growth is vigorous and climbing, and foliage is deep shining green.

Brownell 1940. *D. C. VF. GPJ. — — A.P.Pr. June-July. Hardy.*

CORAL (H.T.) has large double flowers of bright coral-red on a base of buttercup-yellow shading to pale salmon. It is of vigorous growth and flowers with continuity.

Dickson 1931. *D. VG. MF. GPB. — — B. June-September. Hardy.*

CORAL CLUSTER (polyantha pompon) is a coral-pink sport from Orleans Rose and bears its large coral-pink clusters of smallish semi-double flowers on medium to dwarf bushes with rich glossy green foliage which has a tendency to mildew.

Murrell 1920. *D. MG. NF. GPE. — 19/3. B. June-September. Hardy.*

CORAL CREEPER (wichuraiana climber) produces sprays of large semi-double flowers of pale pink deepening to coral at the centre.

Brownell 1938. *D. C. NF. GPJ. — — A.P.Pr. June-July. Hardy.*

CORAL CUP (polyantha pompon) is similar in appearance to the well-known Gloria Mundi, but of coral-pink. The double flowers are freely produced in clusters on vigorous plants with bright green foliage.

Bobbink & Atkins 1936. *D. VG. SF. GPF. — — B.G. June-Sept. Hardy.*

CORALIE (wichuraiana rambler) is a rambler with large double and semi-double flowers of bright coral-red, changing to deep pink, on strong canes bearing deep glossy green foliage.
Paul 1919. *D. C. NF. GPJ. — — P. June-July. Hardy.*

CORIIFOLIA (with hide-like foliage) (S.), Europe and Western Asia, is known as "the Leather-leaf Rose" and is said to be a natural hybrid of R. canina. It makes a thorny bush of some five feet in height, with hard green leaves made up of five or seven leaflets, and produces its pale pink flowers of about two inches in diameter either singly or in small corymbs.
Fries —. D. TG. NF. LPC. — — S. June. Hardy.

CORIIFOLIA VAR. FROEBELII (Froebel's) is also known as Rosa laxa, and has bluish-green foliage and corymbs of small white flowers. It has been used frequently as an understock, but such stocks are under suspicion as being a contributory cause of rust.
— —. D. TG. NF. LPC. — White. S. June. Hardy. Pl. 60.

CORNELIA (Hybrid musk) makes an outstanding bush of some four or five feet in height, with dark green tough foliage borne on purple-brown stems, and produces clustered heads of large strawberry-coloured semi-double flowers flushed with yellow.
Pemberton 1925. *D. TG. VF. LPC. — — S. July-October. Very hardy.*

CORYMBULOSA (producing flowers in corymbs) (S.), China, is a bush of some six feet in height, with its yellowish-green leaves with three to five leaflets borne on green stems tinged with bronzy-red. The single deep-pink flowers with white eyes are as small as a halfpenny, but are borne in many-flowered clusters.
Rolfe —. D. EG. F. LPC. — — S. June-July. Hardy.

COUNTESS OF ELGIN (H.T.) is very similar in shape and habit to Madame Edouard Herriot, the colour of the flowers being salmon-pink with a deeper rose-pink reverse.
Ferguson 1925. *D. VG. MF. GPB. — — B.G. June-September. Hardy.*

COUNTESS OF STRADBROKE (H.T. or Climbing H.T.) can be either a very tall-growing bush rose or a climber, and bears its large double dark red flowers in groups.
Clark 1928. *D. EG. (C.) F. GPC. (LPC.) — — B.G.C. June-Sept. Hardy.*

COUNTESS OF WARWICK (H.T.) is of good strong upright growth and bears its well-formed yellow, pink-edged flowers on upright stems.
Easlea 1919. *D. MG. NF. GPB. — — B.G. June-September. Hardy.*

COURAGE (H.T.) produces from long-pointed buds large double flowers, with conical centre, of deep crimson on a plant of moderate growth but dwarf habit.
McGredy 1923. *D. MG. VF. GPB. — — B.G. June-September. Hardy.*

COURTNEY PAGE (H.T.) has well-formed flowers of great fullness, borne singly, of scarlet-crimson shaded with deep crimson, and remains a very good rose. Foliage is glossy dark green and resistant to disease.
McGredy 1922. *D. VG. VF. GPB. — — B.G. June-September. Hardy.*

COVENT GARDEN (H.T.) has flowers of medium size, of attractive shape and of deep crimson somewhat deeper on the reverse. Each flower is borne on a long strong stem, the general growth is vigorous and upright, and the flowering period continuous.
B. R. Cant 1919. *D. VG. NF. GPB. — 822/3. B. June-Sept. Hardy.*

CRAMOISIE SUPÉRIEURE (see R. chinensis).

CRESTED MOSS (see R. muscosa cristata).

CRIMSON BEAUTY (H.T.) has long-pointed well-formed flowers of deep crimson shaded with maroon, has good healthy green foliage, is vigorous and free-flowering.
Le Grice 1935. *D. VG. F. GPB. — B. June-September. Hardy.*

CRIMSON CONQUEST (wichuraiana climber) produces large clusters of deep crimson-scarlet single flowers in great abundance on vigorous canes bearing glossy green foliage not subject to disease.
Chaplin 1931. *D. C. VF. GPJ. — 822. Pr.A. June-July. Hardy.*

CRIMSON EMBLEM (H.T.) has fully double, bright crimson-scarlet flowers of perfect shape and bears them on long stout stems.
McGredy 1916. *D. VG. NF. GPB. — B. June-September. Hardy.*

CRIMSON GLOBE (see R. muscosa).

CRIMSON GLORY (H.T.) has large full flowers of good shape of deep crimson-velvet, borne on long stems, on very vigorous and bushy growth with much leathery green foliage. Flowers are produced very freely and continuously.
Kordes 1935. *D. VG. VF. GPB. EA.* 821/1 *shot* 824. *G.B.E. June-Sept.*
[Hardy. Pl. 28.

CRIMSON GLOW (wichuraiana climber) is a climber similar in habit to Paul's Scarlet Climber, and produces clusters of very large, full, deep crimson flowers with a white base. The flowers are fragrant and the growth vigorous.
Chaplin 1930. *D. C. MF. GPJ. — — A.Pr. June-July. Hardy.*

CRIMSON ORLEANS (polyantha pompon) is a sport from Orleans Rose, and very vigorous, producing very large clusters of bright crimson smallish semi-double flowers, which are slightly fragrant. The foliage is glossy green, but is subject to mildew in certain localities.
Laxton 1923. *D. VG. SF. GPF. — 24. B.Pot. June-October. Hardy.*

CRIMSON RAMBLER (multiflora rambler) is interesting if only for its contribution to the race of climbers which followed it. Its continued existence demonstrates not only its popularity but its vigour and hardiness. Its sprays of rather small double crimson flowers are produced in late summer on pale green canes with pale green foliage which is subject to mildew.
Turner 1893. *D. C. NF. GPH. — — A.P.Pr. July. Hardy.*

Three Hybrid Tea Roses

Madame Jules Bouché **ABCDFG**
Madame Butterfly **EH**
Orange Nassau **JKNOLMPQ**

Three Dwarf Polyantha Pompon Roses

Glory of Hurst **ABCDE**
Kersbergen **FGHJKLMNR**
Koster's Orleans **OPSTU**

CRISTAL (H.T.) has perfectly-shaped flowers of clearest yellow veined with ochre, produced upon vigorous growth with shiny green foliage. *Gaujard* 1938. *D. VG. F. GPB. EB. — G.B.E. June-September. Hardy.*

CROWN OF GOLD (H.T.) has large double high-pointed flowers of lemon-yellow, deepening to deep golden yellow at the centre, produced upon long stems from very robust plants, with bright green leaves. *Howard & Smith* 1937. *D. VG. SF. GPB. — — B.G. June-Sept. Hardy.*

CRUSADER (H.T.) has very double, full, large flowers of crimson-red, of excellent shape, borne in solitude on long stems, and is in every way a good rose, its vigour and upright growth, combined with its good green foliage, adding to its attractiveness. *Montgomery Co.* 1920. *D. VG. MF. GPB. — — B. June-September.*

CUBA (H.T.) has large semi-double cupped flowers of bright crimson-scarlet, tinted with yellow, paling quickly with age, borne on vigorous bushes with bronze foliage. *Pernet-Ducher* 1926. *D. VG. VF. GPB. — — B. June-September.*

CUPID (H.T.) has single flowers of pale peach-pink, borne in clusters, and makes a large bush which is outstanding in its beauty. *B. R. Cant* 1915. *D. TG. NF. GPC. LPC. — — S. June-July.*

CYNTHIA BROOKE (H.T.) has exceptionally well-shaped fragrant tea-scented blooms with high centres, which open in perfect shape, last well, and are of a fine shade of coppery-yellow. Growth is vigorous and flowering free, and the dark green foliage appears to be resistant to disease. *McGredy* 1942. *D. VG. VF. GPB. EA. — G.B.E. June-September.*

DAILY MAIL ROSE is another name for Madame Edouard Herriot, which see.

DAILY MAIL SCENTED ROSE (H.T.) has medium flowers of fine shape of deep red, of velvet-like texture, with hints of scarlet and maroon, with the reverse of the petals deeper in colour. Growth is variable in some districts, rather moderate in others, vigorous and upright, and the flowers very fragrant. *Archer* 1929. *D. MG. VF. GPB. — — B. June-September. Hardy.*

DAINTY (H.T.). The upright growth, shining green foliage, branching habit, and free-flowering proclivities, added to the long-stemmed large, full, perfectly-formed reflexed flowers of apricot-pink, tinted with cherry, conspire to make this one of the most attractive of all roses. *Dickson* 1921. *D. VG. MF. GPB. — — B. June-September. Hardy.*

DAINTY (polyantha pompon) is another polyantha variety with attractive clustered heads of medium semi-double flowers of salmon-pink *De Ruyter* 1930. *D. VG. NF. GPF. — — B. June-September. Hardy.*

DAINTY BESS (H.T.) produces large single flowers of salmon-pink borne in small clusters, but the most attractive feature of the plant is the delightful contrast afforded by the golden stamens borne upon red filaments.
Archer 1926. *D. VG. VF. GPB.* — 625/2 & 623. *B. June-Sept. Hardy.*

DAINTY DAWN (polyantha pompon) has extremely large clusters of semi-double cerise-pink flowers which persist upon bushes which bear bronzy-green foliage.
Knight 1931. *D. VG. VF. GPF.* — — *B. June-September. Hardy.*

DAINTY MAID (Hybrid polyantha) has large single flowers of rose-pink shaded with carmine, the inside of the flower being clear silvery pink, is very vigorous, its height often exceeding three feet; is disease-free, and does not suffer from rain.
Le Grice 1938. *D. VG. NF. GPG.* — 427-24/3. *B.G.H. June-Sept. Hardy.*
[*Pl.* 15 & 59.

DAKAR (H.T.) has very large flowers borne on long stiff stems, of good shape and lasting powers, of bright silvery-rose shaded and striped with rose-pink.
Pernet-Ducher 1932. *D. VG. VF. GPB.* — — *G.B. June-Sept. Hardy.*

DAMASCENA. The Damask Rose is one of the oldest roses in existence and is possibly a natural hybrid of R. gallica. It is exceptionally hardy, a very strong grower and bears large thorns on green wood, carrying pale green somewhat woolly leaves, usually made up of five leaflets. The flowers are double, very fragrant and borne in small clusters. Their exquisite rose-pink colour, shown mainly in June and July, repeats itself sometimes in the autumn. R. damascena and its hybrids should not be pruned heavily, thinning-out only being permissible.
Miller —. *D. EG. VF. GPG.* — — *S. June-July. Very hardy.*

DAMASCENA MADAME PLANTIER appears to be a pure white form of R. damascena, similar in all other respects.
Plantier 1835. *D. EG. VF. GPG.* — — *S.H. June-July. Very hardy.*

DAMASCENA TRIGINTIPETALA (thirty-petalled) has soft-pink semi-double flowers, and yields the essential oil of the rose: attar of roses.
Dieck —. *D. EG. VF. GPG.* — — *S. June-July. Very hardy.*

DAMASCENA VARIEGATA (York and Lancaster Rose) is a very old variety with semi-double irregular-shaped flowers which may be white, striped with red, or flesh, and sometimes either part or all of any of these colours. The flowers are flat and are produced in clusters, and though it is neither a pretty nor well-shaped rose it is worth growing for its history alone.
Monardes 1551. *D. EG. VF. GPG.* — — *S. June-July. Very hardy.*

DAME CATHERINE (H.T.) is of vigorous bushy upright habit and bears its perfectly-shaped high-centred fully double flowers of bright golden-yellow on long stiff stems. The foliage is plentiful and glossy, and flowering prolific.
B. R. Cant 1937. *D. VG. MF. GPB. EB.* — *G.B.E. June-September.*

DAME EDITH HELEN (H.T.) produces its large double flowers singly on long stems, on vigorous upright and bushy growth with green, resistant foliage. The blooms are of good shape, fully double and of glowing pink and intensely fragrant.
Dickson 1926. *D. MG. VF. GPB. EB.* 625/1 *to* 623/2. *G.B.E. June-Sept.*
[*Hardy. Pl.* 6 & 29.

DANAË (Hybrid Musk) has clusters of large, double, pale yellow flowers borne on vigorous bushes of some four feet in height, with dark green foliage.
Pemberton 1913. *D. TG. VF. GPG. LPC.* — — *S. June-September. Hardy.*

DANCE OF JOY (wichuraiana pompon) makes a rather stong bushy growth, but produces its rather large dazzling velvety red flowers in the fashion of a miniature Paul's Scarlet Climber. May be kept dwarf by pruning.
J. Sauvageot 1932. *D. TG. F. GPF. or GPG.* — — *B. June-Sept. Hardy.*

DAVIDII (David's) (S.), China, is a strong-growing six-foot shrub, protected with strong straight thorns, and bears large, single, rich rose flowers in clusters; the flowers are followed by elongated pear-shaped fruits which are bristly and of the brightest orange-red.
Crepin —. *D. EG. NF. GPJ.* — — *S. June-July. Hardy.*

DAVIDII VAR. ELONGATA is a similar shrub with branches more arching and pendent clusters of single pink flowers, followed by similar fruits of rich red colourings.
— —. *D. EG. NF. GPJ.* — — *S. June-July. Hardy.*

DAVID McKEE (H.T.) has beautifully-shaped flowers, large and full, of bright crimson, is vigorous, hardy and free-flowering and delightfully fragrant.
Dickson 1933. *D. VG. VF. GPB. EB.* — *B.G. June-September. Hardy.*

DAVURICA (Dahurian), Manchuria, is a small very spiny shrub with purplish-pink flowers and light green leaves, which is lax and running in habit.
Pallas —. *D. SG. NF. GPJ.* — — *Banks.S. June-July. Hardy.*

DAYBREAK (H.T.) has many-petalled flowers of high-pointed shape, of salmon-pink and creamy-yellow, and is of exceptionally vigorous growth.
Laxton 1935. *D. VG. SF. GPB.* — — *B.G. June-September. Hardy.*

DAZLA (Pernetiana) produces from a very vigorous bush with glossy mildew-proof foliage long buds which open to huge semi-single flowers of brilliant orange-scarlet with the reverse of golden-yellow flushed with scarlet.
B. R. Cant 1930. *D. VG. MF. GPC.* — 020-6/2. *B.G. June-Sept. Hardy.*

DEAN HOLE (H.T.) still remains with us. The tendency it has to inherit disease fails to detract completely from the charm of its large, double, full-petalled, silvery carmine flowers, flushed with salmon, produced intermittently.
Dickson 1904. *D. SG. MF. GPC.* — — *B.G. June-July. Hardy.*

DECEPTION (H.T.) is a very vigorous rose with upright growth producing its perfectly-shaped large rose-coloured blooms with freedom. *Beckwith* 1923. *D. VG. VF. GPB. —— B.G. June-September. Hardy.*

DECORATOR (H.T.) is a fine bedding rose with loose brilliant carmine flowers, with a base of orange-yellow. The colour of the flowers deepens with age to neyron-rose, and the growth is strong and the leaves resistant to disease. *Dickson* 1936. *D. VG. MF. GPB. —— B. June-September. Hardy.*

DELIGHTFUL (H.T.) has well-shaped, large, double, full flowers of bright rose shaded with yellow, which retain that colour well, is free-flowering and very vigorous, being upright-growing and somewhat taller than most of its type. *McGredy* 1931. *D. VG. MF. GPC. EC. — G.E. June-September. Hardy.*

DE MEAUX (see R. muscosa).

DE MEAUX PINK (see R. centifolia provincialis).

DENISE CASSEGRAIN (polyantha pompon) has large clusters of snow-white, scented flowers on plants of bushy growth. *Grandes Roseraies* 1922. *D. VG. VF. GPF. —— B. June-Sept. Hardy.*

DESMOND JOHNSTON (H.T.) has large long-pointed buds, opening to full double high-centred, perfectly fashioned, flowers of scarlet, heavily flushed with orange and claret, with the reverse of the petals veined with orange. The leaves are glossy green and resistant to disease. *McGredy* 1927. *D. TG. MF. GPA. EA. — G.E. June-September. Hardy.*

DESTINY (H.T.) has well-shaped fully double flowers, with high centres of crimson-scarlet, with darker shading and velvety texture; is very vigorous, of upright habit, with dark green foliage, and is moderately fragrant. *Beckwith* 1935. *D. VG. MF. GPB. —— G.B. June-September. Hardy.*

DIADEM (H.T.) makes a bush of very vigorous upright growth, with green glossy leaves, and bears its large deep crimson, pointed, double flowers, which are suffused with salmon and coppery-yellow, each on a single long stem. *McGredy* 1922. *D. VG. MF. GPB. —— G.B. June-September. Hardy.*

DIANA (Hybrid polyantha) has clusters of single dark orange-yellow flowers, tipped with carmine, on plants of bushy growth, with fine dark-green foliage. *Leenders* 1922. *D. VG. MF. GPG. — 609/3-6/2. B. June-Sept. Hardy.*

DICKSON'S BOUQUET (H.T.) has long-pointed buds which develop into thin double blooms of good shape, of salmon blended with carmine and apricot. The flowers are borne on long strong stems, and the foliage is glossy and resistant to disease. *Dickson* 1938. *D. VG. F. GPC. —— B.G. June-September. Hardy.*

DICKSON'S CENTENNIAL (H.T.) has loosely formed, fully double blooms made up of very large petals of shining crimson, which have deeper shading. The opened petals are strawberry-red. Of exceptionally vigorous and bushy growth, the leaves are plentiful, glossy and resistant to disease.
Dickson 1938. *D. VG. VF. GPC. EC. — G.E. June-September. Hardy.*

DICKSON'S DELIGHT (H.T.) produces well-shaped flowers of double form, of an incomparable blend of orange shaded with rose. Growth is vigorous and free.
Dickson 1938. *D. VG. F. GPC. — — G. June-September. Hardy.*

DICKSON'S PERFECTION (H.T.) has the advantage of producing strong well-balanced stems which soon make a sturdy plant. The large flowers, which are loose, are of shrimp-pink overshot with orange, and the foliage is a good green.
Dickson 1937. *D. MG. F. GPA. — — 022/2. B. June-Sept. Hardy. Pl. 63.*

DICKSON'S RED is the American name for Dr. F. G. Chandler, which see.

DIGNITY (H.T.) has high-centred double flowers of creamy-white, produced from neat but vigorous plants, with tough green foliage.
Le Grice 1940. *D. VG. VF. GPB. — — B.G. June-September. Hardy.*

DIRECTEUR GUÉRIN (H.T.) has the advantage of vigorous and branching habit, combined with large fully double high-centred blooms of creamy-yellow, with the centre deepening to gold. The foliage is glossy green and plentiful and is not subject to disease. If anything, it is better in autumn.
Gaujard 1937. *D. VG. F. GPB. EB. 402/2-407. B.G.E.St. June-Sept.*
[Hardy.

DIRECTEUR PLUMECOCQ (Pern.) has high-centred, very full and double flowers of apricot-yellow borne on long stems. The foliage is glossy green and plentiful, and the plant is very free-flowering.
Gaujard 1931. *D. VG. F. GPB. — — B. June-September. Hardy.*

DIRECTOR RUBIO (H.T.) makes an upright bush with large green, resistant foliage and bears singly, upon long stiff stems, its very large semi-double, very deep pink, sweetly-scented flowers.
Dot 1928. *D. VG. F. GPB. — — G.B. June-September. Hardy.*

DISTINCTION (Hybrid polyantha) has large double flowers of bright rose-pink, deepening at the centre, borne in clusters of some thirty to forty blooms on plants of about eighteen inches in height, with bright green, glossy, disease-resistant foliage.
Turbat 1927. *D. VG. SF. GPG. — — B. June-September. Hardy.*

DOG ROSE (see R. canina).

DOLLY VARDEN (polyantha pompon) is of vigorous growth, bearing, upon bushes of some eighteen inches in height, clustered semi-double flowers of clear pink.
De Ruyter 1930. *D. VG. MF. GPF. — — B. June-September. Hardy.*

DOLLY VARDEN (see R. rugosa).

DONALD MACDONALD (H.T.) has dwarf compact but vigorous growth, with semi-double blooms of medium size of bright orange-carmine borne in clusters.

Dickson 1916. *D. SG. F. GPA. LPA. — — B. June-September. Hardy.*

DONALD PRIOR (Hybrid polyantha) must be one of the finest of all the hybrid polyantha roses. Its large bright crimson-scarlet semi-double flowers are borne in small clusters which are just the right size, its green glossy foliage fits it well, and its fragrance adds weight to the scale. Add the facts that it is not subject to disease, that it is impervious to rain, and that it is vigorous in growth, and one has all the material from which to judge its worth.

Prior 1934. *D. MG. F. GPG. — 822/1. B.G.St. June-Sept. Very hardy.*

DON BRADMAN (H.T.) has many-petalled high-centred flowers of deep coppery-pink, passing with age to pale pink, produced with freedom from vigorous and erect plants of good habit.

Wheatcroft 1938. *D. VG. SF. GPB. — — B.G. June-September. Hardy.*

DORCAS (wichuraiana rambler) has fully double flowers of deep rose-pink, paling to coral-pink within, to yellow at the base, in many-flowered sprays. Foliage is bright green, shiny and almost evergreen.

English 1922. *D. C. NF. GPI. — — A.Pr. July. Very hardy.*

DOREEN THORN (H.T.) has deep green foliage, strong vigorous habit, flowers of perfect shape of deep pink with yellow at the base. Upon development they open and expose a central tassel of anthers of bright gold.

F. Cant 1934. *D. VG. SF. GPC. — — B. June-September. Very hardy.*

DORINA NEAVE (H.T.) has large pointed flowers of globular shape, of silvery pink, borne on long stiff stems, and is of compact habit and vigorous growth. Foliage is dark green and not subject to disease. For bedding purposes it should be planted closely.

Pemberton 1926. *D. MG. F. GPB. EB. — B.E. June-September. Hardy.*

DORIS FINDLATOR (H.T.) is one of those imperturbable roses one finds too seldom. The flowers are shapely and full, of two shades of apricot, the deeper at the base, flushed with reddish-salmon without. Growth is vigorous, foliage good and plentiful, and the plant will flourish almost anywhere.

Dickson 1936. *D. VG. MF. GPB. — — G.B. June-September. Hardy.*

DORIS GRACE ROBINSON (H.T.) has fragrant creamy-white flowers deepening to lemon in the heart of the bloom. The foliage is olive-green, disease-resistant, and the growth vigorous.

Bees Ltd. 1943. *D. VG. MF. GPB. — — E.G.B. June-September. Hardy.*

DORIS TRAYLER (H.T.) forms a vigorous upright compact bush of some two feet in height with glossy green foliage, and bears upon stiff stems full, double, high-pointed flowers of amber-yellow, flushed outside with deep orange.

McGredy 1924. *D. VG. MF. GPB. — — G.B. June-September. Very hardy.*

DOROTHY FOWLER (see R. rugosa).

DOROTHY HODGSON (H.T.) has nicely shaped double flowers of orange-cerise produced upon rather tall vigorous plants.
F. Cant 1930. *D. TG. MF. GPC. —— B. June-September. Hardy.*

DOROTHY HOWARTH (Hybrid polyantha) bears, upon a vigorous bushy plant with glossy green leaves, rather large double flowers of coral-pink shaded with salmon, in clusters.
Bees 1921. *D. VG. NF. GPG. —— B. June-September. Hardy.*

DOROTHY MCGREDY (Pern.) is reminiscent in colouring of an old favourite in Juliet, but in every way a better and finer rose. The flowers are of good size, perfect shape, and are carried erect, and outside are sunflower-yellow, shading to crushed strawberry; within they are vermilion-red, yellow at the base. The growth is vigorous and foliage ample.
McGredy 1936. *D. VG. MF. GPB. — 21, 4, 2. G.B. June-October. Hardy.*
[*Pl.* 68.

DOROTHY PAGE-ROBERTS (H.T.) is an old favourite which still persists and deserves so to do. The very large double flowers of beautiful copper-pink are borne singly on long stiff stems arising from bronzy foliage. Flowering, if not continuous, is at least persistent.
Dickson 1907. *D. VG. MF. GPB. —— B.G. June-September. Hardy.*

DOROTHY PERKINS (wichuraiana rambler) takes me back many years, and raises a memory which seems at least to consist of a perfect cascade of rose-pink. Of very vigorous growth, the clustered, double, rose-pink flowers are borne in profusion on strong canes with green leaves.
Jackson & Perkins 1901. *D. C. MF. GPH. —— A.Pr.H.Wst. July. Hardy.*

DOUBLOONS (see R. setigera).

DR. A. I. PETYT (H.T.) produces a very large, high-pointed, fully-petalled scarlet-crimson rose borne on a strong stem, and is a free- and frequent-flowering plant.
Burrell 1924. *D. VG. F. GPA. EA. — E. June-September. Hardy.*

DR. ECKENER (see R. rugosa).

DR. EDWARD DEACON (H.T.) produces its flowers of salmon-orange in groups of two or three on a stem. The flowers are large, full and double, and pale with age to shrimp-pink. The foliage is glossy green and not liable to disease, borne upon upright bushy growth.
Morse 1926. *D. VG. MF. GPB. EB. — G.E. June-September. Hardy.*

DR. E. M. MILLS (see R. Hugonis).

DR. F. G. CHANDLER (H.T.) has long-petalled flowers of perfect shape, full, double, of bright crimson-scarlet, borne singly upon long stiff stems. The foliage is glossy dark green and growth vigorous.
Dickson 1939. *D. VG. VF. GPB. EB. 824. G.E. June-September. Hardy.*

135

DR. HERBERT HAWKESWORTH (H.T.) has finely shaped medium-size flowers of deep crimson, deepening in intensity in the centre, borne upon long strong stems. The foliage is deep green and proof against mildew.

Bees 1927. *D. VG. VF. GPB. — — B.G. June-September. Hardy.*

DR. KIRK (Pernetiana) has exceptionally large coral-pink flowers of high-pointed form, with orange-yellow shadings, and is of robust growth, with polished green foliage.

Mallerin 1939. *D. VG. SF. GPB. — — B.G. June-September.*

DR. SCHEINER (H.T.) has freely-produced flowers of good shape and size, borne upon vigorous growth bearing dark green foliage. The flowers are fully double, high-centred and of deep velvety red.

Bohm 1933. *D. VG. F. GPB. — — B.G. June-September. Hardy.*

DRUSCHKI RUBRA (H.P.) is a rose which has a marked resemblance to Frau Karl Druschki except in the colour of its flowers, which are crimson-red and slightly fragrant.

Lambert 1929. *D. EG. MF. GPC. — — B.G. June-July. Hardy.*

DR. W. E. HADDEN (H.T.) seems to be always in flower during the season, producing its average-size flowers of perfect shape and of raspberry red, streaked and flushed with yellow, with freedom and continuity. Growth is vigorous and bushy, and the foliage dark green and resistant to the attacks of mildew.

McGredy 1934. *D. VG. MF. GPB. — — G. June-September. Hardy.*

DR. W. VAN FLEET (wichuraiana rambler) is one of the best of all the vigorous ramblers. Its fine glossy green foliage, its large open double flowers of soft, delicate pink make it outstanding.

Van Fleet 1910. *D. C. MF. GPI. — — A.Pr. June-July. Hardy.*

D. T. POULSEN (Hybrid polyantha) has large clusters of large single scarlet-red flowers with white eyes, borne upon vigorous plants with bright green glossy disease-resistant foliage.

Poulsen 1932. *D. VG. NF. GPG. — — B. June-September. Hardy.*

DUCHER (see R. chinensis).

DUCHESS OF ATHOLL (H.T.) produces its perfectly formed large double flowers, of orange shaded with old rose, with great freedom. The flowers are borne singly on long stiff stems from an upright plant with bronze-green foliage. Is unfortunately liable to black spot.

Dobbie 1927. *D. MG. MF. GPB. — B.St. June-September. Hardy. Pl. 30.*

DUCHESS OF MONTROSE (H.T.) has perfectly-formed fragrant large flowers with high centres of vermilion-crimson, upright growth, with dark green resistant foliage, and is an exceptionally good rose for bedding purposes.

Dobbie 1930. *D. VG. MF. GPB. — — B. June-September. Hardy.*

Three Hybrid Tea Roses

Elizabeth Arden **BCFG**

Mabel Morse **JKNO**   Josephine Spiecker **LMPQ**

Max Krause (Hybrid Tea) **BCDG**

Lady Hillingdon (Tea) **EFJK**

Lamia (Hybrid Tea) **KLMPQ**

DUPONTII (comm.) (Hybrid of species) makes a rounded strong-growing thornless bush with light green foliage, of about five feet in height, bearing very large, single, white flowers shaded with pink. The flowers are followed by pear-shaped orange-red fruits.
— 1822. *D. EG. F. GPG. LPC. — — S. June-July. Hardy.*

DUQUESA DE PENARANDA (H.T.) has remarkable long-pointed flowers of coppery-orange borne singly on straight stems, and can be an outstanding rose. The habit is vigorous, and the glossy bright green foliage makes it particularly attractive.
Dot 1931. *D. EG. MF. GPB. — — B. June-September. Hardy.*

DUSKY MAIDEN (formerly Piccaninny) (H.T.) has very dark, glowing red, sweetly-scented flowers carried in clusters. The foliage is deep-green, healthy and abundant.
Le Grice 1947. *D. VG. VF. GPB. — — B.G. June-September.*

EARLDOMENSIS (Hybrid of species) is a hybrid of R. Hugonis with R. omeiensis with the peculiar idiosyncrasy of producing wood both thorny and thornless. The flowers, which appear first in late May, are single and of bright yellow. R. earldomensis makes a bush of some six feet in height, which should be left unpruned.
Courtney Page 1934. *D. TG. NF. Not to be pruned. — — S. May-June*
[and October. Hardy.

EARL HAIG (H.T.) produces large perfectly-formed fully double flowers of deep crimson-red, on stems of medium length. Foliage is green but not plentiful, growth moderate; but this variety will produce splendid roses for exhibition purposes.
Dickson 1921. *D. MG. VF. — EA. — E. June-September. Very hardy.*

EASLEA'S GOLDEN RAMBLER (wichuraiana rambler) has large full flowers of golden-yellow with crimson splashes, in clusters, bears bright green shiny foliage of considerable attraction, and is exceptionally vigorous.
Easlea 1932. *D. VC. MF. GPI. — — P.Pr.A. June. Very hardy.*

EAST ANGLIA (H.T.) is of low diffuse habit and has fully double flowers of good shape of orange-pink.
Morse 1939. *D. MD. GPB. — — B.G. June-September. Hardy.*

EBLOUISSANT (polyantha pompon) is of dwarf growth with glossy bronze-green foliage which withstands disease, and bears large clusters of very double rich deep crimson flowers of average size which retain their colour well.
Turbat 1918. *D. SG. SF. GPF. — — B.Pot. July-September. Hardy.*

ECAE (S.), Afghanistan, has slender spreading branches with solitary buttercup-yellow flowers, and forms an attractive and symmetrical bush of some three feet in height.
Aitcheson —. *D. TG. NF. Not to be pruned. — — S. June-July. Hardy.*

ECLIPSE (H.T.) has very long buds of clear golden-yellow, with foliage of clear green. Outstanding in bud form, the flowers are borne on long strong stems, and its vigorous upright habit and continuous and profuse flowering make it a rose which will provide cut blooms for a long period.
Nicholas 1936. *D. TG. F. GPC. — — Cut. June-September. Hardy.*

ECSTASY (H.T.) has full medium-size flowers borne on stiff stems and produces these pale-yellow cerise-flushed beauties, which are deeper on the outside, with some freedom. Foliage is green and moderate in quantity.
Dickson 1935. *D. MG. VF. GPB. — — B.Cut. June-September.*

EDEL (H.T.) has very large, very double flowers which are of excellent shape, of clear white shading to pale ivory at the base. Flowers well, but is best grown as an exhibition rose.
McGredy 1919. *D. MG. MF. — EB. White. E. June-September. Hardy.*

EDITH BELLENDEN (see R. rubiginosa).

EDITH CAVELL (polyantha pompon) has brilliant scarlet clustered heads of semi-double flowers borne on moderately dwarf bushes with bright green foliage. Has but one drawback, the colours burn in the hot sun.
Spek 1917. *D. SG. SF. GPF. — — B.Pot. June-September. Hardy.*

EDITH CLARK (H.T.) has double, medium-size flowers of rounded outline of bright red, borne on stiff stems. Foliage deep green and resistant.
Clark 1928. *D. SG. SF. GPA. — — B. June-September. Hardy.*

EDITH KRAUSE (H.T.) has large double flowers with pointed centres of greenish-white, singly borne on stout long stems, on vigorous upright bushes with few thorns and plentiful large glossy foliage.
Krause 1930. *D. TG. MF. GPC. EC. White. G.E. June-Sept. Hardy.*

EDITH MARY MEE (H.T.) has full flowers of bright orient-red flushed with orange, with a yellow base, with dark green disease-resistant foliage. Is vigorous and compact in habit and makes a fine bedding variety.
Mee 1936. *D. MG. SF. GPB. — — B. June-September. Hardy.*

EDITH NELLIE PERKINS (H.T.) has somewhat thin blooms of salmon-pink flushed with orange, with the outside of orient-red shaded with cerise. The flowers are very freely produced and the bronzy-green foliage is plentiful. Unfortunately, the flowers rapidly lose their shape in the hotter summers.
Dickson 1928. *D. VG. MF. GPB. — — B.G.St. June-September. Hardy.*

EDITOR McFARLAND (H.T.) has semi-double flowers produced from a long-pointed bud, of rich pink with a yellow base. Has a free and continuous flowering habit and large, leathery, disease-resistant foliage, together with very vigorous growth.
Mallerin 1931. *D. TG. MF. GPC. — — G. June-September. Hardy.*

EDOUARD RENARD (H.T.) produces its long perfectly-shaped buds on long stiff stems, opening to carmine-lake flowers with a yellow base. Growth is vigorous and the foliage plentiful and glossy green.
Dot 1933. *D. VG. MF. GPB.* — — *G.Cut. June-September. Hardy.*

EDUARD SCHILL (Pern.) has full, perfectly-shaped flowers of brick-red shaded with yellow, and shiny green foliage with vigorous upright growth.
Kordes 1931. *D. TG. MF. GPC.* — — *G. June-September. Hardy.*

EFFEKT (H.T.) is scarlet-red with the outside of the petals flushed with golden-yellow; the flowers are large, double and of good shape. Growth is vigorous and upright and the foliage large and dark green in colour. The variety flowers freely and with continuity.
Krause 1935. *D. TG. MF. GPC.* — — *G. June-September. Hardy.*

E. G. HILL (H.T.) produces its fine very large crimson-scarlet flowers, which deepen in the centre, on long strong stems. Foliage is deep green and plentiful, and the flowers fragrant and freely produced.
Hill 1929. *D. VG. VF. GPB.* — *G.B.Pot. June-September. Hardy.*

EGLANTERIA (see R. rubiginosa).

E. J. LUDDING has full double flowers of pointed globular form, of bright carmine-pink shaded salmon, with good green foliage. Though it cannot be said to be profuse in flower, it is very satisfying, and particularly good in autumn.
Van Rossem 1939. *D. VG. F. GPB.* — — *G.B. June-September. Hardy.*

ELEGANCE (wichuraiana climber) has very large flowers of bright cadmium-yellow with strong vigorous growth and shiny green foliage produced in some abundance.
Brownell 1938. *D. G. SF. GPJ.* — — *A.W. June-July. Hardy.*

ELEGANTULA (extra graceful) (S.), Western China, makes a bush of some five to six feet in height with green five- to seven-parted foliage, and produces its small clusters of rich-pink flowers with freedom in June. The flowers are followed by long deep-red fruits.
Rolfe —. *D. EG. NF. GPG.* — — *S. June. Hardy.*

ELFIN (Hybrid polyantha) has large double deep cerise-pink flowers, shaded with orange, borne in clusters from vigorous but dwarf and compact plants.
Archer 1939. *D. NG. NF. GPG.* — — *B.G. June-September. Hardy.*

ELISABETH FAURAX (H.T.) is another white rose of perfect shape, shaded with ivory at the base, full, double, and well pointed. Growth is vigorous and flowers are borne on long strong stems.
Meilland 1937. *D. VG. F. GPB. EB. White. B.G.E. June-Sept. Hardy.*

ELISA ROBICHON (wichuraiana rambler) is of exceptionally vigorous growth, its long canes bearing glossy dark green foliage and clusters of large, semi-double rose flowers shaded yellow. Flowering in summer, it remains so for a very considerable time, its flowers lasting well.
Barbier 1901. *D. C. SF. GPI.* — — *P.Pr.A.Wst. June-July. Hardy.*

ELITE (H.T.) has long-pointed buds with large semi-double flowers of good shape, of glowing orange with rose shading. Growth is vigorous, upright, and leaves green and leathery and resistant to disease.
Tantau 1937. *D. VG. SF. GPB.* 621-620. *B. June-Sept. Hardy. Pl.* 30.

ELIZABETH (polyantha pompon) has small semi-double flowers of deep salmon, borne in large trusses from vigorous but compact plants.
Letts 1937. *D. VG. NF. GPG.* — — *B.G. June-September. Hardy.*

ELIZABETH ARDEN (H.T.) has fine-pointed buds, large very double flowers of purest white borne singly on long stems. Has plenty of large dark green foliage, resistant to disease, on strong vigorous upright growth.
Prince 1929. *D. TG. VF. GPC. EC. White. B.G.E. June-Sept. Very hardy.*
[*Pl.* 49.

ELIZABETH OF YORK (H.T.) produces, upon a plant of vigorous growth, semi-double flowers of good shape with high centres of cerise-pink shaded with orange, and is a very good variety for bedding, the moderately produced glossy green foliage adding to its attractions.
Dobbie 1927. *D. VG. MF. GPB.* — — *B.G. June-Sept. Hardy. Pl.* 77.

ELIZABETH ZEIGLER (wichuraiana rambler) came into being as a sport from Dorothy Perkins and inherits all that rose's vigour and free flowering propensities, together with a deeper rose colour.
Pierson 1917. *D. C. F. GPI.* — — *A.Pr.Wst.H. July. Hardy.*

ELLEN POULSEN (polyantha pompon) has clustered heads of somewhat large, full double flowers of bright cherry-rose, borne on vigorous dwarf bushes with glossy dark green foliage.
Poulsen 1912. *D. VG. MF. GPF.* — *G.St.B.Pot.* 625/3-625/1. *June-Sept.*
[*Hardy. Pl.* 31.

ELLEN WILLMOTT (H.T.) carries a name previously used by Bernaix in 1898, and is one of the finest of all single roses. On a bush of some thirty inches with red-purple stems and glossy foliage the single, wavy-petalled pink, white and lemon flowers are borne. To add to their attraction, they have bright golden anthers and red filaments.
Archer 1936. *D. VG. MF. GPB.* — 625-625/1. *B. June-Sept. Hardy.*

ELLI KNAB (H.T.) has large, double, full flowers of good shape, borne on very vigorous and upright bushes with large leathery green foliage. The flowers have a ground of creamy flesh tone overlaid with bright rose, and tinted and veined with vermilion-red.
Kordes 1934. *D. VG. MF. GPB.* — — *B. June-September. Hardy.*

ELSE CHAPLIN (Hybrid polyantha) resembles Else Poulsen in habit but varies by having its flowers of deep glowing pink and producing them in still larger clusters.
Chaplin 1934. *D. VG. SF. GPG.* — — *B. June-September. Hardy.*

Else Poulsen (Hybrid polyantha) has dark-green, bronzed, glossy foliage and bears its clusters of medium-size bright rose-pink flowers on upstanding stems, and is splendid for bedding purposes.
Poulsen 1924. *D. TG. SF. GPG.* — 625/3-625/1. *B.St. June-September.*
[*Hardy. Pl.* 13 & 34.

Else's Rival (Hybrid polyantha) has fully double flowers of somewhat deeper pink, with the reverse of the petals carmine, and is generally an improved Else Poulsen.
Boer 1937. *D. TG. SF. GPG.* — 25/2-25/1. *B. June-Sept. Hardy. Pl.* 35.

Elsie (wichuraiana rambler) is an exceedingly vigorous rambler with large clusters of single flowers of delightfully soft pink, borne in great profusion. Foliage is very bright glossy green and resistant to disease.
Chaplin 1934. *D. C. NF. GPI.* — — *A.P.Pr.Wst. July. Hardy.*

Elsie Beckwith (H.T.) has high-pointed double flowers of deep glowing rose-pink, with firm petals borne on upright strong stems, and is an exceptionally vigorous plant.
Beckwith 1922. *D. VG. VF. GPB.* — — *B.G.Pot. July-September. Hardy.*

Elvira Aramayo (Pernetiana) has somewhat small double flowers of Indian red, borne on a vigorous upright bushy plant, carried in groups upon short stems, and is a plant profuse in its flowering.
Looymans 1922. *D. VG. NF. GPB.* — — *B. July-September. Hardy.*

Ember Glow (H.T.) is an aptly named rose with large, double, shapely flowers of fiery orange-red, and of robust habit, with shining green foliage.
Grillo 1935. *D. VG. MF. GPB.* — — *B.G. June-September. Hardy.*

Emily Gray (wichuraiana rambler) is a fine climber with large, glossy, dark, bronzy-green holly-like foliage and lovely dark-ochre buds, opening to large semi-double flowers of golden yellow with a pleasant scent. It thrives best with plenty of space in which to ramble, and with the lightest of pruning.
Williams 1916. *D. C. MF. GPJ.* — — *A.P.Pr.W.Wst. June. Not very*
[*hardy.*

Emma Wright (H.T.) has small but perfectly formed semi-double flowers of pure orange, borne upon moderately vigorous bushes bearing rich glossy green, disease-resistant foliage. An exceptionally beautiful and good bedding rose, it is unaffected by wet weather.
McGredy 1917. *D. MG. VF. GPB.* — 512, 616/1. *G.B. June-Sept. Hardy.*

Empire Queen (H.T.) has large, very double, full flowers of brilliant cerise-pink, borne several upon each long strong stem. It is vigorous and upright in growth with plentiful foliage of bright-green colour, but is unfortunately subject to mildew.
Easlea 1925. *D. VG. MF. GPB.* — — *B.E. June-September. Hardy.*

EMPIRE STATE (H.T.) is a delightful rose of American origin with well-shaped pointed double flowers of bright scarlet shaded at the base with gold. It has upright vigorous growth and ample foliage.
Nicolas 1934. *D. VG. MF. GPB. — — B. June-September. Hardy.*

EMPRESS (H.T.) has dark-cerise fragrant flowers of good shape and substance, freely borne on stiff erect stems, and is exceptionally good for bedding purposes.
Chaplin 1933. *D. VG. VF. GPB. — — B.G. June-September. Hardy.*

ENA GLADSTONE (H.T.) has large, double, shapely rounded flowers of deep carmine-pink with a yellow base, and is of moderately robust growth.
Dickson 1936. *D. NG. MF. GPB. — — B.G. June-September. Hardy.*

ENCHANTRESS (see R. rugosa).

ENID (Hybrid polyantha) has perfectly shaped large semi-double flowers of clear salmon-pink borne in small clusters upon vigorous upright-growing bushes.
Prior 1936. *D. TG. MF. GPC. — 625. B.G. June-Sept. Hardy. Pl.* 13.

ERIC B. MEE (H.T.) has fully double, high-centred, huge flowers of excellent shape and perfect form, of very bright cerise, borne on long strong stems upon a vigorous and upright bush with plentiful green foliage which is resistant to disease.
Oliver Mee 1937. *D. VG. MF. GPB. EB. — G.E. June-Sept. Hardy.*

ERNA TESCHENDORFF (polyantha pompon) has small semi-double flowers of bright crimson, borne in clusters on short stems. The habit is very dwarf and compact, the foliage bright green but subject in certain districts to mildew.
Teschendorff 1911. *D. DG. SF. GPF. — — B. June-September. Hardy.*

ERNESTINE COSME (wichuraiana rambler) bears its huge conical clusters of large, single, red flowers, each with its bold white eye, upon very vigorous growth with light green foliage, resistant to disease.
Turbat 1926. *D. C. SF. GPI. — — A.Pr.H. July. Hardy.*

ESPERANTO (H.T.) speaks an international language, intermittently combining its large, very double, sweetly-scented flowers, of clearest yellow, with glossy bronzy-green foliage borne upon an upright compact plant.
Bohm 1932. *D. VG. VF. GPB. — — B.G. June-September. Hardy.*

ESSENCE (H.T.) speaks also to the senses, intriguing both sight and scent. Its semi-full flowers are most attractive in the bud stage, when they are long and well pointed. The colour of rich crimson is matched by the richness of its delightful fragrance.
B. R. Cant 1930. *D. VG. VF. GPB. — — B.G. June-September. Hardy.*

ETERNAL YOUTH (H.T.) has fully double pink flowers with high centres borne upon long strong stems in some profusion upon a vigorous upright-growing bush bearing dark green glossy foliage, and is admirable for bedding.
Aicardi 1939. *D. VG. MF. GPB. — 625/3. B.G. June-Sept. Hardy. Pl.* 36.

ETHEL JAMES (H.T.) is a single rose it would be difficult to do without. The very large single flowers are borne in large clusters and are of soft carmine-red, flushed with orange-scarlet, with a base of clear yellow. Habit is dwarf, bushy and vigorous.
McGredy 1921. *D. VG. VF. GPB. — — B.G. June-September. Hardy.*

ETOILE DE FEU (Pernetiana) bears its full, well-rounded semi-double flowers, of bright salmon-pink and flame, upon vigorous bushy branched plants with glossy reddish-green foliage.
Pernet-Ducher 1921. *D. VG. NF. GPB. — — B. June-September. Hardy.*

ETOILE DE FRANCE (H.T.) has small long-pointed buds and bears its double crimson flowers of moderate size, each upon a long stem. Its growth is vigorous and diffuse, and the foliage of glossy dull green.
Pernet-Ducher 1904. *D. VG. VF. GPB. — — B. June-September. Hardy.*

ETOILE DE HOLLANDE (H.T.) was, and remains, one of the best of all the dark red roses, lacking only perfection of form in the open flower. As a bedding rose it has few equals and no superiors. The flowers are of rich dark crimson with an underlying scarlet glow, and the scent is ineffable.
Verschuren 1919. *D. VG. VF. GPB. — 821/2. B.G.St. June-Sept. Hardy.*

EUGENE FURST (H.P.) is one of the old hybrid perpetual crimson roses with large, full, sweetly scented flowers borne on very vigorous upright free-flowering bushes with bold tough foliage.
Soupert & Notting 1875. *D. TG. VF. GPC. EC. — G.E. June-Aug. Hardy.*

EUGÉNIE LAMESCH (polyantha pompon) bears its small clusters of double flowers of moderate size neatly upon dwarf compact plants with neat glossy deep green foliage. The flowers are clear-yellow edged with rose, and carry the scent of violets, which is at least discernible.
Lambert 1899. *D. SG. MF. GPF. — — G.B. June-September. Very hardy.*

EVA (Hybrid Musk) bears large fragrant, semi-double, carmine-red flowers with white eyes in clusters upon vigorous upright bushes with much disease-proof foliage.
Kordes 1933. *D. TG. GPG. — — S. June-September. Very hardy.*

EVA EAKINS (H.T.) has small long-pointed double flowers of carmine-scarlet, flushed with orange within, and yellow without, borne upon good stems on compact plants with deep-green resistant foliage.
McGredy 1926. *D. MG. SF. GPB. — — B.G. June-September. Hardy.*

EVALINE (polyantha pompon) bears its clusters of small quilled-petalled flowers of light rose-pink, with deeper edges and a yellow base, continuously upon neat bushy plants.
Prosser 1920. *D. MG. SF. GPF. — — B. June-September. Hardy.*

EVA M. DAVIES (H.T.) has brightly coloured buds opening to brilliant orange-scarlet flowers. Has vigorous, branching habit and is sweetly scented.
Bees Ltd. 1943. *D. VG. VF. GPA. EA. — G.B. June-September. Hardy.*

EVANGELINE (wichuraiana rambler) is a vigorous rambler with long sprays of single flowers of pale pink with a white eye, produced with freedom upon vigorous growth with glossy green foliage.
Walsh 1906. *D. G. F. GPH. — — C.A.Pr.Wst. July-August. Hardy.*

EVA TESCHENDORFF (polyantha pompon) has large semi-double white, green-shaded flowers, borne in clusters in great abundance upon thornless bushes with glossy light-green foliage.
Teschendorff 1923. *D. VG. SF. GPF. — B.Pot. — June-August. Hardy.*

EVELYN THORNTON (polyantha pompon) has clusters of moderate-size double flowers of shell-pink shaded salmon, and lemon shaded with orange, borne upon bushes with vigorous growth and shiny bronze-green foliage.
Bees 1919. *D. VG. SF. GPF. — — B. June-August. Hardy.*

EVERBLOOM (Climbing polyantha) is an attractive pillar rose with large clusters of deep pink single flowers, borne upon plants producing vigorous climbing canes, with glossy green foliage.
Archer 1939. *D. C. SF. GPG. — — A.Pr. June-September. Hardy.*

EVEREST (H.T.) is of extraordinary vigour and can be grown as a pillar rose or pruned at will for ordinary culture. The slightly fragrant flowers are immense in size, perfect in shape, full, and of clear white, shading to a creamy-green tinting in the centre, and are borne singly upon long strong stems.
Easlea 1927. *D. EG. SF. GPG. EG. White. B.Pot.E.G. June-Sept. Hardy.*

EVERGREEN ROSE (see R. sempervirens).

EVERT VAN DYK (H.T.) has high-centred full flowers of good shape, of warm bright-pink, with glossy, disease-proof, green foliage upon bushes of vigorous growth.
Van Rossem 1931. *D. VG. SF. GPB. — — B.G.St. June-September. Hardy.*

E. V. LUCAS (H.T.) bears its clusters of semi-double crimson-scarlet flowers with profusion upon vigorous freely branching bushes, and in the bud form is exceptionally attractive.
McGredy 1934. *D. VG. NF. GPB. — — B.G. June-September. Hardy.*

EXCELSA (wichuraiana rambler) produces its double crimson-scarlet flowers in large clusters upon strong stems and has the added attraction of glossy bright-green foliage. Late in flowering, it has the drawback of being subject to mildew in certain districts.
Walsh 1909. *D. C. NF. GPH. — — A.Pr.Wst. July-August. Hardy.*

FABVIER (see R. chinensis).

FACKEL (H.T.) has semi-globular very double flowers of deep crimson, shaded with maroon, borne upon neat but vigorous plants.
Krause 1937. *D. MG. SF. GPB. — — B.G. June-September. Hardy.*

FAIENCE (H.T.) has pointed buds developing to semi-double flowers of deep peach-pink with the backs of the petals lemon-yellow. Closely resembles "Cherry."
Van Rossem 1936. *D. VG. SF. GPB. — 0621 & 3/3. B.G. June-September.*
[Hardy. Pl. 37.

Madame Jean Gaujard (Pernetiana) **ABF**   Viscountess Charlemont (Hybrid Tea)
CDGH

Polly (Hybrid Tea) **EFJKLM**

Pink Dawn (Hybrid Tea) **NORPQTU**

Rosa sertata B
Rosa rubiginosa Flora McIver AEFCGHLP
Rosa rubiginosa Lady Penzance JK

Fairy Rose (see R. chinensis var. minima).

Fairy Cluster (Hybrid polyantha) bears its large loose clusters of pale silvery-pink single blooms upon vigorous upright bushes, and resembles a miniature Dainty Bess with larger clusters of small flowers.
Archer 1934. *D. VG. F. GPG. — — B.G. June-September. Hardy.*

Fargesii (see R. Moyesii var. Fargesii).

Farreri (comm.), China, makes a bush of some five feet in height with arching stems covered with dense fine thorns, and bearing very small eleven-parted light green foliage with a hint of red-bronze and clusters of small light-pink single flowers in late May, followed by small coral-red fruits.
Stapf —. D. TG. SF. GPG. — — S. May-June. Hardy.

Farreri var. persetosa (very bristly) is known as the Threepenny-bit Rose, and has reddish bristly wood and smaller foliage of darker green and still smaller flowers of slightly deeper pink, followed by similar fruits.
Stapf —. D. TG. SF. GPG. — — S. May-June. Hardy.

Fascination (H.T.) has medium-size double flowers of bright cerise shaded with yellow, borne singly on a long strong stem on vigorous upright bushes with dark green glossy foliage.
Chaplin 1927. *D. VG. VF. GPB. — — B.G. June-September. Hardy.*

Federico Casas (H.T.) has pointed buds of bright red, opening to large semi-double flowers of deep rose-pink with yellow reverse, each borne upon a long and strong stem. Growth is vigorous and foliage large, plentiful and of dark green colour.
Dot 1929. *D. VG. VF. GPB. — 22/2 to 20/1. B.G. June-Sept. Hardy.*

Fedtschenkoana (comm.) (S.), Turkestan, makes a tangled many-branched, very thorny bush of about six feet in height, bearing pale green foliage and clusters of smallish single white flowers with golden stamens, followed by rounded dark-red fruits.
Regel —. D. EG. SF. GPG. — — S. June-July. Hardy.

Felicia (Hybrid Musk) produces its double-rosetted china-pink, yellow-based flowers in large upright clusters upon vigorous bushes of upwards of three feet.
Pemberton 1928. *D. TG. VF. GPG. — — B.G.H.S. June-October. Hardy.*

Félicité-et-Perpétue (Sempervirens) is a most vigorous climbing rose of pendulous habit, producing its clusters of very double, flat, creamy-white flowers with great freedom. It is suitable for growing on north walls, and in exposed positions on banks and slopes. It needs only light pruning in February, when tips of laterals should be removed
Jacques 1828. *D. G. NF. Detailed. — A.P.W. June. Very hardy.*

Fellemberg (see R. chinensis).

FEROX (armed with thorns) (S.), Caucasus, is also known as R. horrida and forms a dwarf bush of some three feet in height, clad with small dark green leaves made up of five or seven leaflets, with its straight stems armed with bristly red hooked thorns. The flowers, borne in small corymbs, are about the size of a halfpenny, have orange stamens, and are followed by shiny red fruits.
Bieberstein —. D. VG. SF. GPG. — White. S. June-July. Hardy.

FEU D'ARTIFICE (Climbing H.T.) is a most vigorous climber with deep green glossy foliage with semi-double flowers of bright yellow tinted with hints of coral-red.
Mallerin 1935. D. C. F. GPE. — — W.A.Pr. June-September. Hardy.

FEUERSCHEIN (Hybrid polyantha) has large brilliant-red full flowers borne in large clusters on vigorous plants with dark-green foliage.
Krause 1930. D. VG. SF. GPG. — — B. June-September. Hardy.

FEU JOSEPH LOOYMANS (H.T.) has very large long buds developing to huge, very double, shapely flowers of apricot-yellow tinted with saffron-yellow. It is of vigorous growth and bears plentiful large dark-green glossy leaves.
Looymans 1935. D. VG. SF. GPB. — — B.G. June-September. Very hardy.

FEU PERNET-DUCHER (H.T.) has very large, double, full flowers of exquisite shape and of primrose-yellow, deeper at the centre and slightly flushed with pink, borne upon vigorous upright bushes with good dark-green foliage and with the fragrance of ripe greengages.
Mallerin 1935. D. VG. MF. GPB. EB. — B.G.E. June-September. Hardy.

FIESTA (H.T.) is a vigorous, erect and branching rose, with large double bright-red flowers with a deep pink reverse, freely decked with golden flashes.
Hansen 1940. D. VG. MF. GPB. — — G. June-September. Hardy.

FILIPES (with thread-like stems) (S.), China, is a semi-climbing shrub with long whip-like growths rising to eight feet, with large green leaves divided into five or seven leaflets, and with huge corymbs of rather small, single, white, scented flowers with golden stamens, followed by rounded red fruits.
Rehder & Wilson —. D. EG. VF. GPJ. — White. S. June-July. Hardy.

FIREBRAND (H.T.) has high-centred spiralled flowers of bright crimson-scarlet, borne upon vigorous erect and branching plants, with good foliage.
B. R. Cant 1938. D. VG. VF. GPB. — — B.G. June-September. Hardy.

FIREGLOW (polyantha pompon) has small double flowers of vermilion-red shaded with orange-red, and is a good bright variety of dwarf habit for bedding purposes.
Wezelenberg 1929. D. MG. NF. GPF. — 20. B. June-September.

FISHER HOLMES (H.P.) has pointed buds developing to large full double flowers of bright crimson and of good shape, borne upon long strong stems.
Verdier 1854. *D. VG. MF. GPB. — — G.B. June-July. Hardy.*

F. J. GROOTENDORST (see R. rugosa).

FLAMBEAU (H.T.) has large, double, crimson-scarlet flowers, freely produced from vigorous, branching plants.
Nicolas 1939. *D. VG. MF. GPB. — — B.G. June-September.*

FLAMINGO (H.T.) has high-centred flowers of good shape of bright cerise-red, borne upon vigorous bushes with good grey-green foliage.
Dickson 1929. *D. MG. VF. GPB. — — G.B. June-September. Hardy.*

FLASH (Climbing H.T.) has open globular semi-double flowers of crimson-scarlet, with a bright yellow reverse, borne upon vigorous plants of climbing habit, with deep green polished foliage.
Hatton 1938. *D. VG. MF. GPE. — — A.P. June-July.*

FLAVESCENS (S.) (see R. spinosissima).

FLORA McIVER (see R. rubiginosa).

FLORENCE HASWELL VEITCH (H.T.) has nicely-shaped flowers of bright crimson and is so vigorous as to be suitable for growth either as a bush, pillar or climbing rose.
Paul 1911. *D. G. VF. GPE. — — C.Pr.B. June-July. Hardy.*

FLORENCE L. IZZARD (H.T.) has a long-pointed bud which becomes a large, very double, long-pointed flower of buttercup-yellow, borne upon a long stem from a vigorous plant bearing glossy bronze-green, disease-proof foliage.
McGredy 1923. *D. VG. VF. GPB. — — B.G. June-September. Hardy.*

FLORENTINA (Hybrid polyantha) bears clusters of large single flowers of pale pink, with a deep carmine reverse, upon vigorous plants with deep green leaves.
Leenders 1938. *D. VG. SF. GPG. — — B.G. June-September. Hardy.*

FLOREX (H.T.) has attractive long-pointed buds and large double flowers of coral flushed with orange, borne on upright vigorous bushes with glossy green foliage.
Geiger 1927. *D. VG. VF. GPB. — B.G. June-September. Hardy.*

FLORIBUNDA (see R. gentiliana).

FOETIDA is another name for R. lutea, which see.

FOLIOLOSA (with much foliage) (S.), W. America, is a dwarf of about eighteen inches in height, with shiny foliage divided into seven to nine leaflets, with single bright pink flowers of about one and a half inches in diameter, borne singly or in small clusters and followed by bristly red fruits.
Nuttall 1890. *D. DG. F. GPG. — — S. July. Hardy.*

FOLIOLOSA ALBA is similar in all respects, but has white flowers.
Nuttall 1890. *D. DG. F. GPG. — White. S. July. Hardy.*

FOLKESTONE (Hybrid polyantha) is a large-flowered hybrid polyantha rose with large trusses of bright crimson semi-double flowers freely produced.
Archer 1938. *D. MG. F. GPG. — — B.St. June-September. Hardy.*

FONTANELLE (H.T.) has large high-centred fully double flowers of fine shape with wide petals of lemon-yellow deepening at the centre, borne singly on long and strong stems, with bronzy-green foliage.
Hill 1927. *D. VG. MF. GPB. EB. — B.G.E. June-September. Hardy.*

FORTSCHRITT (Hybrid polyantha) seems really much more akin to the Pernetiana type whilst producing clusters of semi-double salmon flowers, shaded with yellow, on vigorous upright-growing bushes.
Kordes 1933. *D. MG. MF. GPB. — — B. June-September. Hardy.*

FORTUNA (Hybrid Musk) has very large semi-double fragrant flowers of soft rose-pink, with golden stamens, borne in large clusters upon a dwarf bush of some two and a half feet.
Pemberton 1928. *D. VG. VF. GPG. — — B.S.H. June-September. Hardy.*

FORTUNE'S YELLOW (see R. Noisettiana).

FRAGRANCE (H.T.) is, as its name suggests, highly scented and is a high-centred shapely rose with large fully double flowers of deep crimson, and is of exceptionally vigorous growth.
Chaplin 1924. *D. TG. VF. GPC. — — B.P. June-September. Hardy.*

FRAGRANT PILLAR (Climbing H.T.) is, as its name suggests, another scented rose with double flowers of good shape of clear cerise-pink tinted with yellow. Its growth is very vigorous and the foliage of shiny bronze-green.
Allen 1930. *D. C. VF. GPE. — — W.Pr. June-September. Hardy.*

FRANCESCA (Hybrid Musk) produces very large trusses of pale apricot-yellow flowers, upon strong stout bushes, with great continuity.
Pemberton 1922. *D. EG. MF. GPG. — 64/3-64/2. S. June-Sept. Hardy.*
[Pl. 32.

FRANCES GAUNT (H.T.) bears, upon upright strong-growing bushes with shining green, disease-resistant foliage, semi-double flowers of apricot blending to yellow, each upon a long strong stem.
Dickson 1918. *D. VG. VF. GPB. — — B.G. June-September. Hardy.*

FRANCIE SIMMS (H.T.) has high-centred flowers of cerise-red, developing from long-pointed buds. The flowers are flushed at the base with deep yellow, and are freely produced upon vigorous plants with green, disease-resisting foliage.
Dickson 1926. *D. VG. MF. GPB. — — B.G. June-September. Hardy.*

FRANÇOISE BLANDEAU (H.T.) is an exceptionally vigorous plant with stout robust stems and much large deep-green foliage, accompanied by very double, large, deep coral-pink flowers with silver pink reflexes.
Mallerin 1938. *D. VG. SF. GPB. — — B.G. June-September. Hardy.*

FRANÇOIS GUILLOT (wichuraiana rambler) bears its fairly large milky-white double flowers, with pink and yellow tints, in small clusters and is a vigorous climber with glossy green foliage.
Barbier 1907. *D. C. MF. GPI. — — A.P.W. June. Hardy.*

FRANÇOIS JURANVILLE (wichuraiana rambler) produces its large double flowers, of deep salmon-pink with a yellow base, upon vigorous canes with attractive glossy light-bronze foliage, and makes its best display of colour in late June and early July, with adventitious blooms until October. Deliciously scented, it remains outstanding.
Barbier 1906. *D. C. VF. GPI. — — A.P.Wst. June-July. Sept.-October.*
                                                          [Hardy.

FRAU ASTRID SPATH (Hybrid polyantha) has large double flowers of clear carmine-rose produced upon a dwarf vigorous plant with dark green glossy foliage.
Spath 1930. *D. VG. F. GPG. — — B.G. June-September. Hardy.*

FRAU DR. SCHRICKER (see R. chinensis).

FRAU HUGO LAUSTER (H.T.) has moderate-size, double, shapely flowers of pale buttercup-yellow, lightening at the edges, borne upon a vigorous bush with attractive foliage.
Pfitzer 1931. *D. VG. F. GPB. — — B.G. June-September. Hardy.*

FRAU KARL DRUSCHKI (H.P.) remains one of the finest of all white roses, its high-centred very double white flowers being produced in profusion in June and July. Growth is very vigorous and the tree has dark green disease-resistant foliage. Its only shortcoming is that it has no scent.
Lambert 1901. *D. TG. NF. GPC. EC. — B.G.E.St.Pot. June-July. Very*
                                                          [hardy.

FRAXINIFOLIA is another name for R. blanda, which see.

FRAZER ANNESLEY (H.T.) has fully double high-centred flowers of intense carmine, with a base shaded with gold and the outside of the petals of deep orange-yellow, borne upon plants with plentiful bronzy-green foliage which is resistant to disease.
McGredy 1931. *D. VG. F. GPB. — — B.G. June-September. Hardy.*

FRED J. HARRISON (H.T.) has a globular bud developing to a large high-centred fragrant flower of deep cardinal-red, produced upon strong stems on a vigorous bush with ample green foliage.
Dickson 1924. *D. VG. F. GPB. — — B.G. June-September. Hardy.*

FRED WALKER (H.T.) has large fully double high-centred flowers of deep pink with a bronzy-orange base, opening to old rose and gold, borne upon long stems. Foliage is plentiful, dark green and disease-resistant.
McGredy 1935. *D. VG. MF. GPB. — — B.G. June-September. Hardy.*

FRENCH Rose (see R. gallica).

FRIEDA KRAUSE (H.T.) has large, full, double, crimson-scarlet flowers borne upon long strong stems, produced with freedom upon plants bearing tough deep-green foliage.

Krause 1935. *D. VG. MF. GPB. — — B.G. June-September. Hardy.*

FRIEDRICHSRUHE (H.T.) closely resembles Château de Clos Vougeot except in its crimson rather than crimson-scarlet colouring.

Turke 1908. *D. VG. VF. GPB. — — B.G. June-September. Hardy.*

FRIENDSHIP (H.T.) has well-formed fully double flowers of strawberry-red shaded at the base with scarlet, with high centres, and borne upon stout stems upon plants of vigorous growth.

Dickson 1938. *D. VG. F. GPB. — — B.G. June-September. Hardy.*

FRITZ HOGER (H.T.) is another crimson rose with very large high-centred flowers of good shape, borne singly on long strong stems with good bronzy-green foliage, and vigorous growth.

Kordes 1934. *D. VG. F. GPB. EB. — B.G.E. June-September. Hardy.*

FROEBELII (see R. coriifolia). *Pl.* 60.

FUCHSINE GUY (Hybrid polyantha) has double flowers of bright pink borne in large clusters upon dwarf strong-growing plants with green foliage.

Leenders 1932. *D. MG. F. GPG. — — B.G. June-September. Hardy.*

FUJIYAMA Rose (see R. acicularis var. nipponensis).

F. W. LOWE (H.T.) has long-pointed double flowers of deep orange-yellow, borne upon vigorous plants with deep green shining foliage.

Lowe 1936. *D. VG. SF. GPB. — — B.G. June-September. Hardy.*

GAIETY (H.T.) combines the colours of Joseph's coat in a harmony which gives rise to its name. The buds are long and develop to fairly full, cupped flowers of orange, bronzy-red, yellow and pink. To add to its other attractions the flowers are borne on long stems with shiny pale green foliage.

Hill 1928. *D. VG. SF. GPG. — — B.G. June-September. Hardy.*

GALLICA (S.) (the French Rose) has single deep pink or crimson flowers, borne singly on bushes of some three to four feet in height, with thick green foliage composed of from three to five leaflets. It is said to be the rose which originally formed the badge of the House of Lancaster, but is not chronicled as having been introduced into Britain before 1596. Requires good rich soil and very little pruning.

Linnaeus (known in England in 1596). *D. TG. F. GPG. — — S. July.*
[Hardy.

GALLICA VAR. CONDITORUM (of the preserve-makers), W. Asia, has rather larger, paler pink flowers of intense fragrance, and is used as the basis of preserves in the Near East.

Dieck —. *D. TG. VF. GPG. — — S. July. Hardy.*

GALLICA VAR. OFFICINALIS (of the shop) is the Apothecary's Rose, and
is similar with semi-double flowers of pale red. In earlier times it was
used medicinally.
Thory —. *D. TG. VF. GPG.* — — *S. July. Hardy.*

GALLICA VAR. VERSICOLOR (changing colour) is also known as Rosa
mundi, or more correctly Rosemonde, and produces semi-double
white buds which open to flat flowers and are heavily striped with
deep pink.
Vibert 1835. *D. TG. F. GPG.* — — *S. July. Hardy. Pl.* 59.

GARDEN GLOW (H.T.) is one of the newer varieties with long red buds
developing into large, moderately full flowers of good shape, with
large scarlet petals with a bronze base. Foliage is large, ample and
glossy; growth vigorous and upright and flowering persistent.
B. R. Cant 1937. *D. VG. F. GPB.* — — *B.G. June-September. Hardy.*

GARDENIA (wichuraiana rambler) has long-pointed medium-sized buds
opening to semi-double flowers of creamy-white with yellow centre,
borne in small sprays. The foliage is deep glossy green and freely
produced.
Manda 1899. *D. C. NF. GPI.* — — *A.P.Pr. July. Hardy.*

GEHEIMRAT DUISBERG (Pernetiana) produces excellently shaped, very
fragrant flowers of clear golden yellow upon short stems on a
dwarf plant bearing ample green glossy foliage and adds to its other
merits a facility for producing flowers without seeming end.
Kordes 1933. *D. MG. VF. GPA.* — 403/1. *B.G. June-September. Hardy.*

GÉNÉRAL JACQUEMINOT (H.P.) was a friend of my youth and remains
so to-day. Its vigorous growth and intense fragrance remain still
to commend it, in addition to its velvety crimson flowers.
Roussel 1853. *D. VG. VF. GPB.* — — *B.G.St. July. Hardy.*

GENERAL MACARTHUR (H.T.) has the drawback of being somewhat
variable in colour, but can be so outstandingly good both in shape
and in its crimson-scarlet tones as to be worthy of a high place.
The flowers are fully double and borne singly upon short stems clad
with deep green foliage, but have a tendency to flatness.
Hill 1905. *D. MG. VF. GPB.* — — *B.G.St. June-September. Hardy.*

GENERAL SUPERIOR ARNOLD JANSSEN (H.T.) is, curiously enough, a
child of General MacArthur, and is just as attractive, resembling it
in all but colour, which is of deep pink with a deeper reverse.
Leenders 1912. *D. MG. F. GPB.* — — *B.G.St. June-September. Hardy.*

GENTILIANA (comm.) (S.), from Central China, is the Rosa floribunda
of Baker and has curious large foliage resembling that of laurel but
made up of five leaflets borne upon very long, almost climbing, red
stems. The flowers are fragrant, single white and about one inch
in diameter, borne in large many-flowered clusters, and are followed
by small red fruits.
Léveillé —. *D. C. F. GPG.* — *White. W.Pr.S. June-July. Hardy.*

GENTILIS (see R. pendulina).

GEORG ARENDS (H.P.) is a very vigorous rose of the parentage Frau Karl Druschki × La France, which bears its very large, very double, pale pink flowers on long stiff stems. Very fragrant, it does credit to both parents by continuing to persist in spite of parental competition.
Hinner 1910. *D. TG. VF. GPC. —— G.B.St. June-July. Hardy.*

GEORGE DICKSON (H.P.) provided so many perfect and much appreciated flowers in my youth and is bound up with so many happy memories that it is possible I view it with rose-coloured spectacles. To me at least it remains an ideal rose with its intense-crimson, large, perfectly formed flowers and its permeating fragrance. Curiously enough its best blooms come from the side buds, and though the flower stems are sometimes weak and it is prone to mildew badly in certain localities, it remains an outstanding rose, eminently suited to town growth.
Dickson 1912. *D. EG. VF. GPC. EC. 727 and 823. G.E.St. June-July.*
[*Hardy. Pl. 38.*

GEORGE ELGER (polyantha pompon) is a dwarf-growing polyantha rose, with clusters of very double golden-yellow flowers which pale with age, but persist, and are produced with freedom from bushy growth bearing bright green foliage.
Turbat 1912. *D. MG. SF. GPF. —— B.St. June-September. Hardy.*

GEORGE G. WAUD (H.T.) is a rose of dwarf habit with unobtrusive bright green foliage which sets off its freely produced, very large, very double, sweetly-scented flowers of dark rose, with a paler reverse to the petals.
Dickson 1908. *D. NG. VF. GPA. —— G.B. June-September. Hardy.*

GEORGES CHESNAL (H.T.) resembles Feu Joseph Looymans, but bears its large full golden-yellow flowers with copper veinings upon long, strong stems, and is of vigorous growth.
Gaujard 1934. *D. VG. F. GPC. —— B. June-September. Hardy.*

GERALD HARDY (H.T.) and Madge Whipp remain in my memory more from their entrancing beauty under artificial light than for any other reason. True, the lovely shape and delightful fragrance remain unaltered, but the crimson-scarlet flowers under table conditions become so scarlet as to be almost unbelievable, and almost make me believe some of the rose colours portrayed in pictures to be nearly true. A good rose with fine spiral shape, fully double flowers, good habit, strong growth, it is very fragrant and of exceptional freedom in flowering.
Dickson 1936. *D. MG. VF. GPB. — 726. B.G. June-Sept. Hardy. Pl. 27.*

GERBE ROSE (wichuraiana rambler) has large globular double flowers of deep pink, borne on short stems on strong plants with deep green glossy foliage of medium size.
Barbier 1905. *D. C. SF. GPl. —— A.P.Pr. June-July. Hardy.*

Rosa Moyesii var. Fargesii ABEO
Rosa blanda var. michiganensis GH
Rosa Willmottiae CFKLMQ

Hybrid Tea Rose, Madame Henri Guillot

GIGANTEA (giant) (S.), from Burma, is a very vigorous climber with polished green foliage and long pointed yellow buds opening to huge fragrant five-petalled flowers of glistening white often tinted with yellow, but is only suited to a warm unexposed position.
Collett 1888. *D. CF. GPJ. — White. W.T. June-July.*

GIGANTEA × LA FOLETTE is similar, with slender growth and large pink flowers of exceptional charm.
Bushby —. *D. C. F. GPJ. — — W. June-July.*

GIPSY LASS (H.T.) has crimson-scarlet flowers of extremely graceful shape and delightful fragrance freely produced over a long period on vigorous upright bushes.
Dickson 1932. *D. VG. VF. GPB. — — B.G. June-September. Hardy.*

GIRALDII (comm.) (S.), from China, is a climbing rose with grey-green foliage with reddish smooth canes, bearing clusters of rose-pink single flowers with white eyes, followed by small bright red fruits.
Crepin 1912. *D. C. SF. GPJ. — — S.W. June-July.*

GIRALDII VAR. VENULOSA (closely veined) is similar but more dwarf and bushy, with small, single, pink flowers, followed by similar fruits.
Giraldi 1912. *D. EG. F. GPG. — — S. June.*

GIRONA (Pernetiana) has long-pointed buds, fragrant, full, shapely flowers of pale pink, flushed with yellow and red shading. Growth is vigorous, flowering free and continuous, and foliage ample, glossy, and proof against disease.
Dot 1937. *D. VG. VF. GPB. — — B.G. June-September. Hardy.*

GISÈLE ALDAY (H.T.) produces from its pointed buds large, loosely-built flowers of bright rose-pink shaded with salmon-flesh; is of upright habit and produces its flowers in long succession.
Mallerin 1933. *D. VG. F. GPB. — — B. June-September. Hardy.*

GLADYS BENSKIN (H.T.) has long-pointed buds developing to flowers which can be perfect in shape, but often lose shape too rapidly, and prove variable in colour, which at its best is deep salmon-cerise, shaded with gold with yellow veining.
Dickson 1929. *D. VG. F. GPB. — — G. June-September. Hardy.*

GLAMOUR (H.T.) produces its large, many-petalled, high-centred, salmon-pink flowers on long strong stems from vigorous plants with ample green foliage.
Leenders 1939. *D. VG. VF. GPB. EB. — B.E.G. June-September. Hardy.*

GLENN DALE (wichuraiana climber) has large, lemon, semi-double, many-petalled flowers paling to white, produced both singly and in corymbs upon strong canes with dark green, resistant foliage.
Van Fleet 1927. *D. C. SF. GPG. — White. W. June-July. Hardy.*

GLOAMING (H.T.) bears upon long, strong stems its individual high-centred, very double flowers of shining deep pink flushed with salmon produced upon vigorous upright bushes with plentiful dark green foliage.
Nicolas 1935. *D. VG. F. GPB. EB.* 620. *B.E.G. June-Sept. Hardy. Pl.* 23.

GLOIRE DE DIJON (T.) is nearing its centenary and retains all its old appeal and its extraordinary grip upon life. The double golden-buff flowers, which are produced unendingly, are ineffably scented and render it a perfect climber for a north or east wall. Canes should be pruned in April to variable lengths, according to their strength. Stout canes should be pruned to about 6–8 feet; medium ones to 4–6 feet, and basally produced less strong shoots to 2–3 feet.

Jacotot 1850. *D. C. VF. Detailed. —— W.Wst. June-September. Hardy.*

GLOIRE DES MOUSSEUSES (see R. muscosa).

GLOIRE DU MIDI (polyantha pompon) bears its fully double orange-scarlet flowers in large clusters on dwarf well-formed bushes with bright green foliage, and retains its colour well, and is best described as an improved Gloria Mundi.

De Ruyter 1932. *D. VG. SF. GPF. —* 18/1. *B.G.St. June-Sept. Hardy.*
[*Pl.* 42.

GLORIA MUNDI (polyantha pompon) has brilliant orange-scarlet flowers of a similar type.

De Ruyter 1929. *D. VG. SF. GPF. —* 18/1. *B.G.St. June-Sept. Hardy.*

GLORIANA (H.T.) has sulphur-yellow to golden-yellow globular double flowers, occasionally marked with deep pink. Growth is vigorous and branching, and leaves are of polished deep green.

Hillock 1936. *D. VG. SF. GPB. —— B.G.Pot. June-September. Hardy.*

GLORY OF HURST (polyantha pompon) has similar growth with semi-double small flowers of cherry-red borne in large clusters.

Hicks 1921. *D. VG. SF. GPF. —— B.G. June-September. Hardy. Pl.* 48.

GLORY OF ROME (H.T.) has long-pointed buds opening to perfectly shaped double flowers of bright crimson-scarlet; is delightfully scented; bears its flowers singly upon long strong stems, and has plentiful deep green, disease-resistant foliage borne upon vigorous growths.

Aicardi 1938. *D. VG. VF. GPB. EB.* 24 *and* 24/1. *B.G.E. June-Sept. Hardy.*
[*Pl.* 39.

GLORY OF SURREY (H.T.) has large double high-centred flowers of great substance, with golden-yellow flowers of great fragrance borne on vigorous bushes with glossy, disease-resistant foliage.

Ley 1935. *D. VG. VF. GPB. —— B.G. June-September. Hardy.*

GLOWING CARMINE (H.T.) has large rounded double flowers of intense carmine, and is of vigorous growth.

Howard & Smith 1936. *D. VG. SF. GPB. —— B.G. June-September.*

GLOWING SUNSET is the American name for Wilhelm Breder (which see).

GLUTINOSA (sticky) (S.), Eastern Mediterranean region, is a dwarf and compact bush of about a yard in height with bright green scented foliage bearing clusters of small very pale pink flowers, followed by bright red, round, hairy fruits.

Sibthorpe & Smith 1821. *D. VG. F. GPG. —— S. June. Hardy.*

GOLDEN BEAUTY (H.T.) has large semi-double flowers of deep orange-yellow, gaining with age a flush of orange-red. Growth is vigorous and erect and branching, and foliage is bright polished green.
Van Rossem 1937. *D. VG. SF. GPB. — — B.G. June-September. Hardy.*

GOLDEN DAWN (T.) has large well-formed flowers of pale lemon-yellow with the outer petals flushed with rose on the reverse, freely produced upon branching plants with dark-green leathery foliage. It carries the characteristic "tea" perfume, is especially good in the autumn and in towns, but is apt to produce "divided" blooms when partially open.
Grant 1929. *D. VG. F. GPB. EB.* 5/2. *B.G.E.St.Pot. June-Sept. Hardy.*
[*Pl.* 40.

GOLDEN EMBLEM (Pernetiana) has large, double, well-formed flowers of golden-yellow borne singly on long, stiff stems with glossy green foliage. Its faults are its proneness to die-back and black spot.
McGredy 1916. *D. VG. F. GPB. —* 603/2. *B.St. June-September. Hardy.*

GOLDENER GRUSS AN AACHEN (Hybrid polyantha) has large, double, pointed-centred flowers of deep golden- to orange-yellow, borne singly and in few-flowered clusters. Growth is robust and bushy, and foliage deep glossy green.
Kordes 1935. *D. VG. MF. GPG. —* 5/2. *B.G. June-September. Hardy.*

GOLDENER TRAUM (see R. rugosa).

GOLDENES MAINZ (H.T.) has large-cupped double flowers of pure golden-yellow, produced upon upright bushy plants with good green leafage. It is exceptionally free in flowering and delightfully scented.
Kordes 1933. *D. VG. VF. GPB.* 3/2, 4/1. *B.G. June-Sept. Hardy. Pl.* 33.

GOLDEN GLEAM (H.T.) has medium-sized flowers of bright buttercup-yellow streaked with scarlet without, and produced from buds of perfect shape. The foliage is dark green and not subject to disease, growth is good and flowering especially good in autumn, making it a fine variety for bedding purposes.
Beckwith 1926. *D. VG. VF. GPB. — — B.St. June-September. Hardy.*

GOLDEN GLORY (H.T.) is a rather more dwarf variety with very shapely deep golden-yellow flowers produced with great freedom.
Dobbie 1931. *D. MG. F. GPB. — B.G. — June-September. Hardy.*

GOLDEN IDEAL (H.T.) has very large double flowers of brilliant yellow.
Lens 1939. *D. VG. SF. GPB. — — B.E.G. June-September. Hardy.*

GOLDEN KING (see R. rugosa).

GOLDEN MELODY (H.T.) has a somewhat globular-shaped bud of deep yellow verging upon orange, and has fragrance beyond the ordinary. Foliage is deep green, resistant to disease, and growth is strong.
Meilland 1940. *D. VG. VF. GPC. — — B. June-September. Hardy. Pl.* 45.

GOLDEN MOSS (see R. muscosa).

GOLDEN OPHELIA (H.T.) is linked to Ophelia only in parentage; its yellow-centred creamy flowers are borne upon long, strong stems and rise from a vigorous bush with glossy deep green foliage.
B. R. Cant 1917. *D. VG. SF. GPB.* — — *B.Pot. June-September. Hardy.*

GOLDEN RAPTURE is the American name for Geheimrat Duisberg, which see.

GOLDEN SALMON (polyantha pompon) has large clusters of small semi-double pure orange flowers on plants of vigorous growth with pale green leaves.
Cutbush 1926. *D. VG. NF. GPB.* — — *B. June-September. Hardy.*

GOLDEN SALMON SUPÉRIEUR (Golden Salmon Improved) is similar, with flowers of golden-salmon, proof against even the strongest sunlight.
de Ruiter 1930. *D. VG. NF. GPB.* — — *B. June-September. Hardy.*

GOLDEN SASTAGO (Pern.) has large open semi-globular flowers of soft yellow and is otherwise similar to Condesa de Sastago.
Dot 1938. *D. VG. SF. GPB.* — — *B.G. June-September. Hardy.*

GOLDEN STATE (H.T.) has large, very double, semi-globular and reflexed flowers of biscuit-yellow deepening at the centre to orange-yellow, produced upon vigorous and upright plants with glossy green foliage.
Meilland 1937. *D. VG. SF. GPB. EB.* — *B.E.G.Pot. June-Sept. Hardy.*

GOLDFINCH (Climbing polyantha) has semi-double small yellow flowers which pale to white with age, borne in clusters, produced on strong canes with small deep-green foliage.
Paul 1907. *D. C. SF. GPI.* — — *A.Pr. June-July. Hardy.*

GOOILAND GLORY (H.T.) bears upon its upright-growing bushy plants, with dark green shiny foliage, small groups of semi-double large cherry-red flowers shaded with coral, produced consistently throughout the season.
Van Rossem 1925. *D. VG. SF. GPB.* — — *B.G. June-September. Hardy.*

GOOSEBERRY Rose (see R. mirifica).

GORGEOUS (H.T.) produces its large well-formed double flowers on long stems on plants of medium height with soft green leaves. The flowers, which are moderately fragrant, are deep orange-yellow with deep orange veins.
Dickson 1915. *D. MG. MF. GPB.* — — *B.G. June-September. Hardy.*

GOTHA (H.T.) has moderate-size flowers of bronzy-orange with the outside of the petals flushed with carmine. The flowers are borne on long stems on plants which the glossy foliage and upright habit render particularly suitable for bedding purposes.
M. Krause 1932. *D. VG. MF. GPB.* — 612/2-616/1. *B.G.St. June-Sept.*
[*Hardy.*

GRANAT (H.T.) has blackish red buds of long-pointed shape and produces its deep red well-shaped flowers in quick succession.
Krause 1936. *D. VG. VF. GPB.* — — *B.E.G. June-September. Hardy.*

GRATISSIMA (pleasant) (S.), California, makes a many-branched bush of about six feet in height, bearing green leaves generally composed of from five to seven serrated leaflets, and clusters of small pink flowers followed by rounded red fruits.
— —. *D. TG. SF. GPG. — — S. June.*

GREEN MANTLE (see R. rubiginosa).

GRENADIER (H.T.) has fully double crimson-scarlet flowers with stout wide petals of great substance, with glossy, disease-resisting foliage and vigorous branching habit.
Dickson 1930. *D. VG. VF. GPB. — — B.G. June-September. Hardy.*

GRENOBLE (H.T.) proves a variable plant, and the best that can be said about it is that when it is good it is very, very good. The flowers, when the plant is well suited, are large high-centred, scented, crimson-scarlet gloriously formed beauties and are produced singly upon long stems with fine glossy, disease-proof foliage.
Mallerin 1932. *D. VG. MF. GPB. EB. — B.G.E. June-September. Hardy.*

GROOTENDORST SUPREME (see R. rugosa).

GRUSS AN AACHEN (H.T.) has medium-size very double flowers borne in small clusters, salmon-orange at the centre, passing to white at the edges of the petals, with large deep-green foliage, which has a tendency to mildew in certain districts, under unfavourable circumstances.
Geduldig 1908. *D. MG. SF. GPB. — — B. June-September. Hardy.*

GRUSS AN TEPLITZ (H.T.) is another friend of my youth, which has remained so. Its vigorous growth, its intense fragrance, its dark-crimson somewhat flat and loose flowers, the intense brightness of its almost red young growth, and its ability to produce flowers at all times make it a good garden rose especially suited to towns.
Geschwind 1897. *D. TG. VF. GPC. — — B.C.G.H.P.Pr.W. June-Sept.*
[Hardy.

GUARDSMAN (H.T.) has large, double, high-centred flowers of intense crimson-scarlet, on a yellow base. Growth is vigorous but tight, and leaves ample and of polished deep green.
Archer 1937. *D. VG. SF. GPB. — — B.G. June-September. Hardy.*

GUINÉE (Climbing H.T.) produces its large, fully double, deep-crimson, almost black flowers with wavy petals, in trusses of two or three, upon very vigorous canes. It is exceptionally fragrant.
Mallerin 1937. *D. C. VF. GPE. — — A.W.P. June-July. Hardy.*

GURNEY BENHAM (Pernetiana) has perfectly shaped double flowers of golden orange-yellow borne upon strong plants with glossy, mildew-proof foliage.
B. R. Cant 1935. *D. VG. F. GPB. — — B.G. June-September. Hardy.*

GUSTAV GRUNERWALD (H.T.) has full double cup-shaped flowers of deep pink, glossy green foliage, and may be relied upon to do its best always.
Lambert 1903. *D. VG. VF. GPB. — — B.G. June-September. Hardy.*

157

GWYNETH (Hybrid polyantha) has clustered heads of semi-double lemon-white flowers, which develop from red-lined canary-yellow buds. Growth is vigorous, foliage light green, flowering continuous.
Easlea 1923. *D. VG. VF. GPG. — — B.G. June-September. Very hardy.*

GWYNETH JONES (Pernetiana) has carmine-orange semi-double flowers generally grouped in clusters on bushy vigorous green-leaved plants, and is exceptionally good for massing.
McGredy 1925. *D. VG. SF. GPB. — — B.G. June-September. Hardy.*

GYMNOCARPA (bearing naked fruit) (S.), Western North America, can reach ten feet in height, and makes a shapely upright plant with green leaves composed of from five to nine leaflets. The flowers, usually borne singly, are rose-coloured and small, but are followed by small bright-red fruits.
Nuttall —. D. EG. F. GPG. — — S. June-July. Hardy.

GYPSY (H.T.) has nicely shaped dark-crimson flowers with very thick petals and a heavy fragrance.
Evans 1930. *D. VG. VF. GPB. — — B. June-July. Hardy.*

HADLEY (H.T.) has very large well-shaped flowers of deep rich crimson, borne singly on good stems. Its drawbacks are that the flowers have a tendency to blue with age, and in certain districts the deep green foliage is subject to mildew.
Waban Conservatories 1914. *D. VG. VF. GPB. — 827-827/1. B.G.St.Pot.*
[June-Sept. Hardy. Pl. 27.

HAEMATODES (blood-red) (S.) is a very vigorous much-branched species with single flowers of deep pink, borne in clusters, followed by inverted-pear-shaped scarlet fruits.
— —. D. EG. F. GPG. — — S. June-July. Hardy.

HAMBURG (Climbing H.T.) has large semi-double flowers of bright crimson, borne in clusters on very vigorous canes, with bright green foliage. A very good climber, producing its fragrant flowers in long succession.
Kordes 1935. *D. C. SF. GPE. — — W.P. June-August. Hardy.*

HANSA (see R. rugosa).

HARMONY (H.T.) has fully double shapely blooms of deep pink, borne upon plants of vigorous branching habit.
Le Grice 1940. *D. VG. F. GPB. — — B.G. June-September.*

HARRISONII is a hybrid of R. spinosissima and R. lutea (and is sometimes regarded as a variety of R. lutea), and has semi-double pale golden-yellow flowers of about one and a half inches in diameter, borne in clusters on vigorous bushes exceeding four feet in height, with small mid-green foliage.
Rivers 1830. *D. TG. MF. GPG. — — S.H. June. Very hardy.*

HARRISON'S YELLOW (see R. spinosissima).

HARRY KIRK (T.) remains a personal favourite for old associations; its bold double well-shaped flowers, generally borne in groups of there or four, carry the tints of the moonbeam and the soft fragrance of midsummer air. Its plentiful green foliage is subject to mildew and, not so frequently, to black spot, but in spite of its classification it must be said to be hardy, and I have seen it growing magnificently within five miles of Charing Cross.
Dickson 1907. *D. VG. MF. GPB. — — G. June-September.*

HARVEST MOON (H.T.) is an aptly named golden-cream large single-flowered rose, with golden stamens, borne in attractive clusters on vigorous but compact bushes with large deep green leaves.
B. R. Cant 1938. *D. VG. SF. GPB. — — B.G. June-September. Hardy.*

HAVERING (Hybrid Musk) bears its large china-pink double flowers in clusters and is of exceptionally sturdy growth and fragrance.
Bentall 1937. *D. VG. VF. GPG. — — S.H. June-September. Hardy.*

HAWLMARK CRIMSON (H.T.) has long-pointed buds opening to crimson-scarlet semi-double flowers reminiscent of Red Letter Day but darker in colour, and is good variety for bedding purposes.
Dickson 1920. *D. VG. VF. GPB. — — B.G. June-September. Hardy.*

HAZEL ALEXANDER (H.T.) has flowers of Madame Butterfly shape, of bright crimson with deeper shading, is sweetly fragrant and of vigorous bushy growth.
Dickson 1933. *D. VG. VF. GPB. — — B. June-September. Hardy.*

H. C. YOUNG (H.T.) has long-pointed buds and nicely shaped flowers of shrimp-pink deepening to salmon and tinted with deep yellow at the base, the flowers being borne singly on long stiff stems. Foliage is ample and green.
Austin & McAslan 1934. *D. VG. MF. GPB. — — B.G. June-Sept. Hardy.*

HEART OF GOLD (wichuraiana climber) bears its large, single, crimson flowers with white eyes and bold golden stamens in clusters, on strong canes with shiny deep green attractive foliage.
Van Fleet 1925. *D. C. SF. GPG. — — P.Pr.S. June. Hardy.*

HEATHER PATON (H.T.) has deep carmine-pink flowers of good shape, deepening in the centre, borne singly on long strong stems on vigorous and erect plants.
Austin & McAslan 1934. *D. VG. SF. GPB. — — B.G. June-Sept. Hardy.*

HEBE'S LIP (see R. rubiginosa).

HECTOR DEANE (H.T.) produces its double salmon-pink flowers shaded with gold from long-pointed buds on plants of free upright branching habit, and bearing good green foliage.
S. McGredy 1938. *D. VG. VF. GPB. — — B.G. June-September. Hardy.*

HEDE (H.T.) has substantial double flowers of sunflower-yellow borne on long stems from vigorous plants with deep green foliage.
Tantau 1934. *D. VG. SF. GPB. — — B.G. June-September. Hardy.*

HEDGEHOG Rose (see R. rugosa).

HEIDEKIND (see R. rugosa).

HEIDEROSLEIN (Lambertiana) has large salmon-pink single flowers shaded with yellow, borne in clusters on tall, wide, pillar-like plants. *Lambert* 1932. *D. C. VF. GPE. — — S. June-September. Hardy.*

HEINRICH WENDLAND (H.T.) bears large very double pointed flowers of good shape and of nasturtium-red within and golden-yellow without, resistant to bad weather, and produced on vigorous plants with glossy, disease-resistant foliage. *Kordes* 1930. *D. VG. MF. GPB. — — B.G. June-September. Hardy.*

HELENAE (comm.) (S.) grows vigorously, with long slender arching canes with green leaves made up of from seven to nine leaflets, and with large clusters of sweetly fragrant white flowers, each about the size of a penny, and followed by bright orange-scarlet fruits. *Wilson* 1924. *D. EG. VF. GPG. — White. S. June. Hardy.*

HÉLÈNE VACARESCO (H.T.) has large, double, globular flowers of salmon-orange, shaded with coppery-pink. *Chambard* 1939. *D. MG. MF. GPB. — — B.G. June-September. Hardy.*

HELIOS (H.T.) has shapely semi-double medium-size flowers of deep canary-yellow, borne on long strong stems with deep green, disease-resistant foliage. *Leenders* 1935. *D. VG. F. GPB. — — B.G. June-September. Hardy.*

HENRI MARTIN (see R. muscosa).

HENRY NEVARD (H.P.) is one of the more modern hybrid perpetuals and has very large round buds developing to large finely-fashioned flowers of deep crimson-scarlet, borne upon exceptionally vigorous bushes of tall and upright growth, with dark green foliage. *F. Cant* 1924. *D. EG. VF. GPC. — — G. June-September. Very hardy.*

HERMANN LONS (Climbing H.T.) has large single flowers of bright red, borne upon vigorous upstanding canes in clusters, and is well suited for growing as a pillar rose. *Tantau* 1931. *D. C. F. GPE. — — Pr. June-July. Hardy.*

HERMOSA (see R. chinensis).

HEROINE (H.T.) bears it deep salmon-pink, large, fully double flowers on long stems on strong upright plants with dark green foliage. Flowering period is long and continuous. *Krause* 1935. *D. VG. F. GPB. — — B.G. June-September. Hardy.*

HEROS (H.T.) has large, double, very full flowers borne singly upon strong stems of deep glowing red. Habit is bushy and upright, flowers retain their colour, foliage is dark green and profuse, and flowering almost continuous. *Tantau* 1933. *D. VG. VF. GPB. — — B.G. June-September. Hardy.*

160

Hybrid Tea Rose, Margaret McGredy

Hybrid Tea Rose, McGredy's Wonder

HIAWATHA (wichuraiana rambler). When grown in a somewhat sheltered position it is at its best and produces its sprays of bright crimson single flowers with bold white eyes, centred with golden stamens, in great abundance. Unfortunately, its glossy green foliage is subject at times to mildew.
Walsh 1904. *D. C. NF. GPH. — — A.Pr.Wst. July. Hardy.*

HIBERNICA (S.) (the Irish Rose), British Isles, is a natural hybrid of R. spinosissima and R. canina and bears its small clusters of single pale pink flowers, each about the size of a halfpenny, on a compact bush of about four feet in height, with dull red very spiny wood and small bright green leaves. The freely produced flowers are followed by shining dark red fruits.
Smith —. D. TG. SF. GPG. — — S. May-June. Hardy.

HIGHDOWNENSIS (Hybrid of species) was raised as a hybrid of R. Moyesii and forms a particularly graceful bush with long arching stems bearing small green multiple leaves, glaucous beneath, with single flowers of light shining crimson. The fruits which follow prolifically are bright signal-red.
Stern 1928. *D. TG. — GPG. — — S. June. Hardy.*

HILDA (H.T.) is reminiscent of Betty Uprichard, with very large double but somewhat loose flowers of carmine and light pink borne in groups on strong upright-growing plants with good green, disease-resistant foliage.
B. R. Cant 1928. *D. VG. SF. GPG. — — B. June-September. Hardy.*

HILDEBRANDSECK (see R. rugosa).

HILLIERI (H.S.) has both fragrant flowers and foliage. A hybrid of parentage R. Moyesii × R. Willmottiae, it makes a dense bush with long strands of small finely divided foliage and bears its very dark-red single flowers in great profusion in June, followed by its distinctive elongated red fruits. Reaching approximately eight to nine feet in height, it is essentially a specimen shrub.
Hillier —. D. EG. F. GPG. — — S.Sh. June. Hardy.

HINRICH GAEDE (H.T.) is a most vigorous variety with upright habit and bronze-green foliage and large, very shapely, fully double flowers of nasturtium-red shaded with orange-yellow at the base and outside the petals, which retain their colour under all circumstances. It is, unfortunately, liable to black spot.
Kordes 1931. *D. TG. MF. GPB. — 19/2-1. B.G.H. June-Sept. Hardy.*
[*Pl.* 79.

HISPANA (H.T.) is another very large, double, scented, cherry-crimson rose with full, wide petals, dark-green leathery foliage, disease-resistant, and grows to a height of about eighteen inches.
Pahissa 1938. *D. VG. VF. GPC. — — B.G. June-September. Hardy.*

HISPIDA (bristly) (S.), Siberia, makes a shapely bush of some five to six feet in height, with smallish green foliage and very spiny growth, bearing large, single, creamy-white flowers, followed by round blackish fruits.
Sims, Koehne 1780. *D. EG. NF. GPG. —— W.S. May-June. Hardy.*

HOLLANDIA (polyantha pompon) has large clusters of very small, double, bright red flowers which do not fade, and with its bright green foliage and medium growth is one of the best varieties for bedding purposes.
Zigverden 1930. *D. MG. NF. GPF. —— B. June-September. Hardy.*

HOLODONTA (S.), W. China, makes a tall bush exceeding eight feet in height, with dark green almost thornless canes, with green leaves widely dispersed along them, and produces groups of large, single, pink flowers which deepen to rose at the edges and are followed by elongated red fruits.
Stapf —. D. EG. NF. GPG. —— S. June. Hardy.

HOLSTEIN (Hybrid polyantha) is a good deep crimson single-flowered rose, with its flowers borne in large clusters from bushes of moderate height and vigorous growth with deep bronze-green foliage.
Kordes 1927. *D. MG. SF. GPG. —— B.G. June-September. Hardy.*

HOLSTENROSE (H.T.) has large, double, crimson-scarlet flowers of open globular form.
Tantau 1937. *D. VG. VF. GPB. —— B.G. June-September. Hardy.*

HOLT HEWITT (H.T.) is of dwarf but upright growth with good foliage, proof against mildew. The flowers, borne on long stems, are large and perfectly shaped and of rich polished crimson, with a hint of scarlet at the edges and in the veins.
Beckwith 1925. *B. DG. VF. GPA. EA. — June-September. Hardy.*

HOME SWEET HOME (H.T.) is a rose about which there are very mixed opinions. True, the flowers are flat; but they are modest and borne on a long stem. Is of upright growth and the foliage is good and disease-resistant. Fragrance is exceptionally fine, and personally I find the silvery-pink flowers grip the heart in a way in which more flaunting beauties fail.
Wood and Ingram 1939. *D. VG. VF. GPB. — 605/3. B. June-Sept. Hardy.*
[*Pl.* 16.

HOOSIER BEAUTY (H.T.) is a nicely shaped fully double, fragrant, crimson rose, with its flowers borne in groups on short plants, with rather less glossy foliage than seems necessary. It is, however, a good bedding variety.
Dorner 1915. *D. MG. VF. GPB. —— B. June-September. Hardy.*

HORRIDA (see R. ferox).

HORTULANUS BUDDE (H.T.) has nearly all the qualities of a perfect bedding rose, but for a tendency to bend its head. Flowers are large, full, double and of bright carmine-red. Foliage is plentiful, green, and habit upright and vigorous.
Verschuren 1919. *D. VG. MF. GPB. — — B. June-Sept. Hardy. Pl.* 41.

HUGH DICKSON (H.P.) again takes me back to the days of my youth, but remains both in fact and memory a good rose. Growth is very vigorous, foliage ample and green, flowers high-centred, fully double and of good shape and of intense crimson. Growth will reach even eight feet in height under some conditions, and flowering is continuous and prolonged. A fine rose for towns.
Hugh Dickson 1904. *D. EG. VF. GPC. EC. — B.G.E.H.Pr.St. June-Sept.*
[Very hardy.

HUGONIS (S.) is named after Father Hugo (Rev. Hugh Scallon) who discovered it in Western China in 1899. It makes a shapely bush of some eight feet in height, with graceful arching branches bearing grey-green leaves with from five to thirteen leaflets, with a feathery appearance. The flowers, borne at intervals along the strands, are soft yellow with deeper stamens and are fragrant.
Veitch 1908. *D. EG. F. GPG. — — S. April-May. Hardy.*

HUGONIS ALBERT MAUMENÉ (H.S.) bears little resemblance to its parent. The flowers are large, semi-double and salmon-pink shaded with copper and orange, and are borne in long succession on vigorous upright bushes with green foliage.
Sauvageot 1934. *D. TG. F. GPG. — — S.H. June-September. Hardy.*

HUGONIS CANTABRIGIENSIS (H.S.) bears a much greater resemblance to the parent, the large single pale lemon-yellow flowers being similarly produced on somewhat smaller symmetrical bushes with the small feathery foliage of the type.
— —. D. EG. F. GPG. — — S. June. Hardy.

HUGONIS DR. E. M. MILLS (H.S.) makes a fine hedge rose or decorative shrub. The primrose flowers are semi-double and borne on a bush of three to six feet in height with light green foliage.
Van Fleet 1926. *D. TG. F. GPG. — — S.H. June. Hardy.*

HUMILIS (see R. carolina).

HURST GEM (polyantha pompon) has double flowers of orange-red borne in large clusters which retain their colour well and are produced upon dwarf green-leaved bushes of good habit.
Hicks 1931. *D. SG. NF. GPF. — 18. B. June-September. Hardy. Pl.* 42.

H. V. MACHIN (H.T.) has bright green leaves on upright and vigorous growth and bears very large double full flowers of crimson scarlet.
Dickson 1914. *D. VG. SF. GPB. — — B.G. June-July. Hardy.*

HYTHE CLUSTER (Hybrid polyantha) has semi-double flowers of brilliant deep pink, larger than those of Ellen Poulsen, and is a taller variety. Foliage is green and resistant to disease.
Archer 1935. *D. VG. SF. GPC. — — B. June-September. Hardy.*

IAN BRINSON (H.T.) has bright scarlet flowers flushed with deep crimson, heavily scented, and is very free-flowering.
Bees Ltd. 1934. *D. MG. VF. GPB. EB. — B.G. June-July. Hardy.*

IDEAL (polyantha pompon) is dwarf, has dark green glossy foliage, and bears large clusters of fully double small flowers of dark crimson. It is subject to both mildew and black spot, but is a good variety for bedding.
Spek 1922. *D. MG. SF. GPE. — — B. June-September. Hardy.*

ILE DE FRANCE (H.T.) is a name previously used by Nonin in 1922 for a wichuraiana rambler, but is now applied to a large, high-centred, rather loose salmon-pink rose shaded with gold, borne upon good stems, and vigorous plants with plentiful green foliage.
J. Gaujard 1940. *D. VG. MF. GPB. — — B. June-September. Hardy.*

INDEPENDENCE DAY (Pernetiana) has double high-pointed flowers of orange-apricot shaded with flame, borne in groups on vigorous bushes of upright habit with green glossy leaves.
Bees 1919. *D. VG. VF. GPB. — — B.St. June-September. Hardy.*

INERMIS (see R. pendulina).

INFANTE BEATRICE (Pernetiana) has pointed double flowers of orange-yellow on a yellow base with the outside of the petals shaded with carmine. The flowers are borne on good stems on stout vigorous plants.
Guillot 1930. *D. VG. VF. GPB. — — B.G. July-September. Hardy.*

INGAR OLSSON (Hybrid polyantha) is upright and compact but vigorous in its growth, with green disease-resistant foliage, and bears (intermittently) large clusters of semi-double bright cerise-red flowers.
Poulsen 1931. *D. VG. SF. GPG. — — B.G. July-September. Hardy.*

INNOCENCE (H.T.) is one of the finest of the single white roses, its flowers reaching five inches in diameter, with a central zone of red and gold anthers. The green foliage is proof against mildew.
Chaplin 1921. *D. VG. VF. GPC. — White. G. July-September. Hardy.*

INVOLUTA (with curved-in petals) (S.), Eastern Europe, is dwarf in its habit, with almost thornless branches with small multiple pale-green foliage and rather small, single, flowers of pale reddish-pink.
Smith —. D. MG. SF. GPG. — — S. June. Hardy.

INVOLUTA VAR. WILSONII (see R. Wilsonii).

IOLANTHE (H.T.) has large, almost double, open flowers of intense red with the exterior of the petals of bright yellow, on plants of vigorous growth with glossy green foliage.
Gaujard 1940. *D. VG. SF. GPB. — — B.G. June-September.*

IRENE WATTS (see R. chinensis).

IRISH Rose (see R. hibernica).

IRISH ELEGANCE (H.T.) has large single flowers of apricot combined with buds of orange-scarlet, and bronze-green foliage borne on vigorous bushes.
Dickson 1905. *D. VG. MF. GPB. — 420/2. 3/3. B. June-Sept. Hardy.*

IRISH FIREFLAME (H.T.) is similar in appearance but deeper in colour, with its flowers borne on long strong stems on even more vigorous plants. The brilliant single flowers are veined with lemon and crimson.
Dickson 1913. *D. TG. VF. GPB. — 11/3. B. June-September. Hardy.*

ISA (H.T.) has large semi-double flowers of shell-pink, shading off to creamy-white, borne upon dwarf upright-growing almost thornless plants with green ample foliage, and having a delicious fragrance.
Evans 1931. *D. MG. VF. GPB. — — B. June-September. Hardy.*

ISABEL LLORACH (H.P.) has very large semi-double flowers of deep yellow, borne on strong stems on very vigorous plants with glossy dark green foliage resistant to disease. Generally manages to flower again later in the year.
Dot 1929. *D. EG. MF. GPC. — — B. June-July. Hardy.*

ISOBEL (Pernetiana) is a very lovely single-flowered variety with rose-pink flowers flushed with orange, with exceptionally vigorous growth and deep green foliage.
McGredy 1916. *D. TG. VF. GPB. — 34/3. 016/2. B.H. June-Sept. Hardy.*

IVY MAY (H.T.) has medium-size, fairly double, long-stemmed flowers of rose-pink shaded with dull yellow at the base, and is of strong upright habit with dark green foliage and a long flowering succession.
Beckwith 1925. *D. VG. VF. GPB. — — B. June-September. Hardy.*

I.X.L. (wichuraiana rambler) is a child of that disappointing rose, Veilchenblau, the much-vaunted "blue rose" of former years, and has the doubtful characteristic of throwing up long straight stems of terrifying thickness. The flowers are double, fairly large for the type, magenta, slightly scented, and borne in large clusters.
Coolidge 1925. *D. C. SF. GPI. — — A.P.Pr. June-July. Hardy.*

I ZINGARI (Pernetiana) has almost single flowers of orange and scarlet produced almost without ceasing during the season, in fairly large groups, on bright red stems with dark green leaves.
Pemberton 1925. *D. VG. NF. GPB. — — B.G. June-September. Hardy.*

JACK MCCANDLESS (H.T.) has double flowers produced from amber and carmine buds, which open to deep amber flowers splashed and veined with crimson within. Flowers are of medium size and are of good shape, and foliage is small, ample, dark green and mildew-proof. Habit is vigorous and bushy, and flowers produced with great freedom.

McGredy 1935. *D. VG. F. GPB. — — B.G. June-September. Hardy.*

JACOBITE Rose (see R. alba).

JACOTTE (wichuraiana rambler) has large, semi-double, open but rounded flowers of deep coppery-yellow shaded with terracotta-red. Growth is very vigorous with many thorns and dark green foliage which is resistant to disease.

Barbier 1920. *D. C. SF. GPI. — — A.C.P.Pr.Wst. June-July. Hardy.*

JACQUES LA TOUCHE (H.T.) has large very double flowers of good shape, of deep orange-pink with the backs of the petals of clear yellow. Growth is vigorous and upright and bears ample glossy green mildew-proof foliage.

Mallerin 1935. *D. VG. SF. GPB. — — B.G. June-September. Hardy.*

JAMES GIBSON (H.T.) has large, fully double, high-pointed flowers which open well in spite of wet weather and are of crimson-scarlet. The vigorous bushy plants bear ample dark green foliage and produce these attractive flowers with regularity for a long period.

McGredy 1928. *D. VG. SF. GPB. — — B.G. June-September. Hardy.*

JAMES REA (H.T.) produces very large fully double flowers of perfect form, of rose-pink, on plants of moderate growth with dark green foliage, and is eminently suitable for exhibition purposes.

McGredy 1930. *D. MG. VF. GPB. EB. — G.E. June-September. Hardy.*

JAN ABBING (H.T.) is a vigorous rose with upright growth and green ample foliage and large rounded flowers of glowing salmon-rose flushed with yellow, which produces its lasting flowers with some freedom.

Tantau 1933. *D. VG. SF. GPB. — — B.G. June-September. Hardy.*

JAN BOHM (H.P.) is another red rose with a fiery tone and aggressive growth, the well-shaped flowers being carried upon stems of exceptional strength, generally in twos or threes, and accompanied by very large green leaves.

Bohm 1928. *D. EG. VF. GPC. EC. — E.G.H.Pr.St. June-Sept. Hardy.*

JANE THORNTON (H.T.) is a rose of rich velvety crimson, shot with maroon; has an intense old-rose perfume, is very free-flowering and of vigorous growth.

Bees Ltd. 1943. *D. VG. VF. GPA. EA. — B.G. June-Sept. Hardy.*

JANET'S PRIDE (see R. rubiginosa).

JAPANESE Rose (see R. multiflora, R. rugosa).

J. B. CLARK (H.T.) has very large double flowers of crimson-scarlet with darker shading, generally borne in groups upon exceptionally vigorous plants, and is a good rose for growing in towns.
Hugh Dickson 1905. *D. EG. MF. GPC. EC. — E.G.H.P.St.W. June-July.*
[*Hardy.*

J. C. M. MENSING (H.T.) is a variety which missed deserved popularity for no good reason at all. A rose-pink sport of Ophelia, its shape is delightful, colour, fragrance and growth good. So why!
Eveleens 1924. *D. VG. VF. GPB. — — B.G.St.Pot. June-Sept. Hardy.*

J. C. THORNTON (H.T.) has extremely vigorous growth and glossy pale bronze-green foliage with perfectly shaped medium flowers of bright crimson-scarlet, borne on long stems, and has the grace to produce its flowers with freedom and regularity, yet lacks the essential fragrance so necessary to a red rose.
Bees 1926. *D. TG. NF. GPC. — — B.G. June-September. Hardy.*

JEAN COTE (Pernetiana) has the typical shiny disease-resistant foliage on strong vigorous canes and bears very large buds which open to perfectly double amber and old-gold flowers of intense fragrance.
Gaujard 1936. *D. MG. VF. GPB. EB. — B.G.E.St. June-Sept. Hardy.*

JEANNIE DEANS (see R. rubiginosa).

JERSEY BEAUTY (wichuraiana rambler) is an exceptional rambler with very glossy deep green foliage and strong canes, bearing large clusters of single pale yellow flowers which pass to cream.
Manda 1899. *E. C. F. GPI. — — A.C.H.P.Pr. June-July. Hardy.*

JESSIE (polyantha pompon) is a very dwarf bedding rose with bright shining green foliage and rather large semi-double flowers of bright red with white centres borne in large clusters. Has a tendency to fade but is otherwise a good dwarf.
Merryweather 1909. *D. MG. SF. GPE. — — B. June-September. Hardy.*

JESSIE SEAGRAVE (H.T.) may or may not be a novelty which will pass. Its excellently-formed flowers are bright crimson-scarlet with a base of deep yellow with veined markings inside the petals. The flowers are produced with regularity and habit is good.
Oliver Mee 1937. *D. VG. SF. GPB. — — G.B. June-September. Hardy.*

J. G. GLASSFORD (H.T.) is another extra vigorous rose with tall upright growth and large dark green leaves, and high-pointed flowers of deep crimson with reflexed petals.
Hugh Dickson 1921. *D. TG. MF. GPC. EC. — G.E. June-July.*

J. H. BRUCE (H.T.) has high-pointed flowers of brilliant carmine-scarlet of fine shape and with overlapping reflexed petals. The green foliage is proof against disease and the flowers against rain. In artificial light appears to be of intense vivid scarlet.
Bees 1936. *D. MG. MF. GPB. EB.* 24-625. *G.E. June-Sept. Hardy. Pl.* 39.

J. H. PEMBERTON (H.T.) is another tall-growing variety with large double flowers of crimson-scarlet borne in profusion and long succession.

Bentall 1931. *D. TG. MF. GPC. — — B.G. June-September. Hardy.*

JILL (Hybrid polyantha) has large clusters of semi-double flowers of crimson-pink.

Le Grice 1939. *D. VG. SF. GPG. — — B.G. June-September. Hardy.*

JOAN CANT (H.T.) is of vigorous growth and bears full, high-pointed, very double flowers of bright salmon-pink with a paler centre, in groups of two or three, on plants with mid-green foliage which is both large and resistant to disease.

B. R. Cant 1929. *D. VG. VF. GPB. — — G.B. June-September. Hardy.*

JOHANNA ROPCKE (Climbing Hybrid polyantha) is a most vigorous climber with the parentage Dorothy Perkins × Ophelia, and produces flowers like clustered miniatures of Ophelia, with dark green foliage.

Tantau 1931. *D. C. MF. GPH. — — A.P.Pr. June. Hardy.*

JOHANNA TANTAU (Hybrid polyantha) is the result of a similar cross and is in effect a miniature Ophelia, opening pink and paling to white. The flowers are large, nicely shaped and double, borne in clusters and freely produced upon plants of low, spreading habit.

Tantau 1928. *D. SG. MF. GPG. — — G. July-September. Hardy.*

JOHANNISZAUBER (H.T.) has high-centred double flowers of medium size of dark blood-red, which retain their colour well and are produced upon plants of medium upright growth with tough disease-proof foliage.

Tantau 1926. *D. SG. SF. GPB. — B.G. July-September. Hardy.*

JOHN E. SLEATH (H.T.) has fully double high-centred flowers carried on long strong stems, and flowers prolifically for a long period. The carmine-red flowers are tinted with reddish-orange and are invaluable for cutting.

Mee 1937. *D. VG. F. GPB. — — B.G. June-September. Hardy.*

JOHN McNAB (see R. rugosa).

JOHN MOORE (H.T.) has large many-petalled high-coned flowers of biscuit-yellow, with a golden base.

Gaujard 1938. *D. VG. SF. GPB. — — B.G. June-September. Hardy.*

JOHN RUSSELL (H.T.) resembles in character some older hybrid perpetuals with round globular flowers of perfect shape, great substance and size with large thick petals of deep crimson, borne upon strong vigorous plants.

Dobbie 1924. *D. VG. NF. GPB. — — B.G. June-September. Hardy.*

Three Hybrid Tea Roses

Mrs. Henry Bowles **ABEF**   McGredy's Coral **CDGH**
Princess Marina **JKLOP**

Four Hybrid Tea Roses

Mrs. A. R. Barraclough **ABEF**   President Macia **CDGH**
Madame Butterfly **JKNO**   Ophelia **GHLMPQ**

Josef Strnad (H.T.) is not, in spite of its queer arrangement of consonants, a misprint. This Czechoslovakian rose has large, double, high-pointed flowers of dark carmine-red with yellow, orange, and pink flushes. The foliage is dark bronze-green and the growth vigorous and upright.
Bohm 1932. *D. VG. MF. GPB. — — B.G. June-September. Hardy.*

Joseph Guy (Hybrid polyantha) is also known as Lafayette and has large crimson-cerise semi-double flowers borne in very large clusters. Its habit is dwarf and vigorous and foliage is green and glossy and resistant to mildew.
Nonin 1924. *D. MG. SF. GPF. — — B.G. June-September. Hardy.*

Joseph Hill (H.T.) is an old rose which has the drawback of being completely intolerant of wet weather conditions, but produces upon very dwarf growth its medium-size perfectly formed double flowers of bright coppery-yellow, shaded with salmon-pink, above glossy green attractive foliage.
Pernet-Ducher 1903. *D. MG. SF. GPB. EB. — B.G.E.St. June-July.*

Josephine Spiecker (H.T.) has long-pointed buds of rich orange with distinct orange-brown veining and full double fragrant flowers. Foliage is glossy bronze-green, habit branching and vigorous, and it appears to be as good a plant as Mrs. G. A. van Rossem.
Harkness 1938. *D. VG. F. GPB. — 607/1. B.G. July-Sept. Hardy. Pl.* 49.

Joseph Pernet (Pernetiana) has coppery-salmon flowers of good shape, very large and double, borne upon long strong stems, which make them exceptionally good for cutting. Foliage is shiny dark green, and growth vigorous, erect and bushy.
Pernet-Ducher 1934. *D. VG. SF. GPB. — — B.G.St. June-Sept. Hardy.*

Joy (H.T.) is a rose of short growth and has orange-red buds with double high-pointed flowers of rose-pink flushed with red and with a yellow base. Foliage is green and resistant to disease, and growth is vigorous.
Beckwith 1929. *D. MG. SF. GPB. — — B.G. June-September. Hardy.*

Joyous Cavalier (H.T.) is a tall and vigorous plant bearing its full double, large, crimson-scarlet flowers in groups of two or three. Foliage is glossy deep bronze-green, habit bushy and suitable for a hedge.
Archer 1926. *D. TG. F. GPC. — — G.H. June-September. Hardy.*

Judith (H.T.) has cerise-red globular flowers of bright charm, with the reverse of the petals of orange-yellow, accompanied by red-bronze glossy foliage.
Le Grice 1938. *D. VG. VF. GPB. — — B.G. June-September. Hardy.*

Jules Gaujard (Pernetiana) has large globular double flowers of bright orange-red, consistently flushed with carmine, borne singly on long stems. Foliage is green and ample, growth is vigorous.
Pernet-Ducher 1928. *D. VG. VF. GPB. — — B.G. June-September. Hardy.*

JULIA COUNTESS OF DARTREY (H.T.) produces its very high-pointed double flowers of deep rose with a yellow base on long stems, from plants of vigorous erect growth with shiny dark green foliage.
Campbell Hall 1927. *D. VG. VF. GPB. EB. — E.G. June-Sept. Hardy.*

JULIANA (polyantha pompon) makes large clusters of semi-double pale salmon flowers on dwarf sturdy bushes with green foliage.
Den Ouden 1920. *D. MG. NF. GPF. — — B. June-September. Hardy.*

JULIEN POTIN (Pernetiana) has somewhat globular high-pointed flowers of primrose-yellow, large, double, and produced on long and strong stems. Foliage is green, disease-resistant, growth vigorous, erect, and period of flowering prolonged. The best flowers are always produced from side shoots.
Pernet-Ducher 1927. *D. MG. F. GPA. EB. 1/3 to 3/2. B.G.E.Pot. June-Sept.*
[Hardy. Pl. 33.

JULIET (Pernetiana) came with a flourish of trumpets, and can be good, bad and indifferent. The large double flowers are well rounded and of vermilion-rose or deep rich pink, with the reverse of the petals of yellow to old-gold. Habit is tall and vigorous and foliage green, curiously curled, and subject to mildew. Flowers are inclined to quarter.
Paul 1910. *D. TG. F. GPC. — — G.B. June-July. Hardy.*

JUNE (H.T.) has attractive high-centred double flowers of soft flesh-pink, deepening in intensity at the centre.
Archer 1937. *D. VG. MF. GPB. — — B.G. June-September. Hardy.*

KAISERIN AUGUSTE VICTORIA (H.T.) bears its medium-size white, cream-centred, double flowers on weak stems arising from a plant with moderate growth, and green, somewhat attenuated foliage. It remains in cultivation, having many of the good points which make a good rose.
Lambert 1891. *D. MG. SF. GPB. — White. G. June-September. Hardy.*

KARDINAL (H.T.) has full, cup-shaped flowers of good form, fiery-crimson, shaded with darker red, borne upon plants of vigorous but dwarf and compact habit.
Krause 1934. *D. MG. F. GPB. — — B.G. June-September. Hardy.*

KAREN POULSEN (Hybrid polyantha) produces large clusters of large single flowers of bright crimson-scarlet, borne upon vigorous bushes with ample leathery green foliage. Its colour is retained well, and the strong vigorous growths it produces in autumn should be shortened to three to four eyes in order to ripen in September.
Poulsen 1933. *D. VG. NF. GPG. — — B.G.St.Pot. June-September. Hardy.*

KATE RAINBOW (H.T.) has large, full, gracefully-shaped flowers of several shades of pink with gold flushes and red shadings, borne on extra vigorous plants with glossy green, disease-resistant foliage.
Beckwith 1935. *D. TG. VF. GPC. — — B.G. June-September. Hardy.*

KATHARINE ZEIMET (polyantha pompon) bears large, double, pure white flowers on exceptionally dwarf plants of vigorous, erect growth, with bright green plentiful foliage. It is undoubtedly the best double white polyantha pompon.
Lambert 1901. *D. DG. SF. GPF. — White. A.G.Pot.St. June-Sept. Hardy.*

KATHERINE PECHTOLD (H.T.) has fully double shapely flowers of bronzy-orange, flushed rose and gold, borne on long stems, on vigorous plants with green leathery foliage, and is perfect under glass.
Verschuren 1934. *D. VG. F. GPB. — — B.G.Pot. June-September.*

KATHLEEN (Hybrid Musk) has semi-double flowers of blush-pink, borne in large clusters upon upright bushes of vigorous habit, with much green foliage, and exceeding four feet in height, flowering with continuity for a long period.
Pemberton 1922. *D. TG. VF. GPC. — — Pr.H.S. June-September. Hardy.*

KATHLEEN KENNEDY (H.T.) has salmon-pink flowers of good shape and size, flushed with orange and cherry-pink, and is of vigorous growth with green foliage.
Dickson 1939. *D. VG. F. GPB. — — B.G. June-September. Hardy.*

KATHLEEN MILLS (H.T.) has semi-double flowers of silver-pink, borne on vigorous upright-growing bushes with bright green foliage.
Le Grice 1934. *D. VG. F. GPB. — — B.G. June-September. Hardy.*

KEES KNOPPERS (Hybrid polyantha) has large clusters of large semi-double flowers of flushed pale pink, borne upon vigorous bushes with ample green foliage, and flowers continuously.
Leenders 1930. *D. VG. F. GPG. — — B.G. June-September. Hardy.*

KERSBERGEN (polyantha pompon) bears large clusters of semi-double dark-red medium flowers on dwarf bushes of upright and vigorous habit with green, mildew-resistant foliage.
Oosthoeck 1927. *D. DG. NF. GPF. 820-824. B.Pot. June-Sept. Hardy.*
[*Pl.* 48.

KIDWAY (H.T.) has very large, double, high-pointed flowers of sunflower-yellow, tinted and flushed with gold and orange, borne upon long stems on vigorous and bushy plants with large dark bronze-green foliage.
Pernet-Ducher 1933. *D. VG. F. GPB. EB. — B.E.G. June-Sept. Very hardy.*

KING ALEXANDER THE FIRST (H.T.) has very large fully double flowers of golden-copper with a base of bright yellow, borne upon long strong stems on vigorous, erect-growing bushes, with deep bronzy-green foliage on reddish new wood.
Pernet-Ducher 1937. *D. VG. F. GPB. EB. — B.E.G. June-Sept. Hardy.*

KIRSTEN POULSEN (Hybrid polyantha) has clustered single flowers of bright cherry-red, borne upon strong stems and upon strong upright-growing bushes with light green foliage. Can be grown into an exceptionally large bush or used as a hedge.
Poulsen 1925. *D. TG. F. GPC.* — 23. *B.G.H.St.Pot. June-Sept. Very hardy.*
[*Pl.* 34 & 59.

KLONDYKE (H.T.) resembles Lady Forteviot in everything but colour, which is of clear gold.
Le Grice 1934. *D. VG. MF. GPB.* —— *B.G. June-September. Hardy.*

K. OF K. (H.T.) is extremely decorative in effect, producing its semi-double crimson-scarlet flowers in great profusion upon very vigorous erect bushes, for an exceedingly long period.
Dickson 1917. *D. TG. MF. GPC.* — 824. *B.G.S. June-Sept. Very hardy.*

KONIGIN VON DANEMARK (see R. centifolia provincialis).

KONINGIN ASTRID (Queen Astrid) (H.T.) has very large, double, full flowers with high centres, borne on long strong stems, and of apricot and bronze with a red tinge. Growth is erect and vigorous; foliage large, ample and bronze-green. Flowering is free and continuous.
Leenders 1935. *D. VG. MF. GPB.* —— *B.G. June-September. Very hardy.*

KOROVO (H.T.) has large double flowers of rose, shaded with peach-pink, borne upon long stems on vigorous plants with thick green, disease-resistant foliage.
Leenders 1931. *D. VG. F. GPB.* —— *B.G. June-September. Hardy.*

KOSTER'S ORLEANS (polyantha pompon) has small semi-double flowers of crimson-scarlet, borne in large clusters on dwarf but vigorous plants of bushy habit with glossy green foliage.
Koster 1920. *D. MG. SF. GPF.* — 25. *B. June-Sept. Very hardy. Pl.* 48.

KURT SCHOLTZ (H.T.) has large, high-pointed, crimson-scarlet flowers with huge overlapping petals, borne on long strong stems. Growth is erect, very vigorous, with large green, disease-resistant foliage.
Kordes 1936. *D. TG. MF. GPB.* —— *B.G. June-September. Hardy.*

KYSON (Climbing H.T.) has immense single flowers of intense crimson-scarlet, borne in large clusters, and flowers for a long period.
Eacott 1940. *D. C. MF. GPF.* —— *P.W. June-July. Hardy.*

LADDIE (H.T.) has large open, high-centred, full flowers of carmine-red, flushed with orange and crimson which fades to carmine, borne on strong stems from vigorous plants with bushy upright growth and healthy green foliage.
Beckwith 1926. *D. VG. SF. GPB.* —— *B.G. June-September. Hardy.*

LADY ALICE STANLEY (H.T.) has large, double, open flowers of silvery-pink, with the reverse of the petals of rose, borne each upon a long strong stem. Growth is upright and vigorous and foliage plentiful and green.
McGredy 1909. *D. VG. F. GPB. EB.* — *B.E.G. June-September. Hardy.*

172

Lady Ashtown (H.T.) is another old favourite with large, double, high-pointed flowers of clean deep pink, borne singly on long stems. Growth is vigorous and erect, and foliage green, plentiful and subject to mildew.
Dickson 1904. D. VG. SF. GPB. EB. — E.G.St. June-September. Hardy.

Lady Barnby (H.T.) adds to greater modernity perfectly-shaped flowers built of wide deep petals of clear rich pink shaded with intense rose, borne on straight stems and on vigorous, erect plants, with rich green, disease-proof foliage.
Dickson 1930. D. VG. VF. GPB. EB. 625/2-625/1. B.E.G. June-Sept.
[Pl. 23.

Lady Cahn (H.T.) has clear apricot-yellow double flowers with veins of a deeper tone, of good shape and freely borne upon vigorous, upright plants, with healthy ample foliage which is resistant to disease. Is a good variety for cutting.
Pernet-Ducher 1938. D. VG. F. GPB. — — B.G. June-September. Hardy.

Lady Charles Townsend (Pernetiana) has large, double, globular flowers, of deep orange with salmon tints, on erect vigorous plants with dark green foliage proof against disease. Flowering is free and prolonged.
Daniels 1930. D. VG. NF. GPB. — — B.G. June-September. Hardy.

Lady Cunliffe Owen (H.T.) has large, double, perfectly-formed flowers of salmon and cream flushed with carmine, borne on vigorous upright plants of bushy growth, with good green foliage.
Ley 1932. D. TG. MF. GPB. EB. — — E.G. June-September. Hardy.

Lady Dawson Bates (H.T.) has large double, high-centred, semi-globular flowers of butter-yellow heavily flushed with pink. Growth is vigorous and erect.
McGredy 1939. D. VG. MF. GPB. EB. — B.E.G. June-September. Hardy.

Lady Dixon-Hartland (H.T.) produces its full high-pointed flowers on vigorous upright plants with good green foliage. The open flowers shade from pale pink at the edges to deep salmon-pink at the centre.
B. R. Cant 1922. D. VG. MF. GPB. — — B.G. June-September. Hardy.

Lady English (H.T.) has wide-petalled flowers, well reflexed, of bright pink, borne upon strong stems on vigorous bushes with glossy bright foliage.
B. R. Cant 1934. D. VG. SF. GPB. EB. — B.E.G. June-September. Hardy.

Lady Forteviot (Pernetiana) has characteristically large petals forming large shapely semi-double flowers of golden-yellow shaded with apricot; is fragrant, floriferous, bearing its flowers in groups on vigorous plants with attractive dark bronze-green shiny foliage.
B. R. Cant 1928. D. VG. VF. GPB. — 609/2-3/2. B.G.St. June-Sept.
[Hardy.

Lady Frost (H.T.) gets the greatest part of its beauty from its wide overlapping petals which make up its dainty flowers of rose flushed with carmine, which are borne on long stems on vigorous bushes with foliage of olive-green.
Bees 1935. *D. VG. VF. GPB. — — B.G. June-September. Hardy.*

Lady Gay (wichuraiana rambler) is a very vigorous rambler with glossy green foliage and long sprays of double, smallish flowers of deep rose-pink.
Walsh 1905. *D. C. F. GPH. — — A.C.P.Pr.Wst.T. July-August. Hardy.*

Lady Godiva (wichuraiana rambler) is a sport of Dorothy Perkins with medium-sized double flowers of pale blush-pink with a deeper centre, borne in large clusters on canes with deep glossy almost evergreen foliage.
Paul 1908. *D. C. NF. GPH. — — A.P.Pr.Wst.T. July-August. Hardy.*

Lady Hamilton (see R. spinosissima).

Lady Hillingdon (T.) is one of the few tea roses remaining in general cultivation, and has long buds, medium apricot-yellow semi-double flowers, borne on upright plants of moderate growth with unobtrusive bronze-green foliage. Suitable for warm districts.
Lowe & Shawyer 1910. *D. MG. MF. GPB. — 603/1, 604. B.G.St.Pot.*
[*July-Sept. Pl.* 50.

Lady Inchiquin (Pernetiana) is well worth growing in districts where it is known to do well, its rose-pink flowers suffused with orange being so exceptionally attractive. The high-centred, somewhat globular flowers are borne on moderately vigorous, upright plants with glossy green foliage.
Dickson 1921. *D. MG. MF. GPB. EA. — E.G. July-September. Hardy.*

Lady Leconfield (H.T.) has firm-petalled, beautifully formed, long buds of sulphur-yellow opening to creamy-white and turning pure white with age; is highly fragrant and of vigorous growth.
Burbage 1939. *D. VG. VF. GPB. — — E.G. July-September. Hardy.*

Lady Leslie (H.T.) produces its large double, full, high-pointed, carmine-scarlet, saffron-tinted flowers on long strong stems rising from vigorous, erect bushy plants with dark green mildew-proof foliage.
McGredy 1929. *D. VG. VF. GPB. EB. — E.G.B. July-September. Hardy.*

Ladylove (H.T.) has nicely-shaped flowers of rose-pink with a flush of apricot, borne on long stems on plants with erect sturdy growth, and dark green foliage resistant to mildew.
Beckwith 1926. *D. VG. VF. GPB. — — B.G.Pot. June-September. Hardy.*

Lady Mandeville (H.T.) has very double flowers of pointed shape, of clear yellow flushed with orange and veined with vermilion, on long strong stems. Growth is vigorous and foliage good and plentiful.
McGredy 1939. *D. VG. F. GPB. EB. — B.E.G. June-September. Hardy.*

LADY MARGARET STEWART (H.T.) produces its large, very double, high-centred flowers singly upon long strong stems. The colour is deep buttercup-yellow flushed with orange-scarlet, and the flowers fail to open in wet weather. Growth is vigorous and erect, the glossy grey-green foliage being freely produced.
Dickson 1926. *D. VG. VF. GPB. — — B.G. June-September. Hardy.*

LADY MOYRA CAVENDISH (H.T.) has full flowers of intense strawberry-red with reflexed petals of perfect form, borne upon plants with attractive green foliage and moderate upright growth.
McGredy 1938. *D. MG. SF. GPB. — — B.G. June-September. Hardy.*

LADY NUTTING (H.T.) has shapely double, high-centred flowers of diffused salmon-pink. Growth is vigorous and flowering prolific when established.
Wheatcroft 1938. *D. VG. MF. GPB. — — B.G. June-September. Hardy.*

LADY PENZANCE (see R. rubiginosa).

LADY PIRRIE (H.T.) has large double flowers of soft apricot with the reverse of the petals of coppery-salmon, each borne upon a strong stem. Of vigorous growth, with deep green foliage, it is subject at times to mildew and generally to rust. Flowering is continuous and prolific.
Hugh Dickson 1910. *D. VG. MF. GPB. — — B.G.St.Pot. June-Sept.*
[Hardy.

LADY RACHEL VERNEY (H.T.) has medium-size flowers of rose and cerise-pink, of good shape, with conical spiral centres, borne in some profusion upon vigorous and upright plants with good green foliage.
Bees 1936. *D. MG. F. GPB. — — B.G. June-September. Hardy.*

LADY READING (polyantha pompon) has clustered heads of rounded small deep red flowers, borne upon dwarf bushes of vigorous growth with dark green foliage.
Van Herk 1921. *D. MG. NF. GPF. — 23. B.St.Pot. June-Sept. Hardy.*
[Pl. 31.

LADY SACKVILLE (H.T.) has large well-formed double flowers of creamy-white, borne upon upright vigorous plants with good green foliage, and produces its flowers freely and continuously.
B. R. Cant 1933. *D. VG. MF. GPB. — White. B.G. June-Sept. Hardy.*

LADY SYLVIA (H.T.) is a sport of Madame Butterfly, and has high-centred flowers with reflexed wide petals of deep flesh-pink with a yellow base, each borne on a long strong stem. Growth is vigorous and upright, foliage large, green and leathery, subject to occasional mildew and black spot, and the flowering period long.
Stevens 1927. *D. VG. MF. GPB. — 622/3-622/2. B.G.St.Pot. June-Sept.*
[Hardy.

Lady Trent (H.T.) is a many-petalled high-centred shapely rose of reddish-orange with strong growth and deep green shining leaves. *Dot* 1940. *D. VG. MF. GPB. EB. — B.E.G. June-September.*

Lady Ursula (H.T.) has pointed, large, very double flowers of flesh-pink, borne with almost unceasing regularity on strong vigorous upright bushes with glossy green, disease-resistant foliage. An old but charming variety. *Dickson* 1908. *D. TG. MF. GPB. EB. — B.E.G. June-September. Hardy.*

Lady Violet Astor (H.T.) has a full high-centred flower of pink shaded with salmon, which is at its best in hot weather. Growth is vigorous and upright, foliage bright green and freely borne. *B. R. Cant* 1933. *D. VG. MF. GPB. — — B.G. June-September. Hardy.*

Lady Waterlow (Climbing H.T.) has large, shapely, semi-double, salmon-pink flowers with crimson-edged petals, borne upon strong canes, and is very suitable as a pillar rose. *Nabonnand* 1902. *D. C. MF. GPE. — 625/1. Pr. June-Sept. Hardy. Pl.*25.

Lady Worthington-Evans (H.T.) is vigorous, erect and bushy in its growth, with bronze-green foliage and high-centred deep crimson semi-double flowers, borne on long stems, frequently in quantity. *Dickson* 1926. *D. VG. MF. GPB. — — B.G. June-September. Hardy.*

laevigata (smooth) (S.) (China), is the Cherokee Rose and bears upon long flexible canes, clothed with very glossy green leaves, very large, single, white, fragrant flowers with yellow centres. Is suitable for warm sunny positions as a climber. *Michaux* 1803. *D. C. VF. GPC. — White. C. June-July.*

laevigata major (large) (S.) is similar in all respects except in its vigour, which is much greater. *— —. D. C. VF. GPC. — White. C. June-July.*

× laevigata sinica Anemone is a semi-climbing rose with clusters of very large silvery-pink flowers flushed with rose-pink, and glossy green leaves, which requires a similar warm sheltered position. *F. Schmidt* 1895. *D. C. VF. GPC. — S.C. June-July.*

Lafayette (see Joseph Guy).

La Follette (see R. gigantea).

La France (H.T.) was the first of the hybrid tea varieties and has very large, very double, cupped flowers of silvery-pink with a rose-pink reverse, each borne on a long strong stem. Foliage is large, deep green, and growth vigorous and erect. Unfortunately, it no longer seems to be the great rose of thirty to forty years ago, and is best on light soils. *Guillot* 1867. *D. TG. VF. GPC. — — B.G.St. June-September. Hardy.*

Dainty Maid (Hybrid Polyantha) **ABCDEFGK**
Rosa Mundi **LMPQ**
Kirsten Poulsen Improved (Hybrid Polyantha) **JNORSTU**

Three Species Roses

Rosa Andersonii **ABCEFJKH**
Rosa Froebelii **FGL**
Rosa nitida **OPQ**

LAL (H.T.) has large fully double flowers of fine-pointed shape of deep salmon-pink, borne on long strong stems. Growth is vigorous, upright and bushy, with dark green foliage. It is a fine rose for bedding purposes or growing under glass.
Easlea 1933. *D. VG. F. GPB.* — 623. *B.G.St.Pot. June-Sept. Hardy.*
[*Pl.* 29.

LA MÉLUSINE (see R. rugosa).

LAMIA (H.T.) has attractively shaped semi-double flowers of red-orange which retain their shape well, borne on long strong stems with bronze-green foliage, bright red while young, and fine vigorous growth.
Easlea 1918. *D. VG. SF. GPB.* — 609/3, 612/2. *B. June-Sept. Hardy.*
[*Pl.* 50.

LANCASHIRE LASS (H.T.) is exceptionally free-flowering, its semi-double crimson-pink flowers being produced from robust erect plants, with deep green shining leaves.
Archer 1939. *D. VG. SF. GPC.* — — *B.G. June-September. Hardy.*

LANGLEY GEM (Hybrid polyantha) produces clustered heads of open, single, deep cherry-red flowers approaching scarlet in intensity. Growth is vigorous, erect and branching, and leaves of red-bronze.
Eacott 1939. *D. VG. NF. GPG.* — — *B.G. June-September. Hardy.*

LA PARISIENNE (H.T.) has large nearly double flowers of golden-coral borne on long strong stems on vigorous plants with strong green, disease-resistant foliage.
Mallerin 1936. *D. VG. F. GPB.* — — *B.G. June-September. Hardy.*

LAURETTE MESSIMY (see R. chinensis).

LAWRENCE OF ARABIA (H.T.) has large, fully double flowers of pale yellow flushed with orange, borne on long strong stems on plants of moderate growth with green foliage.
Dickson 1938. *D. VG. F. GPB.* — — *B.G. June-September. Hardy.*

LAXA (see R. coriifolia var. Froebelii).

LEADING LADY (H.T.) has large well-shaped flowers of flesh-pink shaded salmon-rose, borne singly upon plants of vigorous habit, with deep-green tough foliage which is resistant to disease.
Dickson 1935. *D. VG. MF. GPB.* — — *B.G. June-September. Hardy.*

LEATHER-LEAF Rose (see R. coriifolia).

LEMANIA (H.T.) is another red rose with long, almost black buds, the flowers full, of good shape and of deep red, shaded outside with an even deeper colour and borne on long strong stems on plants of vigorous habit.
Heizmann 1937. *D. VG. MF. GPB.* — — *B.G. June-September. Hardy.*

LEMON BEAUTY (H.T.) has large finely-formed flowers of creamy-white shaded at the base with lemon-yellow borne upon long strong stems on plants of upright vigorous growth with green foliage.
B. R. Cant 1932. *D. VG. MF. GPB.* — — *B.G. June-September. Hardy.*

LEMON PILLAR (H. Noisettiana) has fully double large shapely flowers of sulphur-yellow, borne on smooth vigorous canes, with very large green leaves, and is very suitable for growth on a pillar.
Paul 1915. *D. C. F. GPE.* — — *Pr. June. Hardy.*

LENI NEUSS (H.T.) has large, full, shapely flowers of hydrangea-pink, shaded with dull rose on the reverse of the petals. Growth is vigorous and upright and foliage ample and large.
Leenders 1928. *D. VG. MF. GPB.* — — *B.G. June-September. Hardy.*

LEONARD BARRON (H.T.) is one of the first of the florists' varieties to have R. nutkana as one of its ancestors. The flowers are exceptionally full, but very flat and large, and of salmon undershot with amber. Habit is somewhat diffuse, and foliage good and sufficient.
Nicolas 1930. *D. MG. MF. GPB.* — — *B.G. June-September. Hardy.*

LEONARD FIFE (H.T.) has pointed, full, very double flowers of coppery-pink, shaded with gold, borne upon long strong stems on vigorous plants with attractive disease-proof foliage.
Dobbie 1942. *D. VG. VF. GPB. EB.* — — *B.E.G. June-September.*

LÉON CHENAULT (H.T.) bears its large, very double, lasting flowers of deep rose-pink with salmon base on long stems, and with frequency, on strong plants with dark green foliage.
Pernet-Ducher 1931. *D. VG. VF. GPB.* — — *B.G. June-September. Hardy.*

LÉONIE LAMESCH (Hybrid polyantha) has semi-double bright copper-red flowers with golden centres, borne singly or in groups upon bushy plants with bright green foliage.
Lambert 1899. *D. MG. F. GPC.* — — *G.S.St. June-September. Hardy.*

LÉONTINE CONTENOT (H.T.) has high-centred double flowers of bright yellow, borne on plants of moderate growth with good glossy foliage.
Ketten 1936. *D. MG. MF. GPB.* — — *B.G. June-September.*

LÉONTINE GERVAIS (wichuraiana rambler) flowers very early, but is somewhat shy, and bears its large double, yellow, rose-tinted flowers in loose sprays on vigorous canes with glossy deep green foliage.
Barbier 1903. *D. C. MF. GPI.* — — *A.C.P.Pr.Wst. June. Hardy.*

LE RÊVE (Climbing Pernetiana) has semi-double medium-size flowers of bright sunflower-yellow in groups, and is a most vigorous climber, with glossy deep green foliage, producing its flowers in abundance.
Pernet-Ducher 1923. *D. C. MF. GPF.* — — *P.Pr.W. June-July. Hardy.*

LESLEY DUDLEY (H.T.) produces its perfectly-shaped large, pointed, nearly full flowers of soft pink, with gold and buff shadings on the outside of the petals. Growth is smooth, erect, moderately vigorous and bushy, and foliage dark green and disease-resistant.
McGredy 1932. *D. VG. F. GPB.* — — *B.G.St. June-September. Hardy.*

LESLIE EVANS (H.T.) has semi-double flowers of rich crimson, borne on long strong stems on vigorous plants very suitable for bedding.
Evans 1927. *D. VG. F. GPB.* — — *B. June-September. Hardy.*

Lestra Hibberd (H.T.) has shapely flowers of deep yellow, borne upon long stems on vigorous plants with glossy green foliage.
Hill 1935. *D. VG. F. GPB.* — — *B. June-September. Hardy.*

Leuchtstern (Climbing polyantha) bears immense clusters of large, single, rose-pink flowers with white eyes upon moderately vigorous canes with medium dark green foliage, subject, under certain conditions, to mildew.
Schmidt 1899. *D. C. SF. GPH.* — — *C.Pr. June-July. Very hardy.*

Li Bures (Pernetiana) has somewhat thin, double, cupped flowers of rose-pink, shaded with scarlet and gold, produced in profusion, with large glossy green foliage resistant to disease, on vigorous upright plants.
Dot 1928. *D. VG. F. GPB.* — — *B.G. June-September. Hardy.*

Lieutenant (H.T.) has pointed cupped, double, bright pink flowers freely produced upon vigorous erect plants with large green foliage.
Burrell 1940. *D. VG. VF. GPB.* — — *B.G. June-September. Hardy.*

Lieutenant Chauré (H.T.) produces its large, double, cupped flowers of crimson-red on long strong stems from vigorous plants with rich green attractive foliage. Is an honest rose, defying rain, retaining its colour, and is good for bedding.
Pernet-Ducher 1910. *D. VG. VF. GPB.* — — *B.G. June-September. Hardy.*

Lilette Mallerin (H.T.) has loose high-centred flowers of crimson-pink with the reverse of the petals creamy-yellow, borne in profusion on long stems on vigorous plants with dark green foliage.
Mallerin 1937. *D. VG. SF. GPB.* — — *B.G. June-September. Hardy.*

Lilian (H.T.) is an attractive shapely, double, pure yellow rose, borne on a long stem from a moderately vigorous plant with green foliage.
B. R. Cant 1930. *D. MG. SF. GPB.* — — *B.G. June-September. Hardy*

Limelight (H.T.) makes an assault upon the eye with its many attractive large semi-double flowers of clear deep yellow, borne upon extra vigorous erect plants with large glossy green foliage.
Appleton 1934. *D. TG. SF. GPC.* — 2/2. *B.G. June-September. Hardy.*

Lise Palais (H.T.) has large, very full, well-formed flowers borne singly upon long strong stems. The flowers are deep cream shaded with pink and shot with gold, and are equally good for exhibition or garden purposes. Growth is vigorous and erect, and foliage strong, green and healthy.
Gaujard 1937. *D. VG. F. GPB. EB.* — *B.E.G. June-September. Hardy.*

Lismore (see R. spinosissima).

Little Dorrit (polyantha pompon) is a dwarf vigorous plant with glossy green foliage and clusters of semi-double large open flowers of coral-salmon.
Reeves 1930. *D. MG. SF. GPF.* — 621/1. *B. June-Sept. Hardy. Pl. 42.*

LITTLE GEM (see R. muscosa).

LITTLE MISS MUFFET (Hybrid polyantha) has clustered heads of large semi-double open deep pink flowers, with cherry-red reverse.
Archer 1939. *D. VG. SF. GPG. — — B.G. June-September. Hardy.*

LITTLE PRINCESS (polyantha pompon) has neat double flowers of pale coral-pink, borne in neat but large clusters on vigorous upright bushes with green glossy disease-resistant foliage.
Knight 1937. *D. VG. SF. GPF. — — B. June-September. Hardy.*

LLEIDA (Pernetiana) bears its double flowers of bright red, with the outside of the petals yellow, on good stems from vigorous erect plants with glossy green foliage.
Dot 1936. *D. VG. SF. GPB. — — B. June-September. Hardy.*

LOCARNO (Hybrid polyantha) is an orange-scarlet sport from Orleans Rose, and has similar large clusters of semi-double flowers on vigorous erect bushy plants with glossy green foliage occasionally subject to mildew.
De Ruyter 1926. *D. VG. SF. GPF. — — B.St.G. June-September. Hardy.*

LOLITA (H.T.) has large double, rounded white flowers which deepen at the centre to cream, and betrays in growth and habit its relation to the great Druschki.
Croibier 1937. *D. VG. NF. GPB. EB. White. B.E.G. June-Sept. Hardy.*

LONGICUSPIS (with long spines) (S.), Western Asia, makes a very pretty bush with red stems, shining green leaves, red beneath, and bears large creamy-white flowers followed by round red fruits.
Bert —. E. TG. SF. GPC. — White. S. June. Hardy.

LONG JOHN SILVER (Hybrid setigera) is the attractive name of an attractive climber of great vigour allied to the beautiful Doubloons, which has white flowers instead of the golden-yellow of that variety.
Horvath 1934. *D. C. F. GPC. — White. A.P.Pr.W. June-September.*

LORD ALLENBY (H.T.) begins another titled series, and is another red rose with little to commend it except its exceptionally double flowers borne upon strong stems.
Dickson 1923. *D. MG. SF. GPB. — — B. June-September.*

LORD CASTLEREAGH (H.T.) has medium-size semi-double flowers of crimson, borne in groups on strong stems on vigorous plants with dark green foliage.
Dickson 1927. *D. VG. VF. GPB. — — B.G.St. June-September. Hardy.*

LORD CHARLEMONT (H.T.) has high-pointed large very double flowers of good shape, crimson-scarlet in colour, borne on long stems on moderately vigorous plants with dark green foliage.
McGredy 1922. *D. MG. NF. GPB. — — B.E.G.St. June-September.*

LORD LONSDALE (H.T.) has large pointed very double flowers of daffodil-yellow, borne on long strong stems on moderately vigorous plants with ample good foliage.
Dickson 1933. *D. MG. VF. GPB. — — B.G. June-September. Hardy.*

LORD PENZANCE (see R. rubiginosa).

LORD ROSSMORE (H.T.) produces its very large, very double pale cream flowers, edged with rose-pink, in clusters on very vigorous erect plants with dull bronze-green leaves.
Campbell Hall 1930. *D. VG. SF. GPB. EB. — B.G. June-Sept. Hardy.*

LORD STAIR (H.T.) has large full double cupped flowers of intense crimson-scarlet, borne upon long stems on upright and branching plants with large green foliage resistant to disease.
Smith 1930. *D. VG. TF. GPB. — — B.G. June-September. Hardy.*

LORNA (H.T.) has double flowers of attractive shape of clear orange flushed with pink, borne upon vigorous plants with upright growth and leaves of mid-green.
B. R. Cant 1936. *D. VG. F. GPB. EB. — B.E.G. June-September. Hardy.*

LOS ANGELES (Pernetiana) produces its large double flame-pink and coral flowers on long stems; and such is the construction of the flower that each one produced is superlatively good. Habit is vigorous and upright, foliage green and subject at times to black spot.
Howard & Smith 1916. *D. VG. SF. GPB. EB.* 621/3-618-603/1. *B.G.E.*
[*June-Sept. Hardy. Pl.* 44.

LOUISE CRETTÉ (H.P.) is of the style of Frau Karl Druschki, of which it is a descendant, and produces its huge high-centred white very double flowers each upon a long strong stem, from a vigorous plant with dark green foliage.
Chambard 1915. *D. VG. SF. GPB. EB. — White. E.G. June-Aug. Hardy.*

LOUISE KRAUSE (H.T.) has very large double high-centred flowers of pale yellow flushed with flesh, borne upon vigorous erect plants with glossy dark green foliage resistant to disease.
Krause 1930. *D. VG. MF. GPB. — — B.C. June-September. Hardy.*

LOUIS WALTER (H.T.) has large, very double, deep golden-yellow flowers freely produced upon vigorous plants with polished green foliage.
Mallerin 1938. *D. VG. SF. GPB. EB. — B.E.G. June-September. Hardy.*

LOVE (Climbing H.T.) has very large semi-double flowers of bright crimson-scarlet, borne in clusters of from three to five on very vigorous canes with good foliage.
Mallerin 1935. *D. C. VF. GPE. — — P.W. June-August. Hardy.*

LUCIE MARIE (H.T.) has large full wide-petalled flowers of buttercup-yellow shaded with salmon, borne upon long stiff stems on vigorous and branching plants with ample large glossy dark green foliage.
Dickson 1930. *D. VG. MF. GPB. — — B.G. June-September. Hardy.*

Lucy Bertram (see R. rubiginosa).

Lucy Nicholas (H.T.) has large very double flowers of reddish coral-salmon with the reverse of the petals yellow, borne on long strong stems on vigorous plants with glossy bronze-green foliage.
Mallerin 1935. *D. VG. F. GPB. —— B.G. June-September. Hardy.*

Luis Brinas (Pernetiana) has long coppery buds which open to high-centred orange and old-rose flowers of cupped shape, borne upon long strong stems. Growth is very vigorous and erect, and foliage of glossy dark bronzy-green.
Dot 1934. *D. TG. VF. GPB. —— B.G. 609/1, 607/3. June-Sept. Hardy.*
[*Pl.* 75.

Lulu (H.T.) has large semi-double flowers of salmon-orange borne in groups on long strong stems. Growth is of moderate height but vigorous, and foliage is bright glossy green.
Easlea 1920. *D. MG. SF. GPC. —— B.G. June-September. Hardy.*

Luna (H.T.) produces its high-pointed large double pale-yellow flowers on long stems. Growth is very vigorous, foliage dark green and resistant to disease.
Poulsen 1925. *D. TG. VF. GPC. —— B.G. June-September. Hardy.*

lutea (yellow) (S.), Eastern Europe, makes a large bush with brown stems and very sharp thorns, and with leaves divided into five to nine leaflets with a rather unpleasant smell. The large single flowers of deep golden-yellow share this characteristic. The Austrian Briars are all subject to black spot and should be planted separately. Pruning consists of cutting out the dead wood.
Miller (*known in England in* 1596). *D. EC. NF. Detailed. 3. S. June.*
[*Hardy. Pl.* 2.

lutea var. bicolor (S.) is also known as lutea var. punicea, is similar in growth and habit but has single flowers of bright copper-red with a yellow reverse.
Gerard 1596. *D. EG. NF. Detailed above.* 18/1. *S. June. Hardy. Pl.* 2.

Mabel Francis (H.T.) has high-centred blooms of glowing pink, sweetly perfumed, and is disease-resistant and of sturdy growth.
Bees Ltd. 1943. *D. MG. MF. GPB. —— B. June-September. Hardy.*

Mabel Morse (H.T.) has full double large well-shaped flowers of rich golden-yellow, borne singly on good stems from moderately vigorous plants with glossy bronze-green disease-resistant foliage.
McGredy 1922. *D. MG. MF. GPB. EB.* 3/2 *and* 603/1. *B.E.G.St. June-*
[*Sept. Hardy. Pl.* 43 & 49.

Mabel Turner (H.T.) produces its large very double flowers of salmon-pink on long strong stems. Growth is vigorous and foliage dull green and resistant to disease, but the buds fail to open in wet weather.
Hugh Dickson 1923. *D. VG. F. GPB. EB. — June-September. Hardy.*

MACARTNEY ROSE (see R. bracteata).

MACOUNII (comm.) (S.), Western U.S.A., makes an upright-growing bush with red wood and pale green foliage, grey beneath, made up of from five to seven leaflets, and bears single flowers about one and a half inches across, of rose-pink, either singly or in groups.
Greene —. D. TG. F. GPG. —— S. July.

MACRANTHA (large-flowered) (S.), W. Europe, is reputed to be a hybrid between R. gallica × R. canina, and makes a very large specimen bush with long whiplike canes and bright green leaves made up of from five to seven leaflets, which bears many very pale pink, rose-flushed, large single flowers of four inches in diameter, followed by bright red fruits.
Desportes —. D. EG. VF. GPG. —— S. May-June. Very hardy.

MACROPHYLLA (large-leaved) (S.), China, is a variable plant, but generally conforming in the following: height about eight feet, large leaves made up of nine to eleven leaflets, single flowers of about three inches in diameter, borne in large clusters. The colour of the flowers varies from white to red, and they are followed by large inverted-pear-shaped fruits with bristly skins of bright red.
Lindley —. D. EG. SF. GPG. —— S. June. Hardy.

MADAME ABEL CHATENAY (H.T.) has high-pointed well-shaped flowers of pale salmon-pink with a deeper centre and with a deeper reverse, borne singly on long stems. Growth is very vigorous and erect, and foliage green and ample; is suitable for towns.
Pernet-Ducher 1895. D. VG. VF. GPB. — 523. B.G.St.Pot. June-Sept.
[Hardy.

MADAME ALBERT BARBIER (H.P.) has large double open flowers of pale salmon with a deeper centre of orange-yellow. Growth is vigorous and erect and flowers are continuously borne. Foliage is glossy mid-green.
Barbier 1824. D. VG. SF. GPB. —— B.G. June-August. Hardy.

MADAME ALBERT GILLES (H.T.) has large very double persistent flowers of light coral-pink, borne singly on long strong stems on plants of vigorous erect growth, with good mid-green foliage.
Mallerin 1934. D. VG. SF. GPB. —— B.G. June-September. Hardy.

MADAME ALFRED CARRIÈRE (see R. Noisettiana).

MADAME ANTHONY KLUIS (polyantha pompon) has clustered heads of large semi-double flowers of salmon-pink flushed with orange, borne upon vigorous erect and bushy plants with bright green foliage.
Kluis 1924. D. VG. NF. GPF. —— B. June-September. Hardy.

MADAME BUTTERFLY (H.T.) is one of the world's greatest roses. A sport from Ophelia, its long high-pointed open double flowers of tender pink, shaded with apricot, are produced more effectively when extensive disbudding is undertaken. Foliage is large, green and tough, and, though subject to occasional mildew and black spot, it has a definite place in any representative collection of garden roses. Growth is vigorous and erect, and good flowers can be cut at all times and in all places.

Hill 1918. *D. VG. VF. GPB.* — 427/1. *B.G.St.Pot. June-Sept. Hardy.* [*Pl.* 12, 47 & 58.

MADAME CAROLINE TESTOUT (see Caroline Testout).

MADAME CHAMOUTON-MURGUE (H.T.) has very large, very double, cupped flowers of carmine, shaded with orange-red, borne on long tough stems. Growth is vigorous, branching and upright, and the attractive green foliage resistant to disease.

Chambard 1925. *D. M. G. BF. GPB. EB.* — *B.E.G. June-Sept. Hardy.*

MADAME CHARLES MALLERIN (H.T.) has double camellia-shaped flowers of coral-vermilion with a yellow reflex, borne on long strong stems on plants of vigorous erect habit with green glossy foliage.

Mallerin 1939. *D. VG. MF. GPB.* — 19/1-618. *B.G. June-Sept. Hardy.*

MADAME COCHET-COCHET (H.T.) has large moderately full flowers of coppery rose-pink shaded with coral, borne on strong stems on vigorous and upright bushes with fine glossy green foliage.

Mallerin 1934. *D. VG. SF. GPB.* — — *B.G. June-September. Hardy.*

MADAME DE LA VALETTE (see R. chinensis).

MADAME EDMOND LABBÉ (H.T.) has full high-pointed flowers of golden-buff shaded with orange, borne upon upright plants of branching habit with dark red foliage and red wood.

Mallerin 1938. *D. VG. VF. GPB.* — — *B.G. June-September. Hardy.*

MADAME EDOUARD HERRIOT (Pernetiana) has moderately full flowers of bright terracotta passing to strawberry-rose, borne on good stems from vigorous plants, with glossy green foliage and many thorns. Is unfortunately liable to black spot.

Pernet-Ducher 1913. *D. VG. SF. GPB.* — — *B.G.St.Pot. June-Sept. Hardy.*

MADAME EMILE DALOZ (H.T.) has very large double flowers of paeony-pink, with the backs of the petals of clear rose-pink, borne on vigorous stems on plants of strong bushy and erect habit.

Sauvageot 1934. *D. VG. VF. GPB.* — — *B.G. June-September. Very hardy.*

MADAME EUGÈNE RESAL (see R. chinensis).

MADAME GEORGES BRUANT (see R. rugosa).

MADAME GRÉGOIRE STAECHELIN (Climbing H.T.) is an outstanding climber and has high-centred large flowers of pale coral-pink shaded with pink, borne upon the laterals from exceptionally vigorous canes with large dark green mildew-proof foliage.

Dot 1927. *D. C. VG. GPE.* — — *A.P.W. June. Hardy.*

Cecil (Pernetiana) ABEF
Poulsen's Pink (Hybrid Polyantha) CDE
Poulsen's Yellow (Hybrid Polyantha) DEJKLNOP
Yvonne Rabier (Hybrid Polyantha) GHMQ

Hybrid Polyantha Rose, Perle d'Or

MADAME HÉLÈNE PARMENTIER (H.T.) produces its semi-double nasturtium-red flowers, which pale to salmon-pink with age, with the reverse of the petals of orange-yellow, on long stems from strong branching plants with large shining deep-green foliage.
Sauvageot 1935. *D. VG. SF. GPB. — — B.G. June-September. Hardy.*

MADAME HENRI GUILLOT (H.T.) is an attractive rose with high-centred flowers, opening round and flat, rather like a camellia, of deep salmon-pink flushed with orange, borne upon vigorous erect plants with glossy green foliage.
Mallerin 1937. *D. VG. MF. GPB. EB.* 19/2, 622, 18/2. *B.G. June-Sept.*
[*Hardy. Pl.* 54.

MADAME ISAAC PEREIRE (see R. bourbonia).

MADAME J. CROIBIER (Pernetiana) produces its persistent flowers of fine shapely form on long stems from moderately vigorous erect plants. Flowers are double and of salmon-pink shaded with carmine with a yellow base.
Gaujard 1936. *D. MG. SF. GPB. — — B.G. June-September.*

MADAME J. D. EISELE (H.T.) has shapely double pointed flowers of bright cerise shaded with scarlet, borne on moderately vigorous erect bushes with good green foliage.
Howard & Smith 1935. *D. MG. F. GPB. — — B.G. June-Sept. Hardy.*

MADAME JEAN GAUJARD (Pernetiana) has long pointed buds developing into shapely high-centred double flowers of golden-yellow shading to orange at the centre, borne singly upon long strong stems from vigorous plants with good glossy green disease-resistant foliage.
Pernet-Ducher 1935. *D. VG. MF. GPB. —* 407/3 *and* 416. *B.G. June-Sept.*
[*Hardy. Pl.* 51.

MADAME JENNY (Climbing polyantha) bears clusters of small globular pale rose-pink flowers upon vigorous canes with dark green foliage.
Nonin 1926. *D. C. MF. GPI. — — A.P.Pr. June. Hardy.*

MADAME J. M. FRUCTUS (H.T.) has moderately large high-centred double flowers of soft carmine shaded with salmon on a yellow base. Growth is moderately vigorous and habit branching stems.
Chambard 1935. *D. MG. F. GPB. — — B.G. June-September. Hardy.*

MADAME JOSEPH PERRAUD (H.T.) has long pointed buds developing to very large, double full flowers with high centres, of deep orange often shaded at the edges with shell-pink, borne on long strong erect stems. Growth is vigorous, upright and branching, and foliage large and polished.
Gaujard 1934. *D. VG. MF. GPB. EB.* 10/3, 13/2. *B.E.G.St. June-Sept.*
[*Hardy.*

Madame Jules Bouché (H.T.) has attractively shaped flowers, fully double and fragrant, borne upon long strong stems, of clear white shaded in the centre with cream. Growth is vigorous and upright, foliage mid-green and flowering continuous. Flowers are inclined to ball in wet weather, and foliage is subject on occasions to mildew, and black spot.
Croibier 1910. *D. VG. MF. GPB. — White. B.G. June-Sept. Hardy. Pl.*47.

Madame Jules Guérin (see Président Charles Hain).

Madame Julien Potin (see R. rugosa).

Madame Louis Lens (H.T.) has very large, very double, high-pointed flowers of pure white, borne upon long strong stems, produced by vigorous plants with upright and branching growth and large green foliage.
Lens 1932. *D. VG. MF. GPB. EB. White. B.E.G. June-Sept. Hardy.*

Madame Lucien Villeminot (see R. rugosa).

Madame Nicolas Aussel (H.T.) has very large double flowers resembling those of Madame Ed. Herriot, of salmon-yellow flushed with carmine. Growth is vigorous, erect and branching; foliage deep green and resistant to disease and flowering continuous.
Pernet-Ducher 1930. *D. VG. VF. GPB. — — B.G. June-September. Hardy.*

Madame Noël Le Mire (H.T.) carries its semi-double bright crimson flowers with yellow reflexes in clusters and is pleasantly fragrant. Growth is very dwarf but vigorous and foliage glossy and green.
Sauvageot 1934. *D. SG. F. GPA. — — B.G. June-September. Hardy.*

Madame Pierre Koechlin (H.T.) bears large, full, double high-pointed flowers of clear pink, shaded with deep pink and orange, with the reverse of the petals of pale pink and yellow. Growth is vigorous and the foliage plentiful and of an attractive green.
Sauvageot 1934. *D. TG. NF. GPC. — — B.G. June-September. Hardy.*

Madame Pierre S. du Pont (H.T.) has moderate-size semi-double flowers of bright golden yellow paling with age, borne in profusion on vigorous plants with plentiful deep green foliage which is resistant to disease.
Mallerin 1930. *D. VG. MF. GPB. — — B.G. June-September. Hardy.*

Madame Plantier (see R. damascena).

Madame Raoul Fauran (H.T.) produces its clusters of semi-double very deep pink flowers shaded with crimson-purple in almost unending succession. Foliage is green, plentiful and attractive, and borne upon vigorous upright and branching stems.
Sauvageot 1934. *D. VG. MF. GPE. — — B.G. June-September. Hardy.*

Madame Ravary (H.T.) is an old favourite with medium-size flowers of orange-yellow, full and double, borne on good stems from vigorous plants of bushy growth with deep green foliage.
Pernet-Ducher 1900. *D. VG. SF. GPB. — — B.G. June-September. Hardy.*

MADAME RAYMOND GAUJARD (H.T.) is also known as Olympiad, and though it has recently fallen from grace it remains a good rose. The double shapely flowers of crimson-scarlet shade to orange-yellow at the base. Habit is moderately vigorous with deep green attractive foliage.
Pernet-Ducher 1931. *D. MG. SF. GPB. EB. — B.E.G. June-Sept. Hardy.*

MADELEINE MONOD (H.T.) has very large double high-centred flowers, salmon with the reverse of carmine, borne upon strong stems from robust plants with bronze-green leaves.
Chambard 1939. *D. VG. MF. GPB. — — B.G. June-September. Hardy.*

MADGE PRIOR (Hybrid polyantha) has large clusters of single flowers of bright claret-red with distinguishing white eyes. Is vigorous in growth, with dark green foliage resistant to mildew, and is suitable for bedding and low hedges.
Prior 1934. *D. VG. SF. GPC. — — B.G.H. June-September. Hardy.*

MADGE WHIPP (H.T.) has medium-size double flowers of bright cerise, composed of stout petals on strong stems. Growth is robust, erect and branching, foliage is deep olive-green, resistant to disease, and the flowering period long. In artificial light the flowers appear intense scarlet.
Bees 1935. *D. VG. F. GPB. — 24. B.G. June-September. Hardy. Pl. 38.*

MADGE WILDFIRE (H.T.) produces its brilliant cerise flowers, which are of exceptional size and of fine shape, on long strong stems from vigorous plants with attractive green foliage, and is exceptionally good for exhibition purposes.
Dobbie 1932. *D. VG. VF. GPB. EB. 24. E.G. June-September. Hardy.*

MAGNIFIQUE (polyantha pompon) makes shapely vigorous bushes with pleasing glossy green foliage, and bears large trusses of large cupped semi-double frilled flowers of bright pink reminiscent of Dorothy Perkins.
De Ruyter 1927. *D. VG. NF. GPF. — — B. June-September. Hardy.*

MAGNUM PERNET (see Président Charles Hain).

MAIDEN'S BLUSH (see R. alba).

MAID MARIAN (H.T.) is a good rose with large many-petalled flowers of bright carmine-rose, the reverse being of pale pink. The wood is freely produced, with many thorns and good light green foliage. Flowering is frequent and prolonged.
Therkildsen 1920. *D. TG. SF. GPB. — — B.G. June-September. Very hardy.*

MAID MARION (Hybrid Musk) has the redeeming feature of differing by one vowel from the foregoing. A pleasing shrubby plant with glossy green foliage on vigorous and upright growth and bearing very large clusters of semi-double medium-size flowers of white, blushing, correctly, with age!
Pemberton 1930. *D. EG. VF. GPG. — — S.H. June-September. Hardy.*

MAID OF KENT (H.T.) has perfectly formed flowers with gracefully reflexing petals of pale samon-pink borne upon vigorous upright and branching plants with green foliage.
Archer 1930. *D. VG. TF. GPB. — — B.G. June-September. Hardy.*

MAISON PERNET-DUCHER (H.T.) is an exceptionally attractive rose, with large, full double flowers of golden-yellow, with veins clearly defined in copper-red. Habit is vigorous, erect and branching, and foliage dark green, glossy and resistant.
Pernet-Ducher 1934. *D. VG. SF. GPG. — — B.G. June-September. Hardy.*

MAJORCA (H.T.) is a modern double, crimson-scarlet rose with large wide-petalled flowers on vigorous plants with varnished red-bronze foliage.
Dot 1938. *D. VG. VF. GPB. EB. — B.E.G. June-September. Hardy.*

MAJOR SHELLEY (H.T.) is an exceptionally good, nearly double rose, with attractively shaped buds of bright crimson-scarlet, opening well. Growth is vigorous, erect and branching, and foliage dark green. This variety is good in artificial light and is exceptionally good in autumn.
Howard & Smith 1938. *D. VG. VF. GPB. — 822/2. B.G.St. June-Sept. [Hardy.*

MALAR ROS (H.T.) has large double, many-petalled, cupped flowers of deep crimson and blood-red, borne upon long strong stems, lasting well but fading in hot sun. Growth is vigorous, foliage is dark green.
Kordes 1932. *D. VG. F. GPB. EB. — B.E.G.St. June-September. Hardy.*

MAMA PECHTOLD (H.T.) produces its long pointed buds on long strong stems, opening to shapely double flowers of rosy salmon-pink. Growth is vigorous and erect, and foliage green and ample.
Verschuren 1938. *D. VG. SF. GPB. — — B.G. June-September. Hardy.*

MARCHIONESS OF LINLITHGOW (H.T.) has finely shaped flowers of spiral form of very deep crimson, outstanding in its intensity, borne upon good stems on plants of moderate height but of free bushy growth. The green foliage is unfortunately subject to mildew late in the year.
Dobbie 1930. *D. MG. VF. GPB. — — B.G. June-September. Hardy.*

MARCIA STANHOPE (H.T.) produces its large very double, white, rounded flowers in small groups. Growth is vigorous, upright and bushy, with ample green foliage, unfortunately subject to mildew in autumn.
Lilley 1922. *D. VG. VF. GPB. — White. B.G. June-September. Hardy.*

MARÉCHAL LYAUTEY (H.T.) has large shapely flowers with many petals of deep red borne upon stout stems on vigorous and upright plants with dark bronze-green leaves.
Croibier 1931. *D. VG. VF. GPB. — — B.G. June-September. Hardy.*

MARÉCHAL NIEL (Climbing Noisettiana) is still one of the outstanding climbers in cultivation, and is best grown under glass in inland districts or on sheltered walls elsewhere. The large full double, golden-yellow flowers are of excellent shape. Growth is vigorous and foliage of an attractive green colour.
Pradel 1864. *D. C. VF. GPE. — — C.W.H.Cut. June-September.*

MARÉCHAL PÉTAIN (H.T.) has fully double flowers of good shape of blood-red, borne on long stems on plants of vigorous growth, with good green foliage.
Reymond 1926. *D. VG. VF. GPB. — — B.G. June-September. Hardy.*

MARGARET ANNE BAXTER (H.T.) is one of the outstanding white roses. The large many-petalled globular full flowers are nicely reflexed with petals of good substance, and borne singly on long strong stems. Growth is upright, branching and vigorous, and the ample foliage is dark green.
Smith 1928. *D. VG. SF. GPB. EB. White. B.E.G.St. June-Sept. Hardy.*

MARGARET DICKSON (H.P.) has a large double flower of medium height, of creamy-white deepening at the heart and base to pale flesh-pink. It is exceptionally vigorous in growth and has large green leaves subject at times to mildew.
Dickson 1891. *D. VG. SF. GPA. — — B. June-September. Hardy.*

MARGARET DICKSON HAMILL (H.T.) makes a vigorous, upright, bushy plant with dark green foliage, bearing upon long strong stems perfectly shaped pale straw-yellow flowers with elegantly reflexed outer petals the exterior of which is tinted with pale carmine. Is one of the outstanding roses for town cultivation.
Dickson 1915. *D. VG. SF. GPB. EB. — B.E.G.St. June-Sept. Hardy.*

MARGARET McGREDY (H.T.) has very large globular, double, high-centred flowers of geranium-lake, borne several on a stout stem on plants of exceptionally vigorous growth, with large green, disease-resistant foliage. The colour fades as the bloom ages, but is always pleasant, and the flowers are produced with regularity and generosity.
McGredy 1927. *D. VG. NF. GPB. EB. 26, 025/2, 020/1. B.E.G.St. June-*
[Sept. Hardy. Pl. 55.

MARGARET TURNBULL (Climbing H.T.) is a charming climbing rose of Australian origin, with strong canes, with green foliage and double, high-centred, large flowers of salmon flushed with yellow.
Clark 1931. *D. C. F. GPG. — — C.P.W. June-September. Hardy.*

MARGUERITE CHAMBARD (H.T.) has large, full, semi-globular flowers of geranium-red, a colour which is well maintained, borne upon strong stems on very vigorous erect branching plants, with green, disease-resistant foliage.
Chambard 1928. *D. VG. VF. GPB. — — G.B. June-September. Hardy.*

MARIANNE (H.T.) has large fully double flowers with high centres of copper-yellow flushed with pink and red, borne upon vigorous bushy plants with good green foliage.
Krause 1933. *D. VG. VF. GPB. —— B.G. June-September. Hardy.*

MARI DOT (Pernetiana) is a vigorous plant with large shining green leaves producing its flowers in groups on strong stems. The buds are brilliant orange-red flushed with yellow, and open to golden-salmon which pales to pink, and stand all weathers with equanimity.
Dot 1927. *D. VG. SF. GPB. —— B.G. June-September. Hardy.*

MARIE GOUCHAULT (wichuraiana rambler) throws up long strong canes of greenish-bronze wood, long laterals and long sprays of double flowers of light red which pale to deep salmon-pink. The attractive shining green foliage is proof against mildew.
Turbat 1927. *D. C. NF. GPI. —— A.P.Pr. June. Hardy.*

MARIE MAASS (H.T.) has very large, very double flowers of ivory white, borne singly upon good strong stems. Growth is vigorous, erect, and branching, and foliage abundant and green.
Maass 1927. *D. VG. MF. GPB. EB. White. B.E.G. June-Sept. Hardy.*

MARIE VAN HOUTTE (T.) has large many-petalled flowers of good high-centred form of lemon-yellow decked with rose, borne singly on somewhat weak stems on vigorous plants with green foliage. Best grown against a south or west wall.
Ducher 1871. *D. EG. TF. GPC. or GPG. —— W. June-September.*

MARIPOSA (polyantha pompon) is an improved form of Orange King with very small clustered flowers of bright orange-red which does not revert to green, and opens well in all weathers. Foliage green, growth vigorous but dwarf.
Allen 1927. *D. SG. NF. GPF. —— B. June-September. Hardy.*

MARJORIE FOSTER (wichuraiana rambler) has large clusters of very double, cupped flowers of crimson-scarlet of medium size, similar to those of Excelsa, borne on moderately vigorous canes with good green foliage not subject to mildew. Begins to flower in late July.
Burbage 1939. *D. C. NF. GPI. GPL. —— A.P.Pr.C.Wst. July-August.*
[Hardy.

MARRETII (comm.) (S.) is a queer bush from the island of Sakhalin with dark-purple wood and green leaves made up of from five to seven leaflets, and with small clusters of rose-pink flowers, followed by attractive red fruits.
Léveillé —. *D. TG. NF. GPC. —— S. June. Hardy.*

MARVLOUS (H.T.) produces its extremely fragrant, large, double, crimson flowers on long strong stems. Growth is very vigorous, upright and branching, the foliage dark green and leathery, and flowering is long and continuous.
B. R. Cant 1931. *D. VG. VF. GPB. EB. — B.E.G. June-Sept. Hardy.*

Mary Hart (H.T.) is a red sport from Talisman, and produces its carmine-red flowers similarly. The large pointed double flowers are borne on long strong stems. Growth is vigorous and foliage glossy and green but subject to mildew.

Hart 1931. *D. VG. VF. GPB. — — B.G. June-September. Hardy.*

Mary Hicks (wichuraiana rambler) has double flowers, rather larger than those of Excelsa, of bright carmine-crimson, borne in large sprays on moderately vigorous canes with good green foliage.

Hicks 1927. *D. C. MF. GPH. GPL. — — A.P.Pr.C.Wst. July-August.*
[*Hardy.*

Mary Lovett (wichuraiana climber) has large, double, snow-white flowers on vigorous climbing canes with bright green, disease-resistant foliage.

Van Fleet 1915. *D. C. F. GPE. — — White. C.A.P. June-Sept. Hardy.*

Mary MacHutchin (Climbing polyantha pompon) has large clusters of bright crimson-scarlet flowers borne upon very strong canes with good bright green foliage.

B. R. Cant 1935. *D. C. SF. GPF. — — A.P.Pr. June-September. Hardy.*

Mary Wallace (wichuraiana rambler) has large semi-double flowers of clear bright rosy-pink borne in small groups. The very vigorous canes are foliated with glossy green, disease-resistant foliage.

Van Fleet 1924. *D. C. MF. GPF. — — A.P.Pr.W. June. Hardy.*

Matador (H.T.) is termed an improved Etoile de Hollande, and almost justly! The crimson-scarlet flowers are large, double and of good shape, intensely fragrant and borne upon vigorous bushy plants with large, tough, green foliage.

Van Rossem 1935. *D. VG. VF. GPB. EB. — B.E.C.St. June-Sept. Hardy.*

Maud Cuming (H.T.) is moderately vigorous, bushy and of dwarf habit, with dark green glossy foliage proof against disease. The large double flowers are borne singly upon long stems and are of good shape, and of coral-pink veined with orange, but ball badly in wet weather.

Dickson 1923. *D. MG. SF. GPB. EB. — B.E. June-September. Hardy.*

Maud E. Gladstone (Hybrid polyantha) has groups of small, double, well-rounded flowers of pale clear pink shaded with coral and flushed with bright yellow. Growth is vigorous, erect and branching, with deep green glossy foliage.

Bees 1926. *D. VG. F. GPG. — — B.G. June-September. Hardy.*

Max Graf (see R. rugosa).

Max Krause (H.T.) has long red-gold buds opening to high-centred very double flowers of clear golden-yellow, borne singly upon long strong stems. The dark green, disease-resistant leaves, borne upon vigorous and erect plants, afford the excellent contrast needed to make it an exceptional rose.

Krause 1930. *D. VG. MF. GPB. EB.* 603/1-604. *B.E.G. June-Sept. Hardy.*
[*Pl.* 50.

MAYFAIR (H.T.) has very large, shapely, double flowers of deep pink, borne on erect strong stems on very vigorous and branching plants with bronze-green foliage.
Bentall 1935. *D. VG. MF. GPB. — — B.G. June-September. Hardy.*

MAYOR CERMAK (H.T.) has very large, shapely, double flowers of deep dark red with even darker shading, borne upon long strong stems. Growth is vigorous and erect, with attractive foliage.
Bohm 1932. *D. VG. MF. GPB. — — B.G. June-September. Hardy.*

MAY WETTERN (H.T.) has large, double, high-centred flowers of bright salmon-pink with a rose-pink reverse borne upon somewhat limp stems. Growth is very vigorous, upright and branching, and foliage large and green.
Dickson 1928. *D. TG. MF. GPB. EB. — B.E.G.St. June-Sept. Hardy.*

McGREDY'S CORAL (H.T.) is an almost indescribable colour basically of coral-pink and salmon with a suffusion of copper. The flowers are large with pointed centres and borne on long stems. Growth is vigorous, erect and branching, and foliage good.
McGredy 1936. *D. VG. SF. GPB. — 024/2, 625/2. B.G. June-Sept. Hardy.*
[*Pl.* 57.

McGREDY'S GEM (H.T.) has moderate-size flowers with full, double, high-pointed flowers of pale pink shaded with white and gold, borne on long stems. Habit is vigorous, erect and branching, and flowering is exceptionally free.
McGredy 1933. *D. VG. TF. GPC. — — G.St. June-September. Hardy.*

McGREDY'S IVORY (H.T.) is a vigorous erect plant with glossy green leaves. The creamy-white large fully double flowers are tinged with yellow at the centre, and are borne variously upon strong stems.
McGredy 1929. *D. VG. SF. GPB. EB.* 403/3 *to* 2/2. *B.E.G.St. June-Sept.*
[*Hardy. Pl.* 45.

McGREDY'S ORANGE (H.T.) has semi-double high-pointed flowers of bright yellow within; outside the petals are orange flushed with salmon. Habit of growth is vigorous and erect, and foliage is glossy bronze and not subject to mildew.
McGredy 1936. *D. VG. TF. GPB. — — B. June-September. Hardy.*

McGREDY'S PEACH (H.T.) has cupped-shape double flowers of creamy-flesh colour flushed with salmon-pink. Growth is strong and upright.
McGredy 1933. *D. VG. TF. GPB. EB. — B.E.G. June-Sept. Hardy.*

McGREDY'S PINK (H.T.) is outstandingly good in its vigorous, erect and branching growth. The flowers, which are fully double, are of good shape, of bright rose-pink shaded with gold, and are freely borne, persisting for a long period under good weather conditions.
McGredy 1936. *D. VG. MF. GPB. EB.* 18/3 *to* 20/2. *B.E.G.St. June-Oct.*
[*Hardy. Pl.* 79.

Three Hybrid Tea Roses

Phyllis Gold **CDFGH**

Dickson's Perfection **FJK** Mrs. G. A. Van Rossem **LMPQ**

Pernetiana Rose, President Herbert Hoover

McGREDY's PRIDE (H.T.) has large many-petalled flowers, perfectly formed, of orange-salmon, with the outside of deep yellow flushed with flesh-pink, borne upon long strong stems. Growth is vigorous, erect and branching, with green foliage resistant to disease. The flowers are undamaged by rain, and last well.
McGredy 1934. *D. VG. MF. GPB. EB. — B.E.G.St. June-Sept. Hardy.*

McGREDY's SCARLET (H.T.) seems variable in its colour, but generally produces its large, full, double flowers of light crimson shaded with orange on long strong stems. Habit of growth erect and branching, with dull green foliage.
McGredy 1930. *D. VG. MF. GPB. EB. — B.E.G. June-Sept. Hardy.*

McGREDY's SUNSET (H.T.) has shapely flowers of medium size, full and double, of buttercup-yellow, shaded with gold and flushed at times at the edges of the petals with crimson. Growth is moderately vigorous and erect and the foliage bronze-green and resistant to disease.
McGredy 1937. *D. MG. SF. GPB. — — B. June-September. Hardy.*

McGREDY's TRIUMPH (H.T.) has high-centred globular, spiral, exceptionally large flowers with reflexed petals of crimson-pink, borne on long strong stems singly and in clusters. The outside of the petals is flushed with orange at the base. Growth is outstandingly vigorous and the foliage deep red-bronze and free of disease. The flowers are freely produced over a long period and are good in all weather.
McGredy 1934. *D. VG. MF. GPB. — 21/2-19/2. B.G. June-Sept. Hardy.*
[*Pl.* 74.

McGREDY's WONDER (H.T.) has large semi-double to double flowers, with high-pointed centres of coppery-orange with orange-scarlet reverse. Growth is erect and vigorous, and foliage is shining pale bronze-green.
McGredy 1934. *D. VG. VF. GPB. — — B.G. June-Sept. Hardy. Pl.* 56.

McGREDY's YELLOW (H.T.) has cupped double flowers of pale yellow of excellent shape and size, produced in abundance over a large period. Growth is upright and vigorous and the foliage, which is not liable to disease, is glossy dark bronze-green.
McGredy 1933. *D. VG. F. GPB. EB. — B.E.G.St. June-Sept. Hardy.*
[*Pl.* 32 & 45.

MELINA (black stem) (S.), Western U.S.A., is a bush of approximately three feet in height with many branches, leaves composed of seven leaflets, and single rose flowers of about two inches in diameter, borne singly.
Greene —. *D. VG. SF. GPG. — — S. June. Hardy.*

MELITA (wichuraiana rambler) has large double flowers of deep coral-pink borne in small trusses upon moderately vigorous growth, with glossy green, disease-resistant foliage. The flowers persist and the colour lasts for a long period.
Easlea 1934. *D. C. SF. GPI. — — P.Pr. July-August. Hardy.*

MÉMÉ BUY (H.T.) has large, double, cupped flowers of reddish-pink shaded with coral, striped lightly with gold. Growth is erect and vigorous and foliage deep bronze-green.
Chambard 1935. *D. VG. MF. GPB. — — B.G. June-September. Hardy.*

MEMORIAL Rose (see R. Wichuraiana).

MEMORY (H.T.) produces its large high-pointed, double, silvery-pink flowers on long strong stems. Growth is vigorous and erect, and foliage is large and deep green.
B. R. Cant 1933. *D. VG. F. GPB. EB. — B.E.G. June-September. Hardy.*

MERCEDES GALLART (Climbing H.T.) is an exceptionally strong climber with large double flowers of two shades of deep pink and glossy green foliage.
Munné 1932. *D. C. VF. GPE. — — A.P.Pr.W. June-September. Hardy.*

MERMAID (see R. bracteata). *Pl.* 4.

MEVROUW G. A. VAN ROSSEM (see Mrs. G. A. van Rossem).

MEVROUW VAN STRATEN VAN NES (see Van Nes).

MICRANTHA (with small flowers) (S.), Western U.S.A., makes a much-branched bush of some six feet in height, with green leaves made up of from five to seven leaflets, and groups of small single flowers of pale pink.
Smith —. *D. EG. SF. GPG. — — S. June. Hardy.*

MICROPHYLLA is R. Roxburghii, which see.

MILDRED CANT (H.T.) has large, double, sweetly scented, pointed flowers of dark crimson, borne upon strong stems on erect and vigorous plants with large green foliage.
B. R. Cant 1935. *D. VG. VF. GPB. — — B.G. June-September. Hardy.*

MINISTR RASIN (Ministre des Finances Rasin) (H.T.) produces its large double flowers of carmine-rose on long strong stems. Growth is vigorous and erect and foliage green and resistant to disease.
Bohm 1930. *D. VG. F. GPB. — — B.G. June-September. Hardy.*

MINNA KORDES (Hybrid polyantha), known in U.S.A. as World's Fair, is a dwarf, semi-double, dark crimson rose bearing its flowers in clusters, and paling with age. Growth is vigorous, bushy and upright, with dark green foliage.
Kordes 1938. *D. VG. VF. GPG. — — B.H. June-September. Hardy.*

MINNEHAHA (wichuraiana rambler) bears its small, double, deep-pink flowers in large clusters on exceptionally vigorous canes. The flowers pale with age, and foliage is glossy deep green.
Walsh 1905. *D. C. SF. GPH. — — A.P.Pr.Wst. June-July. Hardy.*

MINUTIFOLIA (with tiny leaves) (S.), S.W. U.S.A., is a bush of about four feet in height with very small green leaves made up of from five to seven leaflets, with small, single, white or pink flowers borne singly or in clusters and followed by red spheroidal hairy fruits.
Engelmann —. *D. TG. NF. GPG. — — S. May. Hardy.*

MIRIFICA (S.), New Mexico, is also known as R. stellata mirifica, the Sacramento Rose and the Gooseberry Rose, has pale green leaves, very prickly stems, and bears its single very large flowers of clear pink singly, followed by inverted-pear-shaped prickly red fruits. Growth is vigorous and forms a bush of some thirty inches in height.
Greene —. *D. VG. NF. GPG. — —* 527/2-629/1. *S. July-Aug. Hardy.*
[*Pl.* 11.

MISS AMERICA (H.T.) has large fully double flowers of flesh-pink, flushed with salmon, with a base of gold. Growth is upright and vigorous and leaves large and of dark green.
Nicolas 1938. *D. VG. F. GPB. EB.* — *B.E.G. June-September. Hardy.*

MISS AUSTRALIA (H.T.) originated, as its name indicates, in Australia, and has very large, very double flowers of cupped form of rose-pink shaded with salmon towards the centre. Foliage is leathery and growth vigorous.
Knight 1933. *D. VG. VF. GPB. EB.* — *B.E.G. June-September. Hardy.*

MISS C. E. VAN ROSSEM (H.T.) has medium-size, dark red, semi-double flowers which have the advantage of standing up to hot sun, borne upon moderately vigorous plants with dark bronze-green foliage.
Verschuren 1919. *D. MG. MF. GPB. — — B.G. June-September. Hardy.*

MISS EDITH CAVELL (polyantha pompon) produces clusters of double, bright crimson flowers on vigorous erect plants with glossy bright green foliage.
Meiderwyk 1917. *D. VG. SF. GPF. — — B.St. June-September. Hardy.*

MISS ENGLAND (H.T.) has very large double flowers of cream, flushed in the centre with gold, opening to camellia-shaped blooms with tea-scented fragrance. Growth is vigorous and foliage is large and of glossy green.
B. R. Cant 1936. *D. VG. TF. GPB. — — B.G. June-September. Hardy.*

MISS HELYETT (wichuraiana rambler) has very large double flowers, borne in small groups and of bright carmine-pink, shaded with salmon at the centre. Canes are vigorous; foliage mid-green and glossy.
Fauqué 1909. *D. C. SF. GPI. — — A.P.Pr.W. June. Hardy.*

MISS LOLITA ARMOUR (H.T.) produces vigorous erect growth with polished bronzy-green leaves, and bears upon strong stems groups of large globular flowers of bright salmon, flushed with coppery-orange.
Howard & Smith 1919. *D. VG. VF. GPB. — — B.G. June-Sept. Hardy.*

MISS LOWE'S variety (see R. chinensis indica sanguinea).

MISS ROWENA THOM (H.T.) has very large double flowers of good pointed globular shape, with the inside of the petals of pale rose, and outside of bright rose shaded with gold. Growth is vigorous and erect and foliage dark green.
Howard & Smith 1927. *D. VG. SF. GPB. — — B.G. June-Sept. Hardy.*

Miss WILLMOTT (H.T.) produces its large shapely, double, creamy-white flowers on plants of vigorous growth with great continuity.
McGredy 1917. *D. VG. MF. GPB. EB. — B.E.G.St. June-Sept. Hardy.*

MME . . . (see Madame . . .).

MODESTY (H.T.) has large double flowers of good shape with a high centre and of white shading to rose at the centre borne upon vigorous plants of branching habit.
McGredy 1916. *D. VG. VF. GPB. — — B.G. June-September. Hardy.*

MOHAVENSIS (S.), Mohave, California, is a much-branched shrub of some three feet in height which bears solitary single rose flowers about the size of a halfpenny.
Parish —. D. VG. NF. GPG. — — S. June. Hardy.

MOLLIS (soft) (S.), Britain, is a vigorous bush of about six feet in height with somewhat smooth stems with purple bloom and green leaves, with silky tomentum beneath, and large single flowers of bright rose borne either singly or in small clusters, followed by bright red round fruits.
Smith 1818. *D. EG. SF. GPG. — — S. June. Hardy.*

MONARCH (H.T.) has high-centred, very large, double flowers of silvery-pink, borne singly on long stems, on vigorous plants with dark green foliage.
Dobbie 1926. *D. VG. MF. GPB. — — B.G. June-September. Hardy.*

MONSTROSA (see R. chinensis viridiflora).

MONTANA is very similar to R. canina, bearing its pink flowers either singly or in small clusters upon vigorous, erect and branching plants. The flowers are followed by large oval fruits of bright vermilion.
Chaix —. D. EG. SF. GPG. — — S. June. Hardy.

MONTEZUMAE (S.) (Montezuma Rose), Mexico, forms a bush of about four feet in height with almost smooth dark green canes, pale green five- or seven-parted foliage and deep pink single flowers of about one and a half inches in diameter, borne singly or in small clusters.
Humboldt 1825. *D. TG. F. GPG. — — S. June.*

MONTHLY Rose (see R. chinensis).

MOON GLOW (wichuraiana climber) has large very double flowers of white, shading at the centre to primrose-yellow. Growth is vigorous, leaves glossy green and flowering prolific.
Brownell 1937. *D. C. SF. GPI. — — A.P.W. June-August. Hardy.*

MOONLIGHT (Hybrid Musk) has small clustered groups of semi-double, white flowers flushed with lemon-yellow, borne upon vigorous bushes of some four feet in height, with bronzy-red glossy foliage, in the utmost profusion.
Pemberton 1913. *D. TG. F. GPC. GPG. — — G.H.S. July-Sept. Hardy.*

MORNING GLORY (Climbing H.T.) is a climbing sport of Portadown Sally and has semi-double to double flowers of excellent shape, of crimson-carmine with yellow veins and flushes, on a deep yellow base with the reverse of sulphur-yellow. Growth is vigorous, glossy and green.
Beckwith 1937. *D. C. F. GPE. — — C.W. June-September.*

MOSCHATA (S.) (Musk), Mediterranean region, is an exceptionally vigorous climbing rose bearing seven-flowered clusters of single white flowers of about two inches in diameter, pleasantly scented of musk. Generally about twelve feet in height, it has been known to reach a height of nearly thirty feet in this country, and is best when rambling through trees. All dead wood should be cut away and laterals trimmed to two feet.
Miller (known in England in 1596). *D. C. F. Detailed. — White.*
[A.Pr.W. June-July.

× MOSCHATA VAR. ALBA (H.S.) is a hybrid between R. moschata and R. canina and forms a bush of about six feet in height, with large clusters of clear-white large single flowers with golden stamens. Is probably synonymous with R. Dupontii.
— —. D. EG. F. GPG. — White. S. June-July. Hardy.

× MOSCHATA VAR. FLORABUNDA (H.S.) is of vigorous climbing habit with dark green wood and large pale green leaves and bears large clusters of very fragrant white flowers.
— —. D. C. VF. As for moschata. — White. A.Pr.W. June-July.

× MOSCHATA VAR. GRANDIFLORA (S.) is very similar to R. moschata, but has larger flowers and even more vigorous growth.
Bernaix 1886. *D. C. F. As above. — White. A.Pr.W. June-July.*

MOSCHATA VAR. HIMALAYICA (S.) has similar flowers to those of R. moschata, tinged with pink, and is even more vigorous.
Earle —. D. C. VF. As above. — White. A.Pr.W. June-July.

MOSCHATA VAR. PISSARDII (S.) is also known as R. nasturana; has larger white semi-double flowers than those of R. moschata and is of even more vigorous growth. Fruits which follow are small, bright red, and round.
Carriere 1880. *D. C. VF. As above. — White. A.Pr.W. June-September.*

MOSELLIED (Hybrid multiflora) is a fine semi-climbing rose for a pillar, with vigorous growth, clusters of large reddish-purple flowers with white eyes, and dark green mildew-proof foliage.
Lambert 1932. *D. C. VF. GPH. — — Pr. June-July. Hardy.*

MOSS ROSE (see R. muscosa).

MOTHER (H.T.) has very large, pointed, double, white fragrant flowers, borne upon vigorous bushy plants with dark green foliage resistant to disease.
B. R. Cant 1939. *D. VG. VF. GPB. EB. White. G.B.E. June-Sept. Hardy.*

MOUNT OMI ROSE (see R. omeiensis).

MOUSSELINE (see R. muscosa).

MOYESII (comm.) (S.), Western China, makes a large bush up to ten feet in height, with attractive light green leaves made up of from seven to thirteen leaflets, bearing its solitary or twin large single ruby flowers on long strands, followed by oval fruits, narrowing at the neck, of bright sealing-wax-red.

Veitch 1910. *D. EG. NF. GPG. — 822/3. S. June-July. Hardy. Pl. 78.*

MOYESII VAR. FARGESII (S.), China, has flowers somewhat smaller, of deeper red, is less tall, has rounded leaflets of dark green, larger fruits of coral red, and is equally beautiful.

Hesse 1917. *D. TG. NF. GPG. — 819/1. S. June-July. Hardy. Pl. 53.*

MOYESII VAR. ROSEA is another name for R. holodonta, which see.

MRS. AARON WARD (H.T.) is a rose of variable colour, its double Indian-yellow pointed flowers often being flushed salmon and edged with white. Growth is vigorous, but dwarf and compact.

Pernet-Ducher 1907. *D. VG. SF. GPB. — — B.G. June-September. Hardy.*

MRS. ANTHONY SPALDING (H.T.) has large, full, double flowers of strawberry-red flushed with orange, with the outside of the petals of dull deep orange. Growth is spreading and vigorous and foliage mid-green and resistant to disease.

McGredy 1934. *D. MG. SF. GPB. — — G.B. June-September. Hardy.*

MRS. ANTHONY WATERER (see R. rugosa).

MRS. A. R. BARRACLOUGH (H.T.) produces its very large many-petalled flowers of high-centred form upon long stems on very strong upright growth with dark green foliage, at times subject to black spot. The exceptionally fine flowers are of soft carmine-pink shaded with yellow at the base, and are freely produced.

McGredy 1926. *D. VG. SF. GPB. EB. 24. B.E.G.St.Pot. June-October.*
  [Hardy. Pl. 58.

MRS. ARTHUR CURTISS JAMES (wichuraiana climber) is a most vigorous climbing rose with polished green foliage on strong canes, and bears large open high-centred flowers of deep sunflower-yellow with some generosity.

Brownell 1933. *D. C. MF. GPJ. — — A.C.W.T. June-July. Hardy.*

MRS. ARTHUR ROBERT WADDELL (H.T.) has large, semi-double, open flowers of salmon tinged with red, with the reverse of the petals of pale crimson-scarlet. Growth is vigorous and upright, leaves bronze-green and polished.

Pernet-Ducher 1908. *D. VG. SF. GPB. — — B.G. June-September. Hardy.*

MRS. BEATTY (H.T.) has pointed flowers of lemon-yellow, reminiscent of the tones of Maréchal Niel, of globular shape, freely borne upon dwarf and branching but vigorous plants with attractive mildew-proof dark green foliage, and is exceptionally good in dry weather.

B. R. Cant 1926. *D. MG. MF. GPB. EB. — B.E.G. June-Sept. Hardy.*

Mrs. Beckwith (Pernetiana) is another dry-weather rose, with semi-double flowers of buttercup-yellow, paling upon opening to lemon-yellow. Its almost thornless vigorous growth is upright, and foliage is glossy and green.
Pernet-Ducher 1922. *D. MG. SF. GPB. — — B.G. June-Sept. Hardy.*

Mrs. Bosanquet (see R. chinensis).

Mrs. Bryce Allan (H.T.) has large globular, very double flowers of deep carmine-rose-pink, borne in clusters on strong vigorous erect plants.
Dickson 1916. *D. VG. MF. GPB. — — G. June-September. Hardy.*

Mrs. Charles Lamplough (H.T.), as befits a rose related to the great Druschki, produces large, very shapely, many-broad-petalled flowers of very pale lemon-yellow, borne upon strong stems from vigorous plants of upright growth. It is a fine exhibition variety, only at its best during dry periods.
McGredy 1922. *D. VG. MF. GPB. EB. — E.G.Pot. June-Sept. Hardy.*

Mrs. Charles Tennant (H.T.) flowers with exceptional freedom, producing its pointed shapely flowers, of primrose-yellow with deeper tones, upon vigorous branching plants with bronze-green foliage.
F. Cant 1936. *D. VG. MF. GPB. — — B.G. June-October. Hardy.*

Mrs. Courtney Page (H.T.) has very large, high-pointed, many-petalled flowers of orange-cerise, shaded with carmine toward the base. Growth is vigorous, compact and upright; foliage mid-green and subject to disease.
McGredy 1922. *D. MG. MF. GPB. — — G. June-September. Hardy.*

Mrs. Dunlop Best (H.T.) has a diffuse low habit, with bronze-green foliage and large double flowers of apricot, tinted with red, borne upon long stems with polished bronze-green foliage.
Hicks 1926. *D. VG. F. GPC. — — B.G. June-September. Hardy.*

Mrs. Edward Laxton (H.T.) has large high-centred but globular, very double flowers of bright orange-red and old rose, borne upon vigorous plants with dark green foliage.
Laxton 1935. *D. VG. SF. GPB. — — 620/1-621. B.G.St. June-September.*
                                                              [Hardy. Pl. 30.

Mrs. E. J. Hudson (H.T.) produces its very large double flowers in groups on long strong stems. The fragrant flowers of bright pink are borne upon erect vigorous plants with light green foliage.
Lilley 1923. *D. VG. MF. GPB. — — G. June-September. Hardy.*

Mrs. E. J. Manners (H.T.) has shapely pointed double flowers of deep crimson, borne upon long stout stems. Habit is vigorous, branching and erect, and foliage ample and attractive.
Burbage 1938. *D. VG. MF. GPB. — — B.G. June-September. Hardy.*

Mrs. Erskine Pembroke Thom (H.T.) has large perfectly-shaped double flowers of deep butter-yellow, borne upon strong stems on plants of vigorous upright growth, with dark green glossy foliage.
Howard & Smith 1926. *D. VG. MF. GPB. — — B.G. June-Sept. Hardy.*

Mrs. E. Wood (H.T.) adds to the attractiveness of its long pale-yellow double flowers a charming flush of tender salmon-pink and a frequency of production seldom excelled. Growth is vigorous, habit is good and foliage ample and clean.
Dickson 1934. *D. VG. F. GPB. — — B.G. June-September. Hardy.*

Mrs. F. J. Jackson (H.T.) is a bedding rose of exceptional habit, with shapely double flowers of cerise-scarlet, borne with freedom on plants of moderate height with bronze-green foliage.
Le Grice 1933. *D. MG. F. GPB. — — B.G. June-September. Hardy.*

Mrs. Foley Hobbs (T.) has flowers of medium size, which are fully double, of good shape and ivory-white tinged with pink. Growth is vigorous, but this rose is produced best under glass, when its flowers arrive at intervals throughout the season.
Dickson 1910. *D. VG. TF. GPA. EA. — House.E.St. June-September.*

Mrs. Francis King (H.T.) has shapely high-centred, very double, very large, creamy-white flowers, borne upon long strong stems from vigorous plants with dark green foliage.
Nicolas 1936. *D. VG. SF. GPB. EB. — White. B.E.G. June-Sept. Hardy.*

Mrs. Franklin Dennison (H.T.) has large, double, high-centred flowers of white, with primrose-yellow veins, deepening at the base to deep yellow. Growth is vigorous and erect and flowering is free and continuous.
McGredy 1915. *D. VG. F. GPB. — — B.G. June-September. Hardy.*

Mrs. Franklin D. Roosevelt (H.T.) is an exceptionally beautiful sport from the beautiful Talisman. The flower is large and pointedly globular, of brilliant golden-yellow, and borne upon a long strong stem upon plants of vigorous growth with deep green glossy foliage.
Traendly & Schenck 1933. *D. VG. VF. GPB. EB. — B.E.G. June-Sept.*
[Hardy.

Mrs. Frank Verdon (H.T.) has large, double, shapely flowers of creamy-white deepening to rich gold at the base of the petals. Growth is vigorous and erect and foliage is dark green.
Bees 1935. *D. VG. SF. GPB. — — B.G. June-September. Hardy.*

Mrs. G. A. van Rossem (Mevrouw G. A. van Rossem) (H.T.) is an exceptionally beautiful rose with large double flowers of dark golden-yellow shaded with orange, the reverse of the petals shaded and veined with bronze-red. Growth is vigorous and erect, with large deep bronze-green foliage, and flowers long-stemmed and freely produced.
Van Rossem 1926. *D. VG. MF. GPB. — 09/3. B.G.St. June-Sept. Hardy.*
[Pl. 63.

Hybrid Tea Rose, Rose Berkeley

Fruits of Species Roses

Rosa rubiginosa **ABCDEFGH**
Rosa rugosa var. calocarpa **JKLM**
Rosa multibracteata **NOPQRSTU**

Mrs. G. A. Wheatcroft (H.T.) is an improved form of Lady Pirrie with intensified colour. Flowers are of medium size, very double, and of high-centred cupped form. The petals shade from silver-pink to orange-pink within, and salmon to carmine without. Growth is vigorous and erect, foliage bronze-green and resistant to disease, and flowers are borne in groups of three or four.
Wheatcroft 1926. *D. VG. VF. GPB. — — B.G. June-September. Hardy.*

Mrs. George B. Easlea (H.T.) has very large, exceptionally well-formed, high-pointed flowers of bright carmine-pink, borne upon long strong stems. Growth is vigorous and erect and foliage ample and attractive.
Easlea 1939. *D. VG. VF. GPB. EA. — B.E.G. June-September. Hardy.*

Mrs. George C. Thomas (Hybrid Musk) is a good pillar rose with large, semi-double, open flowers of pink shaded salmon, deepening at the centre to orange. Growth is upright and diffuse with attractive sage-green foliage.
Thomas 1925. *D. C. F. GPG. — — Pr. June-September. Hardy.*

Mrs. George Geary (H.T.) has attractively shaped, pointed flowers of scarlet-cerise, developing to full double fragrant flowers which open well in wet weather, and are borne on long, stiff, almost thornless stems from vigorous plants of erect habit with bronze-green leaves.
Burbage 1929. *D. TG. VF. GPB. — — 23-23/1. B.G. June-Sept. Hardy.*
[Pl. 39.

Mrs. George Marriott (H.T.) has very large, double, high-pointed flowers of deep cream flushed and veined with deep pink, borne upon good stems upon moderately vigorous and erect plants with dark green leaves.
McGredy 1918. *D. NG. SF. GPA. EA. — E.G. June-September. Hardy.*

Mrs. Georgia Chobe (H.T.) has very large, high-pointed, double flowers of mid-pink of undeepened tone, borne upon long strong stems on vigorous plants with mid-green foliage.
Howard & Smith 1937. *D. VG. SF. GPB. — — B.G. June-September.*

Mrs. H. A. Verschuren (see Mrs. Verschuren).

Mrs. Henry Bowles (H.T.) has the disadvantage of sometimes being liable to black spot, but is nevertheless an exceptional rose. The large, high-centred, perfectly shaped flowers are of shining rose-pink borne upon good stems and vigorous erect plants, exceptionally good in the colder north.
Chaplin 1921. *D. VG. SF. GPB. EA.* 625/2, 623. *B.E.G.St.Pot. June-*
[Sept. Hardy. Pl. 46 *&* 57.

Mrs. Henry Morse (H.T.) has large high-centred, double flowers of medium rose-pink flushed with salmon, borne upon strong stems. Growth is erect and vigorous, foliage green but subject to mildew.
McGredy 1919. *D. VG. SF. GPB. EB. — B.E.G.St.Pot. June-Sept. Hardy.*

Mrs. Henry Winnett (H.T.) has large, high-pointed, double flowers of deep crimson-red, borne upon long strong stems. Growth is vigorous and erect and branching, with deep green glossy leaves, and flowering has continuity.
Dunlop 1917. *D. VG. VF. GPB. EB. — B.E.G.St.Pot. June-Sept. Hardy.*

Mrs. Herbert Carter (H.T.) has large, double, shapely flowers of apricot-yellow, lined with bronze, deepening at the centre. Growth is moderately vigorous and erect, and foliage good, sufficient and attractive.
F. Cant 1934. *D. MG. MF. GPB. — — G. June-September. Hardy.*

Mrs. Herbert Hoover (H.T.) produces its moderate-size high-pointed flowers with great freedom on long stiff stems upon vigorous plants. The flowers are of deep crimson and are exceptionally sweetly scented, and foliage is deep green and resistant to disease.
Coddington 1928. *D. TG. VF. GPB. — — B.G.Pot. June-Sept. Hardy.*

Mrs. Herbert Stevens (T.) has large high-centred flowers of snow-white, deepening towards the centre to pale fawn, and is a magnificent variety for florists. Growth is vigorous and erect, foliage light green and ample.
McGredy 1910. *D. TG. F. GPB. — White. B.G.St.Pot. June-Sept. Hardy.*
[*Pl.* 32.

Mrs. H. R. Darlington (H.T.) has exceptionally large lemon-white flowers of good form produced upon long strong stems. Growth is vigorous and erect, and flowering free. Unfortunately the flowers are adversely affected by damp weather, but they may be used for exhibition purposes.
McGredy 1919. *D. VG. SF. GPB. EB. — E.G. June-September. Hardy.*

Mrs. J. D. Eisele (H.T.) has large very double flowers of cerise-pink shaded in the centre with scarlet. Growth is moderately vigorous and foliage ample.
Howard & Smith 1933. *D. MG. VF. GPB. — — B.G. June-Sept. Hardy.*

Mrs. J. D. Russell (H.T.) has deep crimson flowers of medium size, shaded with even deeper crimson, of high pointed shape. Growth is vigorous and erect.
Bees 1930. *D. VG. VF. GPB. — — B.G. June-September. Hardy.*

Mrs. J. J. Hedley Willis (H.T.) produces its medium-size flowers of dark crimson, shaded deeper towards the centre, on long strong stems. Growth is moderately vigorous and foliage dark green.
Bees 1930. *D. MG. VF. GPB. — — B.G. June-September. Hardy.*

Mrs. John Bell (H.T.) has high-pointed, double, rounded flowers of reddish-carmine borne upon long stout stems. Habit of growth is vigorous, bushy and erect, with dark green polished foliage.
Dobbie 1928. *D. VG. MF. GPB. — — B.G. June-September. Hardy.*

Mrs. John Laing (H.P.) is one of the most delightful of all the hybrid perpetuals and has very large double flowers of rose-pink on exceptionally vigorous plants of erect growth with bright green foliage. Is impervious to rain and has a long intermittent period of flowering.
Bennett 1887. *D. TG. VF. GPB. EB. — E.G.St.Pot. June–August. Hardy.*

Mrs. J. T. McIntosh (H.T.) has double flowers of good shape of pale apricot, deepening in the centre to a golden-yellow base. Habit is erect and vigorous.
McIntosh 1935. *D. VG. SF. GPB. — — B.G. June–September.*

Mrs. L. B. Coddington (H.T.) bears its large, double, persistent vivid-pink flowers, with golden bases, on long strong stems on exceptionally vigorous plants with attractive green foliage. The flowers last well, are fragrant, and are exceptionally good in hot dry weather.
Coddington 1932. *D. VG. MF. GPB. — 024/2-1. B.G. June–September.*

Mrs. Lovell Swisher (H.T.) has delicacy of form in its very large, double, pale salmon-pink flowers which deepen toward the centre. The flowers are singly and profusely borne on long strong stems. Growth is vigorous, branching and erect, with polished bronze-green foliage.
Howard & Smith 1926. *D. VG. MF. GPB. EB. — B.E.G. June–September.*

Mrs. M. H. Walsh (wichuraiana rambler) sends up long stout canes with bright green glossy foliage sometimes subject to mildew, carries very large trusses of double, white flowers in great quantity, and is good for covering arches, pillars and pergolas.
Walsh 1912. *D. C. NF. GPH. — — A.P.Pr.W. June–July. Hardy.*

Mrs. Oakley-Fisher (H.T.) is one of the most attractive single-flowered varieties, having five-petalled flowers of deep orange-yellow upon vigorous bushy plants with glossy bronzy-green foliage. In its freedom of flowering it is exceptional.
B. R. Cant 1921. *D. VG. MF. GPB. — — B. June–September. Hardy.*

Mrs. Oliver Ames (H.T.) is an exceptionally vigorous and erect plant with large attractive foliage and very double, very large, high-centred globular flowers of lemon-yellow, borne upon long stiff stems.
Verschuren 1940. *D. TG. VF. GPC. EC. — B.G.E. June–September.*

Mrs. Olive Sackett (Hybrid polyantha) is a sport from Else Poulsen, which it resembles in all respects except in colour, which is bright red.
Wirtz & Eicke 1931. *D. TG. SF. GPG. — — B.St. June–Sept. Hardy.*

Mrs. Oswald Lewis (H.T.) has a picoteed edge of flame to its outer petals, which are of softened canary-yellow. The fully double, freely produced flowers have high centres and are carried on long stems. Growth is vigorous and perfume outstanding, and it is indifferent to wet weather.
F. Cant 1936. *D. VG. VF. GPB. EB. — B.G.E. June–September. Hardy.*

Mrs. Oswald Smeaton (H.T.) has exceptionally large, many-petalled, shapely flowers of deep cream, shaded pink at the centre and towards the edges of the petals. Growth is vigorous and flowering profuse.
Easlea 1932. *D. VG. TF. GPB. EB.* — *B.G.E. June-September. Hardy.*

Mrs. Paul Goudie (H.T.) was at one time known as Shining Sun, and has large fully double flowers of good shape and of bold buttercup-yellow edged with carmine. The flowers are borne on long strong stems upon vigorous and bushy plants of easy growth, with dark green shining foliage.
McGredy 1932. *D. VG. MF. GPB.* — — *B.G. June-September. Hardy.*

Mrs. Paul J. Howard (Climbing H.T.) has extra large double flowers of bright crimson, borne freely upon vigorous canes with dark bronze-green foliage.
Howard & Smith 1936. *D. C. F. GPE.* — — *C.A.W. June-August. Hardy.*

Mrs. R. G. Sharman-Crawford (H.P.) makes an almost continuous display of its large, double, globular rosy-pink flowers which are produced upon vigorous and erect bushes with dark green foliage.
Dickson 1894. *D. TG. VF. GPC.* — — *G. June-August. Hardy.*

Mrs. R. M. Finch (Hybrid polyantha) has exceptionally large, double, bright rose-pink flowers, borne in large clusters upon vigorous bushes with large bright green foliage.
Finch 1923. *D. VG. MF. GPG. GPF.* — — *B.G.St. June-Sept. Hardy.*

Mrs. Sam McGredy (H.T.) is one of the most popular roses in existence, its large, very double, high-centred flowers, with reflexed petals of coppery-orange flushed with scarlet, having the added attraction of lasting well, in addition to being freely produced. Growth is vigorous, branching and erect, and the attractive foliage is glossy red-bronze-green. A rose that is impervious to rain and extra good in autumn.
McGredy 1929. *D. VG. SF. GPB.* — — *B.G.St. June-September. Hardy.*

Mrs. S. Paton (H.T.) has large, double, high-centred flowers of excellent shape, borne with freedom and continuity upon vigorous and erect plants of branching habit, with deep bronze-green foliage. The astonishing orange-scarlet to carmine flowers make it a fine variety for bedding purposes.
McGredy 1928. *D. VG. SF. GPB.* — — *B.G. June-September. Hardy.*

Mrs. T. B. Doxford (H.T.) has pointed rose-pink blooms of moderate size with red flushes without, and combines with these attractions attractive habit of growth and good foliage, with a free flowering capacity rendering it conveniently suited to bedding purposes.
Dickson 1932. *D. VG. MF. GPB.* — — *B.G. June-September. Hardy.*

Mrs. Theonville van Berkel (H.T.) has large, very double, pointed pink flowers flushed with yellow upon the backs of the petals, borne upon vigorous plants with attractive dark green foliage.
Buisman 1935. *D. VG. VF. GPB.* — — *B.G. June-September.*

Mrs. Tom Whitehead (H.T.) produces upon long stiff stems its large double cream flowers, with deep veining upon the reverse and deepening to orange at the centre. Growth is vigorous and flowering free.
Beckwith 1938. *D. VG. SF. GPB. —— B.G. June-September.*

Mrs. Tresham Gilbey (H.T.) has large pointed flowers of orange-salmon, borne singly on good stems on very vigorous erect and branching plants with bright green polished foliage.
Chaplin 1923. *D. VG. VF. GPB. —— B.G. June-September. Hardy.*

Mrs. Verschuren (Mrs. H. A. Verschuren, R.M.S. Queen Mary) (H.T.) has double, high-centred flowers of camellia shape, of coppery-orange flushed on the opened petals with salmon. Growth is moderately vigorous, flowering free and generally attractive.
Verschuren 1937. *D. MG. SF. GPB. EB.* 618/1-19/2. *B.E.G.Pot. June-*
[*Sept. Hardy. Pl.* 77.

Mrs. Walter Brace (H.T.) is claimed to be an improved Picture with better shape, if possible, larger and of a deeper, stronger rose-pink. The flowers are of excellent shape, pleasantly reflexed, and resistant to rain. Growth is vigorous, branching and erect and foliage a pleasant light glossy green.
Beckwith 1939. *D. VG. MF. GPB. EB. — B.E.G.St. June-September.*

Mrs. Wemyss Quin (Pernetiana) is, as yellow roses are judged, one of the older varieties, but combines with its somewhat flat globular flowers of chrome-yellow a free and pleasant habit and an ease of growth which endears it to the gardener. The combination of red wood and polished bronze-green foliage adds still further compensations for its tendency to black spot.
Dickson 1914. *D. VG. SF. GPB. —— B.G.St.Pot. June-Sept. Hardy.*

Mrs. W. E. Nickerson (H.T.) is a good autumn variety having conical flowers which are both very large and double, and of rose flushed salmon, shaded with gold. Growth is vigorous and erect, foliage dark green and proof against disease.
McGredy 1927. *D. VG. MF. GPB. —— B.G. June-September. Hardy.*

Mrs. W. H. Cutbush (polyantha pompon) bears clusters of semi-double flowers, of bright but deep pink, on dwarf plants of vigorous growth with glossy green foliage, sometimes subject to black spot. Its fine clusters and dwarf habit render it very suitable for bedding purposes.
Levavasseur 1906. *D. SG. SF. GPF. —— B.G.St.Pot. June-Sept. Hardy.*

Mrs. William Sprott (H.T.) has large, high-centred, double flowers of bright orange-yellow carried on long stems. Growth is erect, bushy and of moderate height, and the attractive foliage is varnished bronze-green.
McGredy 1938. *D. MG. SF. GPB. EB. — B.E.G. June-September. Hardy.*

M. S. HERSHEY (H.T.) has high-centred double flowers of crimson, borne on long stems. Habit is moderately vigorous, erect and branching, and free-flowering.
Coddington 1940. *D. MG. MF. GPB. — — B.G. June-September.*

MULTIBRACTEATA (many-bracted) (S.), W. China, has thin, very spiny graceful whip-like branches with pretty ferny leaves, made up of from seven to nine leaflets, with solitary or clustered bright-pink flowers of about the size of a halfpenny, followed by small orange-red fruits.
Hemsley & Wilson —. D. EG. NF. GPG. — 30/2-30/1. June-Sept. Hardy.
[*Pl.* 26 & 66.]

MULTIFLORA (many-flowered) (S.), Japan, forms a semi-climbing or widely diffuse bush with green leaves made up of from five to eleven leaflets, and bearing clusters of small white flowers emitting a most attractive scent of honey.
Thunberg 1781. *D. TG. VF. GPG. — White. S. June-September. Hardy.*

MURIELAE (comm.) (S.), W. China, makes a tall branching bush with small very pointed green foliage on very spiny canes with reddish-pink spines, and bears clusters of white to pale-pink flowers of about one inch in diameter, followed by oval orange-red fruits.
Rehder & Wilson —. D. TG. SF. GPG. White. S. June-July. Hardy.

MURRAY HILL (H.T.) has long-pointed buds which open to semi-double flowers of clear canary-yellow, borne upon vigorous and erect plants with good green foliage.
Coddington 1939. *D. VG. NF. GPB. — — B.G.Pot. June-Sept. Hardy.*

MUSCOSA. The Moss Roses are exceptionally attractive descendants of the Cabbage Rose with enlarged and enmossed calices and sepals, and are outstandingly charming in the bud stage. Generally flowering in June and July, a few varieties flower again in the autumn. Pruning consists of removing the old and dead wood, leaving only the strong base shoots and the best of the two-year-old wood, which should be shortened to between four and six eyes, so that the bush approximates to a symmetrical growth of about two feet in height. All are pleasantly fragrant. Among the most attractive of the varieties are:—

× BARON DE WASSENAER, with double crimson flowers.
Verdier 1854. *D. VG. MF. Detailed. — S. June-July. Hardy.*

× BLANCHE MOREAU, with double white flowers.
Moreau-Robert 1880. *D. VG. MF. Detailed. — S. June-July. Hardy.*

COMMUNIS, the old Pink Moss, has rounded, pale-rose, double flowers.
— 1596. D. VG. MF. Detailed. — S. June-July. Hardy.

× CRIMSON GLOBE, with double crimson flowers.
Paul 1890. *D. VG. MF. Detailed. — S. June-July. Hardy.*

CRISTATA (Chapeau de Napoléon), with double deep pink flowers with very heavy mossing.
Vibert 1827. *D. VG. MF. Detailed. — S. June-July. Hardy.*

× DE MEAUX, double blush-pink with deeper centre.
Sweet 1814. *D. VG. MF. Detailed. — S. June-July. Hardy.*

× GLOIRE DES MOUSSEUSES has large double flesh-pink flowers.
Laffay 1852. *D. VG. MF. Detailed. — S. June-July. Hardy.*

× GOLDEN MOSS has very double peach-yellow flowers produced with appropriate shyness.
Dot 1932. *D. VG. F. Detailed. — S. June-July. Hardy.*

× HENRI MARTIN (the Red Moss) has semi-double crimson flowers.
Laffay 1863. *D. VG. MF. Detailed. — S. June-July. Hardy.*

× LITTLE GEM is a dainty double pale cherry-red miniature.
Paul 1880. *D. VG. MF. Detailed. — S. June-July. Hardy.*

× MOUSSELINE has white double flowers deepening to blush-pink at the centre.
Moreau-Robert 1880. *D. VG. MF. Detailed. — S. June-July. Hardy.*

× ŒILLET PANACHÉ has double white flowers striped with red.
Dupont 1880. *D. VG. MF. Detailed. — S. June-July. Hardy.*

× SALET has double pink flowers and generally succeeds in flowering twice.
Lacharme 1864. *D. VG. MF. Detailed. — S. June-September. Hardy.*

× WHITE BATH has clusters of double white flowers.
Salter 1810. *D. MG. NF. Detailed. — S. June-July. Hardy.*

× WILLIAM LOBB has double flowers of carmine shaded with violet.
Laffay 1855. *D. VG. MF. Detailed. — S. June-July. Hardy.*

× ZENOBIA produces large, soft, pale rose double flowers with freedom.
Paul 1892. *D. VG. MF. Detailed. — S. June-July. Hardy.*

MUSETTE (Hybrid polyantha) is a vigorous bushy plant with dark green foliage and clusters of large single flowers of bright crimson-cerise.
Tantau 1936. *D. VG. SF. GPG. — — B. June-September. Hardy.*

MUSK ROSE (see R. moschata; see also R. Brunonii).

NANCY (H.T.) has semi-double flowers of bright crimson-scarlet produced in abundance throughout the season, on vigorous plants with erect and branching habit with good green foliage.
Ferguson 1930. *D. VG. MF. GPB. — — B.G. June-October. Hardy.*

NAOMI (H.T.) produces its high-pointed double flowers of coppery-buff on long strong stems from vigorous plants with dark green attractive foliage.
Pemberton 1926. *D. VG. MF. GPB. — — B.G. June-September. Hardy.*

NASTURANA (see R. moschata var. Pissardii).

NATALIE NYPELS (polyantha pompon) creates large clusters of large double flowers of orange-red, fading to soft pink, on vigorous bushes with bronzy-green foliage.
Leenders 1919. *D. VG. MF. GPF. — — B. June-September. Hardy.*

NEIGE PARFUM (H.T.) has high-centred, large, double flowers of clear white, shading to creamy-yellow at the centre, borne upon vigorous stout long stems. Growth is vigorous, foliage green and perfume exceptional.
Mallerin 1939. *D. VG. VF. GPB. EB. White. B.E.G. June-Sept. Hardy.*

NELLIE E. HILLOCK (H.T.) is of dwarf and diffuse growth, with dark green foliage. The flowers are of good globular shape and of pale pink with an orange base, with the reverse of the petals of deep pink
Hillock 1934. *D. SG. MF. GPA. — — B.G. June-September.*

NELLIE PARKER (H.T.) has double flowers of clear creamy-white shaded at the centre with copper, borne upon vigorous plants with green foliage.
Dickson 1916. *D. VG. SF. GPB. — — G. June-September. Hardy.*

NEON (H.T.) has large, double, high-centred flowers of even crimson-scarlet, produced freely upon vigorous branching plants of moderate height, with dark green, resistant foliage, and flowers well under bad conditions, retaining its colour perfectly.
Nicolas 1936. *D. MG. MF. GPB. — — B.G. June-September. Hardy.*

NEPAL ROSE (see R. Brunonii).

NESTOR BOLDERDIJK (H.T.) has large, double, pointed flowers of camellia outline of pale maize with a deeper shading at the base, and with the reverse of the petals tinted with salmon-pink. Habit is erect and vigorous and leaves large and glossy green.
Leenders 1938. *D. VG. SF. GPB. EB. — B.E.G. June-September. Hardy.*

NEVILLE CHAMBERLAIN (H.T.) has large, pointed, double flowers of bright salmon, merging to orange at the centre, borne upon long strong stems. Growth is vigorous and erect and foliage glossy bronze-green.
Lens 1939. *D. VG. SF. GPB. — — B.G. June-September.*

NEW CENTURY (see R. rugosa).

NEW HAVEN QUEEN (H.T.) is a vigorous-growing sport from Token, with large double flowers of tangerine-orange. Habit is branching and foliage glossy green.
Grillo 1939. *D. VG. F. GPB. — — B.G.Pot. June-September.*

NIGHT (H.T.) has double globular flowers of very deep even crimson, borne upon long stems from vigorous erect plants with dark green foliage, and has the right to be termed one of the darkest red roses in cultivation.
McGredy 1930. *D. VG. MF. GPB. — — G. June-September. Hardy.*

Fruits of Rosa rugosa

Dorothy McGredy (Pernetiana) **ABEF**   Signora (Hybrid Tea) **CDGH**
Violinista Costa (Hybrid Tea) **KLOP**

NIGRETTE (H.T.) has open double flowers of even deeper crimson when
light and weather are suitable, but cannot be said either to be a
good rose or to justify its right to the name of the Black Rose.
Krause 1934. *D. MG. VF. GPB. — — G. June-September. Hardy.*

NINON VALLIN (Pernetiana) is an excellent rose, with large double
flowers of deep apricot within and clear yellow without. The habit
is vigorous and perpetual, with shiny light green foliage well matured.
Gaujard 1936. *D. VG. MF. GPB. — — G. June-October. Hardy.*

NIPPY (H.T.) is a vigorous rose of moderate height and dark green
foliage with double flowers of bright canary-yellow splashed on the
reverse with carmine. Its prolific flowering and neat habit make it
suitable for bedding.
B. R. Cant 1932. *D. MG. MF. GPB. — — B. June-September. Hardy.*

NITIDA (shining) (S.), Eastern North America, is a very dwarf species
with whip-like strands of red stems with many bright red thorns,
glossy bronze-green foliage of feathery lightness, and single rose-pink
flowers with bright yellow centres, borne either singly or in small
clusters on short stalks.
Willdenow 1807. *D. SG. MF. GPG. — — S. June-July. Hardy. Pl.* 60.

NOISETTIANA. This is the Noisette rose, a hybrid of R. moschata and
R. chinensis, which invariably is of climbing habit, bearing its
flowers in clusters, and sweetly scented.

The best-known types are:—

FORTUNE'S YELLOW has semi-double orange-yellow flowers splashed
with red, borne in clusters, and needs the protection of a wall, or
to be grown under glass.
Fortune 1845. *D. C. F. GPE. — — W. June-July.*

MADAME ALFRED CARRIÈRE, which has double, sweetly-scented
flowers of blush-white, is of very vigorous growth.
Schwartz 1873. *D. C. VF. GPE. — — Pr.W. June-September.*

MARÉCHAL NIEL produces its best flowers on the lateral shoots of
the previous year's growth, and has large double flowers of golden-
yellow, with a very sweet fragrance.
Pradel 1864. *D. C. VF. GPE. — — C.W.H.Cut. June-September.*

WILLIAM ALLEN RICHARDSON has deep apricot-yellow flowers which
vary considerably in tone, and are equally pleasantly fragrant.
Ducher 1878. *D. C. VF. GPE. — — A.P.W. June-September.*

NONIN (H.T.) has large flowers with high-pointed centres of deep
cream shaded with gold and tinted with coral. Growth is vigorous
and erect, with red wood and sage-green glossy leaves, and the
flowers are tea-scented, and undamaged by rain.
Mallerin 1938. *D. VG. VF. GPB. — — B.G. June-September. Hardy.*

NORFOLK HARMONY (H.T.) has very shapely, high-centred, large double flowers of bright cerise of even tone, borne upon long stems from vigorous erect plants with dark green glossy foliage.
Le Grice 1940. *D. VG. MF. GPB. — — B.G. June-September. Hardy.*

NORMAN (H.T.) has attractively-shaped double flowers of bright crimson-scarlet, borne upon vigorous and erect plants with perpetual flowering propensities.
Dickson 1934. *D. VG. MF. GPB. — — B.G. June-September. Hardy.*

NORMAN LAMBERT (H.T.) has large, double, high-pointed flowers of orange-salmon flushed with bronze and paler toward the base, with the reverse of the petals of golden-yellow. Growth is vigorous and erect, and leaves are large, glossy green, and resistant to disease.
McGredy 1926. *D. VG. SF. GPB. — — B.G. June-September. Hardy.*

NORMAN'S 137B (H.T.) is a grand new red rose of fine solid appearance and exquisite colour and scent. Foliage is deep green and resistant to disease.
Norman 1940. *D. VG. VF. GPC. — — B. June-Sept. Hardy. Pl. 10.*

NOTTINGHAM (H.T.) has double high-centred flowers of clear yellow, deepening at the centre to orange, borne upon vigorous, erect plants with glossy green foliage.
Robinson 1938. *D. VG. MF. GPB. — — B.G. June-September. Hardy.*

NOVA ZEMBLA (see R. rugosa).

NUMA FAY (H.T.) has large many-petalled flowers of pale pink, deepening at the centre to orange, borne on long stems from plants of vigorous and erect growth with large green leaves.
Meilland 1938. *D. VG. F. GPB. — — B.G. June-September. Hardy.*

NURIA DE RECOLONA (H.P.) has very large, very double, white flowers of perfect shape, borne upon long stems from leafy plants of very vigorous growth.
Dot 1933. *D. TG. VF. GPB. EB. White. B.G.E. June-September. Hardy.*

NUR MAHAL (Hybrid Musk) bears its bright-crimson semi-double flowers in large clusters on vigorous and erect bushy plants with small disease-resistant foliage.
Pemberton 1923. *D. TG. VF. GPG. — — S.H. June-September. Hardy.*

NUTKANA (S.) (the Wasatch Rose), Western North America, has whip-like green stems almost devoid of thorns, with attractive green foliage, and bears singly or in small clusters its large single pink flowers, which are followed by bright red very round fruits. It is a large shrub, often exceeding eight feet in height.
Presl 1888. *D. EG. F. GPG. — 427-627/2. S. June. Hardy.*

NUTKANA VAR. HISPIDA (bristly) (S.) differs only in having the fruits covered with bristly protuberances.
— —. D. EG. F. GPG. — — S. June. Hardy.

NYPEL'S PERFECTION (Hybrid polyantha) has large semi-double flowers of hydrangea-pink borne in large clusters upon vigorous plants of attractive habit with light green foliage.
Leenders 1930. *D. VG. SF. GPG. — — B.G. June-September. Hardy.*

OAKINGTON RUBY (see R. chinensis var. minima).

OAKLEY (H.T.) has large, double, high-centred flowers of flesh-pink deepening gradually towards the centre to deep pink and bright red. Growth is erect and vigorous.
Fairhead 1937. *D. VG. VF. GPB. — — B.G. June-September. Hardy.*

ODINE (H.T.) has large, high-centred, fully double flowers of creamy white tinted at the edge with rose, borne upon strong stems on vigorous and erect plants with sage-green foliage.
Ketten 1937. *D. VG. SF. GPB. — — B.G. June-September. Hardy.*

ŒILLET PANACHÉ (see R. muscosa).

OLD CRIMSON CHINA (see R. chinensis).

OLD GOLD (H.T.) has semi-double flowers of large size, of apricot and orange, borne upon erect plants with bronze-green glossy foliage.
McGredy 1913. *D. MG. SF. GPB. — — B.G. June-September. Hardy.*

OLIVE COOK (H.T.) has very large, high-pointed, double flowers of perfect form, of clear white deepening to cream at the centre, borne upon long strong stems. Foliage is glossy green, habit vigorous, and flowering free.
F. Cant 1934. *D. VG. F. GPB. EB. White. E.G. June-September. Hardy.*

OLIVER MEE (H.T.) produces its large, high-centred, double, deep salmon-pink flowers upon good stems from plants of good vigorous branching habit. It has the additional advantages of being un-affected by damp weather, and immune from disease.
Dickson 1923. *D. VG. F. GPB. EB. — E.G. June-September. Hardy.*

OLYMPIA (H.T.) has its large, double, bright red shapely flowers borne upon long strong stems from plants of vigorous and erect growth.
Tantau 1936. *D. VG. F. GPB. — — B.G. June-September. Hardy.*

OLYMPIAD is the name by which Mme Raymond Gaujard is known in America.

OMEIENSIS (S.) (the Mount Omi Rose), China, differs from most other single roses by having only four petals, arranged in the shape of a cross. Habit is vigorous and branching, the strong six- to seven-foot shoots having red thorns and graceful small foliage made up of from seven to eleven leaflets. The flowers are followed by elliptical red and orange fruits.
Rolfe 1886. *D. EG. NF. GPG. — White. S. June. Hardy.*

OMEIENSIS CHRYSOCARPA (golden fruit) differs only in having fruits of golden-yellow.
Rehder —. *D. EG. NF. GPG. — White. S. June. Hardy.*

OMEIENSIS PTERACANTHA is similar in all respects except that its young
wood has immense flat spines which are of translucent blood-red,
and render the growth of great beauty.
Franchet 1889. *D. EG. NF. GPG. — White. S. May. Hardy.*

OMEIENSIS PTERACANTHA LUTEA is similar, with flowers of canary-yellow.
— —. D. EG. NF. GPG. — — S. May-June. Hardy.

OPHELIA (H.T.) is one of the best known of all roses, and the parent
of many exceptional varieties. The flowers are of perfect shape,
double, open, of pale salmon-flesh shaded with rose, and with an
apricot heart, and are borne upon long stiff stems. Growth is
vigorous and erect, with ample green foliage, which is sometimes
subject to black spot.
Paul 1912. *D. VG. MF. GPB. —* 523/2. *B.G.St.Pot. June-Sept. Hardy.*
[*Pl.* 5 & 58.

ORANGE CHEER (polyantha pompon) has clustered heads of semi-
double orange flowers, borne upon vigorous plants with attractive
glossy green foliage.
Letts 1937. *D. VG. SF. GPF. — — B.G. June-September. Hardy.*

ORANGE NASSAU (H.T.) has exceptionally attractively shaped high-
centred double flowers with gracefully reflexed petals. The flowers,
which are normally of medium size, are of orange-yellow and
vermilion-red; but growth is very moderate and best suited to
indoor culture.
Spek 1939. *D. MG. SF. GPA. EA. — E.Pot.House. June-Sept. Pl.* 47.

ORANGE PERFECTION (polyantha pompon) has double, globular flowers
of orange-red, borne in very large trusses, and is very free-flowering.
Growth is vigorous and erect and foliage is dark glossy green.
Spek 1927. *D. VG. SF. GPF. — — B.G. June-September. Hardy.*

ORANGE TRIUMPH (Hybrid polyantha) produces clusters of rather small
semi-double, globular flowers, of salmon-red with orange, in great
profusion. Growth is vigorous and erect, with glossy green foliage.
Kordes 1938. *D. VG. SF. GPG. —* 22. *B.G.St.Pot. June-Oct. Hardy. Pl.* 31.

ORIENTAL QUEEN (see R. chinensis).

ORLEANS IMPROVED (polyantha pompon) has clustered heads of semi-
double flowers of bright rose-pink on vigorous, erect, moderately
tall plants with glossy green foliage.
Norfolk Nurseries 1931. *D. VG. SF. GPF. — — B.G. June-Sept. Hardy.*

ORLEANS ROSE (polyantha pompon) produces its clustered heads of
semi-double rosy-crimson flowers intermittently throughout the
season, upon vigorous but dwarf plants with glossy green foliage.
Levavasseur 1909. *D. MG. SF. GPF. — — B.G.St. June-Sept. Hardy.*

OSWALD SIEPER (H.T.) has exceptionally large very double flowers of high-pointed shape, with large stiff petals of creamy-white tinted lemon at the centre, borne upon long strong stems. Growth is vigorous, erect and branching, foliage green and glossy and not subject to disease.
Krause 1932. D. VG. MF. GPB. EB. White. B.E.G.St. June-Sept. Hardy.

OTTO KRAUSS (H.T.) makes a vigorous branching plant with glossy bronze-green foliage, and bears large, double, coned flowers of copper-yellow.
Weigand 1931. D. VG. MF. GPB. — — B.G. June-September. Hardy.

OUR ANNIE (H.T.) has large, rounded, double flowers of bright orange-red, borne upon vigorous erect plants with glossy green foliage.
Letts 1937. D. TG. MF. GPB. — — B.G. June-September. Hardy.

OXYODON (sharp-toothed) (S.), Caucasus, makes a compact bush with glossy green leaves with deeply serrated edges and bears solitary single flowers of rose-pink, followed by large round, pendulent, dark red fruits.
Boissier —. D. VG. F. GPG. — — S. June. Hardy.

PALACKY (H.T.) is of vigorous growth with glossy green foliage and bears large single flowers of intense orange-yellow.
Bohm 1936. D. VG. VF. GPB. — — B.G. June-September. Hardy.

PALUSTRIS (S.) (Swamp Rose), Eastern North America, has upright red canes with few thorns, rising to about eight feet, with long green narrow-pointed leaves made up of seven leaflets, and bears clusters of large rose-pink single flowers, followed by scarlet fruits. R. palustris grows best in moist positions.
Marshall —. D. EG. F. GPG. — — S. June-August. Hardy.

PALUSTRIS NUTTALLIANA (S.) is similar in growth, has pale green wood which ripens to red, and bears sharp-pointed thorns and produces somewhat large pink flowers which persist for a longer period.
Rehder —. D. EG. F. GPG. — — S. June-September. Hardy.

PAPA KLEIN (H.T.) has large double flowers with deckled-edged petals of salmon-pink, upon vigorous plants with deep green foliage.
Ketten 1934. D. VG. MF. GPB. — — B.G. June-September. Hardy.

PARIS (polyantha pompon) has clustered heads of double red flowers which persist without fading upon the vigorous plants with green foliage which bear them.
De Ruyter 1929. D. VG. SF. GPF. — — B.G. June-September. Hardy.

PATIENCE (H.T.) has large, double, high-centred flowers of a quaint mixture of orange-carmine and scarlet blended together, borne in clusters on moderately vigorous plants with deep green glossy foliage resistant to disease.
McGredy 1927. D. MG. MF. GPB. — — G. June-September. Hardy.

PATRICK ANDERSON (H.T.) has large, double, conical-centred flowers of deep rose-pink, borne upon strong stems and vigorous plants with dark green foliage. The outstanding scent makes it a lovely rose.
McGredy 1938. *D. VG. VF. GPB. EB. — B.E.G. June-September. Hardy.*

PAUL BOUCLAINVILLE (H.T.) is an exceptionally vigorous plant with dark bronze-green foliage, which is resistant to disease and bears with appropriate caution its semi-double flowers of bright carmine with a yellow base, with the reverse of the petals of white tinted pink and yellow.
Buatois 1930. *D. TG. VF. GPC. — — G. June-September. Hardy.*

PAUL BUATOIS (Climbing H.T.) has large, double, globular flowers of deep carmine and red, with a yellow base. Growth is vigorous and flowering free.
Buatois 1931. *D. C. VF. GPE. — — A.P.W. June-August. Hardy.*

PAUL CRAMPEL (polyantha pompon) has the same colour as the geranium of the same name, with flowers a little bigger and less double than Gloria Mundi, but with a tiny white eye. It retains its colour well, but like all roses of this type, has a marked tendency to throw numerous sports of varying colours. Growth is vigorous, erect, and foliage light green.
Kersbergen 1930. *D. VG. SF. GPF. — — B.St.G. June-September. Hardy.*

PAUL DUVIVIER (H.T.) has semi-double flowers shading from bright yellow at the centre to deep carmine at the edges. Growth is very vigorous, with bronze-green foliage.
La Perrière 1932. *D. TG. VF. GPB. — — G. June-September. Hardy.*

PAUL'S CARMINE PILLAR (see Carmine Pillar).

PAUL'S LEMON PILLAR (see Lemon Pillar).

PAUL'S SCARLET CLIMBER (wichuraiana climber) is one of the most attractive of all climbers with its clusters of large semi-double flowers of crimson scarlet. Growth is very vigorous and hardy and flowers last well and are unaffected by wet weather.
Paul 1916. *D. C. SF. GPJ. — — A.P.W.Wst.House. July-August. Hardy.*

PAX (Hybrid Musk) has exceptionally large, semi-double, white flowers, with golden anthers prominently displayed, borne in very large clusters on vigorous erect bushes with attractive foliage much larger than that of the ordinary Musk rose.
Pemberton 1918. *D. EG. VF. GPG. — White. B.G.St.S.H.W. June-Sept.*
[*Hardy.*

PAX AMANDA (Hybrid blanda) introduces a new parent in the form of R. blanda, designed to impart fortitude and hardiness to its children. The features of the hybrids are their clustered flowers, extremely vigorous growth, general toughness, and thornlessness. Pax Amanda has clustered heads of pale pink semi-double flowers paling with age to white. Growth is tall and suitable for a pillar rose.
Hansen 1938. *D. EG. SF. GPG. — — Pr. June-July. Hardy.*

PAX APOLLO (Hybrid blanda) has similar flowers of deep pink.
Hansen 1938. *D. EG. SF. GPG. — — Pr. June-July. Hardy.*

PAX IOLA (Hybrid blanda) has slightly fuller flowers of shell-pink,
fading paler.
Hansen 1938. *D. EG. SF. GPG. — — Pr. June-July. Hardy.*

PEACE (H.T.) has been hailed as the finest rose of all; not all of this
claim is derived from its name, for it has large flowers of great substance, of creamy white deepening to yellow, and sweetly scented,
with the added charm of an occasional margin of pink edging the
petals.
Meilland 1946. *D. VG. SF. GPC. — — B. June-September. Hardy.*

PEACHGLOW (H.T.) has large double flowers of deep shell-pink, borne
upon strong stems from vigorous plants with glossy green foliage.
Coddington 1937. *D. VG. F. GPB. — — B.G. June-September. Hardy.*

PEARL S. BUCK (H.T.) has very large, many-petalled, high-centred
flowers of pale orange, borne upon long stems. Growth is vigorous
and erect and foliage dark green.
Kordes 1940. *D. VG. SF. GPB. — — B.G. June-September. Hardy.*

PEERLESS (H.T.) has very large, double, high-pointed flowers of intense
carmine scarlet, borne upon long strong stems. Growth is very
vigorous and erect, and foliage dark green and plentiful.
Hill 1935. *D. TG. SF. GPC. — — B.G.Pot. June-September. Hardy.*

PEGGY (H.T.) has high-centred double flowers of deep rose-pink, borne
upon vigorous plants of erect growth with pale-green foliage.
Bees 1934. *D. VG. VF. GPB. — — B.G. June-September. Hardy.*

PEGGY ANN LANDON (wichuraiana climber) bears its large, double,
conical-centred flowers of pale orange, deepening toward the centre,
on vigorous plants with dark green glossy foliage. Is profuse in
flowering and a good hardy climber.
Brownell 1938. *D. CF. GPF. — — A.P.Pr.W. June-July. Hardy.*

PEMBRIDGE (H.T.) is a sport from Roselandia with deeper orange
colouring, the perfection of shape of that variety being fully retained.
Stevens 1934. *D. VG. MF. GPB. — — B.G. June-September. Hardy.*

PENDULINA (pendulous) (S.), Central Europe, has as synonyms R.
alpina, R. gentilis, and R. inermis, and is a tall bush with thornless
stems, rather coarse green foliage made up of from seven to nine
leaflets, and bears large single flowers of bright pink of about two
inches in diameter, either singly or in small groups, followed by
inverted-pear-shaped hanging red fruits.
Linnaeus 1753. *D. TG. VF. GPG. — — S. May-June. Hardy.*

PENDULINA VAR. PLENA is of similar but more robust and diffuse habit,
and bears double flowers of deep pink with deeper veins, followed
by similar fruits.
— —. D. TG. F. GPG. — — S. May-June. Hardy.

PENDULINA VAR. PYRENAICA, S. Europe, is a very dwarf variant best grown in poor soil, bearing bright rose-pink single flowers succeeded by long scarlet fruits.
Keller —. D. DG. SF. GPG. — — S. May-June. Very hardy.

PENELOPE (Hybrid Musk) has clustered double flowers of shell-pink shaded with salmon, borne upon vigorous erect bushes with dark-green ample foliage. It is sweetly fragrant, impervious to damp weather, and long-flowering.
Pemberton 1923. D. TG. VF. GPC. — — B.G.H.S. June-September. Hardy.

PENNSYLVANIA (H.T.) has large semi-double flowers of salmon-pink splashed with deep pink, blending to deep apricot at the centre. Growth is vigorous, foliage dark green, and flowering profuse.
Neuner 1934. D. VG. MF. GPB. — — B.G. June-September. Hardy.

PEON (see R. chinensis var. minima).

PEONY OF FRAGRANCE (H.P.) is a modern hybrid perpetual with large globular paeony-like flowers of bright pink, freely borne on long strong stems. Growth is extra vigorous and perfume good.
Pahissa 1933. D. VG. VF. GPC. — — B.G. June-September. Hardy.

PERCY IZZARD (H.T.) has perfectly shaped double, high-centred, cupped flowers of cream, deepening to maize-yellow at the centre. The flowers are borne upon long stems and open well in all weathers. Growth is vigorous, foliage bronze-green and resistant to disease.
Robinson 1936. D. VG. VF. GPB. EB. 403/3-407/3. E.G. June-Sept. Hardy.
[Pl. 43.

PERFUME (H.T.) has semi-double flowers of deep crimson, freely borne upon strong branching plants, and is exquisitely scented.
Marriott 1927. D. VG. VF. GPB. — — B.G. June-September. Hardy.

PERLE D'OR (Hybrid polyantha) has exquisitely shaped buds and clustered double flowers of pale orange-pink deepening at the centre. Growth is dwarf but vigorous, foliage green and flowers continuous and fragrant.
Dubreuil 1884. D. DG. VF. GPG. — — B.G.St. June-Sept. Hardy. Pl. 62.

PERMANENT WAVE is the American name for Van Nes, which see.

PETER PAN (H.T.) has small but perfectly shaped buds of deep terracotta, opening to resemble a deeper-toned Emma Wright. Growth is strong and erect with dark green foliage.
Wheatcroft 1929. D. VG. MF. GPB. — — B.G.St. June-September. Hardy.

PETITE DE HOLLANDE (see R. centifolia provincialis).

PHYLLIS BIDE (Climbing Hybrid polyantha) bears its loose clusters of pale-gold double flowers, edged with carmine, on very vigorous canes with deep green foliage resistant to disease.
Bide 1924. D. C. MF. GPJ. — — G.H.Pr.W.Wst. July-Sept. Hardy. Pl. 14.

Ulrich Brunner (Hybrid Perpetual) **ABECDH**
Silver Jubilee (Hybrid Tea) **JKNOFGLPQ**

Three Species Roses

Rosa rubrifolia **AEF**

Rosa Claribel **BCGLMPQ**
Rosa blanda var. michiganensis **JKNODH**

PHYLLIS BURDEN (H.T.) has large, double, globular flowers of bright coral shaded with orange towards the base, with vigorous growth and varnished light green foliage.
B. R. Cant 1935. *D. VG. SF. GPB. — B.G. June-September. Hardy.*

PHYLLIS GOLD (H.T.) has perfectly shaped cupped flowers with broad petals and high centres, variable in colour but generally of golden-yellow at the centre, paling towards the edges of the petals. Growth is exceptionally vigorous and upright, and foliage of olive-green. The flowers seem unaffected by rain, and the plant free of disease.
Robinson 1934. *D. VG. MF. GPB. EB. 2. B.E.G.St.Pot. June-Sept. Hardy.*
[*Pl.* 63.

PICARDY (see R. rugosa).

PICCANINNY (H.T.) has large single, open, maroon-red flowers, purple-red on the reverse, centred with golden stamens. The very fragrant flowers are borne upon vigorous plants with varnished dark green foliage.
Lammerts 1941. *D. VG. VF. GPB. — — B.G. June-September.*

PICCANINNY (see also Dusky Maiden).

PICTURE (H.T.) has high-centred flowers of clear rose-pink with pleasantly reflexed petals, which are generally of perfect form. Growth is moderately dwarf but strong and branching. Foliage is dark green, free of disease, the flowers open well in all weathers, and are freely produced.
McGredy 1932. *D. MG. SF. GPB. — — B.Cut.G.Pot. June-Sept. Hardy.*

PIERRE AGUETANT (H.T.) has very large, open, double flowers of maize-yellow, borne upon stout stems. Growth is vigorous and upright and foliage of dark green.
Gaujard 1938. *D. VG. F. GPB. — — B.G. June-September.*

PILARÍN VILELLA (H.T.) is an exceptionally good bedding rose with double, deep red flowers of globular shape, freely produced upon vigorous plants with dark green foliage.
Dot 1936. *D. VG. VF. GPB. — — B.G. June-September. Hardy.*

PILAR LANDECHO (H.T.) has high-centred shapely double flowers of deep orange shaded with pink. Growth is very vigorous and branching. Foliage is good and free of disease; generally an outstanding variety in its ease of growth.
Nadal 1939. *D. VG. F. GPB. — — B.G. June-September. Hardy.*

PIMPINELLIFOLIA is another name for R. spinosissima, which see.

PINELIENSIS (H.S.) is a natural hybrid of R. rubiginosa and R. canina, and makes a tall shapely bush with clusters of bright pink single flowers in May, followed by typical red fruits.
— —. D. TG. F. GPG. — 530. *S.H. May. Hardy. Pl.* 21.

PINK CLUSTER (H.T.) bears very large clusters of double salmon-pink flowers shaded with gold. Growth is exceptionally vigorous and suitable for a hedge. Is resistant to disease and impervious to wet weather.

Morse 1938. *D. TG. SF. GPB. — — G.H.S. June-September. Hardy.*

PINK DAWN (H.T.) has large, many-petalled, high-pointed flowers of salmon-pink shaded with rose, borne on good stems from vigorous and erect plants with attractive green foliage. Seems indifferent to wet conditions and flowers exceptionally well in autumn.

Howard & Smith 1937. *D. TG. F. GPB. — 427/3-23/2. G.B.S. June-Sept.*
[Hardy. Pl. 51.

PINK DELIGHT (Hybrid polyantha) bears clusters of large, single, shell-pink flowers with golden stamens, on plants of vigorous growth with green foliage.

Laxton 1922. *D. VG. SF. GPG. — 23/3-23/2. B.G. June-September. Hardy.*

PINK DRUSCHKI (H.T.) resembles its great namesake in form and habit of growth, producing its well-formed flowers of clear rose-pink upon exceptionally vigorous plants.

Felberg-Leclerc 1929. *D. EG. SF. GPC. — — G. June-August. Hardy.*

PINK GROOTENDORST (see R. rugosa).

PINK GRUSS AN AACHEN (H.T.) is a rose with polyantha blood, producing small clusters of clear salmon-pink double flowers on plants of dwarf but vigorous and erect habit, with rich green foliage.

Kluis 1930. *D. MG. SF. GPB. — — B.G. June-September. Hardy.*

PINK JEWEL (Hybrid polyantha) has large, semi-double, globular flowers, borne in large clusters, of deep dark pink, shading to paler pink at the centres. Growth is vigorous and foliage green and attractive.

Kordes 1940. *D. VG. SF. GPG. — — B.G. June-September.*

PINK KAREN (Hybrid polyantha) is a bright rose-pink sport of Karen Poulsen, differing only in its bright single flowers.

Poulsen 1936. *D. VG. NF. GPG. — 527/2-601/3. B.G.St.Pot. June-Sept.*
[Hardy.

PINK MOSS (see R. muscosa communis).

PINK PEARL (H.T.) makes a vigorous plant with erect growth and large dark green foliage, and spirally shaped flowers with wide petals of deep pink with a salmon base, borne upon long strong stems.

Leenders 1924. *D. VG. VF. GPG. — — B.G. June-September. Hardy.*

PINK PRINCESS (H.T.) is an exceptionally vigorous rose of erect growth with dark green glossy foliage and long-stemmed large, double, rose-pink flowers shaded with yellow, and is outstandingly hardy.

Brownell 1939. *D. TG. VF. GPC. — — G.H. June-September. Hardy.*

PINK PROFUSION (Hybrid setigera) has small, double, rounded flowers of pale pink with a deeper reverse, borne in clusters on long stems. Growth is extra vigorous and foliage shining green.

Horvath 1938. *D. TG. SF. GPG. — — G.H. June-September. Hardy.*

Pink Prosperity (Hybrid Musk) produces its large clusters of double pink flowers in long succession upon erect and very vigorous bushes with dark green foliage.
Pemberton 1931. *D. TG. VF. GPG. — — G.H. June-September. Hardy.*

pisocarpa (with pea-like fruits) (S.), Western North America, forms a very tall bush with graceful upright and branching smooth canes, small mid-green leaves made up of five to seven leaflets, and bears large clusters of single rose-pink flowers about the size of a halfpenny. The clusters of small red pea-like fruits which follow in autumn are particularly attractive.
Gray 1877. *D. EG. SF. GPG. — — S. June-August. Hardy.*

Pissardii (see moschata var. Pissardii).

Pius XI (H.T.) is a rose of upright and diffuse growth with deep green varnished foliage, and large, very double, creamy-white flowers with high pointed centres, deepening to creamy-yellow.
Leenders 1925. *D. MG. MF. GPC — — B.G. June-September. Hardy.*

Poinsettia (H.T.) is the attractive name of a large, double, high-centred rose of brilliant crimson-scarlet, borne on vigorous and branching plants of moderate height, with glossy green foliage.
Howard & Smith 1938. *D. MG. SF. GPC. — — B.G. June-September.*

Polly (H.T.) has large, double, high-centred flowers of perfect shape and blended blush-pink, paling at the edges of the petals to cream and flushed at the centre with gold, the extent of this flush being variable. Growth is vigorous, erect and branching, the foliage attractive, and the flowers borne upon long strong stems.
Beckwith 1928. *D. VG. MF. GPB. EA. — B.E.G. June-Sept. Hardy. Pl.* 51.

polyantha (see R. multiflora in Glossary and p. 16).

pomifera (bearing apple-like fruits) (S.), Central Europe, bears small clusters of large pink single flowers upon an erect but branching shrub with its young green growth turning red with age. The green five- to seven-parted leaves are well retained and form a good foil for the large bright-red, round, apple-like fruits in autumn.
Hermann 1762. *D. EG. SF. GPG. — 27/1. S. June. Hardy.*

Pompon Rose (see R. centifolia provincialis nana).

Pompon de Paris (see R. chinensis var. minima).

Pompon de Saint François (see R. centifolia var. parvifolia).

Poppy (H.T.) has double flowers with notched petals borne in small groups on vigorous branching and erect plants. The flowers open bright coral and fade to pale pink.
Archer 1939. *D. VG. VF. GPB. — — B.G. June-September. Hardy.*

Portadown Bedder (H.T.) produces its medium-size, double, pointed flowers of excellent shape, and of orange-yellow flushed with cerise, upon vigorous branching and erect plants with deep green polished foliage, which is resistant to disease.
McGredy 1929. *D. VG. MF. GPB. — — B.G. June-September. Hardy.*

PORTADOWN FRAGRANCE (H.T.) has large, double, pointed-centred flowers of blended orange-salmon-pink and crimson-scarlet, borne upon moderately vigorous plants of diffuse habit with bronze-green foliage. It is very fragrant, indifferent to wet weather and resistant to disease.
McGredy 1931. *D. MG. VF. GPB. EB.* — *B.E.G. June-September. Hardy.*

PORTADOWN GLORY (H.T.) has double shapely flowers of bright canary-yellow, borne upon vigorous erect plants with bright shining green leaves.
McGredy 1932. *D. VG. MF. GPB.* — — *B.G. June-September. Hardy.*

PORTADOWN SALLY (H.T.) has semi-double flowers of high-pointed form, of carmine-crimson with a yellow suffusion, with the reverse of the petals of sulphur-yellow. Habit is vigorous and erect and the foliage of glossy deep green.
McGredy 1931. *D. VG. MF. GPB.* — — *B.G. June-September. Hardy.*

PORTO (H.T.) has large double flowers of light crimson-purple shaded with scarlet, borne upon good stems. Growth is vigorous and erect and flowering profuse.
Mallerin 1934. *D. VG. SF. GPB.* — — *B.G. June-September. Hardy.*

POULSEN'S COPPER (Hybrid polyantha) has small light green foliage upon vigorous and erect plants with clustered, double, high-pointed flowers of coppery-rose-pink with a yellow base.
Poulsen 1940. *D. VG. SF. GPC.* — — *B. June-September.*

POULSEN'S PINK (Hybrid polyantha) has loosely clustered, semi-double, rounded flowers of creamy-yellow, deepening to pink at the edges of the petals. Growth is vigorous and erect and foliage is light shining green and profuse.
Poulsen 1939. *D. VG. MF. GPG.* — 407/3-420/1. *B.Pot. June-Sept. Hardy.*
[*Pl.* 61.

POULSEN'S SCARLET (Hybrid polyantha) has large double flowers of the same type, borne in the same way in loose clusters and of bright deep rose.
Poulsen 1941. *D. VG. SF. GPG.* — — *B. June-September.*

POULSEN'S YELLOW (Hybrid polyantha) has semi-double cupped flowers of pale buttercup-yellow, borne in loose sprays upon vigorous glossy green-leaved plants of moderate height.
Poulsen 1938. *D. MG. VF. GPG.* — 1/3-2/1. *B. June-Sept. Hardy. Pl.*61.

PRAIRIE ROSE (see R. setigera).

PRESIDENT BOONE (H.T.) is a rose of which I have seen but few flowers, and each left a definite impression of intense blood-scarlet rounded form. Habit is vigorous and flowering profuse, but beauty hangs its shapely head.
Howard & Smith 1935. *D. VG. VF. GPB.* — — *B. June-September.*

PRÉSIDENT BRIAND (Pernetiana) combines with deep glossy green foliage and vigorous growth its large, double, high-pointed flowers of pink with salmon flushes, which it produces with freedom and regularity.
Mallerin 1930. *D. VG. MF. GPB. — — B. June-September. Hardy.*

PRÉSIDENT CHARLES HAIN (H.T.) lives under a multiplicity of names, to wit, Amelia Earhart, Magnum Pernet, and Madame Jules Guérin, and if size and quality justify them, deserves them all! The huge yellow flowers are very double and are borne in quantity upon vigorous plants with upright growth, but require an umbrella in wet weather.
Reymond 1929. *D. VG. MF. GPB. EB. — B.E.G. June-September. Hardy.*

PRÉSIDENT COCHET-COCHET (H.T.) has very large double flowers of deep crimson-scarlet, borne upon vigorous plants of erect growth.
Mallerin 1937. *D. TG. MF. GPB. — — B.G. June-September. Hardy.*

PRÉSIDENT FÉRIER (H.T.) produces its double, deep coppery-pink flowers in some profusion on vigorous plants with erect growth and very green foliage.
Gaujard 1938. *D. VG. VF. GPB. — — B.G. June-September. Hardy.*

PRESIDENT HERBERT HOOVER (Pernetiana) has shapely double flowers of golden-yellow, paler towards the edges of the petals, the outsides of which are shaded with pink, produced with generosity upon very vigorous spreading plants with polished bronze-green foliage. It has the advantage of producing its best blooms in autumn, and is an outstanding variety for bedding purposes.
Coddington 1930. *D. VG. MF. GPB. — 407/2-407/1. B.G. June-Sept.*
[Hardy. Pl. 64.

PRESIDENT JAC SMITS (H.T.) has large semi-double flowers, generally borne in small groups, of bright but intense red. Growth is vigorous but of moderate height and foliage of bronze-green. A most effective rose for close planting.
Verschuren 1928. *D. MG. SF. GPB. — — B.G. June-September. Hardy.*

PRESIDENT MACIA (H.T.) has large full flowers of rose-pink with the reverse of the petals of salmon, closely resembling others of the same colouring, but being of sufficiently strong growth to warrant inclusion in the garden.
Leenders 1933. *D. VG. F. GPB. EB. 625/3-622/3. B.E.G. June-Sept.*
[Hardy. Pl. 58.

PRESIDENT VAN OOST (Pernetiana) has large, double, golden-yellow flowers paling towards the centre, produced upon long strong stems. Habit is vigorous, and foliage glossy green.
Lens 1934. *D. VG. MF. GPB. — — B.G. June-September. Hardy.*

PRIDE OF HURST (polyantha pompon) has clusters of very small, very double flowers of coral-pink, on vigorous plants of moderate height with rich green glossy foliage.
Hicks 1926. *D. MG. NF. GPF. — — B.G. June-September. Hardy.*

PRIMAVERA (H.T.) has attractively formed flowers of bright salmon-pink, borne upon vigorous plants with good green foliage.
Robichon 1936. *D. VG. MF. GPB. —— B.G. June-September. Hardy.*

PRIMROSE (Primevère) (wichuraiana climber) bears its large, double, many-petalled flowers of primrose-yellow, paling to canary-yellow, upon vigorous climbing canes, with bright green glossy foliage.
Barbier 1929. *D. C. SF. GPJ. —— A.Pr.W.T. June. Hardy.*

PRINCE BERNHARD (H.T.) has high-centred double flowers of bright red, shaded cerise-red, borne upon vigorous erect plants with dark green foliage.
Van Rossem 1937. *D. VG. VF. GPB. —— B.G. June-September. Hardy.*

PRINCE CAMILLE DE ROHAN (H.P.) has shapely, very deep-cupped maroon-red flowers which are intensely fragrant and remains, in spite of its age, one of the darkest of the red roses.
Verdier 1861. *D. VG. VF. GPB. —— B. June-July. Hardy.*

PRINCE CHARLIE (H.T.) has large double, cupped, persistent flowers of coral-pink and salmon, with a base of orange, borne upon vigorous erect and branching plants with bronze-green foliage, produced with freedom and continuity.
Dobbie 1932. *D. VG. MF. GPB. —— June-September. Hardy.*

PRINCE FÉLIX DE LUXEMBOURG (H.T.) has double flowers of smooth carmine-red, borne freely and continuously upon plants of strong upright and bushy growth with dark green foliage.
Ketten 1930. *D. VG. MF. GPB. EB. — B.E.G. June-September. Hardy.*

PRINCESS BEATRIX (H.T.) has very large, double, globular flowers of terracotta-red flushed with pale orange, borne on long stems. Growth is vigorous, erect and branching, and foliage of deep bronze-green.
Morse 1940. *D. VG. VF. GPB. EB. — B.E.G. June-September.*

PRINCESSE AMÉDÉE DE BROGLIE (H.T.) has cupped high-centred flowers of bright orange-red, borne upon long stems. Growth is vigorous and foliage of deep varnished green.
Mallerin 1936. *D. VG. MF. GPB. —— B.G. June-September. Hardy.*

PRINCESS JULIANA (H.T.) produces its double deep-crimson flowers in small groups upon vigorous plants with dark green glossy foliage, and is a good variety for bedding purposes.
Leenders 1918. *D. VG. VF. GPB. —— B.G. June-September. Hardy.*

PRINCESS MARGARET ROSE (H.T.) is of exceptionally strong growth, with double, cupped flowers of soft salmon-pink, with attractively dainty foliage, proof against mildew.
B. R. Cant 1932. *D. VG. SF. GPB. —— B.G. June-September. Hardy.*

PRINCESS MARINA (H.T.) has perfectly shaped double flowers of apricot veined with salmon and produced upon long stiff stems. Growth is vigorous and branching, and flowering prolonged.
Robinson 1936. *D. VG. SF. GPB. —— B.G. June-Sept. Hardy. Pl.* 57.

PRINCESS OF ORANGE (Prinses van Oranje) (Climbing polyantha pompon) is a vigorous climbing sport of Gloria Mundi with clustered heads of double flowers of bright orange-scarlet with bright green glossy foliage.
De Ruiter 1933. *D. C. NF. GPJ.* — — *4.Pr. July-September.*

PRINCESS ROYAL (H.T.) has exceptionally large, wide-petalled, double flowers of hydrangea-pink, borne upon good stems. Growth is strong, erect and branching, with deep green glossy foliage.
Dickson 1935. *D. VG. VF. GPB. EB.* — *B.E.G. June-September. Hardy.*

PRODANA NEVESTA (polyantha) possesses a curious name which may be anglicised into "The Bartered Bride," and forms a bush of about five feet in height, with large clusters of very fragrant white flowers shaded yellow.
Bohm 1934. *D. EG. VF. GPG.* — *White. S. July-September.*

PROFESSEUR DEAUX (H.T.) bears its large, double, pale-yellow flowers, splashed with maize, on long stems. Robust growth and polished dark bronze-green foliage combine to make it a good plant.
Pernet-Ducher 1935. *D. VG. SF. GPB.* — — *B.G. June-September. Hardy.*

PROFESSOR IBRAHIM (Hybrid macrantha) is a climbing rose with large clustered rose-pink flowers, borne on robust canes with much green foliage.
Krause 1937. *D. C. VF. GPJ.* — — *A.Pr. June-July. Hardy.*

PROFUSION (H.T.) has large, double, high-centred flowers of carmine-lake with a yellow base and a bronzy-carmine reverse. Growth is vigorous and erect and the flowering starts early and finishes late.
Dickson 1939. *D. VG. F. GPB. EB.* 621. *B.E.G. June-Sept. Hardy. Pl. 29.*

PROMISE (Climbing H.T.) provides a delightful contrast with its clusters of single salmon-pink flowers with central golden stamens and its bright green foliage.
F. Cant 1923. *D. C. SF. GPE.* — — *A.Pr. June-August.*

PROSPERITY (Hybrid Musk) has large, double, white flowers produced in large trusses upon erect and vigorous plants with glossy dark green foliage.
Pemberton 1919. *D. TG. F. GPG.* — — *G.Pr. July-September. Hardy.*

PROVENCE Rose (see R. centifolia var. provincialis).

PRUDENCE (Climbing H.T.) is a rose of Australian origin producing semi-double salmon-pink flowers of large size on exceptionally vigorous canes, with some continuity.
Hazlewood 1938. *D. C. VF. GPE.* — — *W.A.P. July-August.*

PUMILA is another name for R. chinensis var. minima, which see.

PUNICEA (see R. lutea var. bicolor).

Purity (Climbing H.T.) has large, shapely, semi-double white flowers borne on vigorous stems with light green foliage.
Hoopes & Thomas 1917. *D. C. SF. GPE. — White. A.P.W. June-July.*

Queen Alexandra (see The Queen Alexandra).

Queen Astrid (see Koningin As.rid).

Queen Dorothy Bell (H.T.) has very double, rounded, smooth crimson-scarlet high-centred flowers, borne on very vigorous plants with bright green glossy foliage.
Stell 1940. *D. VG. VF. GPC. EC. — B.E.G. June-September.*

Queen Frances Connally (H.T.) has shapely semi-double flowers of yellow edged with red, with the interior of bright red with a bright yellow base. Growth is vigorous and flowering continuous.
Stell 1939. *D. VG. SF. GPB. — — B.G. June-September.*

Queen Louise Boren (H.T.) has exceptionally vigorous growth and bears upon long stems its very double soft pink flowers flushed with salmon.
Nicolas 1935. *D. TG. VF. GPC — — B.G. June-September.*

Queen Mab (see R. chinensis).

Queen Marie of Jugoslavia (H.T.) has very shapely flowers of bright yellow with a pink flush, borne upon long stems. Growth is vigorous and branching, and foliage large and leathery.
Hicks 1935. *D. VG. MF. GPB. — — B.G.Cut. June-September. Hardy.*

Queen of Bath (H.T.) produces its medium-size, double, buttercup-yellow flowers, which are shaded with paler yellow, on long stems borne by vigorous free-flowering plants with polished bronze-green foliage.
Bees 1931. *D. VG. MF. GPB. — — B.G. June-September. Hardy.*

Radiance (H.T.) bears its large clear-pink, very double, cupped flowers on long stems, upon extra vigorous erect and branching plants with large tough green foliage.
Cook 1908. *D. TG. VF. GPC. — — G. June-September. Hardy.*

Radio (Pernetiana) has large semi-globular flowers, borne upon vigorous, erect, free-flowering plants with glossy green foliage. The basic colour of the flowers is primrose-yellow and each flower is differently striped and splashed with carmine.
Dot 1937. *D. VG. VF. GPB. — 20, 4, 2. B.G. June-September. Hardy.*

Raffles Bruce (H.T.) is a rose with rich glowing apricot (flushed copper-orange) petals, yellow outside and sweetly perfumed. Has glossy green foliage and is of free growth.
Bees Ltd. 1943. *D. MG. MF. GPB. — — B.G. June-September. Hardy.*

Pernetiana Rose, Souvenir de Georges Pernet

Hybrid Rugosa Rose, F. J. Grootendorst

RAMÓN BACH (H.T.) bears its large, double, brilliant orange flowers on stout stems on robust plants with varnished deep green foliage. The flowers lessen in intensity towards the edges of the petals, which have pale coppery-orange backs.
Dot 1938. *D. VG. VF. GPB. — — B.G. June-September. Hardy.*

RAPA is R. virginiana plena, which see.

RAPTURE (H.T.) resembles Madame Butterfly, of which it is a sport, but has a greater intensity of colour in its blending of coral, rose, apricot and gold, and similar habits of growth.
Traendly & Schenck 1926. *D. VG. VF. GPB. — — B.Cut.G. June-Sept.*
[Hardy.

RED ADMIRAL (Hybrid polyantha) bears a topically significant name, with semi-double flowers of intense red borne in clusters upon green-leaved plants of moderate growth.
Archer 1940. *D. MG. SF. GPG. — — B. June-September.*

RED BOY (H.T.) has semi-double few-petalled flowers of orange-red passing to deep pink, freely and continuously borne upon exceptionally vigorous plants with deep green glossy foliage.
Hansen 1939. *D. TG. SF. GPC. — — B.G. June-September.*

RED LETTER DAY (H.T.) has neatly formed semi-double scarlet-crimson flowers borne in profusion upon short stems, on erect robust plants with grey-green foliage.
Dickson 1914. *D. VG. SF. GPB. — 822. June-September. Hardy.*

RED MOSS (see R. muscosa × Henri Martin).

RED RIDING HOOD (see Rodhatte).

RED VELVET (Hybrid polyantha) has clustered, semi-double, globular flowers of bright crimson, borne upon plants of vigorous, erect and branching growth with light green foliage.
Kordes 1939. *D. VG. SF. GPG. — — B. June-September.*

REFULGENCE (see R. rubiginosa).

REGINA ELENA (H.T.) is a sport of Briarcliff and has exceptionally large, very double, deep rose-pink flowers carried on long strong stems, borne almost continuously on vigorous, erect and branching plants with dark green, disease-resistant foliage.
Grillo 1938. *D. VG. VF. GPB. EB. — B.E.G. June-September.*

REINE DES VIOLETTES (H.P.) is a very vigorous plant with double violet-purple flowers, shaded with mauve and red, of medium size. It has been claimed to be a "blue" rose, and is probably the nearest approach that has yet been attained to an object which is quite undesirable.
Millet-Malet 1860. *D. TG. SF. GPC. — — G. June-July. Hardy.*

RENÉ ANDRÉ (wichuraiana rambler) has semi-double saffron-yellow flowers shaded with orange-red. Growth is vigorous and climbing, and flowers are freely produced in June.

Barbier 1900. *D. C. MF. GPI. — — A.Pr.W.Wst. June. Hardy.*

RENÉE BRIGHTMAN (H.T.) has double crimson-scarlet flowers shaded with orange, with golden streaks on the backs of the petals, and is a free-flowering rose with robust growth.

Hurran 1934. *D. VG. F. GPB. — — B.G. June-September. Hardy.*

REPENS (see R. arvensis).

RÊVE D'OR (N.) has vigorous climbing habit, with attractive green foliage and somewhat small double flowers of buff-yellow, produced with most freedom in the autumn when placed on a sheltering south or west wall.

Ducher 1869. *D. C. F. GPJ. — — A.W. June-September.*

RÉVEIL DIJONNAIS (Climbing Pernetiana) possesses the typical glossy bronze-green foliage of its class, clothing vigorous erect stems, and bears its semi-double cherry-red flowers in short-stemmed clusters. These have the outside of the petals of golden yellow splashed with carmine.

Buatois 1931. *D. C. F. GPJ. — — P.Pr. June-July.*

REV. F. PAGE-ROBERTS (H.T.) possesses most of the good points of a rose suitable for exhibition. The orange-yellow to saffron-yellow flowers are very large, full-petalled and of excellent shape, and the colour does not fade. Foliage is of medium size and of bronze-green, and habit of growth is bushy and vigorous.

B. R. Cant 1921. *D. VG. VF. GPB. EB. — G.E.Pot. June-Sept. Hardy.*

REWARD (H.T.) has attractive spiralled flowers of a charming blend of pale rose, light yellow and orange. Growth is vigorous, branching and erect and foliage dark shining green.

Dickson 1934. *D. VG. SF. GPB. — — B.G. June-September.*

REX ANDERSON (H.T.) develops its flowers in loose clusters on stout long stems arising from vigorous erect plants with glaucous green disease-proof foliage. The perfectly shaped flowers are large, very double and of very pale yellow, shading to light gold at the base of the petals.

McGredy 1934. *D. VG. F. GPB. EB. 1/3. B.E.G.St.Pot. June-Sept. Hardy.*

RHEINGOLD (H.T.) is a Mabel Morse seedling with large many-petalled golden-yellow flowers of attractive shape combined with dwarf and branching but vigorous growth, clothed with light green glossy foliage.

Leenders 1934. *D. DG. VF. GPB. — — B.G. June-September. Hardy.*

RIA WENNING (H.T.) provides its moderate-size, carmine-red, semi-double flowers with such freedom upon robust but compact plants as to justify a place in the sun.

Leenders 1932. *D. MG. VF. GPB. — — B.G. June-September. Hardy.*

RICHMOND (H.T.) is an old favourite with medium-size, double, light-crimson flowers produced singly upon virile stems. Growth is vigorous, the foliage dark green and flowers abundant.
Hill 1905. *D. VG. NF. GPB. — — B.G. June-September. Hardy.*

RIVIERA (H.T.) has large, very double, semi-globular flowers of bright orange-red with the outside of the petals of deep orange. Growth is vigorous, erect and branching, and foliage deep shining green.
Dot 1939. *D. VG. SF. GPB. — — B.G. June-September.*

R.M.S. QUEEN MARY is the unaccepted name of Mrs. H. A. Verschuren, which see.

ROBIN HOOD (Hybrid Musk) resembles a polyantha rose, having large clusters of rather small, semi-double, cherry-red flowers, borne upon upstanding bushes of exceptionally vigorous growth.
Pemberton 1927. *D. TG. F. GPG. — 24. B.G. July-September. Hardy.*

ROCHEFORT (H.T.) has large, double, many-petalled, orange flowers shot with old rose, borne upon good stems. Growth is vigorous and flowering free.
Mallerin 1935. *D. VG. VF. GPB. — — B. June-September. Hardy.*

ROCHELLE HUDSON (H.T.) has attractions. The semi-double carmine flowers shade to yellow at the base and provide a picture improving with age. Growth is robust, flowers abundant, and foliage deep green.
Moore 1937. *D. VG. SF. GPB. — — B. June-September.*

ROCKET (H.T.) is exceptionally vigorous in growth, with stout canes clothed with dark bronze-green foliage. The large, double, pointed-centred flowers are of crimson, intensifying at the centre to crimson-scarlet.
Nicolas 1935. *D. TG. VF. GPC. — — G. June-September.*

RODHATTE (Hybrid polyantha) is sometimes known as Red Riding Hood and has large semi-double cherry-red flowers, borne in large clusters upon dwarf and compact plants with cool green foliage.
Poulsen 1912. *D. MG. NF. GPG. — — B. June-September. Hardy.*

ROEBUCK RAMBLER (see R. arvensis capreolata).

ROI ALEXANDRE (see King Alexander I).

ROMANA (H.T.) has very large double flowers of purplish-red, freely borne upon very vigorous plants with polished dark green foliage.
Ringdahl 1938. *D. VG. SF. GPB. — — B. June-September. Hardy.*

ROMEO (wichuraiana climber) has exceptionally attractively formed miniature double flowers of deep crimson, borne in small clusters with glossy deep green foliage.
Easlea 1919. *D. C. SF. GPJ. — — A.P.Pr. June-July. Hardy.*

RONALD HEALY (H.T.) has high-centred, double, old-rose flowers shaded and flushed with salmon and yellow. Growth is moderately vigorous and branching, with shining green foliage.
Dobbie 1932. *D. MG. MF. GPB. — — B.G. June-September. Hardy.*

Ronsard (Pernetiana) has dark green tough foliage, clothing vigorous plants which give rise to semi-double flowers of bright red, the reverse of the petals shading from cream to yellow. Habit is good and flowering profuse and intermittent.
Gaujard 1937. *D. VG. SF. GPB. — — B. June-September.*

Rosaleen (Hybrid Musk) has double, dark-red flowers produced in large clusters upon tall vigorous bushes which flower continuously.
Bentall 1932. *D. TG. F. GPC. — — B.H. June-September. Hardy.*

Rosaleen Dunn (H.T.) bears its large, double, wide-petalled crimson flowers of good high-centred form on strong stems. Growth is vigorous and branching and foliage of deep green.
McGredy 1939. *D. VG. VF. GPB. EB. — B.E.G. June-September.*

Rosa Mundi (see R. gallica var. versicolor).

Rose Anne (Climbing H.T.) is a very vigorous climber producing its semi-double apricot-yellow flowers intermittently throughout the season. Foliage is an attractive glossy green.
Thomas 1938. *D. C. SF. GPE. — — A.W. June-September.*

Rose à Parfum de L'Hay (see R. rugosa).

Rose Apples (see R. rugosa).

Rose Bampton (H.T.) has very double, high-centred, bright crimson-scarlet flowers with gracefully reflexed petals, borne upon plants of robust growth.
Van Rossem 1940. *D. VG. MF. GPB. — — June-September. Hardy.*

Rose Berkeley (H.T.) has large, pointed-centred, deep salmon-pink flowers suffused with orange, made up of many petals, nicely reflexed, and is of vigorous growth with deep green foliage.
McGredy 1928. *D. VG. MF. GPB. EB. 625/2 to 623. B.E.G. June-Sept.*
[*Hardy. Pl.* 65.

Rosebud (wichuraiana rambler) has clusters of very double flowers of pale pink, deepening at the edges, and is a vigorous and free-flowering variety.
Hurran 1934. *D. C. SF. GPI. — — A.P.Pr. June-July. Hardy.*

Rose d'Amour (H.T.) has ovoid double flowers of deep peach-pink inside, and old gold outside, and bears them on vigorous plants with varnished bronze-green foliage.
Gaujard 1936. *D. VG. F. GPB. — — B.G.St. June-October. Hardy.*

Rose Dawn (H.T.) is still a good rose with very large, double, high-centred cream and blush-pink flowers. It is vigorous, erect and branching, flowering is continuous and foliage an attractive polished deep green not subject to disease.
Towill 1924. *D. VG. VF. GPB. — — B.G. June-September. Hardy.*

Rose d'Or (Pernetiana) is a vigorous, erect and branching plant, with varnished bronze-green foliage, giving rise to attractive double golden flowers, the outer petals of which seem to have red blood coursing through their veins.
Gaujard 1940. *D. VG. SF. GPB. — — B.G. June-September.*

Rose du Barri (H.T.) has large single flowers of coppery-pink with a deep pink reverse; habit is vigorous, foliage good, and the flowers are moderately fragrant.
Archer 1940. *D. VG. MF. GPB. — — B. June-September. Hardy.*

Roselandia (H.T.) produces a succession of perfectly shaped high-centred flowers of deep creamy gold with golden-apricot centres, but does so with greater certainty, if somewhat paler colour, under glass. Its relation to Ophelia is clearly shown in the shape of its exquisite flowers.
W. Stevens 1924. *D. VG. MF. GPB. — — G.Pot. June-September.*

Rosella (Hybrid polyantha) has semi-double, deckled salmon-rose-pink flowers borne in very large clusters. Its vigorous habit and attractive green, disease-resistant foliage make it exceptionally good for bedding purposes.
Prior 1930. *D. VG. SF. GPG. — — B. June-September. Hardy.*

Rose Marie (H.T.) is the possessor of large double, ovoid, rose-pink flowers of excellent shape. Growth is robust and branching, the flowering period extended, and foliage an attractive glossy bronze-green.
Dorner 1919. *D. VG. F. GPB. — — B.G. June-September. Hardy.*

Rosenelfe (Hybrid polyantha) is attractive from the moment its clustered pointed buds spring into existence. The delightful miniature perfectly-formed high-centred, double, pale-pink flowers are borne in clusters with quite long individual stems. Vigour is self-evident in the erect and branching growth, clad with shining light green foliage.
Kordes 1937. *D. VG. SF. GPG. — 622/3. B.G.St. June-September. Hardy.*

Rosenwunder (see R. rubiginosa).

Roseraie de L'Hay (see R. rugosa).

Rosette (H.T.) combines very good shapely bushy habit with equally shapely moderate-size rose-red flowers shaded with orange.
Dickson 1934. *D. VG. MF. GPB. — — B.G. June-September. Hardy.*

Roslyn (H.T.) has golden-yellow semi-double flowers of moderate size, but of excellent shape, sometimes splashed with red on the backs of the petals. Growth is robust and compact, flowers produced with freedom, the foliage proof against disease, small and of bright polished green.
Towill 1929. *D. VG. SF. GPB. — — B.G.St. June-September. Hardy.*

ROTARY-LYON (H.T.) has semi-double very large flowers of deep orange-yellow shaded with carmine, with the backs of the petals of clear yellow, and is of vigorous, erect and branching growth, with tough dark green foliage.
Chambard 1936. *D. VG. SF. GPB. — — B.G. June-September. Hardy.*

ROUGE (Hybrid polyantha) bears large clusters of semi-double crimson-scarlet flowers for a long period on dwarf but vigorous plants with good green tough foliage.
Verschuren 1934. *D. MG. SF. GPG. — — B. June-September. Hardy.*

ROUGE MALLERIN (H.T.) couples excellent habit with freedom of flowering and exquisite shape. The large, double, high-pointed flowers are of bright crimson-scarlet and are intensely fragrant, and borne upon compact and vigorous erect plants.
Mallerin 1934. *D. VG. VF. GPB. EB. — B.E.G. June-September. Hardy.*

ROULETTII (see R. chinensis var. minima).

ROXANA (H.T.) makes a strong moderately tall bushy plant, with fragrant semi-double orange-yellow flowers shaded with bright cerise.
Dickson 1933. *D. MG. MF. GPB. — — B.G. June-September. Hardy.*

ROXBURGHII (S.), Japan, is also known as the Chestnut Rose and makes a graceful bush of some six feet in height, with green leaves made up of seven to fifteen small leaflets, with very large, single, pale rose-pink flowers borne singly or in small clusters.
Roxburgh 1824. *D. EG. F. GPG. — — S. June-July. Hardy.*

ROXBURGHII VAR. HIRTULA differs only in having hairy fruits.

ROXBURGHII VAR. PLENA has double pale pink flowers.

ROYAL BEAUTY (H.T.) has dark crimson double flowers of high-centred shape, borne upon very vigorous plants with tough dark green foliage.
Coddington 1940. *D. TG. SF. GPC. — — B.G.Pot. June-September.*

ROYAL SCARLET (wichuraiana climber) is an excellent pillar rose with semi-double crimson-scarlet flowers in small clusters upon vigorous canes.
Chaplin 1926. *D. C. SF. GPJ. — — A.Pr.Wst. June-July. Hardy.*

ROYAL SCOT (H.T.) combines hardiness, sturdy erect habit, with freely produced, semi-double, golden-yellow flowers lightly tipped with crimson. Growth is quite strong, with tough dark foliage.
Dobbie 1928. *D. VG. F. GPB. — — B.G. June-September. Hardy.*

ROYAL VISIT (H.T.) is a very attractive double flower of tangerine, paling slightly towards the edges of the petals, the backs of which are apricot and coral. Growth is vigorous, erect and branching, and foliage tough dark shining green.
Eddie 1939. *D. VG. SF. GPB. — — B.G. June-September.*

RUBIGINOSA (rusty) (S.), Great Britain, is also known as Rosa eglanteria, and is the Sweet Briar, making good hedges with scented foliage and single flowers of bright pink, followed by bright red fruits. It has given rise, chiefly as a result of the work of the late Lord Penzance, to the hybrids which are noted below, and form large distinctive bushes, or can be employed to form hedges.

× RUBIGINOSA

AMY ROBSART. Semi-double deep rose	*Penzance* 1894
ANNE OF GEIERSTEIN. Single deep red	*Penzance* 1894
BRENDA. Peach-pink	*Penzance* 1894
CATHERINE SEYTON. Soft rose-pink	*Penzance* 1894
EDITH BELLENDEN. Single soft rose	*Penzance* 1895
FLORA McIVER. Single pink, white eye. *Pl.* 52.	*Penzance* 1894
GREEN MANTLE. Single red, white eye	*Penzance* 1895
HEBE'S LIP. Semi-double white, purple edge ...	*Penzance* —
JANET'S PRIDE. White, red edge	*Whitwell* 1862
JEANNIE DEANS. Semi-double, rose-crimson ...	*Penzance* 1895
LADY PENZANCE. Single copper, yellow centre. *Pl.* 52	*Penzance* 1894
LORD PENZANCE. Single fawn, gold centre ...	*Penzance* 1894
LUCY BERTRAM. Single crimson, white eye ...	*Penzance* 1895
REFULGENCE. Semi-double, crimson-scarlet ...	*Paul* 1909
ROSENWUNDER. Semi-double, very large, rose-red	*Kordes* 1934

(*Various.*) *D. EG. F. GPG. — —. H.S. June-July. Hardy. Pl.* 66.

RUBRIFOLIA (with red leaves) (S.), Central Europe, makes a tall bush with thornless canes and purplish-red leaves composed of seven to nine leaflets, and bears rather small single flowers of deep reddish-pink in small clusters, followed by flattened round scarlet fruits.
Villars 1814. *D. EG. SF. GPG.* — 625/2. *S. June-July. Hardy. Pl.* 70.

RUBY MANWARING (H.T.) is a sport of Betty Uprichard with similarly shaped flowers of crimson-scarlet, paling on opening to cerise-red. Growth is extra vigorous, foliage light green and glossy, and flowering exceptional in autumn.
Longley 1932. *D. TG. F. GPC.* — 622/024. *B.G. June-September. Hardy.*

RUBY TALISMAN (H.T.) is a Talisman sport, with high-centred, double, ruby-red flowers, with reflexed petals. Growth is as lusty as that of its parent, and foliage deep green.
Eddie 1935. *D. VG. F. GPB. — — B.G. June-September. Hardy.*

Rudolf Kluis Superior (polyantha pompon) has the colour of Paul's Scarlet Climber, and double crimson-scarlet flowers, borne in large clusters on dwarf robust plants with bright green glossy foliage. *Kluis* 1927. *D. MG. MF. GPF. — — B. June-September. Hardy.*

Rufus (polyantha pompon) has double intense-crimson flowers in large clusters, retaining their colour well, and not so prone to "sport" as many of the more recent varieties. *Allen* 1925. *D. VG. SF. GPF. — — B. June-September. Hardy.*

rugosa (wrinkled) (S.) is the Japanese or Hedgehog Rose from Eastern Asia and forms a massive bush with stout, very thorny stems, rising to about six feet in height, with deeply veined or wrinkled leaves of shining green made up of from five to nine leaflets and bearing large four-inch flowers of magenta, either singly or in few-flowered clusters, followed by flattened rounded fruits of bright brick-red deepening with age. R. rugosa and its hybrids should be pruned but very lightly. *Thunberg* 1844. *D. EG. VF. GPG. — 629. S. June-Sept. Hardy. Pl.* 66 [*& 67.*

rugosa var. alba is similar but has white flowers.

rugosa var. calocarpa has rose flowers. 627.

rugosa var. Chamissoniana has few bristles.

rugosa var. kamtchatica has smaller flowers and fruits.

rugosa var. plena has double magenta flowers.

The following hybrids derived from Rosa rugosa are noteworthy, and where any deviation from the habit of the type is outstanding it is noted.

rugosa Agnes has large double flowers of amber-yellow	*Saunders* 1900. *June-July*
„ Agnes Emily Carman. Double crimson	*Carman* 1898. *June*
„ Amélie Gravereaux. Double carmine...	*Gravereaux* 1903. *June*
„ Arnold. Single crimson ...	*Dawson* 1893. *June*
„ atropurpurea. Double maroon	*Levavasseur* 1910. *June*
„ Belle Poitevine. Semi-double magenta-pink	*Bruant* 1894. *June-July*
„ Berger's Erfolg. Single crimson-scarlet	*Berger* 1925. *June-August*
„ Blanche Double de Coubert. Double to semi-double white. H.	*Cochet-Cochet* 1892. *June*

Hybrid Tea Rose, Sam McGredy

Hybrid Tea Rose, McGredy's Triumph

RUGOSA CARMEN. Single crimson ... *Lambert* 1907. *June*

,, CONRAD F. MEYER. Large double, very tall silver-pink. *H.* ... *Muller* 1899. *June-July*

,, DOLLY VARDEN. Apricot-pink... *Paul* 1914. *June-August*

,, DOROTHY FOWLER. Semi-double clear pink ... ... *Skinner* 1938. *June*

,, DR. ECKENER. Semi-double yellow flushed copper, fading pink *Berger* 1930. *June*

,, ENCHANTRESS. Double blood-red, taller ... ... *(Origin unknown.) June*

,, F. J. GROOTENDORST. Fringed double deep-pink flowers ... *de Goey* 1918. *June-July.* [*Pl.* 72

,, GOLDENER TRAUM. Large double yellow ... ... *Turke* 1932. *June-Sept.*

,, GOLDEN KING. Semi-double clear-yellow ... ... *Beckwith* 1935. *June-July*

,, GROOTENDORST SUPREME. Double crimson carnation-like flowers *Grootendorst* 1936. *June-July*

,, HANSA. Large double purple ... *Schaum* 1905. *June*

,, HEIDEKIND. Large double salmon-pink ... ... *Munch & Haufe* 1931. *June-* [*September*

,, HILDEBRANDSECK. Semi-double bright carmine... ... ... *Lambert* 1909. *June-October*

,, JOHN MCNAB. Double pink ... *Skinner* 1938. *July*

,, LA MÉLUSINE. Double deep rose-pink ... ... *Spath* 1906. *June-July*

,, MADAME GEORGES BRUANT. Loose double white. *H.* ... *Bruant* 1887. *June-October*

,, MADAME JULIEN POTIN. Double flesh-pink ... ... *Gravereaux* 1913. *June-Aug.*

,, MADAME LUCIEN VILLEMINOT. Pale pink ... ... *L'Hay* 1903. *June-July*

,, MAX GRAF. Single pink ... *Bowditch* 1919. *June-July*

,, MRS. ANTHONY WATERER. Semi-double deep crimson ... ... *Waterer* 1896. *June-July*

,, NEW CENTURY. Double flesh-pink, deeper centre ... ... *Van Fleet* 1900. *June-July*

,, NOVA ZEMBLA. Double white, flushed pink ... ... *Mees* 1906. *June-July*

,, PICARDY. Blood-red inside, yellow outside ... ... *Gaujard* 1936. *June-Sept.*

RUGOSA PINK GROOTENDORST. A lighter pink counterpart of F. J. Grootendorst, which it resembles in other respects. 625/1	*Grootendorst* 1925. *June-July*	
,,	ROSE À PARFUM DE L'HAY. Double carmine	*Gravereaux* 1903. *June-July*
,,	ROSE APPLES. Semi-double deep rose	*Paul* 1906. *June-July*
,,	ROSERAIE DE L'HAY. Single crimson, fading magenta ...	*Cochet-Cochet* 1901. *June*
,,	RUSKIN. Very double crimson...	*Van Fleet* 1928. *June*
,,	SANGUINAIRE. Semi-double deep red	*Gillot* 1933. *June-July*
,,	SARAH VAN FLEET. Semi-double wild-rose-pink	*Van Fleet* 1926. *June-October*
,,	SCHNEELICHT. Single pure white. H.	*Geschwind* 1894. *June*
,,	SCHNEEZWERG. Semi-double white. Dwarf	*Lambert* 1912. *June-August*
,,	SCHWABENLAND. Double mauve-pink. Dwarf	*Berger* 1928. *June-August*
,,	SIR THOMAS LIPTON. Double white, moderately tall... ...	*Van Fleet* 1900. *June-August*
,,	SOUVENIR DE PHILÉMON COCHET. Double white rose centre ...	*Cochet-Cochet* 1899. *June*
,,	STELLA POLARIS. Single white...	*Jenson* 1900. *June*
,,	STERN VON PRAG. Double dark crimson	*Berger* 1924. *June-August*
,,	TETONKAHA. Deep pink double	*Hansen* 1912. *July*
,,	THUSNELDA. Semi-double rose	*Muller* 1889. *June*
,,	VIRA. Bright red	*Bohm* 1936. *June*
,,	WASAGAMING. Double rose. Dwarf	*Skinner* 1938. *June-August*

RUSKIN (see above).

RUTH (H.T.) has a dwarf habit with compact growth, with dark green glossy foliage, and large double flowers of orange flushed with carmine, held upright.
Pemberton 1921. *D. MG. MF. GPB.* —— *B.G. June-September. Hardy.*

RUTH ALEXANDER (Climbing H.T.) is a vigorous climber with large semi-double orange flowers paling towards the centre. Growth is vigorous and foliage is shining bronze-green.
Wilber 1937. *D. C. VF. GPE.* —— *A.P. June-July.*

SACRAMENTO Rose (see R. mirifica).

SALET (see R. muscosa).

SALLY (H.T.) has long shapely buds, high-centred double flowers of clear pink, borne upon stiff stems, and is of vigorous, erect and branching growth.
Spandikow 1928. *D. VG. MF. GPB. — — B.G. June-September. Hardy.*

SALMON SPRAY (Hybrid polyantha) has single and semi-double flowers of pale salmon-pink, shaded with carmine on the reverse of the petals, and is of robust bushy growth, with bright green attractive foliage.
Grant 1925. *D. VG. SF. GPG. — 23/2-24/3. B.G. June-Sept. Hardy. Pl. 34.*

SAM MCGREDY (H.T.) is one of the largest of roses, producing many exceptional flowers when grown for exhibition purposes. The cream petals building the shapely flowers deepen in intensity to pale biscuit-yellow in the centre. Growth is moderately strong and the rose is best suited to exhibition purposes or indoor pot culture, although it can be very successful under ordinary garden conditions.
McGredy 1937. *D. MG. SF. — EB. 403/3-412/2. E.G.B. June-Sept. Pl. 73.*

SAMMY (Hybrid Musk) has semi-double flowers of bright carmine, borne in clusters, and forms a robust tall bush with shining bronze-green foliage, flowering continuously through the season.
Pemberton 1921. *D. TG. VF. GPG. — — H. June-September. Hardy.*

SAMUEL PEPYS (H.T.) produces its semi-globular very large double flowers of very pale creamy-yellow, deepening at the centre, upon moderately vigorous bushes of dwarf character.
B. R. Cant 1934. *D. MG. MF. GPB. EB. — E. June-September. Hardy.*

SANDERS' WHITE (wichuraiana rambler) has rather small-rosetted double white flowers, borne in large clusters upon very vigorous canes with bright green glossy foliage.
Sanders 1915. *D. C. MF. GPH. — White. A.P.Pr.Wst. June-July. Hardy.*

SAN DIEGO (H.T.) has shapely, double, deep orange-yellow flowers which pass to apricot and pale maize; growth is robust and erect, and foliage is attractively varnished and green.
Hieatt 1937. *D. VG. VF. GPB. — — B.G. June-September.*

S. AND M. PERRIER (H.T.) possesses an unusual name and has unusually robust growth, with very thick stems. The many-petalled flowers are high-pointed and spiralled, and of pale satin-rose with reflexes of gold. Foliage is glossy green.
Mallerin 1936. *D. TG. SF. GPB. EB. — B.E.G. June-September. Hardy.*

SANGUINAIRE (see R. rugosa).

SAN JOSÉ (Pernetiana) attractively combines its glossy foliage with vigorous and erect growth, together with large, double, salmon-orange flowers tinged with gold.
Denoyel 1931. *D. VG. MF. GPB. — — B.G. June-September. Hardy.*

SANTA ANITA (H.T.) has high-pointed double flowers of softly silvered pink produced freely upon robust, erect and branching plants with attractive bright green foliage.
Howard 1940 *D. VG. MF. GPB. —— B.G. June-September.*

SAPHO (H.T.) has very large, double, orange and cream flowers very heavily veined with cerise-red. Foliage is dark green and glossy, growth bushily robust and flowering continuous.
Pernet-Ducher 1933. *D. VG. VF. GPB. —— B.G. June-September. Hardy.*

SARAH DARLEY (H.T.) has shapely double flowers formed of wide stiff petals of golden-yellow. Growth is vigorous and branching, and foliage of dark bronze-green.
Wheatcroft 1938. *D. VG. SF. GPB. —— B.G. June-September. Hardy.*

SARAH VAN FLEET (see R. rugosa).

SATURATA (fruitful) (S.), China, makes a tall bush of some six to eight feet, with almost smooth wood, bearing large bright green leaves and dark reddish-pink single solitary flowers about two inches in diameter, followed by coral-red round to oval fruits.
Baker —. D. EG. NF. GPG. —— S. June. Hardy.

SATURNIA (Pernetiana) has large, double, bright crimson-scarlet flowers flushed with gold. Growth is very strong and branching and foliage is dark green and polished.
Aicardi 1935. *D. VG. MF. GPB. —— B.G. June-September. Hardy.*

SAVERNE (see Ville de Saverne).

SCARLANO (Hybrid setigera) makes a bushy plant with dark green foliage and semi-double cherry-red flowers borne in clusters.
Horvath 1938. *D. VG. SF. GPG. —— B.G. June. Hardy.*

SCARLET BEAUTY (H.T.) bears its large, double, high-centred flowers of crimson-scarlet on very vigorous and erect plants with green foliage.
Vestal 1934. *D. TG. SF. GPC. —— B.G. June-September. Hardy.*

SCARLET QUEEN (Hybrid polyantha) has large, double, bright crimson-scarlet flowers borne in clusters on plants of robust growth with Shiny bronze-green leaves.
Kordes 1939. *D. VG. SF. GPG. —— B.G. June-September. Hardy.*

× SCHARNKEANA (H.S.) is a natural hybrid between R. nitida and R. californica, and makes a shapely bush of thirty to forty inches in height, with single purplish-rose flowers borne in small clusters.
Garebner —. D. VG. SF. GPG. —— S. June. Hardy.

SCHILLER (Hybrid Musk) has large clusters of small semi-double flowers of peach-blossom pink, which fade to white, upon tall bushes with good glossy green foliage.
Lambert 1913. *D. TG. VF. GPG. —— Pr. June-September. Hardy.*

SCHNEELICHT (see R. rugosa).

SCHNEEZWERG (see R. rugosa).

SCHWABENLAND (see R. rugosa).

SCHWERIN (Hybrid Musk) is a semi-climber with clusters of large, double, crimson-pink flowers upon exceptionally vigorous plants with healthy, tough bronze-green foliage.
Kordes 1937. *D. EG. MF. GPG. — — Pr. June-September. Hardy.*

SCORCHER (Climbing H.T.) is a remarkably fine rose of Australian origin, bearing its very large, semi-double, bright crimson-scarlet flowers, from exceptionally strong canes, with great profusion during the early summer.
Clark 1922. *D. C. SF. GPE. — — P.W. June. Hardy.*

SCOTS Rose (see R. spinosissima).

SCOTT'S COLUMBIA (H.T.) is a sport of the famed Columbia, with exceptionally well-formed flowers of clear pink produced singly upon long stems from plants with vigorous growth, with dark green foliage. Flowering is free and almost without interruption.
Scott 1928. *D. VG. SF. GPB. — — B.G.Pot.Cut. June-September. Hardy.*

SEMPERFLORENS is R. chinensis, which see.

SEMPERVIRENS (evergreen) (S.), Southern Europe, is a somewhat tender climbing rose with glossy evergreen foliage made up of from five to seven large leaflets, bearing clusters of single white flowers about two inches in diameter. In pruning, only the dead wood should be removed.
Linnaeus (known in 1629). *E. C. SF. Detailed. — White. W. June-July.*
[Hardy only in sheltered positions in South.

SÉNATEUR POTIÉ (H.T.) is of vigorous branching growth and bears semi-double flowers of open globular shape of bright orange-yellow in conjunction with deep bronze-green foliage.
Dot 1937. *D. VG. SF. GPB. — — B.G. June-September. Hardy.*

SENATOR J. T. ROBINSON (H.T.) is another good, very deep-crimson double rose of semi-globular shape, combined with robust growth.
Vestal 1938. *D. VG. VF. GPB. — — B.G. June-September. Hardy.*

SENIOR (H.T.) is an excellent rose for general or pot culture. The shapely crimson flowers of moderate size are borne on long stems on very vigorous plants with very attractive green foliage.
Spanbauer 1932. *D. VG. MF. GPB. — — G.Cut.Pot. June-Sept. Hardy.*

SEÑORA GARI (Pernetiana) is an exceptionally large, double, high-centred cadmium-yellow rose, with traces of buff and apricot, very robust but diffuse habit, and glossy bronze-green foliage. It has proved of some difficulty, but is nevertheless well worth growing.
Dot 1934. *D. MG. SF. GPB. EB. — E.G. June-September.*

SENSATION (H.T.) has large, fragrant, double, semi-globular crimson-scarlet flowers with deeper markings and is of vigorous, erect and branching habit, generally exceptionally good in autumn.
Hill 1922. *D. VG. MF. GPB. — — B.G. June-September.*

Senta Schmidt (polyantha pompon) bears large clusters of rather small, semi-double, coppery-orange flowers. Growth is moderately vigorous and dwarf, and foliage is light green.
Schmidt 1930. *D. DG. NF. GPF. — — B. June-September. Hardy.*

sepium (see R. agrestis).

Sequoia (H.T.) has large, double, semi-globular flowers of creamy pink shaded with salmon, with deep bronze-green foliage. Growth is moderately vigorous and of medium height.
Verschuren 1938. *D. MG. SF. GPB. — — B.G. June-September.*

Seraphinii (comm.) (S.), Mediterranean region, forms a bush of moderate height (thirty inches), with five- to seven-parted bright-green deeply-serrated rounded leaflets, and bears solitary, single, cupped one-inch flowers of bright pink, followed by oval to round brownish-red fruits.
Viviani 1894. *D. VG. SF. GPG. — 27/2. S. June. Hardy. Pl.* 78.

Sergeant Ulmann (H.T.) is a very vigorous bedding rose with exceptionally large, semi-double, ruby-red flowers, brightened with touches of scarlet, produced with great freedom. Foliage is deep bronze-green.
Mallerin 1932. *D. TG. SF. GPC. — — B.G. June-September. Hardy.*

sericea (silky) (S.), India, is another four-petalled rose, closely resembling R. omeiensis, forming a bush of up to ten feet in height, with large thorns, and graceful leaves divided into seven to eleven leaflets. It flowers in May and June, producing its single creamy-white solitary flowers, of about one and a half inches in diameter, most profusely.
Lindley 1822. *D. EG. SF. GPG. — White. S. May-June. Hardy.*

sericea var. xanthocarpa (yellow-fruited) is similar except in the colour of its fruits.

sertata (garlanded) (S.), Central China, is a rose with smooth green canes turning red with age, with neat graceful deep-green leaves divided into seven to eleven leaflets and bearing single rose-coloured flowers varying from one to two inches in diameter, in small groups or singly, followed by round deep-red fruits.
Rolfe —. *D. EG. NF. GPG. — 627/1. S. June. Pl.* 52.

setigera (bearing bristles) (S.) is the Prairie Rose of North America, and makes a very tall bush with climbing branches, and grey-green leaves made up of three to five large leaflets. The flowers, which are about two inches in diameter, are deep pink and fade to white, and are produced in small clusters and followed by small round red fruits.
Michaux 1800. *D. EG. NF. GPG. — — S. July-August. Very hardy.*

SETIGERA × DOUBLOONS is a very free-flowering climbing rose with large, double, very fragrant flowers of deep golden-yellow, borne upon a very hardy plant with glossy green foliage.
Horvath 1934. *D. C. VF. GPE. — — A.P.Pr.W. June. Hardy.*

SETIGERA VAR. TOMENTOSA (hairy) (S.) is similar to the type, with leaves covered beneath with dense short hair.
Gray —. D. EG. NF. GPG. — — S. July-August.

SETIPODA (with bristly foot) (S.), Central China, is a close-growing, vigorous rose with green leaves, divided into seven to nine leaflets, and bearing large clusters of single deep-pink flowers about two inches in diameter, followed by rounded hanging deep-red fruits with a long narrow neck.
Hemsley & Wilson 1889. *D. EG. NF. GPG. — — S.H. June-July. Hardy.*

SHEILA (polyantha pompon) bears large clusters of semi-double salmon-orange flowers which pale to a pleasing tone of salmon-pink. Growth is vigorous, foliage bright green, and it is a good plant for bedding or forcing.
Walsh 1930. *D. VG. NF. GPF. — — B.Pot. June-September.*

SHENANDOAH (Climbing Nutkana Hybrid) is of vigorous growth with large semi-double flowers of bright crimson, and attractive shining green foliage.
Nicolas 1934. *D. C. VF. GPE. — — A.Pr.W. June. Hardy.*

SHINING SUN (Pernetiana) has rather flat semi-double flowers of deep yellow, overlaid with reddish-orange in the centre. Growth is vigorous and foliage deep shining bronze.
Van Rossem 1932. *D. VG. VF. GPB. — — B.G. June-September. Hardy.*

SHINING SUN (see also Mrs. Paul Goudie).

SHOT SILK (H.T.) has shapely high-pointed, cerise-pink, double flowers shot with orange-salmon, borne on stiff stems of medium length. Growth is moderately vigorous, erect and branching, and foliage is shining, glossy deep green, resistant to mildew. Best planted eighteen inches apart for bedding purposes.
Dickson 1924. *D. MG. VF. GPB. — 23/2 to 18/3 and 3/2 at base. B.G.St.*
                                        [June-Sept. Hardy. Pl. 1.

SHOWER OF GOLD (wichuraiana rambler) is a very vigorous climber with glossy deep green foliage, and bears round, double, golden-yellow flowers, paling with age to light yellow and flowering freely in early July.
Paul 1910. *D. C. NF. GPI. — — A.P.Pr. July. Hardy.*

SIGNET (H.T.) is a free-flowering plant of extra vigorous growth with tough green foliage, and bears high-centred double flowers of clear deep pink on good stems.
Montgomery 1938. *D. TG. VF. GPB. — — B.G. June-September. Hardy.*

SIGNORA (H.T.) is also known as Signora Piero Puricelli, and has very shapely high-centred flowers with reflexed outer petals, and a pleasant combination of deep cerise-pink flushed with salmon and orange, with veins clearly marked. Growth is very vigorous and erect, and foliage glossy green.

Aicardi 1936. *D. VG. MF. GPB. EB.* 20/2-1, 16/2. *B.G.E.St. June-Sept.*
[*Pl.* 68.

SILVER JUBILEE (H.T.) is an all-purpose variety with very large, very double, high-pointed flowers of pale yellow, deepening to pale golden-yellow at the centre. Growth is vigorous, erect and branching, and foliage shining deep green.

Dickson 1937. *D. VG. MF. GPB. EB.* 403/3, 3/1. *B.G.E. June-Sept.*
[*Pl.* 69.

SILVER MOON (wichuraiana climber) calls for the use of superlatives. An attractive climber with very large, semi-double, open creamy-white flowers, borne in large clusters. Growth is exceptionally vigorous, and the foliage is of the deepest glossy green.

Van Fleet 1910. *D. C. SF. GPI. — — A.P.W. June. Hardy.*

SILVIA LEYVA (Pernetiana) is another dwarf rose of vigorous diffuse growth with shining bronze-green foliage. The double, high-centred, semi-globular flowers are of bright crimson-red.

Dot 1933. *D. VG. VF. GPB. — — B.G. June-September.*

SIMEROSE (Pernetiana) combines the now popular deep orange-red petal faces with golden-yellow backs in shapely flowers, freely borne on vigorous plants with glossy green foliage.

Meilland 1939. *D. VG. MF. GPB. — — B.G. June-September.*

SIMONE GUÉRIN (Pernetiana) has large high-pointed double flowers of golden-buff, shaded with pink, freely borne upon branching erect robust plants with glossy deep green foliage, resistant to disease.

Mallerin 1932. *D. VG. MF. GPB. — — B.G.St. June-September. Hardy.*

SIMON MAYERY (H.T.) combines its very large globular flowers of creamy white, deepening to deep yellow at the centre, with attractive clear bronze-green foliage.

Chambard 1937. *D. VG. MF. GPB. — — B.G. June-September. Hardy.*

SIMPLICITY (H.T.) is aptly named, its single clear white flowers of moderate size being produced upon neat and compact plants of erect growth, with varnished green foliage.

Dickson 1910. *D. MG. SF. GPB. — — B. June-September. Hardy.*

SINCERITY (H.T.) has semi-double high-centred flowers of flesh-pink shaded with gold, borne upon plants of moderate erect growth, with attractive dark green foliage. Flowering is very free and protracted.

Le Grice 1940. *D. VG. SF. GPB. — — B.G. June-October. Hardy.*

SIR BASIL MCFARLAND (H.T.) produces its high-centred double flowers of orange-pink, flushed and veined with yellow, on vigorous and erect plants of branching habit, with tough green foliage.

McGredy 1931. *D. VG. SF. GPB. — — B.G. June-September.*

Trigo (Hybrid Tea) **BCFGJKN**

Luis Brinas (Pernetiana) **LMPQ**

Hybrid Polyantha Rose, Van Nes
(also known as Permanent Wave)

Sir David Davis (H.T.) has three outstanding characteristics: form, fragrance and freedom of growth. Flowers are of medium size, high-pointed and double, and of fragrant deep crimson.
McGredy 1926. *D. VG. VF. GPB. —— B.G. June-September. Hardy.*

Sir Henry Seagrave (H.T.) couples outstanding size and shape with excellent colour and moderately free growth. The large double high-pointed lemon-yellow flowers deepen in the centre, and if they fail to open in wet weather amply compensate for this failure under better conditions.
Dickson 1932. *D. MG. MF. GPB. EB. — B.E.G. June-September. Hardy.*

Sir Thomas Lipton (see R. rugosa).

Sister Therese (Sœur Thérèse) (H.T.) possesses both vigour of growth and freedom of flowering in no small degree. The flowers are large and semi-double, open golden-yellow, pale to clear yellow, and are borne upon robust and erect plants with deep bronze-green foliage.
Gillot 1930. *D. VG. SF. GPB. —— B.G. June-September. Hardy.*

Sky Rocket (see Wilhelm).

Smiles (Hybrid polyantha) is the attractive and fitting name for a semi-double flesh-pink rose, borne in clusters on plants of compact and strong growth of moderate height.
Nicolas 1937. *D. MG. SF. GPG. —— B.G. June-September. Hardy.*

Snowflake (wichuraiana rambler) has double, white, open flowers, borne in large clusters upon vigorous climbing plants with glossy deep green foliage.
F. Cant 1922. *D. C. SF. GPI. —— A.P.Pr. July-August. Hardy.*

Sonia (H.T.) has semi-double round-domed flowers of cerise-red, with an orange-red centre, on plants of vigorous and branching growth, with glossy green foliage.
Horvath 1938. *D. VG. SF. GPB. —— B.G. July-August. Hardy.*

Sonnengold (H.T.) has large double flowers of golden-yellow. Growth is vigorous, erect and branching, and foliage is varnished bright green.
Kordes 1936. *D. VG. SF. GPB. —— B.G. June-September. Hardy.*

Soulieana (comm.) (S.), China, is an attractive, very tall, very thorny semi-climbing rose with grey-green leaves, made up of seven leaflets, bearing creamy-white single flowers in very large clusters, followed by similar clusters of brilliant orange-red small spheroidal fruits.
Crepin 1895. *D. EG. SF. GPG. —— S. July. Hardy.*

Southport (H.T.) has large, fairly full, high-centred flowers of bright crimson-scarlet, borne upon vigorous, erect and branching plants with attractive green foliage. It is equally good for bedding or exhibition, and was, and remains, an exceptional rose, as it is both free from disease and tolerant of damp weather.
McGredy 1933. *D. VG. SF. GPB. EB.* 724. *B.E.G. June-Sept. Hardy.*

Souvenir de Claudius Denoyel (H.T.) is a climbing rose with large double crimson flowers produced intermittently throughout the season, and is suitable for growing as a pillar rose.
Chambard 1920. *D. C. MF. GPE. — — Pr. June-September. Hardy.*

Souvenir de Claudius Pernet (H.T.) has exceptionally large, double, high-centred flowers of sunflower-yellow, produced on good stiff stems from upright and branching plants with shining deep green foliage.
Pernet-Ducher 1920. *D. VG. MF. GPB. — — B. June-September. Hardy.*

Souvenir de Denier van der Gon (H.T.) has high-pointed, very shapely double flowers of deep apricot-yellow, paling to golden-yellow, borne upon upright, robust and freely branching plants, with glossy green foliage.
Verschuren-Pechtold 1935. *D. VG. MF. GPB. — — B.G. June-Sept. Hardy.*

Souvenir de George Beckwith (Pernetiana) is another rose of vigorous and erect growth, with large glossy bronze-green foliage, bearing large, double, semi-globular flowers of shrimp-pink, tinted with clear yellow.
Pernet-Ducher 1919. *D. VG. SF. GPB. — — B.G. June-September. Hardy.*

Souvenir de Georges Pernet (Pernetiana) has high-centred double flowers of spiral shape and of deep carmine-pink with a yellow base, borne upon strong stems from lusty plants with erect and branching growth and deep bronze-green foliage.
Pernet-Ducher 1931. *D. VG. MF. GPB. EB. — B.E.G.St. June-Sept.*
[Hardy. Pl. 71.

Souvenir de H. A. Verschuren (H.T.) produces its large shapely double yellow flowers with conical centres, on good stems from vigorous plants with glossy green foliage. The flowers are of sunflower-yellow, shading to deep orange-yellow at the centre.
Verschuren 1922. *D. VG. MF. GPB. — B.G. June-September. Hardy.*

Souvenir de Henri Venot (H.T.) has exceptionally fragrant, large, bright red, very double flowers borne upon long stems on vigorous and erect plants, with dark green foliage.
Lens 1931. *D. VG. VF. GPB. — — B.G. June-September. Hardy.*

Souvenir de J. B. Weibel (H.T.) combines shapely, double, semi-globular flowers of deep carmine-pink, produced freely, with good growth and large dark green foliage.
Sauvageot 1930. *D. VG. SF. GPB. — — B.G.St. June-September. Hardy.*

Souvenir de Jean Soupert (H.T.) is another golden-yellow rose, with very large semi-double globular flowers, healthy and erect growth, with attractive ample bronze-green leaves, and a prolonged flowering period, adding great fragrance to its other attractions.
Soupert & Notting 1929. *D. VG. VF. GPB. — B.G. June-Sept. Hardy.*

Souvenir de la Malmaison (see R. Bourbonia).

Souvenir de Madame Boullet (H.T.) has large, double, deep cadmium-yellow flowers of excellent high-centred form, very freely produced upon robust and diffuse plants, with good tough green foliage.
Pernet-Ducher 1921. *D. VG. SF. GPB. — — B.G.St.Pot. June-Sept. Hardy.*

Souvenir de Madame C. Chambard (H.T.) has large, nearly double, high-centred, deep rose-pink flowers, with reflexed outer petals, deepening at the centre and flushed with gold. Growth is good and branching, foliage tough and mid-green.
Chambard 1931. *D. VG. MF. GPB. EB. — B.E.G. June-Sept. Hardy.*

Souvenir de Madame Salati-Mongellaz (H.P.) is one of the modern hybrid perpetuals, and holds its place by reason of its exceptionally large, very double, pale rose-pink flowers, which are produced freely upon stout stems for a long period.
Croibier 1937. *D. TG. SF. GPC. EC. — B.E.G. June-September. Hardy.*

Souvenir de Marie Clotilde (H.T.) resembles Madame Abel Chatenay in habit and form, but has flowers of white deepening to maize-yellow at the centre, sometimes with a tinge of pink.
Carneiro 1934. *D. VG. SF. GPB. — — B.C.G.St.Pot. June-Sept. Hardy.*

Souvenir de Philémon Cochet (see R. rugosa).

Souvenir du Capitaine Ferrand (Pernetiana) again combines the popular orange-red petal face with golden-yellow reverse in shapely semi-double flowers, borne upon robust and erect plants with glossy green foliage.
Gaujard 1939. *D. VG. SF. GPB. — — B.G. June-September.*

Souvenir of the Old Rose Garden (H.T.) has exceptionally large very double soft rose-pink flowers, with the outside of the petals of silver-pink, of good globular form, borne in few-flowered clusters. Growth is very robust and erect, and foliage is of bright green and heavily polished.
B. R. Cant 1929. *D. VG. VF. GPB. — — B.G.St. June-September. Hardy.*

Sparkler (polyantha pompon) is a very dwarf bedding rose, with exceptionally large clusters of small, semi-double, brilliant red globular flowers, upon neat and compact bushes with light green foliage.
de Ruiter 1930. *D. DG. NF. GPF. — — B.Pot. June-September. Hardy.*

spinosissima (the most spiny) (S.) (the Burnet Rose), Europe, is variable in its growth, sometimes scarcely exceeding a few inches in height, and at other times reaching over three feet. Its erect bushy growth carries many rising branches, clad with small leaves, made up of from five to eleven leaflets, and bears from the nodes solitary milky-white or cream single flowers, of about one and a half inches in diameter, in great profusion, followed by small round black fruits. It is much neater when starved in light soil.
Linnaeus —. D. VG. NF. GPG. — — S. May-June. Very hardy.

SPINOSISSIMA VAR. ALBO PLENA is similar but has double white flowers.

SPINOSISSIMA VAR. ALTAICA, Siberia, has larger single pale lemon flowers in May, and is fragrant, well suited by its growth to the formation of a hedge. (*Rehder.*)

SPINOSISSIMA VAR. ANDREWSII has double red flowers. (*Willmott.*)

SPINOSISSIMA VAR. HISPIDA (bristly) has rather larger flowers of sulphur-yellow. (*Koehne.*)

SPINOSISSIMA VAR. INERMIS (unarmed) has single pink flowers and few spines. (*Rehder.*)

SPINOSISSIMA VAR. LUTEA has single bright-yellow flowers. (*Bean.*) *Pl.* 2.

SPINOSISSIMA VAR. LUTEA PLENA has double bright-yellow flowers.

SPINOSISSIMA VAR. MAXIMA LUTEA has very large single yellow flowers.

SPINOSISSIMA VAR. MYRIACANTHA (myriad-spined) has very small single white flowers. (*Koehne.*)

The following hybrids are notable; all make good low hedges.

× SPINOSISSIMA BRIGHTNESS, double crimson-purple.
    „   FLAVESCENS, double pale yellow.
    „   HARRISON'S YELLOW, double deep yellow. Tall.
    „   LADY HAMILTON, semi-double pale cream, shaded pink.
    „   LISMORE, double very pale pink.
    „   STANWELL PERPETUAL, large double pale blush.

× SPINULIFOLIA (having spiny leaves) (H.S.), Alps, is a natural hybrid of R. pendulina and R. tomentosa, and makes a stately upstanding bush of about six feet in height, with green almost thornless stems, and bears many large single pink flowers either singly or in small groups.
Dematra —. D. EG. VF. GPG. — — S. June. Hardy.

SPLENDOUR (H.T.) has large, double, semi-globular flowers of bright orange-red, turning redder, shaded and veined with orange, and with a salmon-pink reverse. Habit of growth is robust, erect and branching, and the large leaves are tough shining green.
Sauvageot 1934. *D. VG. MF. GPB. — — B.G. June-September. Hardy.*

SPRINGTIME (Hybrid polyantha) has pale pink nine-petalled flowers with white eyes, borne in very large clusters on bushes of moderate height and growth, with green foliage resistant to disease.
Howard & Smith 1935. *D. MG. SF. GPB. — — B.Pot. June-Sept. Hardy.*

STAATPRASIDENT PATS (H.T.) varies considerably in the depth of its colour, which at best is deep maize-yellow. The flowers are large, very double and of high-centred form; growth is vigorous, erect and branching; foliage is dark green and resistant to disease.
Weigand 1937. *D. VG. VF. GPB. — — B.G.St. June-September. Hardy.*

STAMMLER (H.T.) has large, high-pointed, very double flowers of glowing rose-pink, borne upon vigorous, erect and branching plants, with shining green foliage.
Tantau 1930. *D. VG. VF. GPB. — — B.G. June-September. Hardy.*

STANWELL PERPETUAL (see R. spinosissima).

STARGOLD (H.T.) is an aptly named yellow rose with double high-pointed flowers which are often touched with red. Growth is vigorous, erect and branching, when established, with dark green polished foliage.
Brownell 1936. *D. TG. VF. GPC. EG. — B.E.G.St. June-October. Hardy.*

STARLIGHT (H.T.) has semi-double flowers of buff, deepening to orange at the centre, freely produced upon vigorous, erect and branching plants with attractive green foliage.
Wood & Ingram 1934. *D. VG. VF. GPB. — — B.C.G. June-Sept. Hardy.*

STELLA POLARIS (see R. rugosa).

STELLATA MIRIFICA (see R. mirifica).

STERLING (H.T.) has semi-double pink flowers with a deep yellow base, borne upon vigorous plants with shining green foliage.
Hill 1933. *D. VG. MF. GPB. — — B.C.G. June-September.*

STERN VON PRAG (see R. rugosa).

STRATFORD (H.T.) is an exceptionally vigorous rose of tall and branching growth, with large, double, shining pink flowers flushed with salmon.
Nicolas 1936. *D. TG. VF. GPC. — — G. June-September. Hardy.*

SUMMER SNOW (wichuraiana rambler) bears large clusters of semi-double open flowers of snow-white, upon exceptionally vigorous plants of climbing habit.
Couteau 1936. *D. C. SF. GPH. — — P.Pr. June-July. Hardy.*

SUNBURST (H.T.) varies considerably in its colour, often bearing several shades of bright yellow flowers on single plants at the same time. The general colour is pale yellow, deepening in the centre to orange, and the flowers are semi-globular and double.
Pernet-Ducher 1911. *D. MG. SF. GPB. — — B.G.Pot. June-Sept. Hardy.*

SUNGLOW (H.T.) closely resembles McGredy's Orange, having flowers of similar shape, and of bright orange, flushed with salmon.
Wheatcroft 1936. *D. VG. MF. GPB. — — B.G. June-September. Hardy.*

SUN GLOW (H.T.) has large, double, high-pointed flowers of deep salmon-pink, with a fine fragrance, and vigorous, erect and branching growth, and shining dark green leaves.
Florex Gardens 1934. *D. VG. VF. GPB. — — B.G. June-September. Hardy.*

SUNGOLD (Climbing H.T.) is a very vigorous climbing rose with strong canes, deep green foliage, and rather large golden-yellow double flowers.
Thomas 1939. *D. C. MF. GPE. — — A.W. June-August. Hardy.*

Sunny Days (H.T.) has large, double, high-pointed flowers of lemon-yellow, deepening in intensity at the centre. Growth is vigorous and erect, and leaves are dark green and tough in texture.

Verschuren 1938. *D. VG. SF. GPB. — — B.G. June-September. Hardy.*

Sunnymount (H.T.) has a low-centred, large, many-petalled sunflower-yellow flower of camellia shape, borne upon a shapely vigorous plant with large dark green foliage.

Grillo 1936. *D. VG. VF. GPB. EB. — B.E.G.St. June-September. Hardy.*

Sunny South (H.T.) is another rose of Australian origin, with large semi-double pink flowers, with a deeper flush and deep yellow shading at the base of the petals. Growth is vigorous and erect, and leaves are bright green and resistant to disease.

Clark 1918. *D. VG. MF. GPB. — — B.G. June-September. Hardy.*

Sun-Ray (H.T.) has neat habit and produces its semi-double golden-yellow flowers in great profusion upon neat and compact plants, eminently suited to bedding.

Bentall 1932. *D. MG. MF. GPB. — — B.G. June-September. Hardy.*

Sunrise (H.T.) has double, large, high-pointed flowers of spiralled open form, of bright salmon, shaded orange and gold, borne upon vigorous branching plants with deep bronze-green polished foliage; is exceptionally floriferous and not prone to disease.

Dot 1939. *D. VG. SF. GPB. — — B.G. June-September. Hardy.*

Sunshine (polyantha pompon) has dwarf growth, shining bright green leaves, and small double flowers of pale orange, borne in large clusters.

Cutbush 1928. *D. DG. MF. GPF. — — B.G. June-September. Hardy.*

Sunstar (H.T.) is a plant of moderate growth with good light-green foliage, bearing shapely semi-double flowers of salmon-red, shaded with yellow.

Dickson 1921. *D. MG. VF. GPC. — — B.St. June-September. Hardy.*

Suntan (H.T.) has large many-petalled flowers of orange-yellow, paling with age, borne upon exceptionally vigorous, erect plants, with deep bronze-green foliage, and a protracted period of flowering.

Hansen 1939. *D. VG. SF. GPB. EB. — B.E.G.St. June-October. Hardy.*

Super-Rouge (H.T.) is claimed to be an improved Rouge Mallerin, with exceptionally fine-shaped very double blooms of deep crimson-scarlet, deepening towards the edges of the petals. Growth is vigorous, erect and branching when established.

Mallerin 1936. *D. VG. VF. GPB. EB. — B.E.G.St. June-Sept. Hardy.*

Suzanne Michela (H.T.) has outstandingly large double flowers of golden-yellow shaded with pale carmine, of semi-globular shape. Growth is vigorous, erect and branching.

Chambard 1932. *D. VG. MF. GPB. EB. — B.E.G. June-Sept. Hardy.*

Suzanne Villain (H.T.) has large, many-petalled flowers of peach-blossom-pink, with deeper flushes, and a salmon reverse. Growth is robust, upright and branching, and leaves of healthy deep green.
Ketten 1935. *D. VG. SF. GPB. EB. — B.E.G. June-September. Hardy.*

Swamp Rose (see R. palustris).

Swansdown (H.T.) has attractively spiralled, double flowers of creamy-white. Growth is robust, of moderate height, foliage of pale bronze-green, and flowering profuse and protracted.
Dickson 1929. *D. MG. SF. GPB. EB. White. B.E.G.St. June-Sept. Hardy.*

Sweet Briar (see R. rubiginosa).

Sweet Memorie (H.T.) is an exceptionally vigorous, erect-growing rose, with large, semi-double, globular flowers of reddish-pink, with a yellow base.
Hieatt 1927. *D. TG. VF. GPC. — — G. June-September. Hardy.*

Sweetness (H.T.) has a spiralled double flower of lemon-yellow, suffused with cerise-pink, produced from plants of moderate growth with glossy green foliage.
Dickson 1937. *D. MG. MF. GPB. — — B.G. June-September. Hardy.*

Sweet Sue (H.T.) has single flowers of coral-pink, borne in few-flowered clusters, upon extra vigorous plants with attractive green foliage.
Lammerts 1940. *D. TG. MF. GPC. — — G. June-September.*

Sweginzowii (comm.) (S.), China, is a dense bush with wood covered with flat brown spines, and with small leaves, made up of from seven to eleven leaflets, and bright pink flowers of about one and a half inches in diameter, borne in few-flowered clusters, followed by elongated bright red fruits.
Koehne —. D. EG. NF. GPG. — — S. June. Hardy.

Symphony (H.P.) is a modern hybrid perpetual with very large, double, flesh-pink flowers, deepening at the centre. Growth is vigorous and erect, and flowering free and long; leaves are large and deep green.
Weigand 1935. *D. TG. NF. GPC. — — G. June-September. Hardy.*

Syracuse (H.T.) has large, very double, globular flowers, composed of an exceptional number of crimson-scarlet petals; is of vigorous branching and erect growth with dark green foliage, and has a protracted period of flowering.
Mallerin 1930. *D. VG. MF. GPC. — — G. June-September. Hardy.*

Syringa (wichuraiana rambler) is a climber of most vigorous habit bearing extremely large clusters of single white flowers very like those of the shrub from which it takes its name.
Browning 1931. *D. C. SF. GPI. — White. June-July. Hardy.*

Talisman (H.T.) has pointed-centred double flowers of coppery-red, varying to scarlet or pink, with the reverse of lemon-yellow. Growth is vigorous and erect, with deep green foliage. It is a good rose for bedding purposes, for cutting and for growing in pots under glass.
Montgomery 1929. *D. VG. VF. GPB. — 23/1-1/3. B.G.Pot. June-Sept.*
[Hardy.

247

Tango (H.T.) has double, shapely flowers of bright crimson-scarlet, with the reverse of bronze, lightened with gold at the base of the petals. Growth is vigorous, erect and branching.
Howard & Smith 1940. *D. VG. MF. GPB. — — B.G. June-September.*

Tantallon (H.T.) is a rather dwarf rose with compact vigorous growth and dark green polished foliage, with medium-size double flowers of salmon-pink, with the reverse of cherry-red.
Dobbie 1934. *D. MG. MF. GPB. — — B.G. June-September. Hardy.*

Tapis Blanc (polyantha pompon) has large, double, creamy-white flowers, borne in clusters on dwarf, branching and vigorous plants, with bright green foliage.
Turbat 1927. *D. DG. SF. GPF. — White. B. June-September. Hardy.*

Tarantella (H.T.) combines its shapely globular golden-yellow double flowers with attractively crinkled bright green foliage. Growth is vigorous, upright and branching, and flowering free and prolonged.
Tantau 1936. *D. VG. SF. GPB. — — B.G. June-September. Hardy.*

Tatik Brada (H.T.) has exceptionally large double flowers of deep reddish-orange, produced upon vigorous bushes with erect and branching habit, with deep green glossy foliage.
Bohm 1934. *D. VG. SF. GPB. — — B.G. June-September. Hardy.*

Tausendschon (wichuraiana rambler) includes in its thousand beauties a slight but sweet fragrance, soft pink double flowers flushed with rose, soft green attractive foliage which fittingly frames its huge clusters of flowers; and among such beauty no thorn appears to mar.
Schmidt 1907. *D. C. SF. GPH. — — P.Pr. June-September. Hardy.*

Tea Rambler (wichuraiana rambler) has double flowers of coppery-pink, borne in clusters in early summer. Growth is vigorous and climbing, and foliage bright green.
Paul 1903. *D. C. NF. GPI. — — A.H.P.Pr. June. Hardy.*

Temno (H.T.) is an exceptionally deep red rose, with medium-size double, very dark red flowers, borne upon very robust branching plants.
Bohm 1934. *D. VG. MF. GPB. EB. — B.E.G. June-September. Hardy.*

Tess (wichuraiana rambler) has double deep rose-pink flowers, borne in large clusters. Growth is vigorous and foliage bright green.
Beckwith 1939. *D. C. MF. GPI. — — A.P.Pr. June-July. Hardy.*

Tetonkaha (see R. rugosa).

Texas Centennial (H.T.) has long pointed buds opening to high-centred double flowers of bright carmine-red, shaded with gold, and passing to deep pink with age. Growth is exceptionally vigorous, very thorny, and foliage bright rich green.
Watkins 1935. *D. VG. MF. GPB. — 027/3-027/2. B.G.St. June-Sept.*
[*Hardy.*

Three Hybrid Tea Roses

Ville de Saverne **ABEJKNO**

Elizabeth of York **CDGH**
Mrs. Verschuren **LMPQ**

Three Species Roses

Rosa Moyesii **ABFGKLO**

Rosa Seraphinii **EJK**   Rosa virginiana **CDGHLMPQ**

Texas Gold (H.T.) is another sport of President Herbert Hoover, similar to Texas Centennial except in the colour, which is of golden-yellow, sometimes touched with pink. Habit of growth is similar.
Wolfe 1935. *D. VG. MF. GPB. — — B.G.St. June-September. Hardy.*

The Beacon (wichuraiana rambler) has single and semi-double flowers of bright crimson-scarlet with a white eye, borne in very large clusters. Growth is very vigorous and foliage an attractive shining green.
Paul 1922. *D. C. NF. GPI. — — A.P.Pr. June-July. Hardy.*

The Bishop (H.T.), as its name suggests, has freely produced, ponderous double crimson-red flowers of splendid form and intense fragrance, coupled with robust and branching growth and dark green foliage.
Dickson 1937. *D. VG. VF. GPB. EB. — B.E.G. June-September. Hardy.*

The Chief (H.T.) is of exceptionally robust habit with very upright and branching growth, with glossy deep bronze-green foliage. The large double flowers, produced upon long strong stems, are of bright coral, mutating to orange.
Lammerts 1940. *D. VG. MF. GPC. EC. — B.E.G. June-September.*

The Doctor (H.T.) is one of the finest roses ever introduced and is of easy culture. The huge double flowers are of bright silvery-rose, and are perfectly shaped, and lasting. Foliage is plentiful and of good light green and free of disease. Growth is moderately vigorous, flowers are intensely fragrant and open well in all weathers. Is temperamental only in one respect, which need not worry the gardener; it defied the photographer in the studio. Many attempts were made to photograph it in colour, but petal movement was so great that the results always failed to do this great rose the justice it deserves.
Howard & Smith 1939. *D. MG. VF. GPB. EB.* 625/1-625/2. *B.E.G.St.*
[*June-Oct. Hardy.*

The Fairy (wichuraiana polyantha) has small double flowers of pale coral-pink, borne upon very dwarf and compact bushes, with exceptionally attractive deep green foliage.
Bentall 1932. *D. DG. NF. GPF. — — B.G. June-September. Hardy.*

The General (H.T.) has vigorous, erect and branching growth of moderate height with ample dark bronze-green foliage. The large double pointed, semi-globular, blood-crimson flowers are flushed with orange and are freely produced for a long period.
Pemberton 1920. *D. MG. VF. GPB. EB. — B.E. June-October. Hardy.*

Thelma (wichuraiana rambler) has large semi-double flowers of delicate coral-pink flushed with carmine-pink, in freely produced moderate-sized clusters, which retain petals and colour for a long period. Foliage is polished green, and attractive, and canes are robust.
Easlea 1927. *D. C. SF. GPI. — — A.H.P.Pr. July. Hardy.*

THE NEW DAWN (wichuraiana climber) is a moderately growing sport from Dr. van Fleet, and is one of the finest of all ramblers. The double perfectly-shaped flowers of shell-pink are produced in large clusters, and seem always in being. Foliage is deep glossy green and is not one of the least attractions of a remarkable rose.

Dreer 1930. *D. C. MF. GPJ. — 622/3. P.Pr.Wst. July-October. Hardy.*

THE PRINCESS ELIZABETH (Pernetiana) has the attractions of vigour and beauty. Growth is robust, erect and branching, with dark bronze-green foliage, completely resistant to disease. The large double flowers are of orange-yellow, flamed and edged with cerise-pink.

Wheatcroft 1927. *D. VG. SF. GPB. — B.G. June-September. Hardy.*

THE PRINCESS MARGARET ROSE (H.T.) is another rich crimson-scarlet bedding rose of medium size and of free-flowering characteristics. Foliage is green and attractive.

Evans 1932. *D. MG. MF. GPB. — B.G. June-September. Hardy.*

THE QUEEN ALEXANDRA ROSE (Pernetiana) is of exceptionally vigorous growth with double nicely-shaped flowers of bright vermilion with the reverse of the petals of old gold. Foliage is dark, glossy green, but sometimes the plant suffers from die-back.

McGredy 1917. *D. VG. MF. GPC. — — B. June-September. Hardy.*

THÉRÈSE BONNAVIET (H.T.) is of vigorous branching habit with coppery-bronze foliage and bears large double flowers of clear pink, shading to copper at the centre.

Chambard 1934. *D. VG. MF. GPB. — — B.G. June-September. Hardy.*

THISBE (Hybrid Musk) bears large clusters of dull-yellow full flowers upon vigorous tall bushes with attractive green foliage.

Pemberton 1918. *D. TG. VF. GPG. — — H.S. June-September. Hardy.*

THOMAS A. EDISON (H.T.) has very large, semi-globular, pointed flowers of cameo-pink, deepening towards the centre. Growth is vigorous, erect and branching, and flowering period extended.

Bernaix 1931. *D. VG. VF. GPB. — — B.G.St. June-September. Hardy.*

THOR (Climbing H.T.) has large, double, crimson flowers borne upon extremely vigorous plants of climbing habit with attractive deep green foliage.

Horvath 1940. *D. C. VF. GPE. — — A.P.W. June.*

THORESBYANA (see R. arvensis Bennett's Seedling).

THORNLESS Rose (see Zéphirine Drouhin).

THORNLESS BEAUTY (H.T.) is devoid of thorns, as its name suggests, bears high-centred, double, many-petalled flowers of bright crimson-scarlet upon robust, upright and branching plants with tough dark green foliage.

Grillo 1938. *D. VG. VF. GPB. — — B.G.St. June-September.*

THREEPENNYBIT Rose (see R. Farreri var. persetosa).

THUSNELDA (see R. rugosa).

TILFORD (H.T.) is an exceptionally fine sport of President Herbert Hoover, the young flowers of which are crimson and open to carmine and gold. Growth and other characteristics are identical with those of the parent.
Norman 1939. *D. VG. VF. GPB. — — B.G.St. June-September. Hardy.*

TOKEN (H.T.) is a rose of outstanding beauty with large open double flowers of apricot-orange, borne on long stems from erect and vigorous bushes, with glossy bronze-green foliage. Requires good cultivation but repays it and is a good rose for growing in pots.
Montgomery 1933. *D. VG. MF. GPB. — — B.C.St.Pot. June-Oct. Hardy.*

TOM BARR (H.T.) has double, high-centred flowers of orange-bronze, perfect in shape and freely produced upon erect, robust plants with bright green foliage, and is equally good for garden or exhibition.
McGredy 1932. *D. VG. MF. GPB. EB. — B.E.G. June-Sept. Hardy.*

TOMENTOSA (woolly) (S.), Europe, grows into a bush of some six feet in height with strong canes, with grey-green leaves made up of from five to seven leaflets, and bears either solitary, or few-flowered clusters of, pale-pink or white single flowers about one and a half inches in diameter.
Smith —. *D. TG. SF. GPG. — — S. June. Hardy.*

TOM THUMB (see R. chinensis var. minima Peon).

TONY SPALDING (H.T.) is an exceptionally fine bedding rose with medium-size double flowers of bright crimson-scarlet. Growth is robust and branching, and foliage is an attractive glossy green.
McGredy 1933. *D. VG. VF. GPB. — — B.G.St. June-September. Hardy.*

TOPAZ (Hybrid polyantha) has small but perfectly shaped, double, cream flowers, intensifying at the centre to lemon-yellow. Growth is exceptionally dwarf, foliage small to fit, and tough green.
Tantau 1934. *D. VG. SF. GPG. — — B.G. June-September. Hardy.*

TREASURE ISLAND (H.T.) has large, double, pointed flowers, of pale salmon-pink, with the backs of the petals of bright orange-pink. Habit of growth is very vigorous, erect and branching, and foliage bronze-green.
Raffel 1938. *D. TG. MF. GPC. EC. — B.E.G. June-September. Hardy.*

TRIER (Hybrid Musk) is a tall, upright, semi-climbing rose, suitable for a pillar, with semi-double creamy-white flowers, edged with fawn, borne in large clusters with deep green foliage.
Lambert 1904. *D. EG. MF. GPG. — — Pr. June. Hardy.*

TRIGO (H.T.) has large double, rather thin, high-pointed flowers of Indian yellow, shaded with cerise. Growth is vigorous, erect and branching, and foliage shining bronze-green; generally an excellent rose for bedding purposes.
Dickson 1930. *D. VG. MF. GPB. — 601/3, 407/3. B.G. June-Sept.*
[Hardy. Pl. 75.

Twyford (H.T.) has high-centred, spiralled, double flowers of salmon-pink, with the reverse of deeper colour, borne upon vigorous plants of bushy growth with red-bronze foliage.
Waterer 1939. *D. VG. MF. GPB. — — B.G. June-September. Hardy.*

Uhland (Hybrid Musk) is a taller pillar rose with clusters of orange-yellow double flowers with slightly fringed petals and attractive pointed green foliage.
Lambert 1916. *D. EG. MF. GPG. — — Pr. June-September. Hardy.*

Ulrich Brunner (H.P.) is a very vigorous hybrid perpetual with semi-globular double flowers of dark carmine-red, producing its flowers very freely. Growth is very erect and vigorous, foliage tough green, resistant to mildew, and suitable for growing in towns. In addition, the fragrance is exceptional.
Levet 1882. *D. TG. VF. GPB. EB.* 27/1. *G.E. June-Sept. Hardy. Pl.* 69.

Una Wallace (H.T.) has double, shapely, high-centred flowers of even cherry-rose, retaining their colour exceptionally well. Growth is vigorous, erect and branching, and foliage dark green.
McGredy 1921. *D. VG. MF. GPB. — — B.G. June-September. Hardy.*

Unique Blanche (see R. centifolia var. provincialis).

Urdh (H.T.) has very large, high-pointed, very double flowers of pale pink, boern upon good stems and robust erect plants with good green foliage.
Tantau 1930. *D. VG. VF. GPB. EB. — B.G. June-September. Hardy.*

Vainqueur (H.T.) produces from full, well rounded buds huge double flowers of deep blood-red touched with purple, upon long stems and vigorous and erect plants with bright green foliage.
Heizmann 1937. *D. VG. VF. GPB. EB. — B.E.G. June-September. Hardy.*

Valerie (Hybrid polyantha) has semi-double flowers of bright sun-flower-yellow, paling to creamy-yellow, carried in very large trusses upon very upright vigorous plants with bright green foliage.
Chaplin 1932. *D. VG. SF. GPG. — B.G. June-September. Hardy.*

Van der Gon (see Souvenir de Denier van der Gon).

Vanity (Hybrid Musk) is a very tall bushy plant with large semi-double rose-pink flowers borne in large clusters with exceptionally pronounced musky fragrance. Is suitable for pillars or hedges, and has attractive bright green foliage.
Pemberton 1920. *D. EG. VF. GPG. — — H.Pr.S. June-September. Hardy.*

Van Nes (Hybrid polyantha) is the British name for Mevrouw van Straten van Nes, or Permanent Wave, as it is known in America. The flowers, which are of reddish-carmine, are semi-double with frilled petals and borne in large clusters on erect, robust plants with large shining dark green foliage. Sometimes reverts in colour and shape.
Leenders 1934. *D. VG. SF. GPG. — B.H.St.Pot. June-Sept. Hardy. Pl.* 76.

Van Rossem's Jubilee (H.T.) has shapely double flowers of bright carmine-pink, shaded coral, varying considerably, borne upon robust bushes with shining coppery-green foliage.
Van Rossem 1937. *D. VG. SF. GPB. — — B.G. June-September. Hardy.*

Veilchenblau (Climbing polyantha) resembles Crimson Rambler, except that its crimson semi-double flowers pass with age to a particularly dirty magenta-blue. It is exceptionally vigorous, with bright green foliage, but by no means worthy of any select or special place in the sun.
Schmidt 1909. *D. C. NF. GPH. — — A.P.Pr. June. Hardy.*

Velsheda (H.T.) has large double, perfectly formed flowers of soft rose-pink, shaded slightly at the base of the petals, which are firm and cupped. Growth is robust and branching, foliage dark-green, and the flowers carry the fragrance of the old rose.
F. Cant 1936. *D. VG. VF. GPB. EB. — B.E.G.St. June-September. Hardy.*

Vera Allen (H.T.) bears its large, double, shapely flowers on long stems. The attractive flowers are of primrose, shaded with rose within, and the reverse of the petals is of cream shaded with soft pink. Growth is vigorous when established.
Dickson 1939. *D. VG. VF. GPB. EB. — B.E.G. June-September. Hardy.*

Vera Cruz (H.T.) has large, double, pointed flowers of pink, shaded with magenta, and flushed with crimson and yellow. Growth is vigorous and branching and foliage of mid-green.
da Silva 1938. *D. VG. SF. GPB. — — B.G. June-September. Hardy.*

Vestal's Coral Gem (H.T.) is another rose of vigorous growth, with attractive bright green foliage and shapely double flowers of salmon-pink with a deep carmine reverse.
Vestal 1939. *D. VG. SF. GPB. — — B.G. June-September. Hardy.*

Vestal's Red (H.T.) has double semi-globular flowers of bright red, again borne upon plants of vigorous branching growth with bright green foliage.
Vestal 1937. *D. VG. SF. GPB. — — B.G. June-September. Hardy.*

Vestal's Torchlight (H.T.), as befits a blood relation of President Herbert Hoover, has shapely double flowers of gold, touched with red, borne upon vigorous plants with good bronze-green foliage.
Vestal 1939. *D. VG. SF. GPB. — — B.G. June-September. Hardy.*

Vesuvius (H.T.) is a single-flowered rose of very vigorous branching growth, with flowers of intense crimson-scarlet, and bright green foliage.
McGredy 1923. *D. VG. SF. GPB. — — B.G.St. June-September. Hardy.*

Victor Ferrant (H.T.) has large very double flowers of magenta-carmine, paling to pale magenta, with the base of the petals of deep yellow. Growth is vigorous and bushy and foliage is dark glossy green.
Ketten 1933. *D. VG. SF. GPB. — — B.G. June-September. Hardy.*

VICTOR HUGO (H.P.) is a very old-fashioned globular, double, bright crimson rose of moderate growth best suited by cultivation expressly for exhibition purposes.
Schwartz 1884. *D. MG. VF. — EB. — E. June. Hardy.*

VICTORIA (H.T.) has large, double, pointed semi-globular flowers of bright rose-pink, shaded with cerise at the centre, and is of vigorous growth with dark green foliage.
Prince 1924. *D. VG. VF. GPB. — — B.G. June-July. Hardy.*

VICTORIA REGINA (H.T.) has double, high-centred flowers of golden-yellow with the reverse of reddish bronze-yellow, and is of robust growth but tidy and compact habit.
Hillock 1938. *D. VG. SF. GPB. — — B.G. June-September. Hardy.*

VIERLANDEN (H.T.) has even larger, double, shapely flowers of deep even salmon-pink, is ineffably scented and is vigorous in growth with bright green foliage.
Kordes 1932. *D. VG. VF. GPB. — — B.G. June-September. Hardy.*

VIKTORIA ADELHEID (H.T.) has double flowers of bright golden-yellow edged with orange-red, which spreads as the flowers age. Growth is vigorous and foliage of bright shining green.
Kordes 1932. *D. VG. VF. GPB. — — B.G. June-September. Hardy.*

VILLE D'ANGERS (H.T.) has large, semi-double, bright red flowers of semi-globular shape. Growth is vigorous, branching and erect, and foliage an attractive deep green.
Lens 1929. *D. VG. SF. GPB. — — B.G. June-September. Hardy.*

VILLE DE MALINES (Pernetiana) has semi-double flowers of yellow, shaded with cherry-red, with the faces of the petals of orange, produced with great freedom, and is exceptionally good for bedding purposes.
Lens 1929. *D. VG. SF. GPB. — — B.G. June-September. Hardy.*

VILLE DE PARIS (Pernetiana) is an attractive rose with large semi-double, semi-globular flowers of sunflower-yellow, slightly deeper in the centre, retaining its colour well. The flowers are produced from vigorous plants with red-bronze shining foliage resistant to mildew.
Pernet-Ducher 1925. *D. VG. SF. GPB. — — B.G.Pot. June-Sept. Hardy.*

VILLE DE SAVERNE (H.T.) has exceptionally large flowers of high-centred, spiralled and reflexed form, very variable in colour, crimson-pink in the bud, becoming paler with age but developing golden gleams in the petals. Growth is vigorous, erect and branching, and foliage bright glossy green.
Heizmann 1937. *D. VG. SF. GPB. EB. 20/2, 20/1. B.E.G. June-Sept.*
[Hardy. Pl. 8 & 77.

VILLE DU HAVRE (H.T.) has double flowers of creamy-white, flushed
with pink, blending to apricot-yellow at the centre. Growth is
vigorous, branching and erect, and the dark green foliage is ample.
Cayeux 1931. *D. VG. SF. GPB. — B.G. June-September. Hardy.*

VINCENT VERDAGUER (see Viuda Verdaguer).

VIOLET SIMPSON (H.T.) is a moderately vigorous rose with deep reddish-
purple foliage and double very shapely flowers of deep even apricot-
pink, with a yellow base.
Simpson 1928. *D. MG. VF. GPB. EB. — B.E.G. June-September. Hardy.*

VIOLETTE (Climbing polyantha) is an improved Veilchenblau with a
colour much less objectionable; at times of intense violet.
Turbat 1921. *D. C. SF. GPH. — — A.P.Pr.H. June-July. Hardy.*

VIOLINISTA COSTA (H.T.) has shapely, high-centred, double flowers with
imbricated petals of variable pink, beginning at carmine-red and
passing to strawberry-pink, touched with orange to orange-pink.
Flowers are large, borne upon long stems, and growth is vigorous
and branching, with bright green glossy foliage.
Nadal 1937. *D. VG. VF. GPB. EB.* 621. *B.E.G.St. June-Sept. Hardy.*
[*Pl.* 3 & 68.

VIRA (see R. rugosa).

VIRGINIANA (from Virginia) (S.), Eastern North America, makes a
shapely bush of about six feet in height, with shining green leaves
made up of seven or nine leaflets, and bearing either singly or in
few-flowered groups its single variable pink flowers of about two
inches in diameter, which are followed by round red persistent fruits.
Miller 1724. *D. TG. NF. GPG. —* 25/2, 712/2. *S.H. June-July. Hardy.*
[*Pl.* 24 & 78.

VIRGINIANA ALBA (S.) is similar in all respects save in its white flowers.
Ehrhardt 1789. *D. TG. NF. GPG. — — S.H. June-July. Hardy.*

VIRGINIANA PLENA (S.) has double, bright rose-pink flowers and makes
a magnificent hedge.
Rehder —. *D. TG. NF. GPG. — — S.H. June-July. Hardy.*

VIRIDIFLORA (see R. chinensis viridiflora).

VISCOUNTESS CHARLEMONT (H.T.) has very shapely flowers of pale
salmon-rose, with the base of the petals and reflexes of deep yellow, at
their best in cooler weather. Growth is vigorous and branching, and
the fragrant flowers are borne on long stems.
McGredy 1937. *D. VG. VF. GPB. EB.* 416/3, 18/2. *B.E.G. June-Sept.*
[*Hardy. Pl.* 51.

VIUDA VERDAGUER (Pernetiana), sometimes Vincent Verdaguer in
Britain, has large, double, open flowers of orange-ochre, freely borne
upon very vigorous plants with dark green glossy foliage.
Dot 1934. *D. VG. MF. GPB. — — B.G. June-September. Hardy.*

von Liliencron (Hybrid Musk) is a semi-climber suitable for growing as a pillar rose, with large clusters of semi-double white flowers, shaded with pink, freely produced. Growth is vigorous and foliage shining bronze-green.
Lambert 1915. *D. EG. MF. GPG. — — Pr. June-September. Hardy.*

Vorbergii (S.) is a hybrid between R. foetida and R. spinosissima, making a dwarf bush of approximately two feet in height, with creamy white single flowers with a yellow flush, borne singly.
Graebner —. D. MG. SF. GPG. — — S. May-June. Hardy.

W. A. Bilney (H.T.) has large semi-double flowers of pale apricot-yellow shaded with primrose, borne upon long stems from vigorous plants with erect growth and dark green foliage.
Easlea 1927. *D. VG. MF. GPB. — — B.G.Pot. June-September. Hardy.*

Wadeii (H.S.) is a hybrid of R. rugosa and R. Moyesii and makes a round compact thorny bush of about thirty inches in height, with small pale green foliage, and bears large bright pink single flowers of about three inches in diameter.
Hurran —. D. MG. MF. GPG. — — S. May-June. Hardy.

Walter Bentley (H.T.) is a remarkable rose. It can, and does, produce very large, perfectly-shaped double flowers with beautifully reflexed petals of deep carmine-pink, flushed, at times, with coppery-orange. It is apt to quarter, and seems to be variable in its growth, ranging from vigorous to weak, but it seems to be destined to be a rose particularly for the expert. Foliage is glossy dark green.
Robinson 1938. *D. MG. F. GPB. EB.* 623/1-621, *base* 1/2. *E.G. June-*
[*Sept. Hardy. Pl.* 9.

Waltham Cross (H.T.) is a semi-double rose of crimson-scarlet, moderate height, and of continuous flowering propensities, which make it an admirable rose for bedding purposes, probably better than K. of K.
Chaplin 1927. *D. MG. VF. GPB. —* 824/1. *B. June-September. Hardy.*

Warrawee (H.T.) is a fascinating rose of Australian origin, with high-pointed, double, shell-pink flowers which open flat to show the central golden stamens. Foliage is dark green, but bronze-green when young.
Hazlewood 1935. *D. VG. VF. GPB. — — B.G. June-September. Hardy.*

Wasagaming (see R. rugosa).

Wasatch Rose (see R. nutkana).

Watsoniana (comm.) (S.), Japan, forms a bush of about three feet in height with red and green almost thornless arching canes, and blue-green leaves made up of three to five narrow leaflets completely without serrations, and with curiously waved margins. The small single white and pink flowers of about half-inch diameter are borne in large clusters and are followed by tiny round reddish fruits.
Crepin —. D. VG. SF. GPG. — — S. May-June.

Three Hybrid Tea Roses

McGredy's Pink **BCDFGH**
Hinrich Gaede **EJKLMPQ**
Weigand's No. 4701 **NORSPQTU**

Hybrid Tea Rose, William Moore

WEBBIANA (comm.) (S.), Himalayas, makes a graceful thorny bush of some six feet in height with green leaves composed of five to nine very small leaflets, bearing, either singly or in few-flowered clusters, pale pink single flowers of about two inches in diameter, followed by oval red fruits.
Wallich 1820. *D. TG. MF. GPG. — — S. June. Hardy.*

W. E. CHAPLIN (H.T.) is an excellent crimson rose which does not discolour or damage in wet weather, its very large, high-centred, globular flowers being very profusely produced from robust, upright and branching plants with much deep-green foliage.
Chaplin 1931. *D. VG. SF. GPB. EB.* 727-030-828. *B.E.G. June-Sept.*
[*Hardy. Pl.* 38.

WEIGAND'S No. 4701 (H.T.) remains under its producer's number, and is an exceptional crimson rose with large, double, many-petalled flowers of camellia shape, produced from plants of vigorous and branching growth with dark green foliage.
Weigand 1939. *D. VG. VF. GPB. EB.* 724/1. *B.E.G. June-Sept. Hardy.*
[*Pl.* 79.

WENDY BARRIE (polyantha pompon) has nicely shaped, very double flowers of soft orange-salmon, borne freely in large clusters on dwarf but vigorous plants with bright green foliage, and not inclined to sport excessively.
Beckwith 1936. *D. MG. NF. GPF. — — B. June-September. Hardy.*

WESTFIELD SCARLET (Pernetiana) has very large, double, high-centred flowers of vivid crimson-scarlet produced upon long stems from moderately vigorous plants with glossy bright green foliage.
Morse 1931. *D. MG. SF. GPB. EB. — B.E.G. June-September. Hardy.*

W. F. DREER (H.T.) has exceptionally well-formed, double, pointed flowers of yellow, shaded with peach-pink, variable in extent. Growth is vigorous and erect, flowering profuse and extended, and foliage light green.
Howard & Smith 1920. *D. VG. VF. GPB. — B.G.St.Pot. June-Sept.*
[*Hardy. Pl.* 46.

WHITE Rose (see R. alba).

WHITE BATH (see R. muscosa).

WHITE BRIARCLIFF (see Madame Louis Lens).

WHITE ENSIGN (H.T.) is a very double, high-centred, semi-globular white rose with a cream centre which behaves well in all weathers. Growth is vigorous, erect and branching, and foliage glossy green, liable in some districts to mildew and black spot.
McGredy 1925. *D. VG. SF. GPB. — White. B.G. June-September. Hardy.*

WHITE FINCH (Hybrid polyantha) for its type has large flowers, each being a shapely miniature, double, high-centred rose of clear white. *Easlea* 1939. *D. VG. MF. GPG or GPF. White. B.G.St. June-Sept. Hardy.*

WHITE PAT (see R. chinensis).

WHITE PROVENCE (see R. centifolia provincialis alba Unique Blanche).

WICHURAIANA (comm.) (S.), Eastern Asia, is a prostrate or trailing plant with shining green leaves composed of seven to nine leaflets and which bears large clusters of fragrant single white flowers of two inches in diameter. It is evergreen in suitable positions, and useful for covering banks. One of the parents of the wichuraiana ramblers and climbers detailed. *Crepin* —. *E. VG. MF. GPG.* — *White. Banks. July-September. Hardy.*

WIELAND (Hybrid Musk) has clustered single flowers of yellow flushed with red, borne upon vigorous and erect bushes with green glossy foliage. *Lambert* 1916. *D. EG. MF. GPG.* — — *Pr. July-September. Hardy.*

WILHELM (Hybrid Musk), known in the U.S.A. as Sky Rocket, makes a large bush or pillar rose with huge clusters of large, double, pointed flowers of dark red. Growth is very vigorous and erect, and foliage is glossy green. *Kordes* 1934. *D. EG. VF. GPG.* — — *S.Pr. June-October. Hardy.*

WILHELM BREDER (Pernetiana) is known in the U.S.A. as Glowing Sunset, and has large, double, open flowers of orange shot with deep pink and yellow. Growth is vigorous and erect and foliage is glossy bronze-green. *Kordes* 1933. *D. VG. VF. GPB. EB.* — *B.E.G. June-September. Hardy.*

WILHELM KORDES (H.T.) has large double flowers of bright golden-yellow, flushed at the edges of the petals with orange-red, borne upon stout stems from vigorous, erect and branching plants with shining bronze-green foliage. *Kordes* 1922. *D. VG. SF. GPB. EB.* — *June-September. Hardy.*

WILLIAM ALLEN RICHARDSON (see R. Noisettiana).

WILLIAM F. DREER (see W. F. Dreer).

WILLIAM LOBB (see R. muscosa).

WILLIAM MOORE (H.T.) is a very beautiful shapely rose with large double, high-centred, rounded deep-pink flowers with attractively reflexed petals, paling slightly with age. The flowers are borne upon long stems on vigorous, erect and branching plants, with a little light-green foliage. *McGredy* 1935. *D. VG. VF. GPB. EB.* — *B.E.G. June-Sept. Hardy.*
[*Pl.* 80.

WILLIAM ORR (H.T.) has very shapely double, large, high-pointed flowers of deep crimson, with attractively reflexed petals. Growth is moderately vigorous and bushy, foliage is light green, and the flowers freely produced for a protracted period in good years.
McGredy 1931. *D. VG. VF. GPB. EB. — B.E.G.St. June-October. Hardy.*

WILLMOTTIAE (comm.) (S.), China, makes a very large erect dense bush with red canes and profuse lateral branches, with fragrant sage-green leaves composed of seven to nine small leaflets bearing solitary single flowers of rose-purple, about one inch in diameter, and followed by small orange-red flattened round fruits.
Hemsley 1907. *D. EG. NF. GPG. — 26/1. S. June. Hardy. Pl.* 53.

WILL ROGERS (H.T.) has shapely double flowers of very deep crimson with even deeper shading, freely borne upon vigorous plants with mid-green foliage. Flowers are exceptionally good and retain their colour best in autumn.
Howard & Smith 1936. *D. VG. VF. GPB. EB. — B.E.G. June-Oct. Hardy.*

WILSONII (S.) is also R. involuta var. Wilsonii and a natural hybrid of R. tomentosa and R. spinosissima, and makes a bush of some forty inches in height, with almost thornless canes, bearing large green leaves made up of seven to nine leaflets with large single white flowers, borne singly or in few-flowered clusters.
Baker —. D. TG. SF. GPG. — — S. June. Hardy.

WINDERMERE (wichuraiana rambler) is a good pillar rose with rather stiff upright canes and glossy green leaves, bearing large clusters of semi-double carmine flowers of medium size.
Chaplin 1932. *D. C. SF. GPJ. — — Pr.A. June-July. Hardy.*

WINSOME (Climbing H.T.) is a vigorous climbing rose with large, double, cerise-red flowers, freely produced in summer on long stems, accompanied by medium green foliage.
Dobbie 1931. *D. C. VF. GPE. — — W. June-July. Hardy.*

WINTONIENSIS (H.S.) makes a tall bush like R. Moyesii with fragrant foliage and single rose-pink flowers, borne in small clusters, and followed by bright red pitcher-shaped fruits.
Hillier 1928. *D. EG. VF. GPG. — — S. June-July. Hardy.*

WOLFGANG VON GOETHE (H.P.) is a modern hybrid perpetual rose with very large double and shapely flowers of brilliant apricot-pink, borne upon vigorous plants with deep green foliage.
Weigand 1933. *D. TG. SF. GPC. EC. — B.E.G. June-September. Hardy.*

WOODSII (comm.) (S.), North America, makes a four-foot bush with smooth red-brown canes and small light green leaves made up of five or seven leaflets, and bearing solitary single pink flowers about the size of a halfpenny, followed by small round red fruits.
Lindley —. D. TG. SF. GPG. — — S. June-July. Hardy.

WORLD'S FAIR is the American name for Minna Kordes, which see.

XANTHINA (of golden-yellow colour) (S.), Korea, forms a bush exceeding six feet in height with small soft green fragrant leaves made up of seven to nine leaflets, and which bears freely, on the lateral from the old wood, double golden-yellow solitary flowers.
Lindley 1820. *D. EG. VF. GPG.* —— *S. June-July. Hardy.*

XANTHINA KOKANICA (S.), from Turkestan, is a much dwarfer plant with red-brown thorny canes, small rounded very fragrant foliage and solitary small, single, pale yellow flowers.
Rehder —. *D. VG. MF. GPG.* —— *S. June-July. Hardy.*

XANTHINA SPONTANEA (S.), Korea, is the wild species with grey-green foliage and large flat, single, golden-yellow flowers.
Rehder —. *D. EG. VF. GPG.* —— *S. June-July. Hardy.*

YELLOW CREST (H.T.) has rather small but perfectly formed double flowers of canary-yellow produced from vigorous, erect and branching plants with pale green glossy foliage.
Le Grice 1935. *D. VG. SF. GPB.* —— *B.G. June-September. Hardy.*

YELLOW DOT (H.T.) is a vigorous branching plant with dark green foliage, with small globular double flowers of pale orange, with the reverse of the petals of dark apricot-pink.
Hill 1938. *D. VG. SF. GPB.* —— *B. June-September. Hardy.*

YELLOW HOOVER (H.T.) resembles President Herbert Hoover in all respects save in its uniform pure yellow colour.
Western Rose Co. 1933. *D. VG. MF. GPC.* —— *B.G. June-Sept. Hardy.*

YELLOW JOANNA HILL (H.T.) has double, high-centred flowers of pure yellow, borne upon long strong stems, from plants with vigorous growth and bright green foliage.
White 1932. *D. VG. SF. GPB.* —— *B.G.Pot. June-September.*

YORK AND LANCASTER (see R. damascena variegata).

YOSEMITE (H.T.) has double, semi-globular flowers of carrot-red shaded red-gold and orange, paling with age to bright coral-pink. Growth is vigorous, erect and branching, and foliage deep green.
Nicolas 1934. *D. VG. MF. GPB.* —— *B.G. June-September. Hardy.*

YOUTH (Pernetiana) has very large, many-petalled, high-pointed flowers of cream, flushed at the base with deep pink. Growth is vigorous, erect and branching, and foliage deep green.
Cook 1935. *D. VG. TF. GPB.* —— *B.G. June-September. Hardy.*

YVONNE MILLOT (H.T.) has very large, full, high-centred flowers of yellow, tinted and shaded with apricot, produced with freedom on vigorous, erect and branching plants with deep green glossy foliage.
Mallerin 1934. *D. VG. SF. GPB.* —— *B.G. June-September. Hardy.*

YVONNE PRINTEMPS (H.T.) has shapely double flowers of orange with deeper veining, with the reverse of the petals of clear golden-yellow. Growth is vigorous and branching, and foliage bronze-green and shining.
Gaujard 1939. *D. VG. SF. GPB.* —— *B.G. June-September. Hardy.*

YVONNE RABIER (Hybrid polyantha) has double flowers of white shaded cream at the base, borne in large clusters from dwarf but robust plants with bright green shining foliage.

Turbat 1910. *D. MG. MF. GPG. — — B.G.S. June-Sept. Hardy. Pl.* 61.

ZENOBIA (see R. muscosa).

ZÉPHIRINE DROUHIN (Hybrid Bourbonia) is the so-called Thornless Rose, with large semi-double rose-pink flowers of good shape and form, produced freely upon very vigorous canes with attractive foliage.

Bizot 1873. *D. C. VF. GPE. —* 627. *H.B.P.Pr.S.W. July-Sept. Hardy.*
[*Pl.* 7.

ZULU QUEEN (H.T.) has large, double, pointed flowers of deep crimson-maroon, borne upon vigorous, erect and branching plants with deep green foliage.

Kordes 1939. *D. VG. GPB. — — B.G. June-September.*

A	B	C	D
E	F	G	H
J	K	L	M
N	O	P	Q
R	S	T	U

To use the template place it over the plate, with the top white line coincident with the top edge of the plate. The letters beside the name of the rose at the foot of the plate will then indicate in which squares the rose will be found. Thus in Plate 25, the rose

CAROLINE TESTOUT is in squares A, B, E and F;
LADY WATERLOW in squares C, D, G and H;
and COMMON CHINA BLUSH in squares K, L, M, O, P and Q.